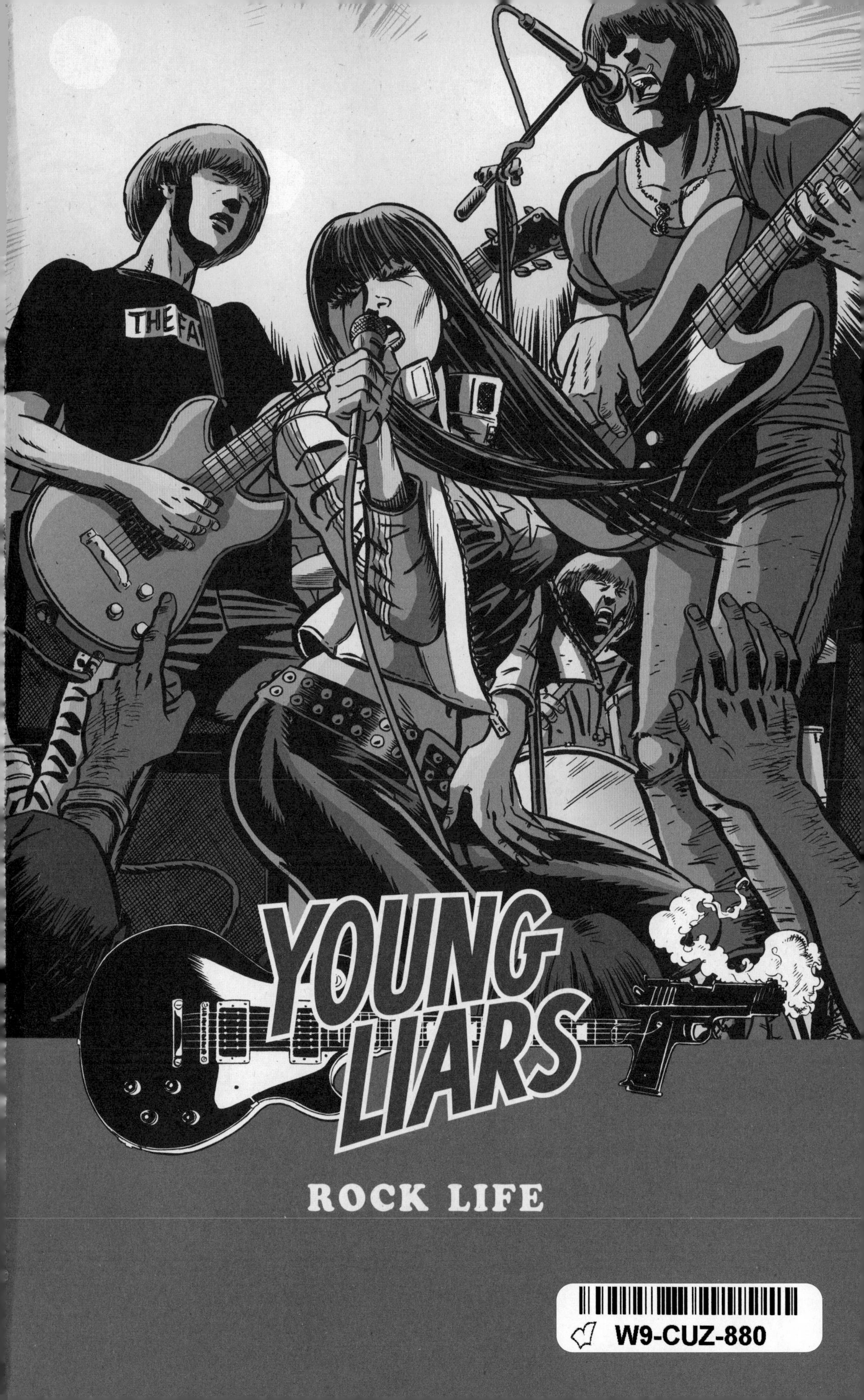
THE FA

YOUNG LIARS

ROCK LIFE

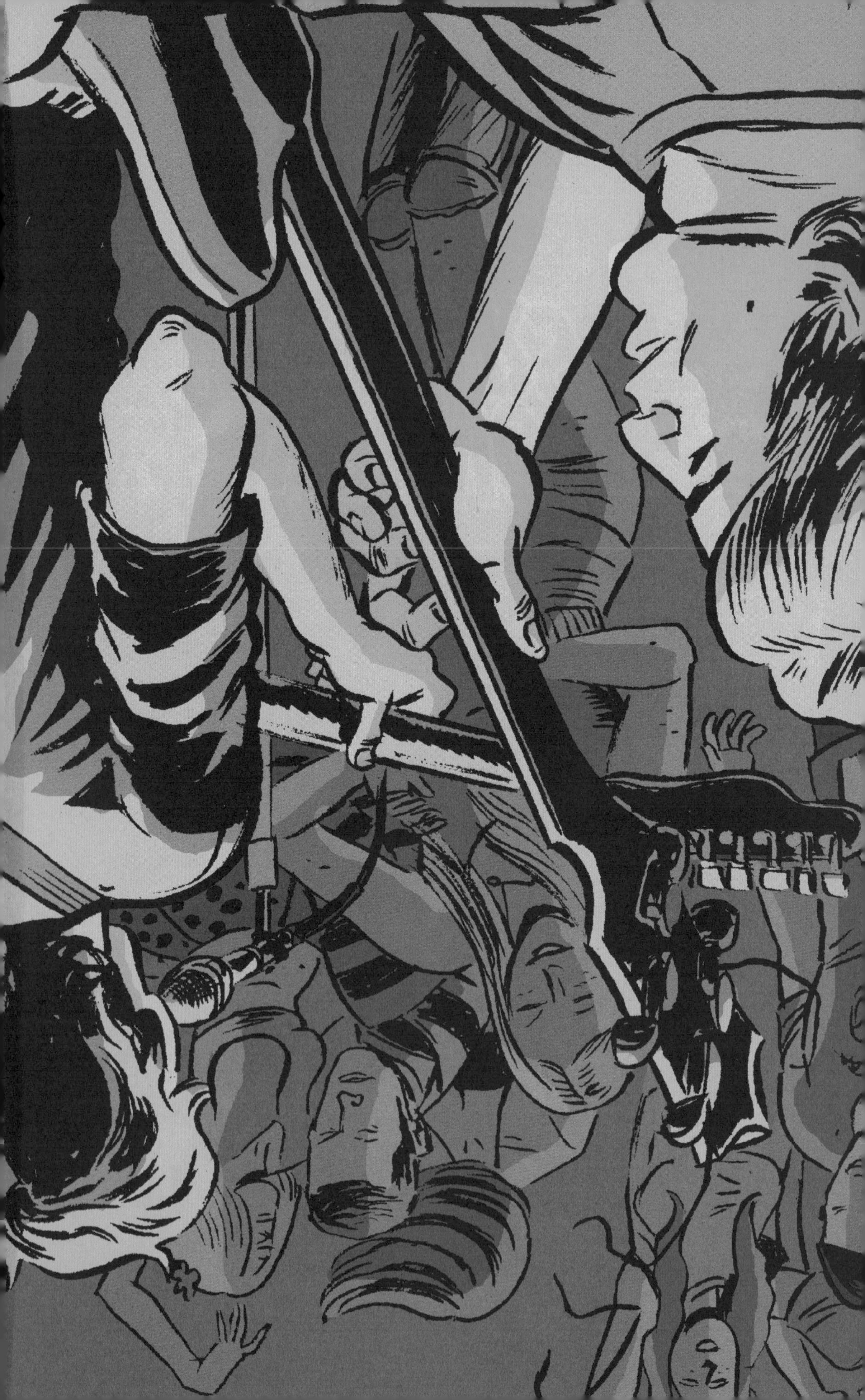

YOUNG LIARS

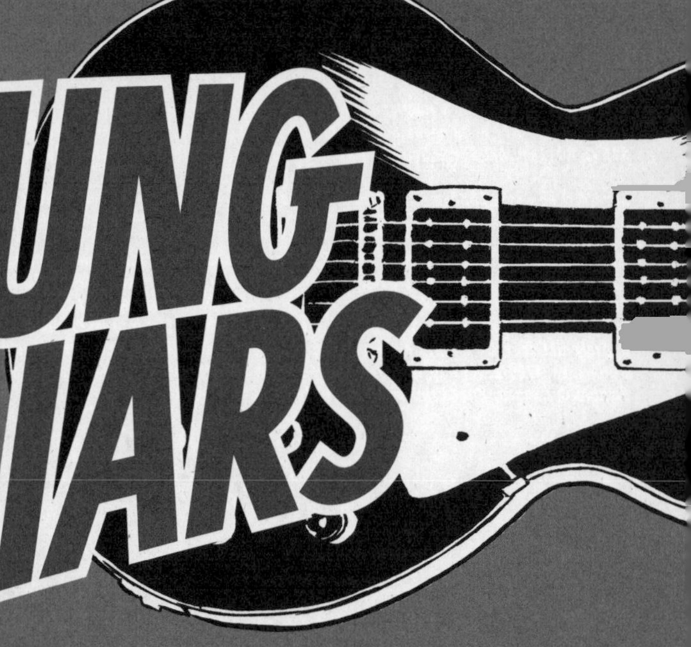

ROCK LIFE

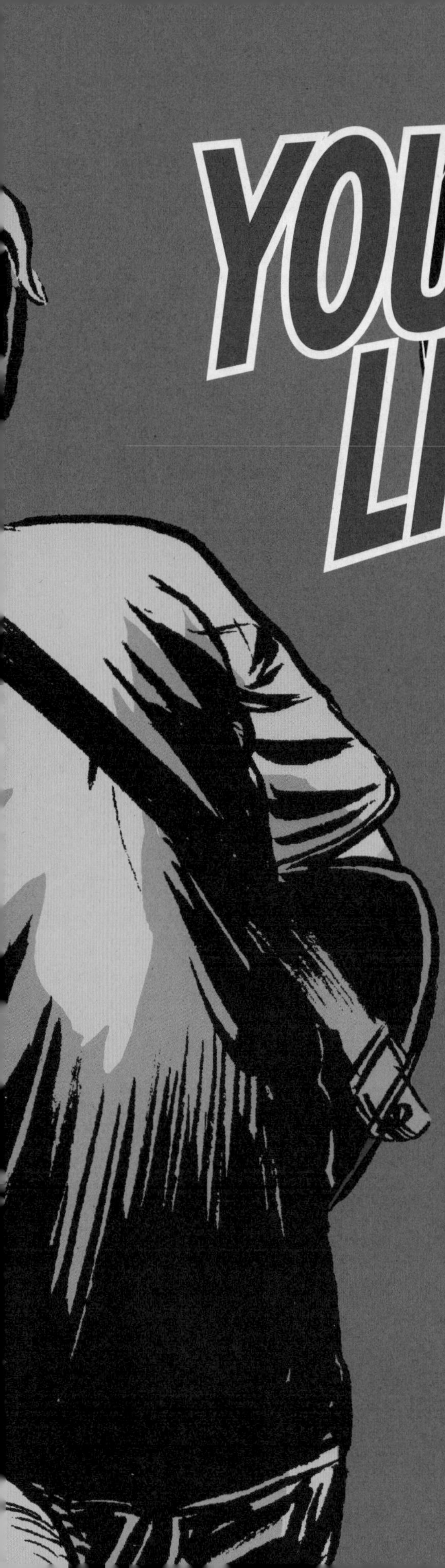

David **Lapham**

Writer, Artist and Cover Artist

Lee **Loughridge**

Colorist

Jared K. **Fletcher**

Letterer

YOUNG LIARS created by

David **Lapham**

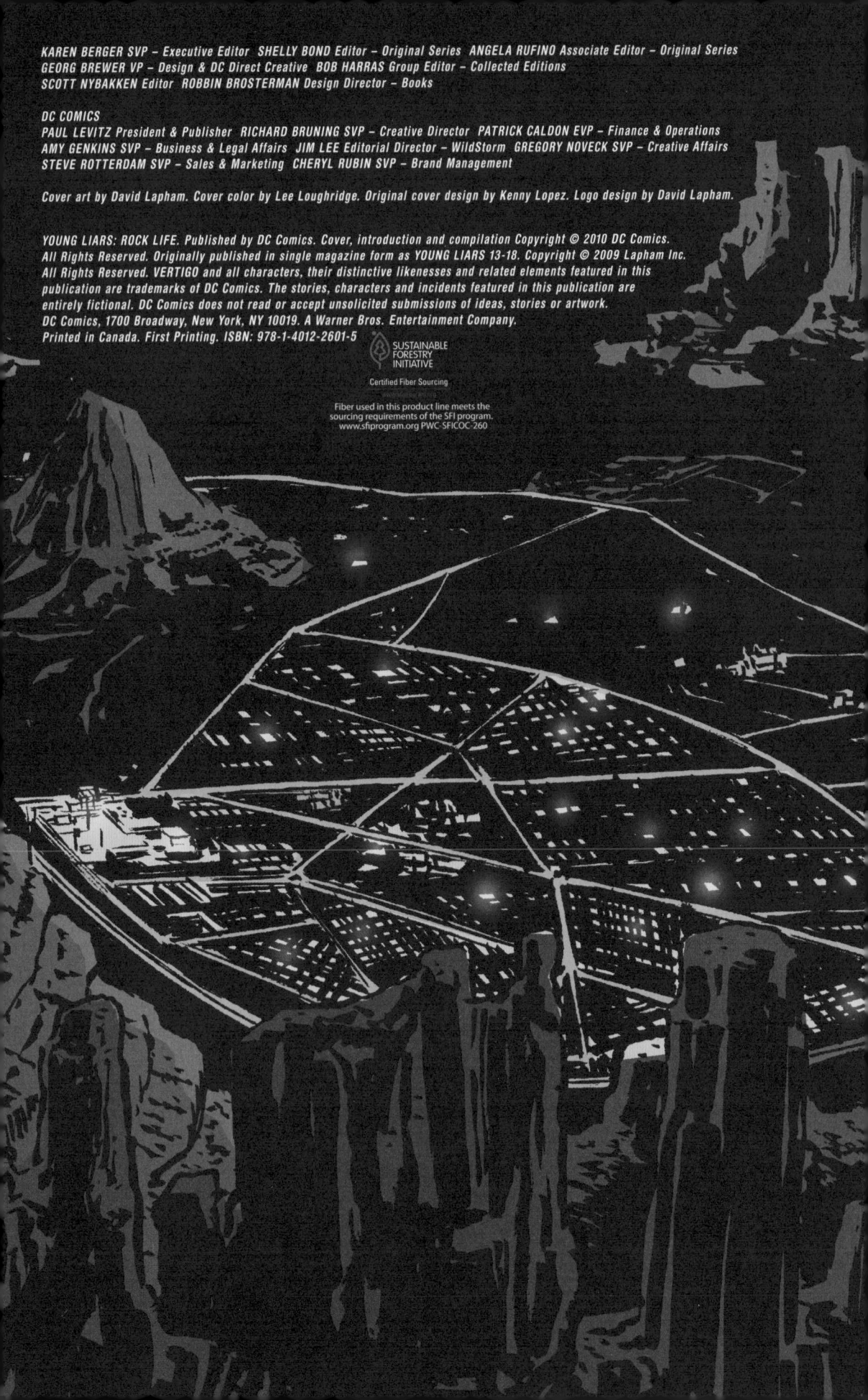

KAREN BERGER SVP – Executive Editor SHELLY BOND Editor – Original Series ANGELA RUFINO Associate Editor – Original Series
GEORG BREWER VP – Design & DC Direct Creative BOB HARRAS Group Editor – Collected Editions
SCOTT NYBAKKEN Editor ROBBIN BROSTERMAN Design Director – Books

DC COMICS
PAUL LEVITZ President & Publisher RICHARD BRUNING SVP – Creative Director PATRICK CALDON EVP – Finance & Operations
AMY GENKINS SVP – Business & Legal Affairs JIM LEE Editorial Director – WildStorm GREGORY NOVECK SVP – Creative Affairs
STEVE ROTTERDAM SVP – Sales & Marketing CHERYL RUBIN SVP – Brand Management

Cover art by David Lapham. Cover color by Lee Loughridge. Original cover design by Kenny Lopez. Logo design by David Lapham.

DC Comics, 1700 Broadway, New York, NY 10019. A Warner Bros. Entertainment Company.
Printed in Canada. First Printing. ISBN: 978-1-4012-2601-5

SUSTAINABLE FORESTRY INITIATIVE
Certified Fiber Sourcing
Fiber used in this product line meets the sourcing requirements of the SFI program.
www.sfiprogram.org PWC-SFICOC-260

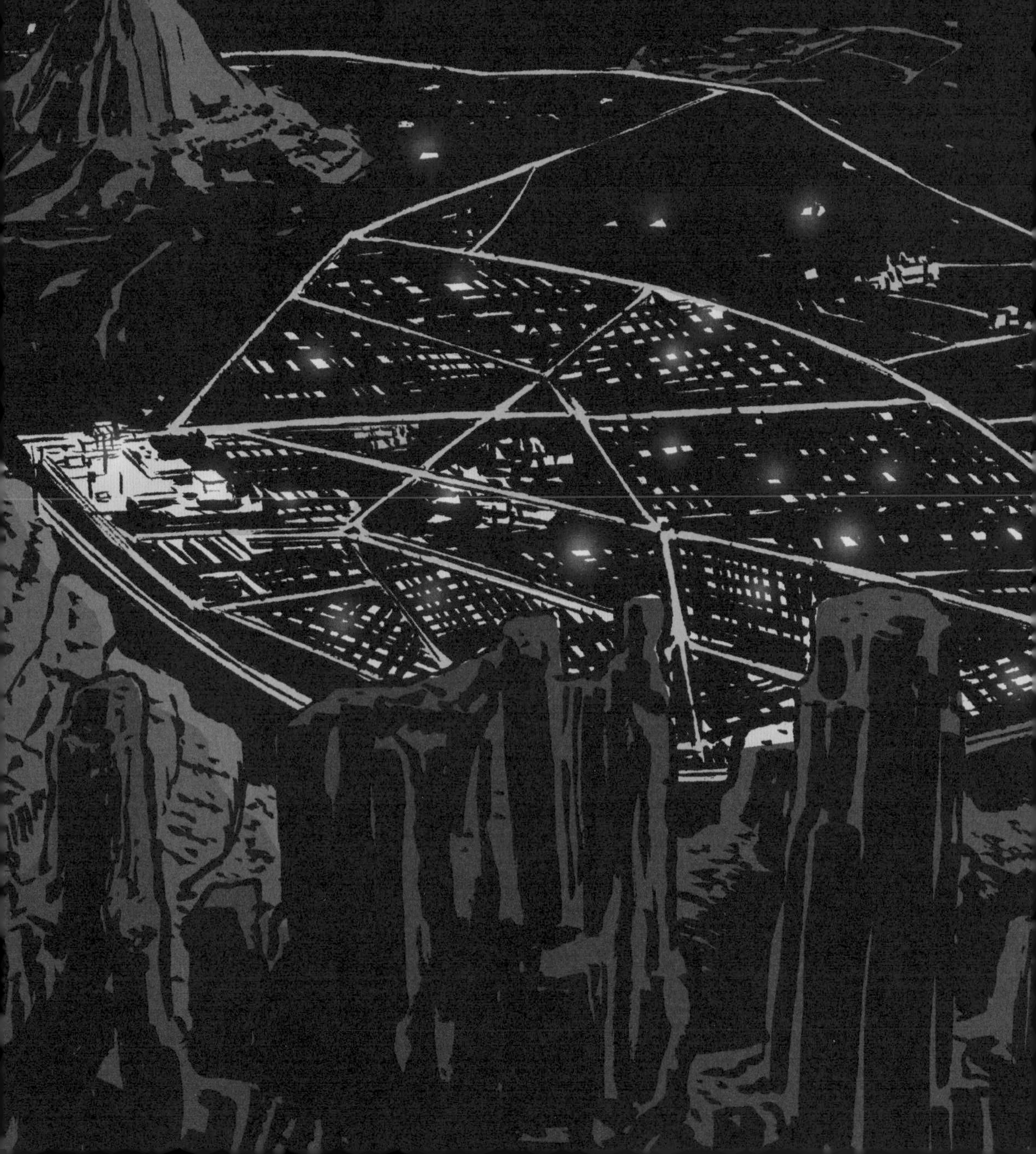

What is ROMANCE?

I'm allowed to ask that question because I believe I'm an old man, and being one, I miss what I once thought I knew. And being an old man who is in love — profoundly — I have the perspective to assure you that romance and love are not the same thing.

See, love is buried in the soul, but romance is pure heart/groin. Romance is being in love with the idea of being in love. And trust me, there's much of that to go around. You can romance one person — or just as easily another — purely based on smell. Or a glimpse, or whatever... a memory. You can be romantically involved with an idea, a situation, a cause. You can give yourself over to romance because the moment strikes you, and falls out the next. Love binds, but romance is freeing.

ROMANCE IS EXCITING, BRIEF, AND SO, SO INTENSE. LIKE A SONG.

And that's what YOUNG LIARS always strikes me as: songs. This is the third album. The swan one. Six songs about being in love. About immediacy, about longing, about confusion... about romance.

Don't be afraid to embrace a song, or how it makes you feel. Remember the person you were with when it touched you, or where you were. Have the courage to cry when you hear it again — even years down a road you haven't yet had the opportunity to travel. Be brave, and love the romance you felt.

What David Lapham has done with YOUNG LIARS is Romance with a capital R — and yet, a labor of love. He's a brutally honest creator, I wouldn't expect anything less.

This book is what makes lives (with a small l) worth living. I'm begging you: be young, and lie. And know an old man envies you.

— BRIAN AZZARELLO
October 2009

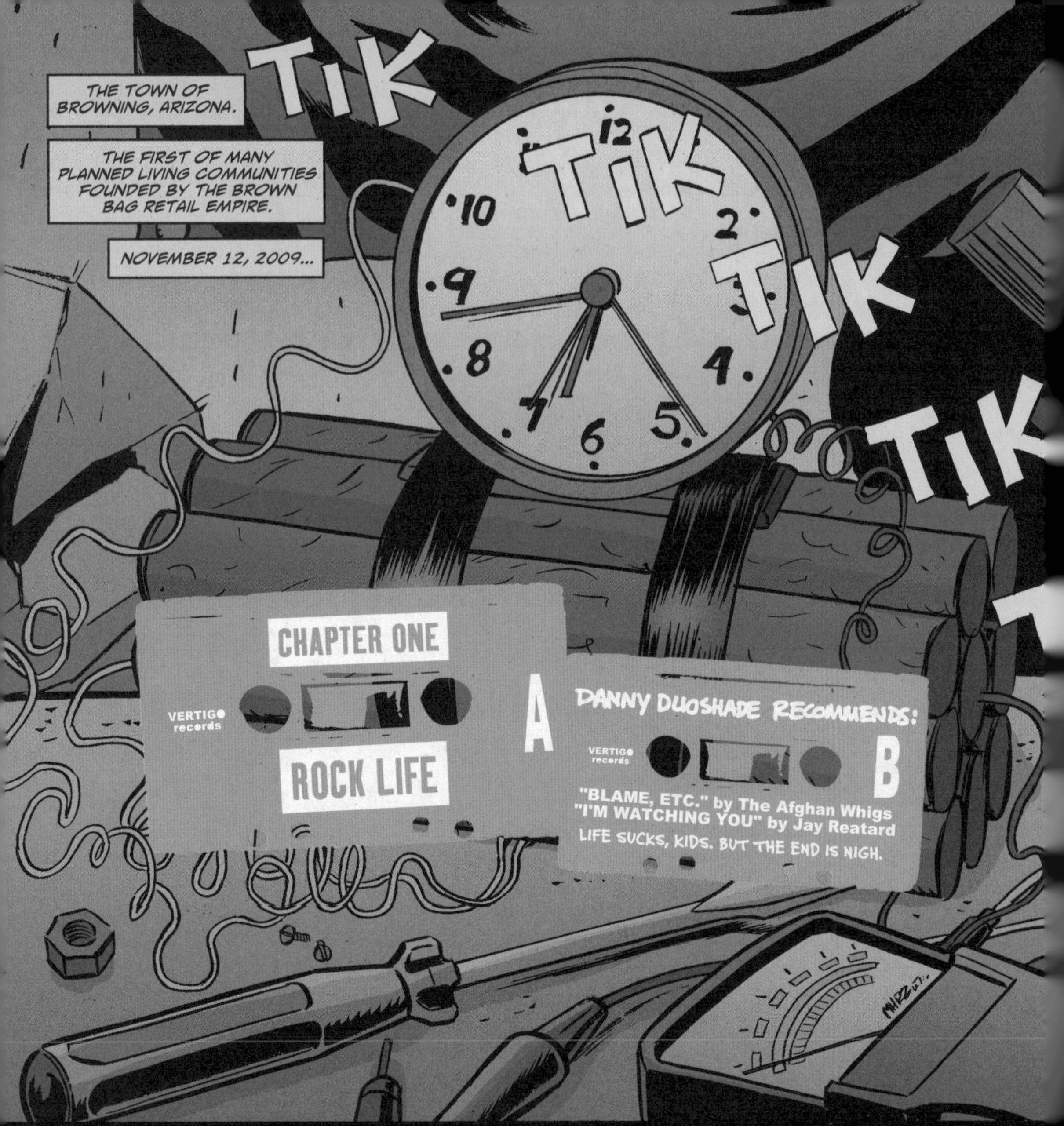
THE TOWN OF BROWNING, ARIZONA.
THE FIRST OF MANY PLANNED LIVING COMMUNITIES FOUNDED BY THE BROWN BAG RETAIL EMPIRE.
NOVEMBER 12, 2009...
TIK
TIK
TIK
TIK
CHAPTER ONE
A
VERTIGO records
ROCK LIFE
DANNY DUOSHADE RECOMMENDS:
VERTIGO records
B
"BLAME, ETC." by The Afghan Whigs
"I'M WATCHING YOU" by Jay Reatard
LIFE SUCKS, KIDS. BUT THE END IS NIGH.

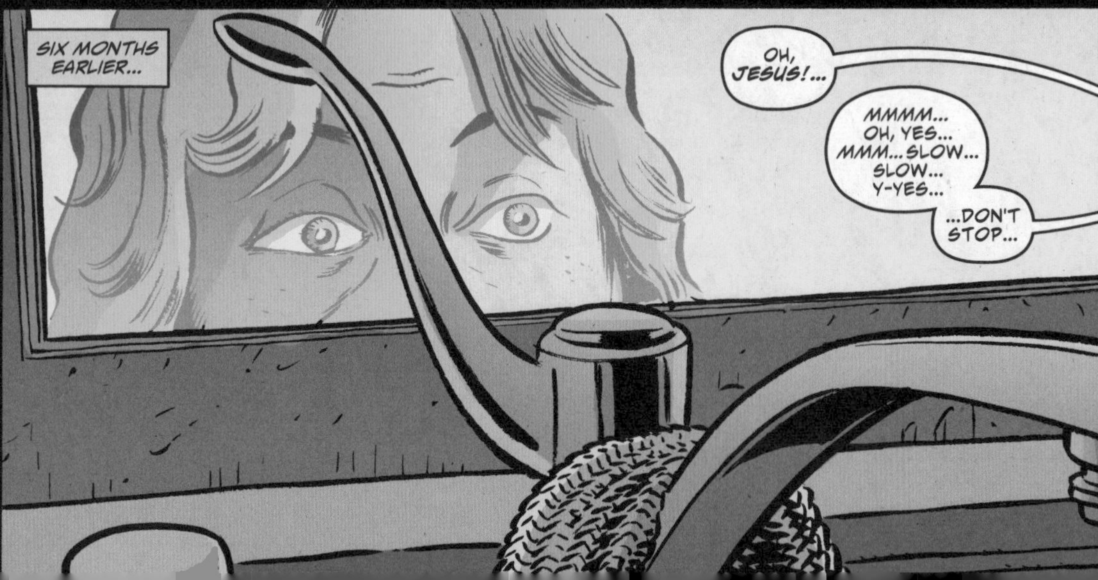
SIX MONTHS EARLIER...
OH, JESUS!...
MMMM... OH, YES... MMM...SLOW... SLOW... Y-YES...
...DON'T STOP...

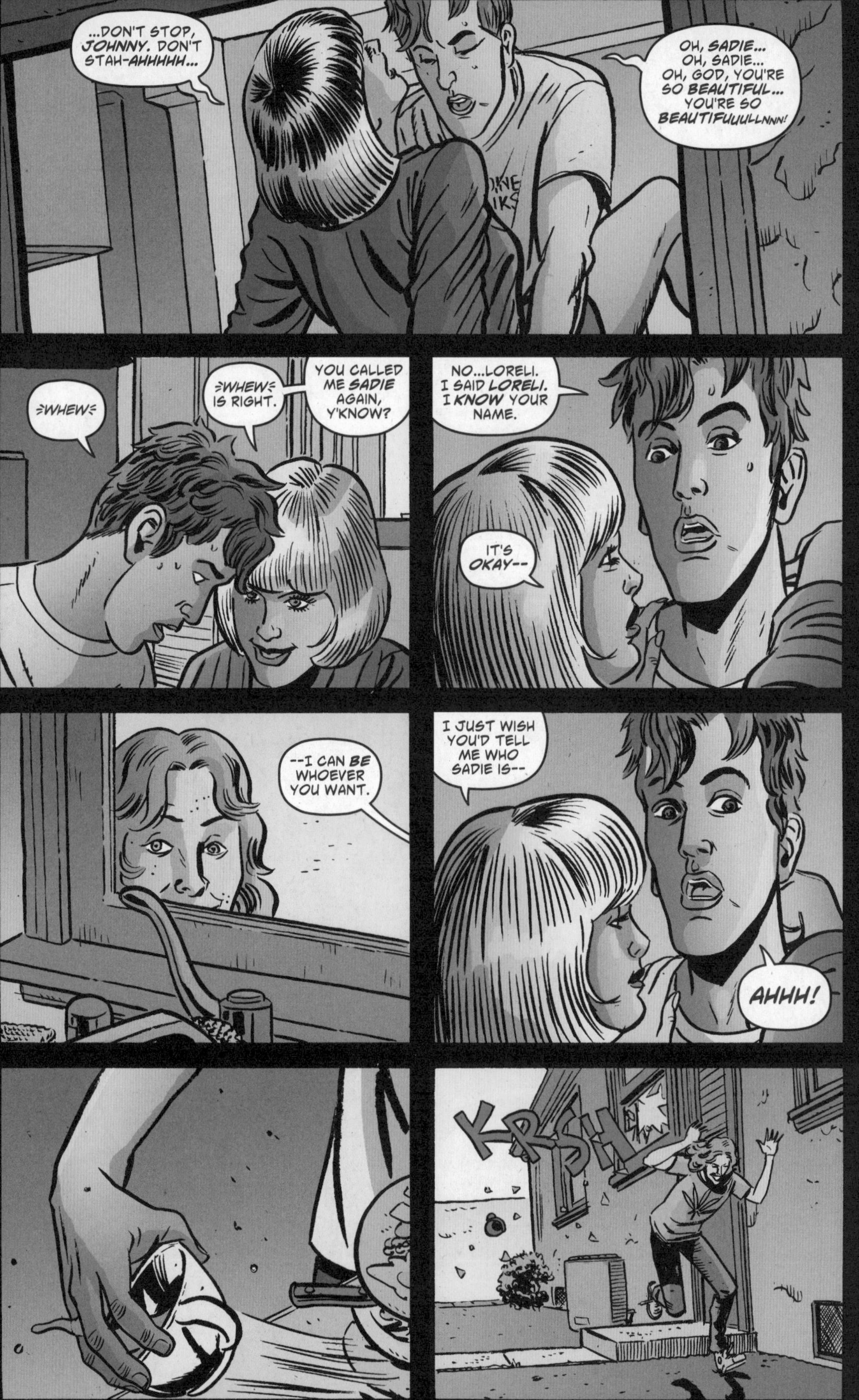
...DON'T STOP, JOHNNY. DON'T STAH-AHHHHH...
OH, SADIE... OH, SADIE... OH, GOD, YOU'RE SO BEAUTIFUL... YOU'RE SO BEAUTIFUUULLNNN!
≈WHEW≈
≈WHEW≈ IS RIGHT.
YOU CALLED ME SADIE AGAIN, Y'KNOW?
NO...LORELI. I SAID LORELI. I KNOW YOUR NAME.
IT'S OKAY--
--I CAN BE WHOEVER YOU WANT.
I JUST WISH YOU'D TELL ME WHO SADIE IS--
AHHH!
KRSH

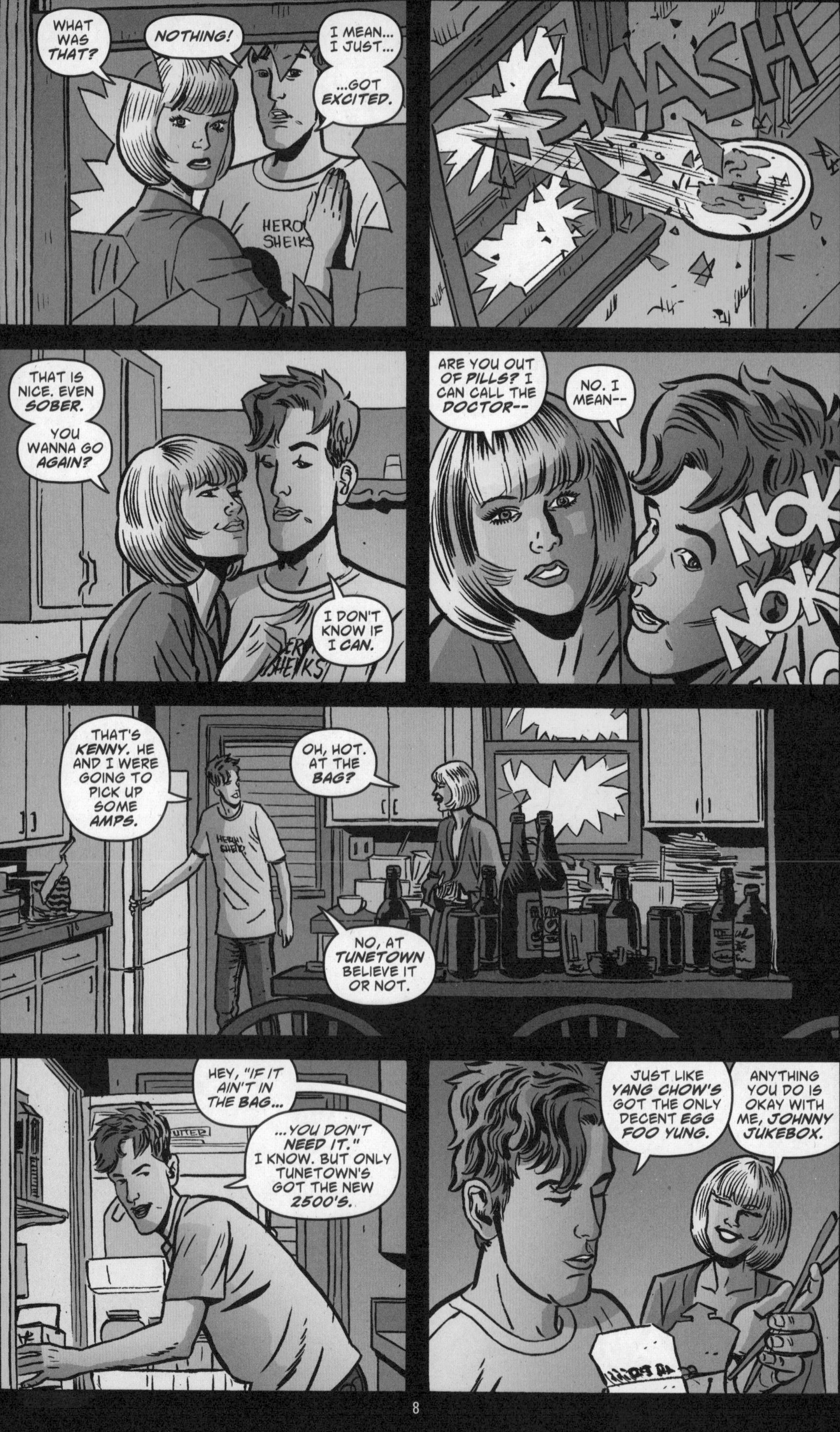

WHAT WAS THAT?
NOTHING!
I MEAN... I JUST...
...GOT EXCITED.
HERO SHEIKS
SMASH
THAT IS NICE. EVEN SOBER.
YOU WANNA GO AGAIN?
I DON'T KNOW IF I CAN.
ARE YOU OUT OF PILLS? I CAN CALL THE DOCTOR--
NO. I MEAN--
NOK NOK
THAT'S KENNY. HE AND I WERE GOING TO PICK UP SOME AMPS.
OH, HOT. AT THE BAG?
NO, AT TUNETOWN BELIEVE IT OR NOT.
HEY, "IF IT AIN'T IN THE BAG...
...YOU DON'T NEED IT." I KNOW. BUT ONLY TUNETOWN'S GOT THE NEW 2500'S.
JUST LIKE YANG CHOW'S GOT THE ONLY DECENT EGG FOO YUNG.
ANYTHING YOU DO IS OKAY WITH ME, JOHNNY JUKEBOX.

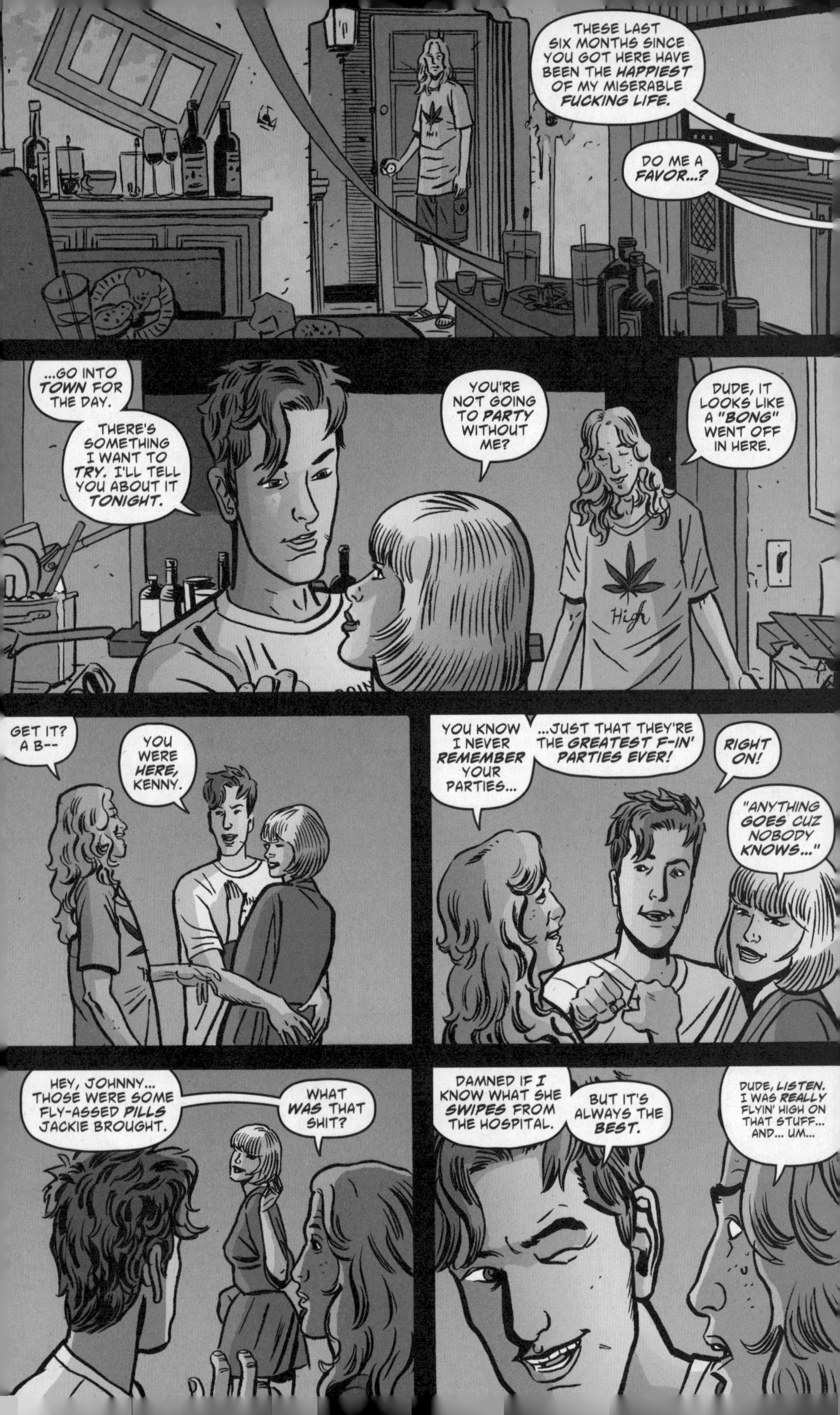

THESE LAST SIX MONTHS SINCE YOU GOT HERE HAVE BEEN THE HAPPIEST OF MY MISERABLE FUCKING LIFE.
DO ME A FAVOR...?
...GO INTO TOWN FOR THE DAY.
THERE'S SOMETHING I WANT TO TRY. I'LL TELL YOU ABOUT IT TONIGHT.
YOU'RE NOT GOING TO PARTY WITHOUT ME?
DUDE, IT LOOKS LIKE A "BONG" WENT OFF IN HERE.
GET IT? A B--
YOU WERE HERE, KENNY.
YOU KNOW I NEVER REMEMBER YOUR PARTIES...
...JUST THAT THEY'RE THE GREATEST F-IN' PARTIES EVER!
RIGHT ON!
"ANYTHING GOES CUZ NOBODY KNOWS..."
HEY, JOHNNY... THOSE WERE SOME FLY-ASSED PILLS JACKIE BROUGHT.
WHAT WAS THAT SHIT?
DAMNED IF I KNOW WHAT SHE SWIPES FROM THE HOSPITAL.
BUT IT'S ALWAYS THE BEST.
DUDE, LISTEN. I WAS REALLY FLYIN' HIGH ON THAT STUFF... AND... UM...

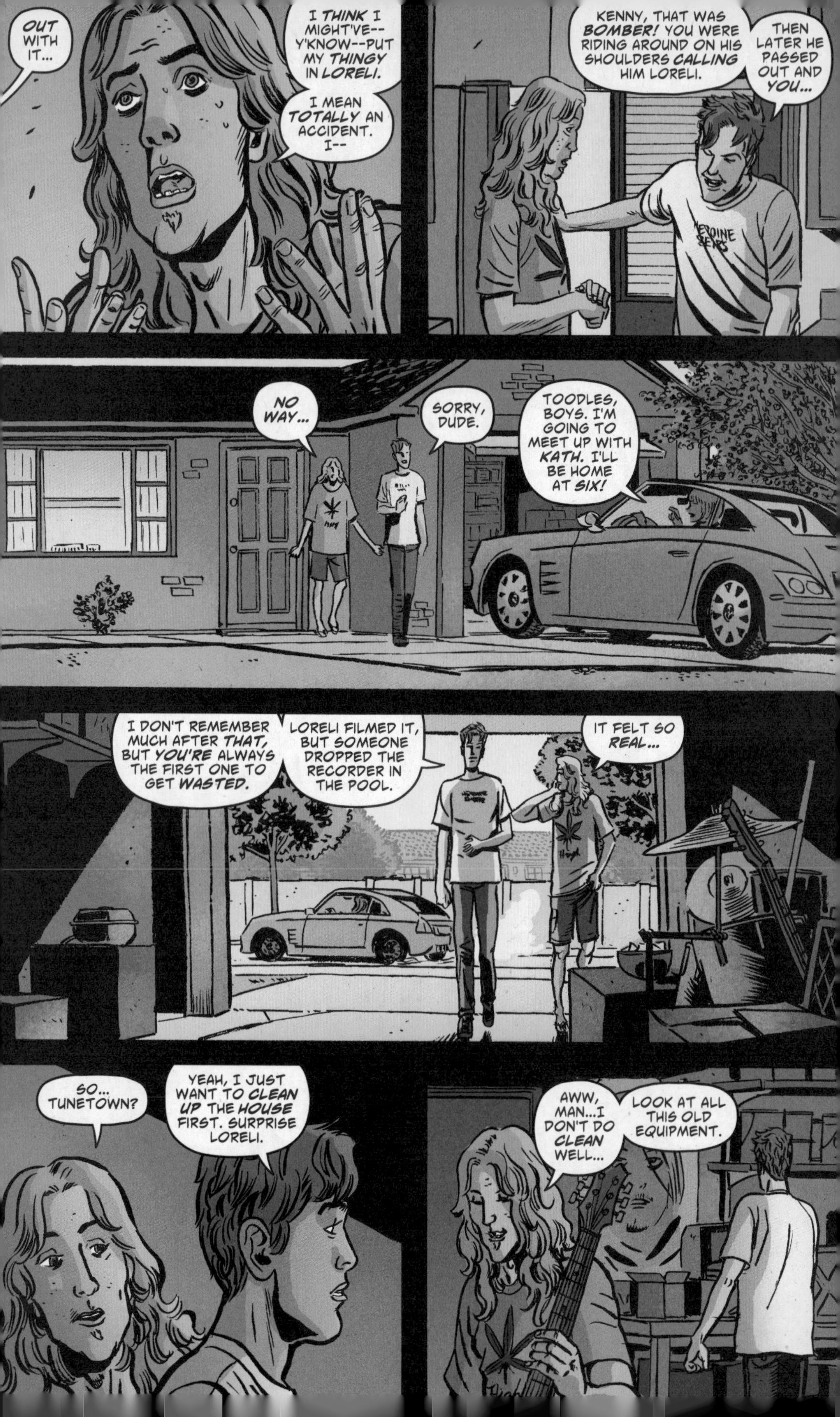

OUT WITH IT...
I THINK I MIGHT'VE--Y'KNOW--PUT MY THINGY IN LORELI.
I MEAN TOTALLY AN ACCIDENT. I--
KENNY, THAT WAS BOMBER! YOU WERE RIDING AROUND ON HIS SHOULDERS CALLING HIM LORELI.
THEN LATER HE PASSED OUT AND YOU...
NO WAY...
SORRY, DUDE.
TOODLES, BOYS. I'M GOING TO MEET UP WITH KATH. I'LL BE HOME AT SIX!
I DON'T REMEMBER MUCH AFTER THAT, BUT YOU'RE ALWAYS THE FIRST ONE TO GET WASTED.
LORELI FILMED IT, BUT SOMEONE DROPPED THE RECORDER IN THE POOL.
IT FELT SO REAL...
SO... TUNETOWN?
YEAH, I JUST WANT TO CLEAN UP THE HOUSE FIRST. SURPRISE LORELI.
AWW, MAN...I DON'T DO CLEAN WELL...
LOOK AT ALL THIS OLD EQUIPMENT.

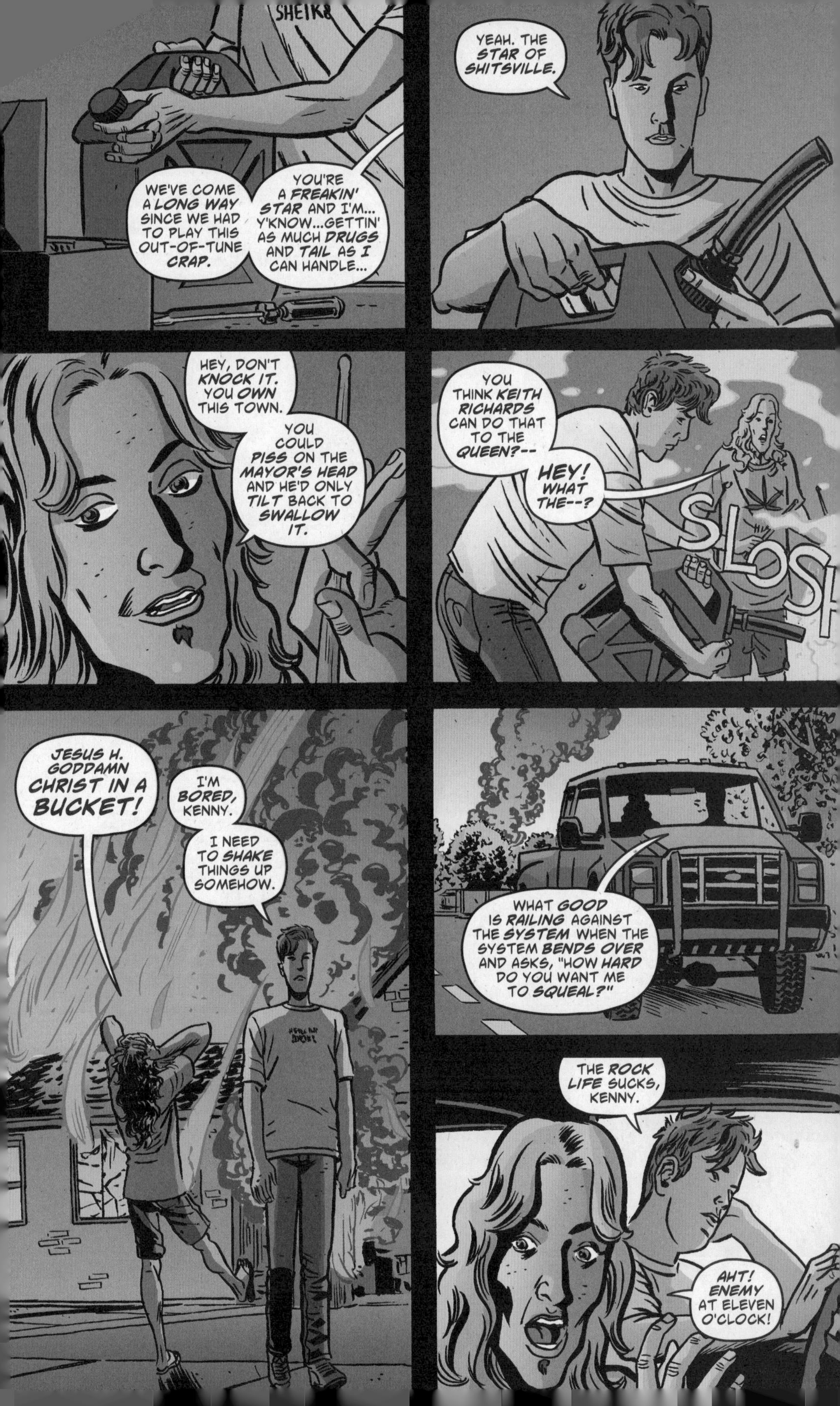
SHEIK8
WE'VE COME A LONG WAY SINCE WE HAD TO PLAY THIS OUT-OF-TUNE CRAP.
YOU'RE A FREAKIN' STAR AND I'M... Y'KNOW...GETTIN' AS MUCH DRUGS AND TAIL AS I CAN HANDLE...
YEAH. THE STAR OF SHITSVILLE.
HEY, DON'T KNOCK IT. YOU OWN THIS TOWN.
YOU COULD PISS ON THE MAYOR'S HEAD AND HE'D ONLY TILT BACK TO SWALLOW IT.
YOU THINK KEITH RICHARDS CAN DO THAT TO THE QUEEN?--
HEY! WHAT THE--?
SLOSH
JESUS H. GODDAMN CHRIST IN A BUCKET!
I'M BORED, KENNY.
I NEED TO SHAKE THINGS UP SOMEHOW.
WHAT GOOD IS RAILING AGAINST THE SYSTEM WHEN THE SYSTEM BENDS OVER AND ASKS, "HOW HARD DO YOU WANT ME TO SQUEAL?"
THE ROCK LIFE SUCKS, KENNY.
AHT! ENEMY AT ELEVEN O'CLOCK!

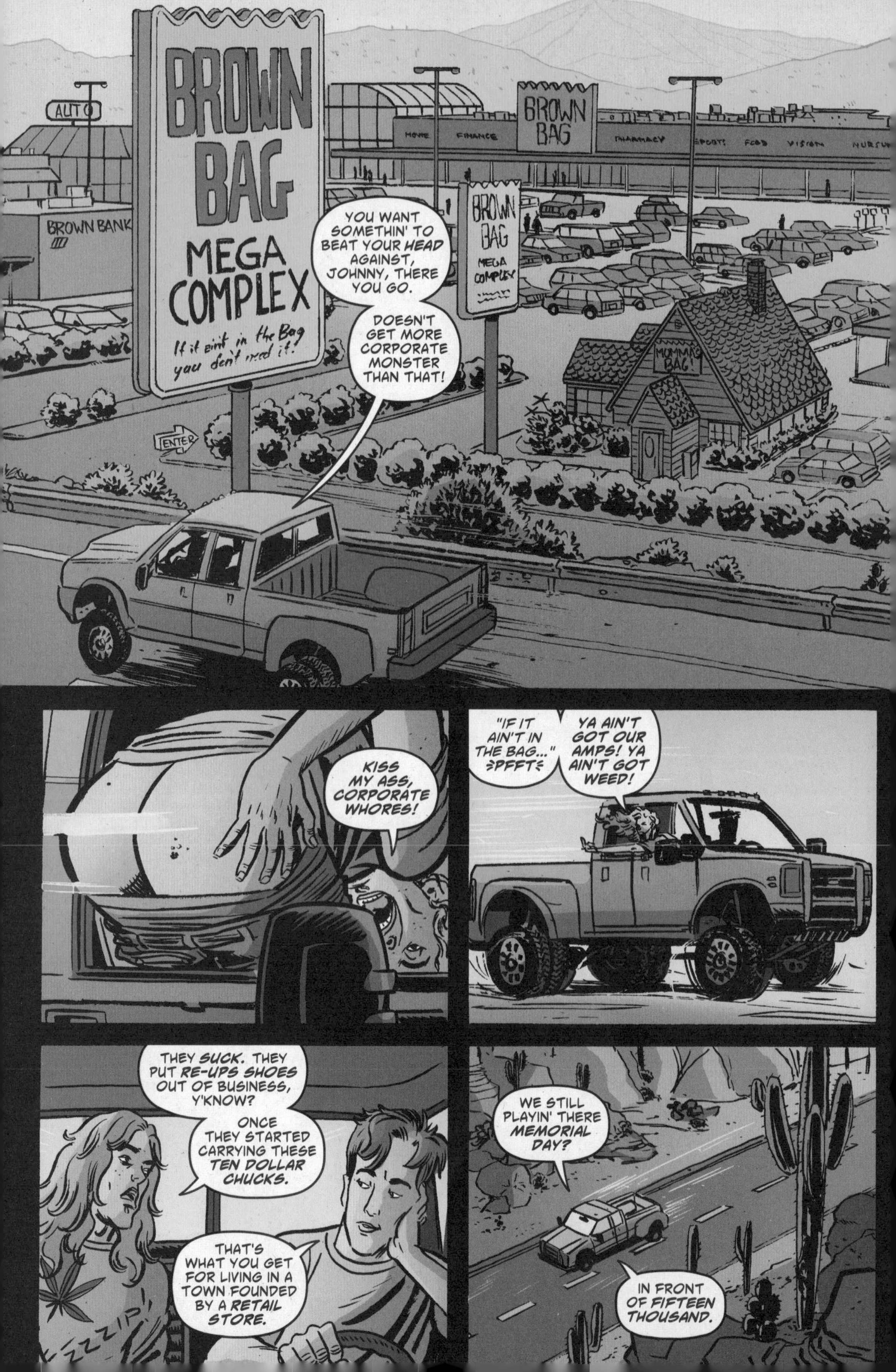
BROWN BAG
MEGA COMPLEX
If it ain't in the Bag you don't need it!
AUTO
BROWN BANK
BROWN BAG
MOVIE FINANCE PHARMACY SPORTS FOOD VISION NURSERY
BROWN BAG MEGA COMPLEX
MOMMA'S BAG
ENTER
YOU WANT SOMETHIN' TO BEAT YOUR HEAD AGAINST, JOHNNY, THERE YOU GO.
DOESN'T GET MORE CORPORATE MONSTER THAN THAT!
KISS MY ASS, CORPORATE WHORES!
"IF IT AIN'T IN THE BAG..." PFFT
YA AIN'T GOT OUR AMPS! YA AIN'T GOT WEED!
THEY SUCK. THEY PUT RE-UPS SHOES OUT OF BUSINESS, Y'KNOW?
ONCE THEY STARTED CARRYING THESE TEN DOLLAR CHUCKS.
THAT'S WHAT YOU GET FOR LIVING IN A TOWN FOUNDED BY A RETAIL STORE.
ZZZZIP
WE STILL PLAYIN' THERE MEMORIAL DAY?
IN FRONT OF FIFTEEN THOUSAND.

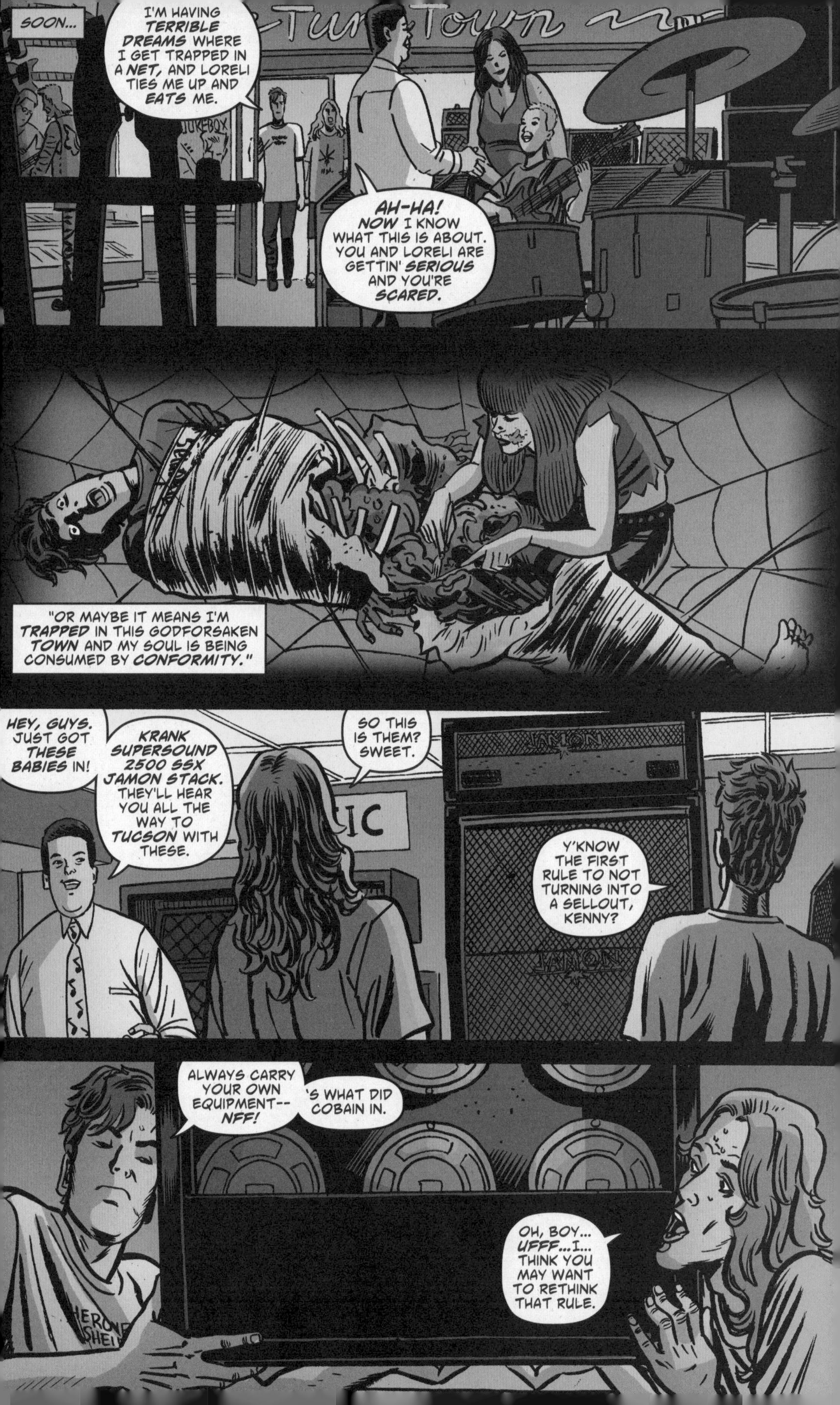
SOON...
I'M HAVING TERRIBLE DREAMS WHERE I GET TRAPPED IN A NET, AND LORELI TIES ME UP AND EATS ME.
AH-HA! NOW I KNOW WHAT THIS IS ABOUT. YOU AND LORELI ARE GETTIN' SERIOUS AND YOU'RE SCARED.
"OR MAYBE IT MEANS I'M TRAPPED IN THIS GODFORSAKEN TOWN AND MY SOUL IS BEING CONSUMED BY CONFORMITY."
HEY, GUYS. JUST GOT THESE BABIES IN!
KRANK SUPERSOUND 2500 SSX JAMON STACK. THEY'LL HEAR YOU ALL THE WAY TO TUCSON WITH THESE.
SO THIS IS THEM? SWEET.
Y'KNOW THE FIRST RULE TO NOT TURNING INTO A SELLOUT, KENNY?
ALWAYS CARRY YOUR OWN EQUIPMENT-- NFF!
'S WHAT DID COBAIN IN.
OH, BOY... UFFF...I... THINK YOU MAY WANT TO RETHINK THAT RULE.

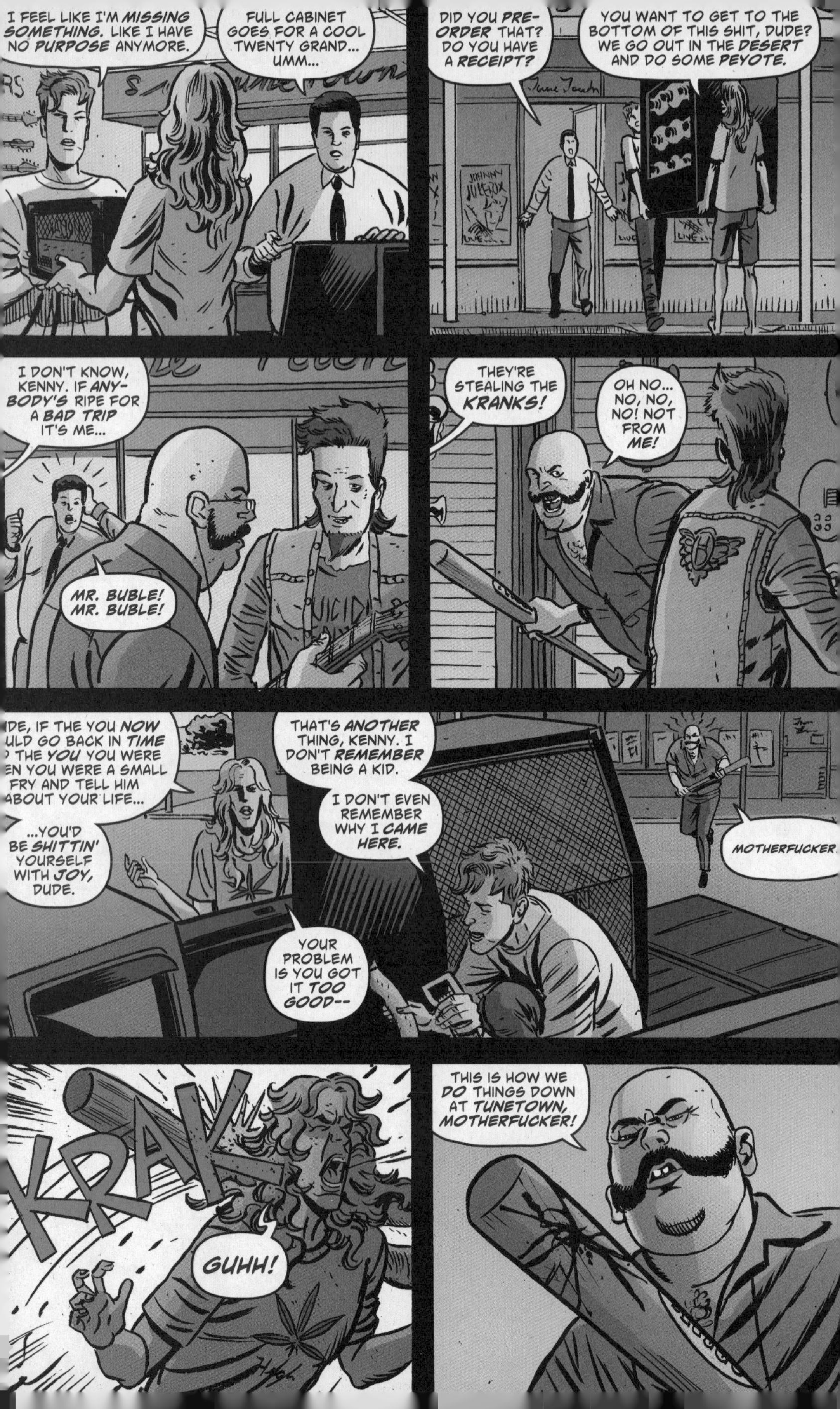
I FEEL LIKE I'M MISSING SOMETHING. LIKE I HAVE NO PURPOSE ANYMORE.
FULL CABINET GOES FOR A COOL TWENTY GRAND... UMM...
DID YOU PRE-ORDER THAT? DO YOU HAVE A RECEIPT?
YOU WANT TO GET TO THE BOTTOM OF THIS SHIT, DUDE? WE GO OUT IN THE DESERT AND DO SOME PEYOTE.
I DON'T KNOW, KENNY. IF ANYBODY'S RIPE FOR A BAD TRIP IT'S ME...
MR. BUBLE! MR. BUBLE!
THEY'RE STEALING THE KRANKS!
OH NO... NO, NO, NO! NOT FROM ME!
...YOU'D BE SHITTIN' YOURSELF WITH JOY, DUDE.
THAT'S ANOTHER THING, KENNY. I DON'T REMEMBER BEING A KID.
I DON'T EVEN REMEMBER WHY I CAME HERE.
YOUR PROBLEM IS YOU GOT IT TOO GOOD--
MOTHERFUCKER
KRAK
GUHH!
THIS IS HOW WE DO THINGS DOWN AT TUNETOWN, MOTHERFUCKER!

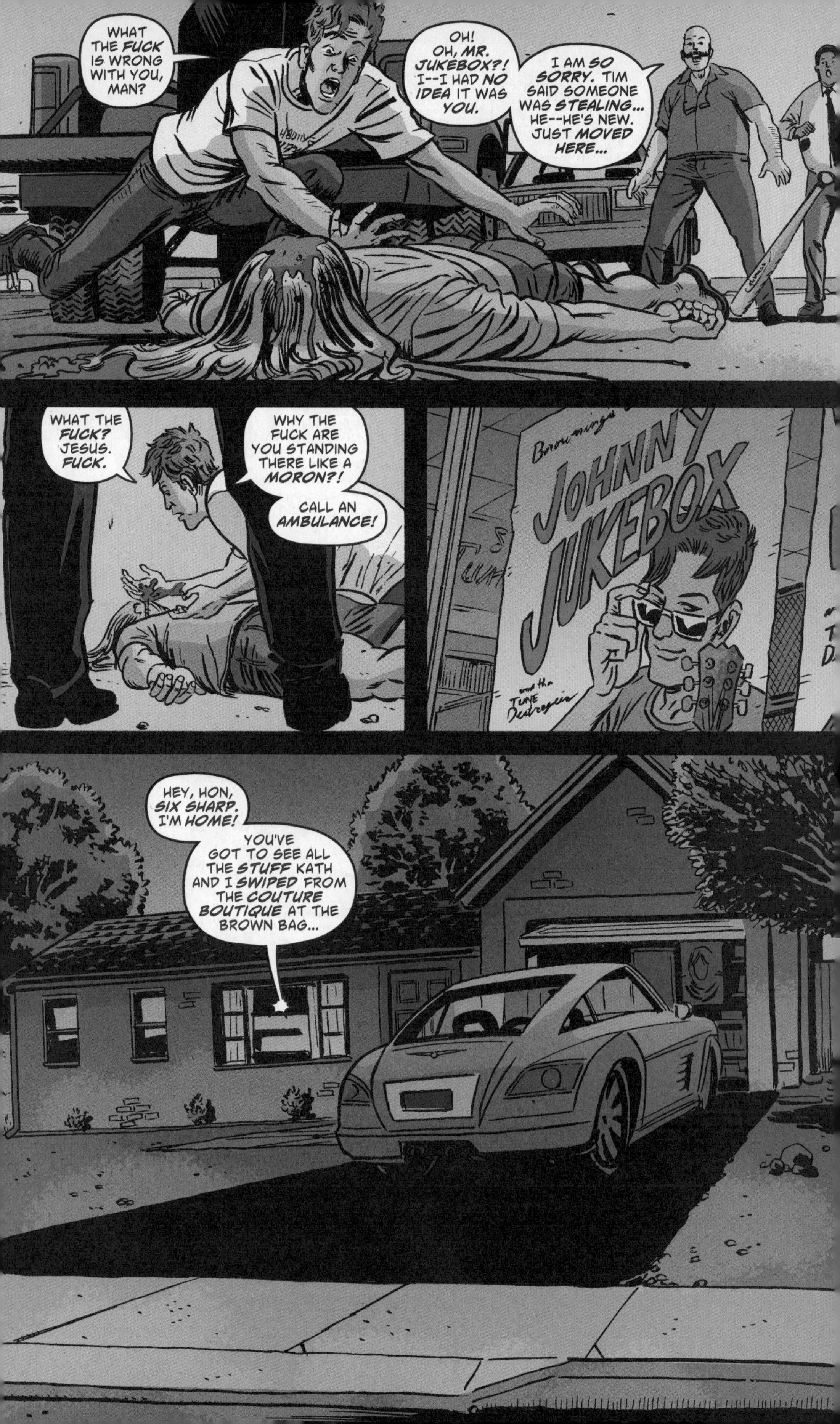
WHAT THE FUCK IS WRONG WITH YOU, MAN?
OH! OH, MR. JUKEBOX?! I--I HAD NO IDEA IT WAS YOU.
I AM SO SORRY. TIM SAID SOMEONE WAS STEALING... HE--HE'S NEW. JUST MOVED HERE...
WHAT THE FUCK? JESUS. FUCK.
WHY THE FUCK ARE YOU STANDING THERE LIKE A MORON?!
CALL AN AMBULANCE!
JOHNNY JUKEBOX
HEY, HON, SIX SHARP. I'M HOME!
YOU'VE GOT TO SEE ALL THE STUFF KATH AND I SWIPED FROM THE COUTURE BOUTIQUE AT THE BROWN BAG...

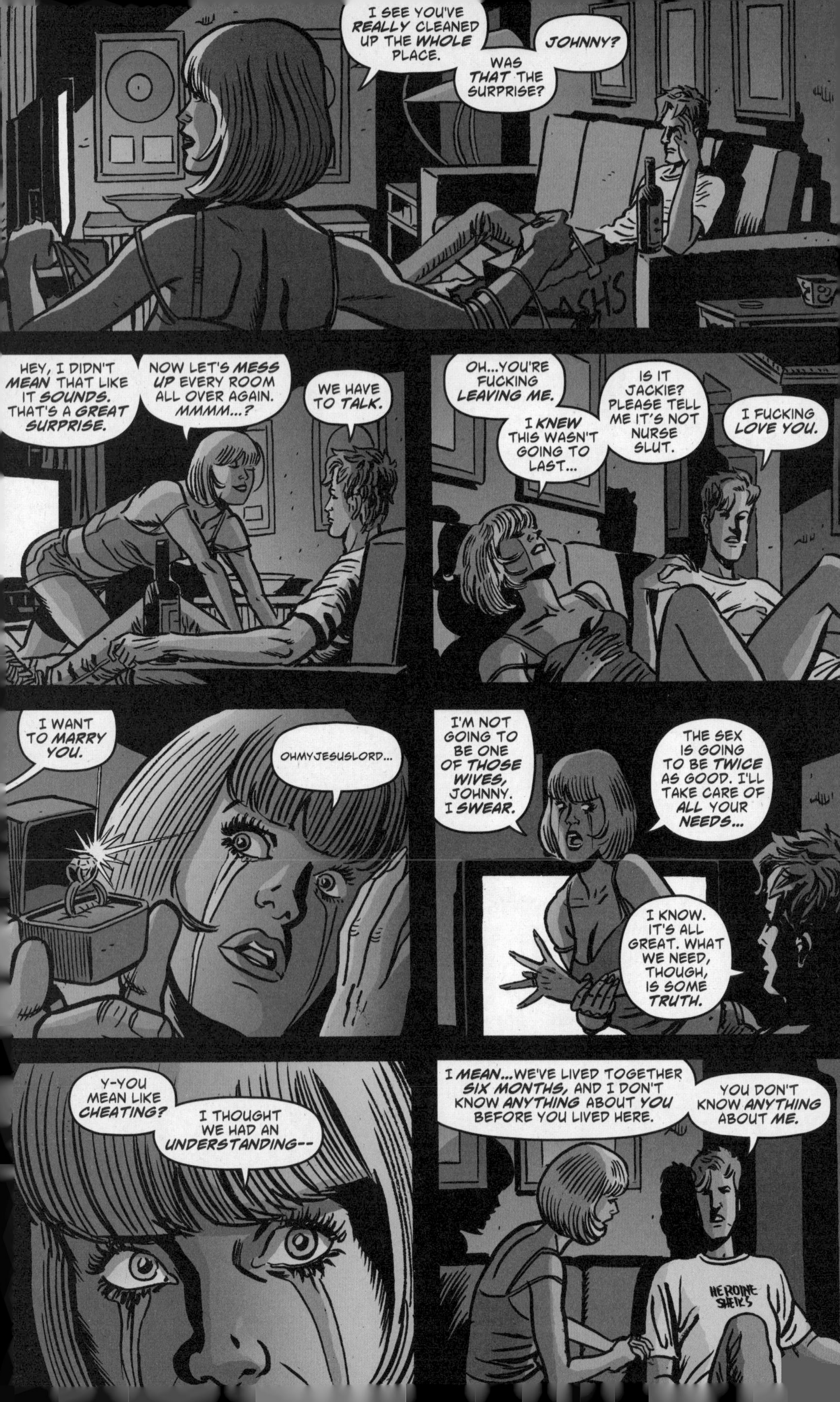
I SEE YOU'VE *REALLY* CLEANED UP THE *WHOLE* PLACE.
WAS *THAT* THE SURPRISE?
JOHNNY?
HEY, I DIDN'T *MEAN* THAT LIKE IT *SOUNDS*. THAT'S A *GREAT SURPRISE*.
NOW LET'S *MESS UP* EVERY ROOM ALL OVER AGAIN. *MMMM...?*
WE HAVE TO *TALK*.
OH...YOU'RE FUCKING *LEAVING ME*.
I *KNEW* THIS WASN'T GOING TO LAST...
IS IT JACKIE? PLEASE TELL ME IT'S NOT NURSE SLUT.
I FUCKING *LOVE YOU*.
I WANT TO *MARRY YOU*.
OHMYJESUSLORD...
I'M NOT GOING TO BE ONE OF *THOSE WIVES*, JOHNNY. I *SWEAR*.
THE SEX IS GOING TO BE *TWICE* AS GOOD. I'LL TAKE CARE OF *ALL* YOUR *NEEDS...*
I KNOW. IT'S ALL GREAT. WHAT WE NEED, THOUGH, IS SOME *TRUTH*.
Y-YOU MEAN LIKE *CHEATING?*
I THOUGHT WE HAD AN *UNDERSTANDING--*
I *MEAN*...WE'VE LIVED TOGETHER *SIX MONTHS*, AND I DON'T KNOW *ANYTHING* ABOUT *YOU* BEFORE YOU LIVED HERE.
YOU DON'T KNOW *ANYTHING* ABOUT *ME*.
HEROINE SHEIKS

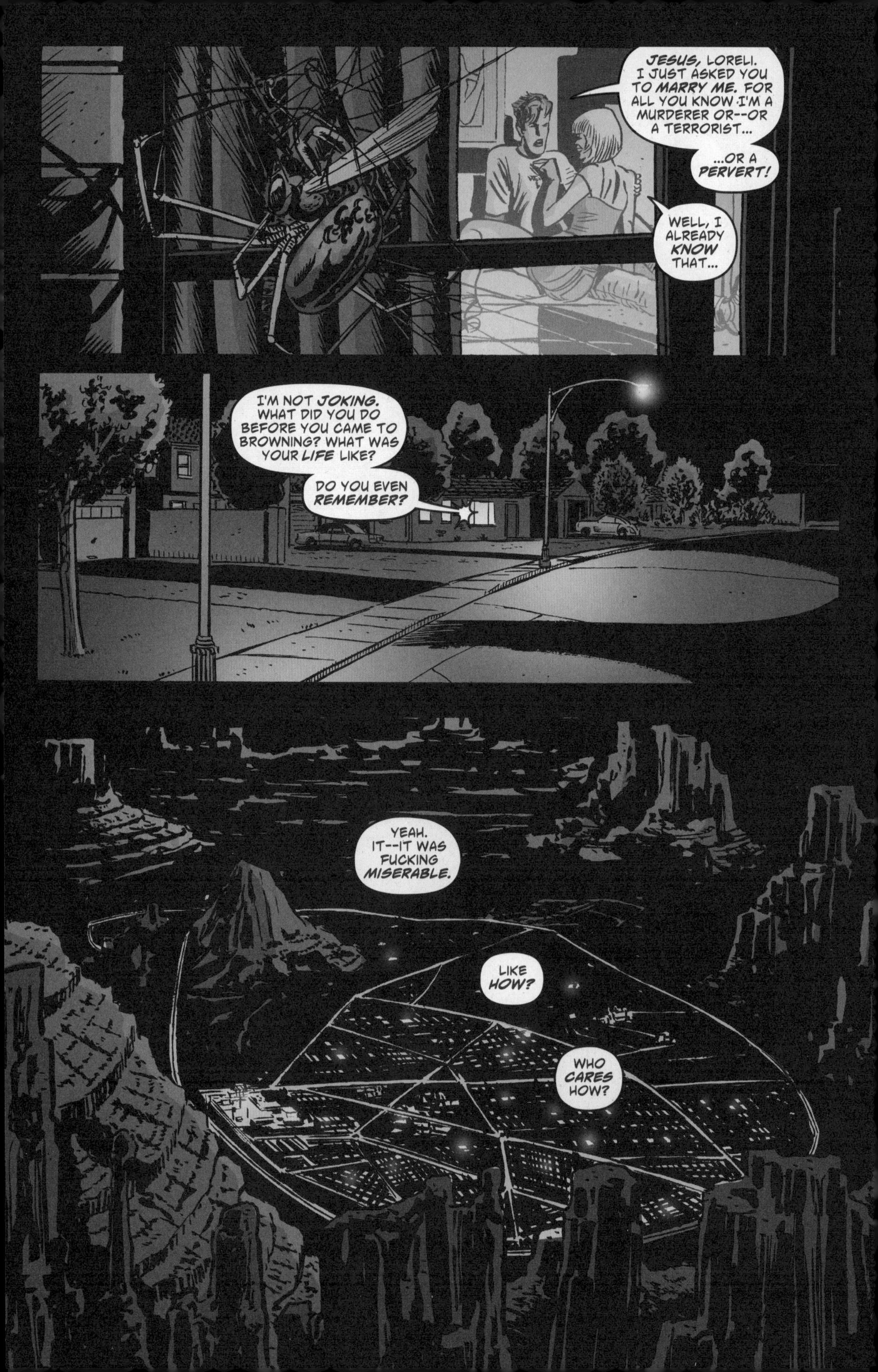
JESUS, LORELI. I JUST ASKED YOU TO MARRY ME. FOR ALL YOU KNOW I'M A MURDERER OR--OR A TERRORIST...
...OR A PERVERT!
WELL, I ALREADY KNOW THAT...
I'M NOT JOKING. WHAT DID YOU DO BEFORE YOU CAME TO BROWNING? WHAT WAS YOUR LIFE LIKE?
DO YOU EVEN REMEMBER?
YEAH. IT--IT WAS FUCKING MISERABLE.
LIKE HOW?
WHO CARES HOW?

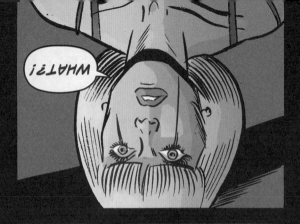

WHAT?!

JOHNNY, YOU TOOK HOW MANY DRUGS LAST NIGHT? ASK KENNY. I BET HE SAYS YOU LOOPED OUT.

KENNY'S DEAD.

I POURED GASOLINE OVER EVERYTHING AND LIT THE WHOLE THING UP.

OH, HA, HA.

OKAY... Y'KNOW I DIDN'T CLEAN UP THE HOUSE. I BURNED DOWN THE HOUSE.

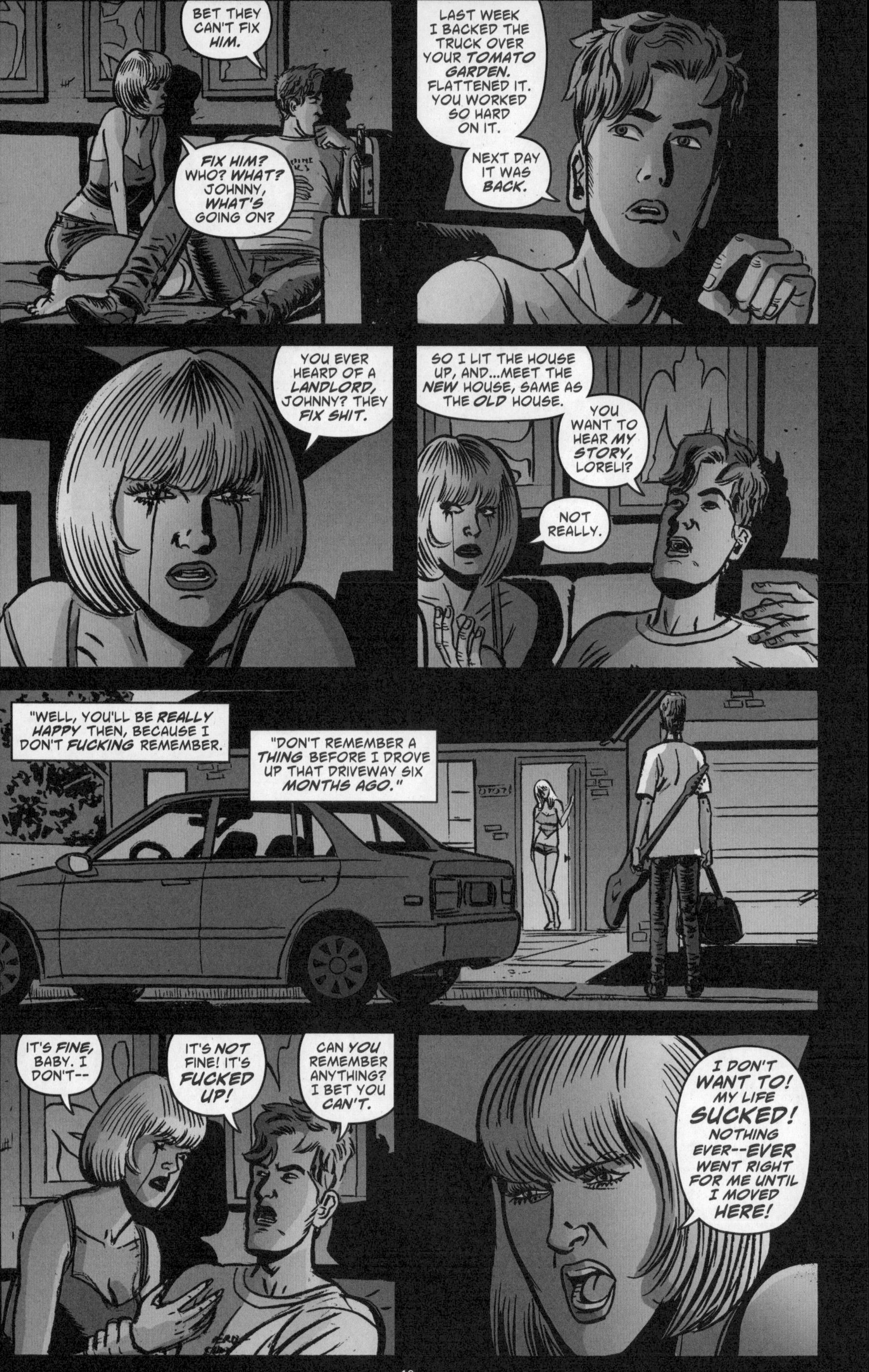
BET THEY CAN'T FIX *HIM.*
FIX HIM? WHO? *WHAT?* JOHNNY, *WHAT'S* GOING ON?
LAST WEEK I BACKED THE TRUCK OVER YOUR *TOMATO GARDEN.* FLATTENED IT. YOU WORKED SO HARD ON IT.
NEXT DAY IT WAS *BACK.*
YOU EVER HEARD OF A *LANDLORD,* JOHNNY? THEY *FIX SHIT.*
SO I LIT THE HOUSE UP, AND...MEET THE *NEW* HOUSE, SAME AS THE *OLD* HOUSE.
YOU WANT TO HEAR *MY STORY,* LORELI?
NOT REALLY.
"WELL, YOU'LL BE *REALLY HAPPY* THEN, BECAUSE I DON'T *FUCKING* REMEMBER.
"DON'T REMEMBER A *THING* BEFORE I DROVE UP THAT DRIVEWAY SIX *MONTHS AGO.*"
IT'S *FINE,* BABY. I DON'T--
IT'S *NOT* FINE! IT'S *FUCKED UP!*
CAN *YOU* REMEMBER ANYTHING? I BET YOU *CAN'T.*
I DON'T **WANT TO!** MY LIFE **SUCKED!** NOTHING EVER--**EVER** WENT RIGHT FOR ME UNTIL I MOVED **HERE!**

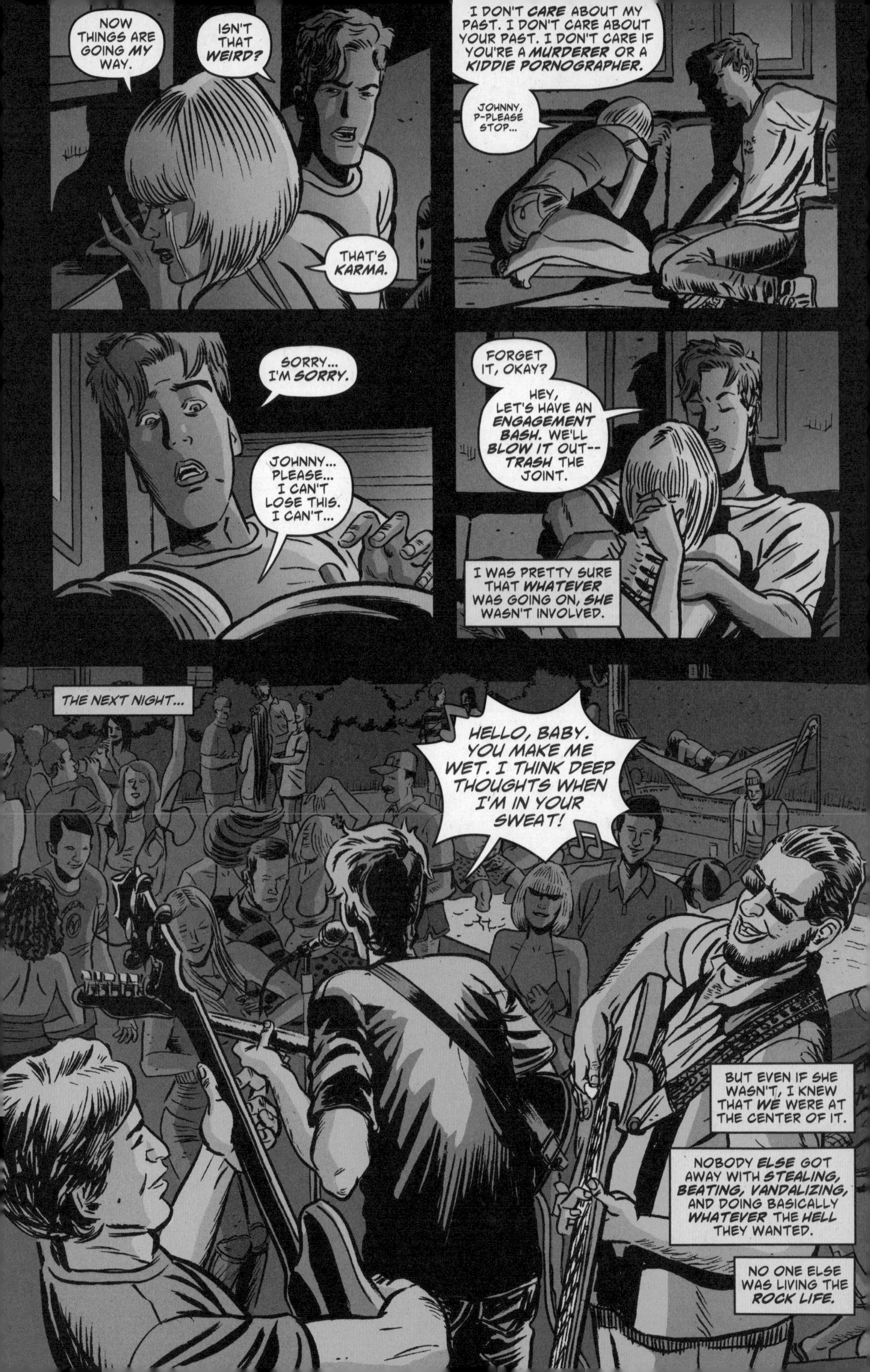
NOW THINGS ARE GOING MY WAY.
ISN'T THAT WEIRD?
THAT'S KARMA.
I DON'T CARE ABOUT MY PAST. I DON'T CARE ABOUT YOUR PAST. I DON'T CARE IF YOU'RE A MURDERER OR A KIDDIE PORNOGRAPHER.
JOHNNY, P-PLEASE STOP...
SORRY... I'M SORRY.
JOHNNY... PLEASE... I CAN'T LOSE THIS. I CAN'T...
FORGET IT, OKAY?
HEY, LET'S HAVE AN ENGAGEMENT BASH. WE'LL BLOW IT OUT-- TRASH THE JOINT.
I WAS PRETTY SURE THAT WHATEVER WAS GOING ON, SHE WASN'T INVOLVED.
THE NEXT NIGHT...
HELLO, BABY. YOU MAKE ME WET. I THINK DEEP THOUGHTS WHEN I'M IN YOUR SWEAT!
BUT EVEN IF SHE WASN'T, I KNEW THAT WE WERE AT THE CENTER OF IT.
NOBODY ELSE GOT AWAY WITH STEALING, BEATING, VANDALIZING, AND DOING BASICALLY WHATEVER THE HELL THEY WANTED.
NO ONE ELSE WAS LIVING THE ROCK LIFE.

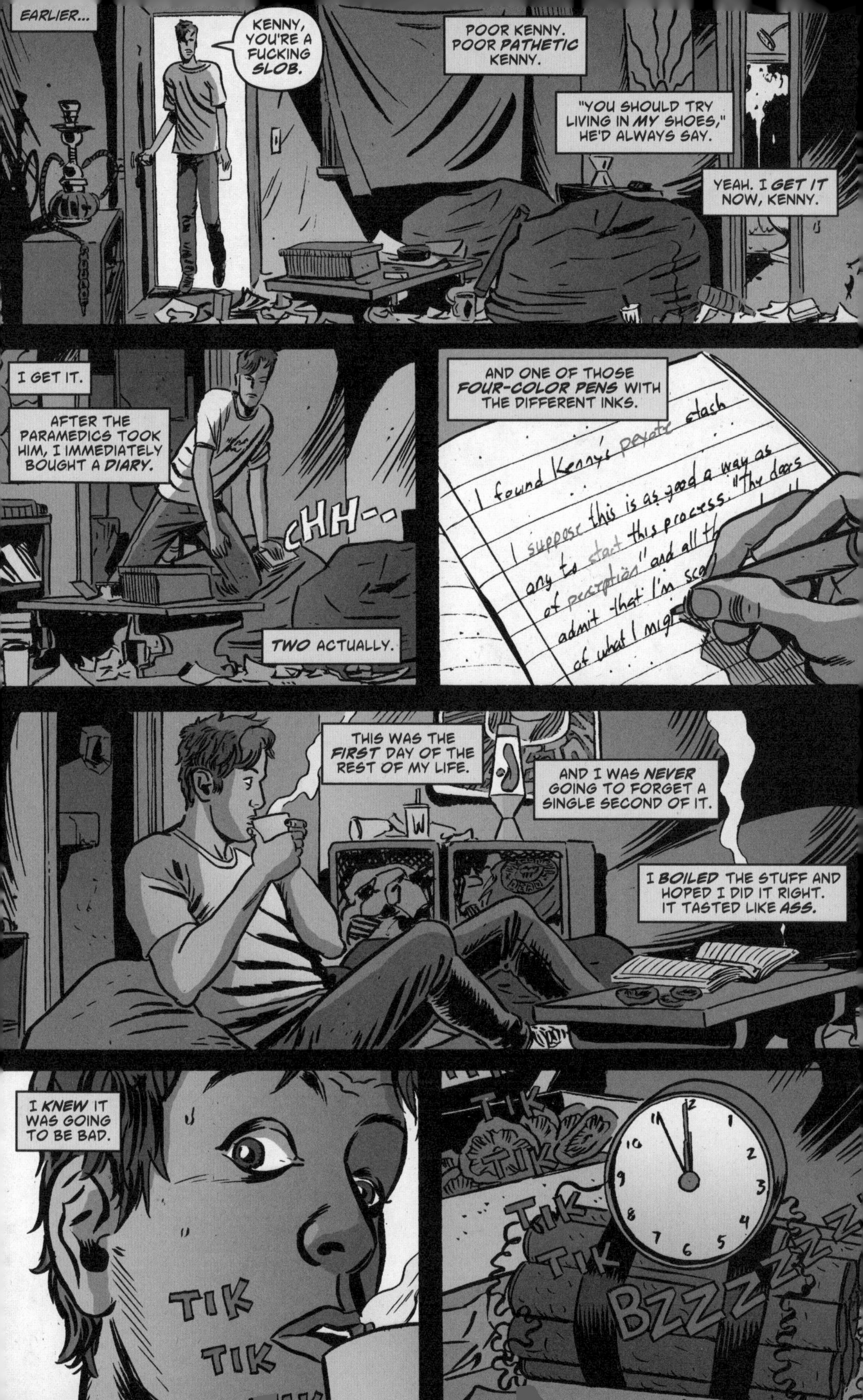
EARLIER...
KENNY, YOU'RE A FUCKING SLOB.
POOR KENNY. POOR PATHETIC KENNY.
"YOU SHOULD TRY LIVING IN MY SHOES," HE'D ALWAYS SAY.
YEAH. I GET IT NOW, KENNY.
I GET IT.
AFTER THE PARAMEDICS TOOK HIM, I IMMEDIATELY BOUGHT A DIARY.
CHH--
TWO ACTUALLY.
AND ONE OF THOSE FOUR-COLOR PENS WITH THE DIFFERENT INKS.
I found Kenny's peyote stash
I suppose this is as good a way as
any to start this process. "The doors
of perception" and all th
admit that I'm sca
of what I mig
THIS WAS THE FIRST DAY OF THE REST OF MY LIFE.
AND I WAS NEVER GOING TO FORGET A SINGLE SECOND OF IT.
I BOILED THE STUFF AND HOPED I DID IT RIGHT. IT TASTED LIKE ASS.
I KNEW IT WAS GOING TO BE BAD.
TIK
TIK
TIK
TIK
TIK
BZZZZZ

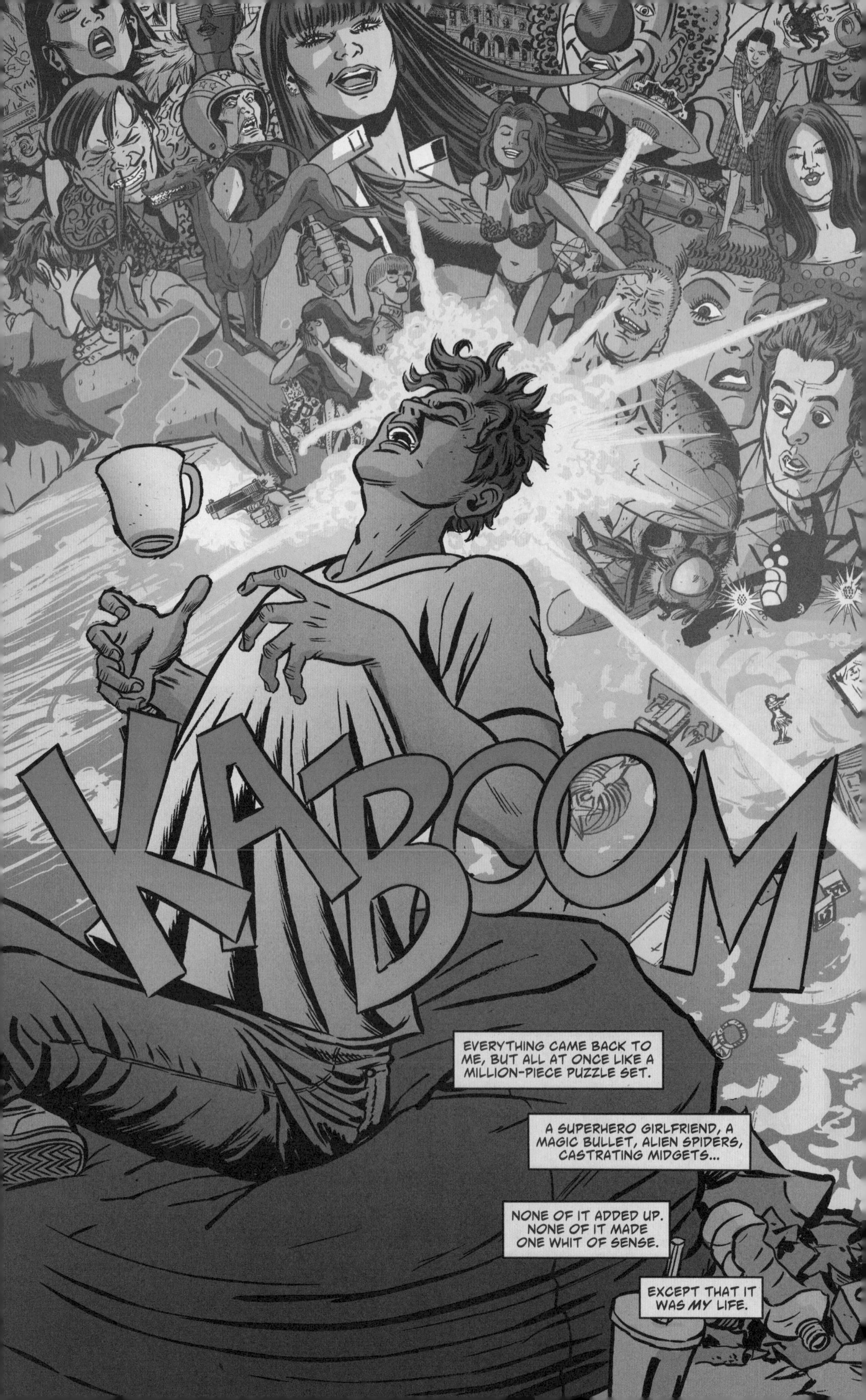
KA-BOOM
EVERYTHING CAME BACK TO ME, BUT ALL AT ONCE LIKE A MILLION-PIECE PUZZLE SET.
A SUPERHERO GIRLFRIEND, A MAGIC BULLET, ALIEN SPIDERS, CASTRATING MIDGETS...
NONE OF IT ADDED UP. NONE OF IT MADE ONE WHIT OF SENSE.
EXCEPT THAT IT WAS *MY* LIFE.

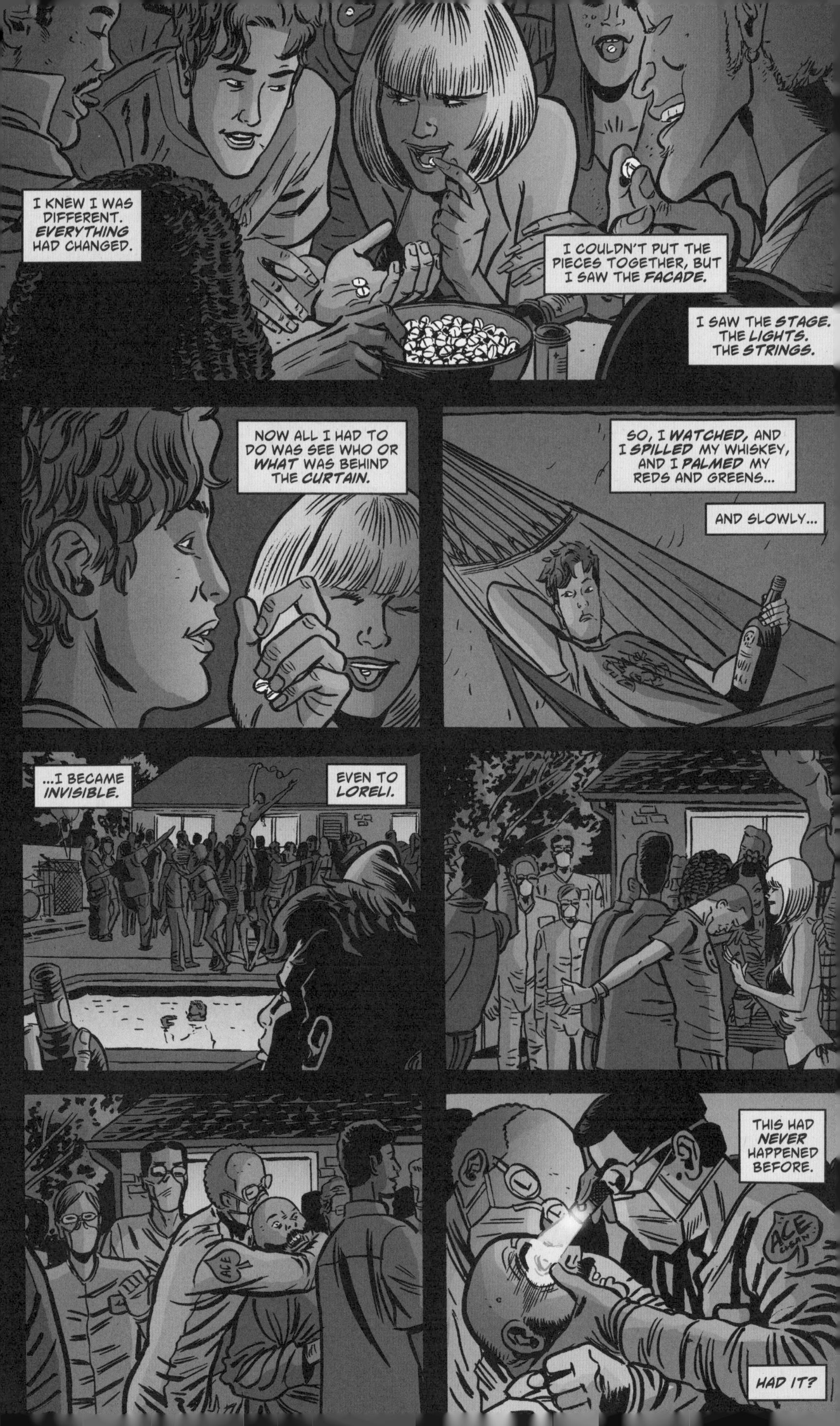
I KNEW I WAS DIFFERENT. EVERYTHING HAD CHANGED.
I COULDN'T PUT THE PIECES TOGETHER, BUT I SAW THE FACADE.
I SAW THE STAGE. THE LIGHTS. THE STRINGS.
NOW ALL I HAD TO DO WAS SEE WHO OR WHAT WAS BEHIND THE CURTAIN.
SO, I WATCHED, AND I SPILLED MY WHISKEY, AND I PALMED MY REDS AND GREENS...
AND SLOWLY...
...I BECAME INVISIBLE.
EVEN TO LORELI.
THIS HAD NEVER HAPPENED BEFORE.
HAD IT?

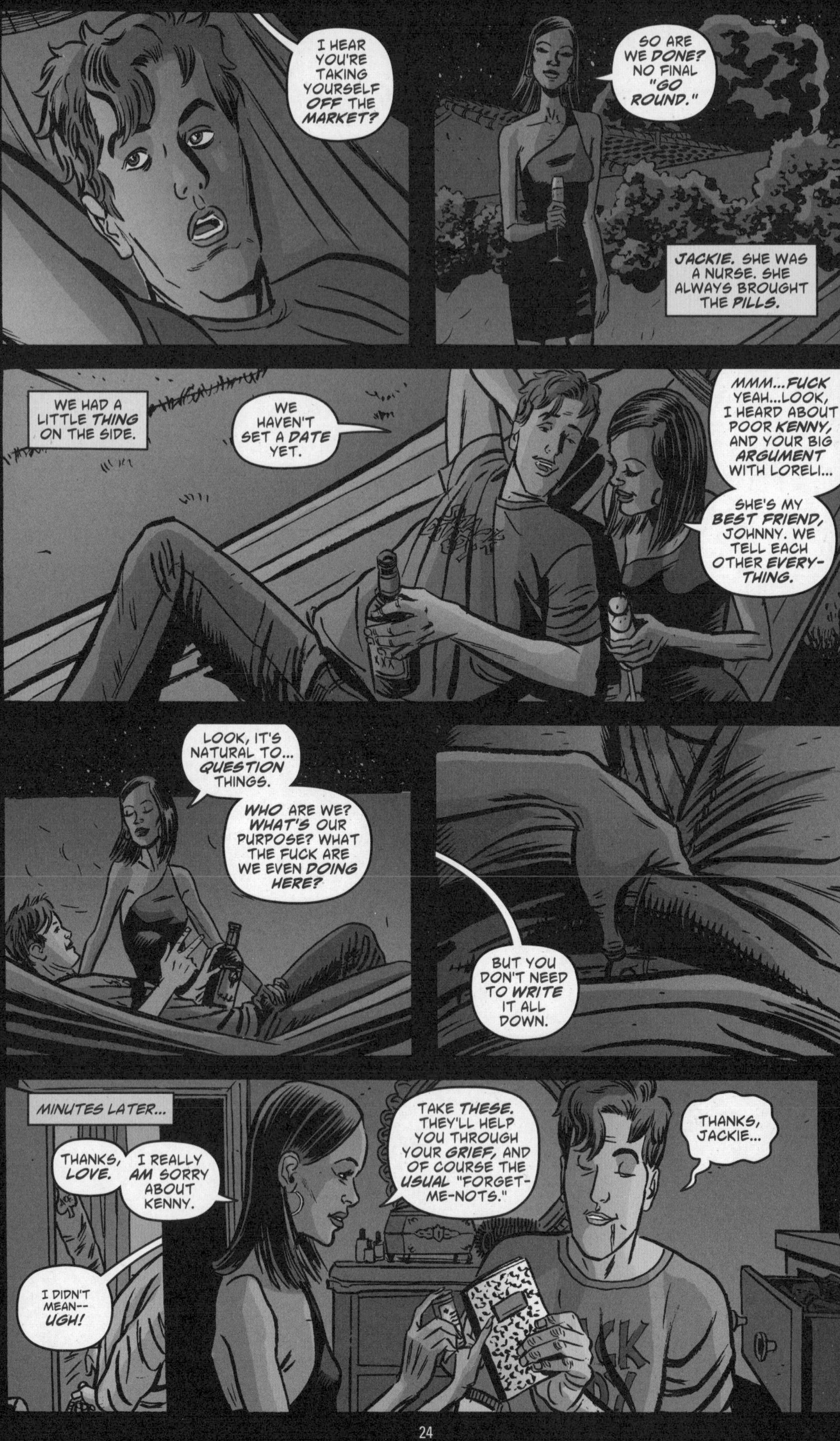
I HEAR YOU'RE TAKING YOURSELF OFF THE MARKET?
SO ARE WE DONE? NO FINAL "GO ROUND."
JACKIE. SHE WAS A NURSE. SHE ALWAYS BROUGHT THE PILLS.
WE HAD A LITTLE THING ON THE SIDE.
WE HAVEN'T SET A DATE YET.
MMM...FUCK YEAH...LOOK, I HEARD ABOUT POOR KENNY, AND YOUR BIG ARGUMENT WITH LORELI...
SHE'S MY BEST FRIEND, JOHNNY. WE TELL EACH OTHER EVERY-THING.
LOOK, IT'S NATURAL TO... QUESTION THINGS.
WHO ARE WE? WHAT'S OUR PURPOSE? WHAT THE FUCK ARE WE EVEN DOING HERE?
BUT YOU DON'T NEED TO WRITE IT ALL DOWN.
MINUTES LATER...
THANKS, LOVE.
I REALLY AM SORRY ABOUT KENNY.
I DIDN'T MEAN-- UGH!
TAKE THESE. THEY'LL HELP YOU THROUGH YOUR GRIEF, AND OF COURSE THE USUAL "FORGET-ME-NOTS."
THANKS, JACKIE...

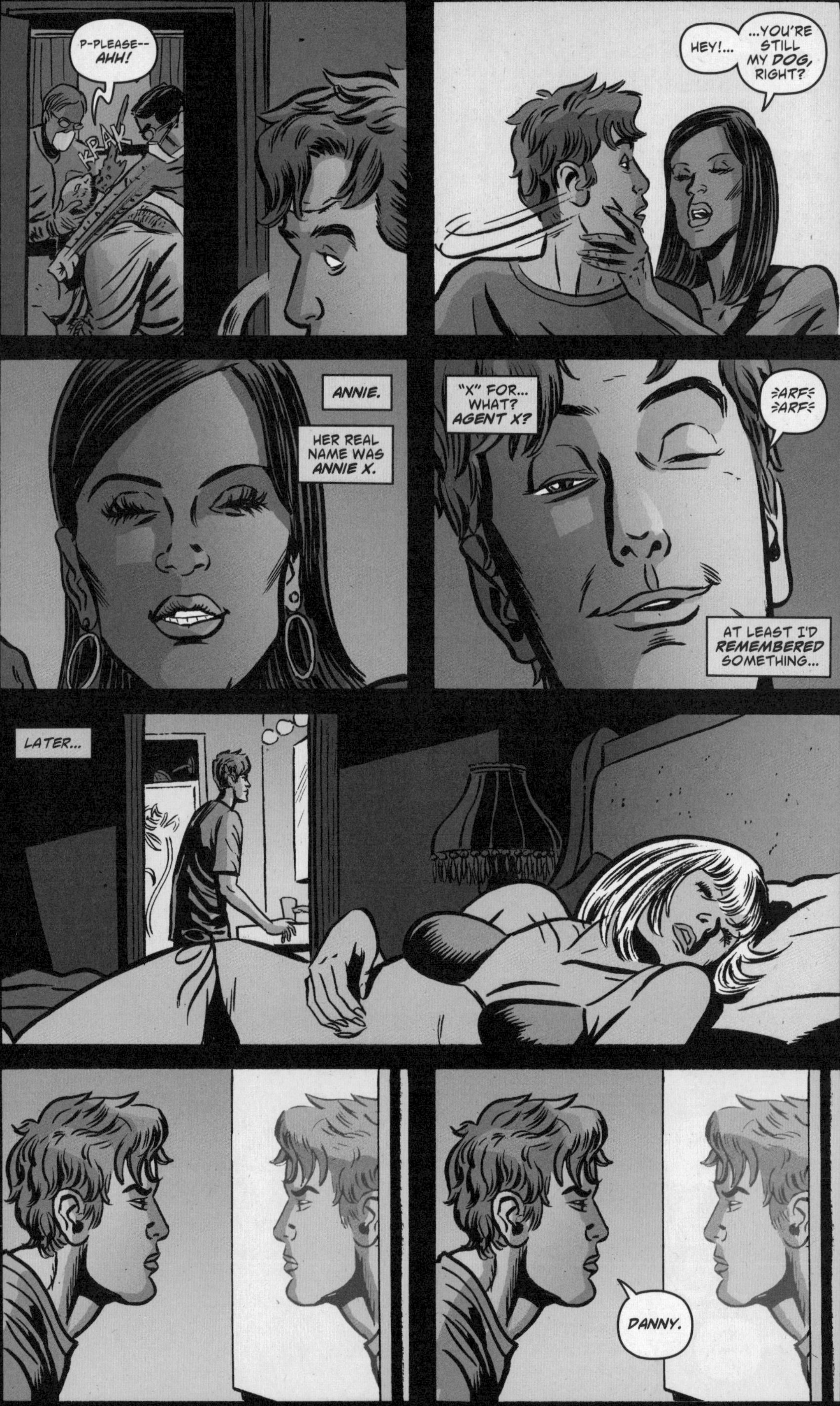
P-PLEASE--
AHH!
KRAK
HEY!...
...YOU'RE STILL MY DOG, RIGHT?
ANNIE.
HER REAL NAME WAS ANNIE X.
"X" FOR... WHAT? AGENT X?
ARF ARF
AT LEAST I'D REMEMBERED SOMETHING...
LATER...
DANNY.

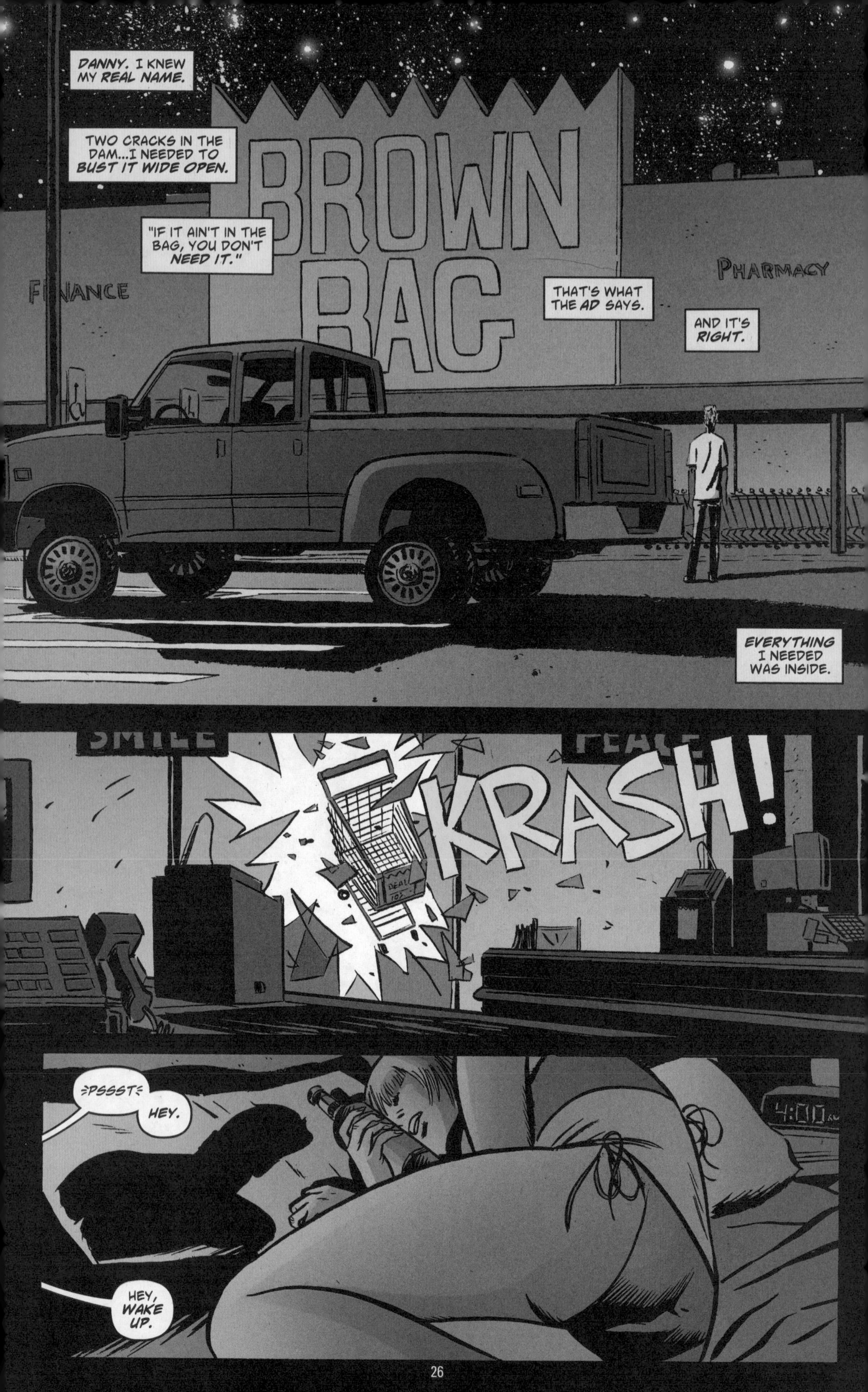
DANNY. I KNEW MY REAL NAME.
TWO CRACKS IN THE DAM...I NEEDED TO BUST IT WIDE OPEN.
BROWN BAG
"IF IT AIN'T IN THE BAG, YOU DON'T NEED IT."
FINANCE
PHARMACY
THAT'S WHAT THE AD SAYS.
AND IT'S RIGHT.
EVERYTHING I NEEDED WAS INSIDE.
KRASH!
=PSSST= HEY.
4:00 AM
HEY, WAKE UP.

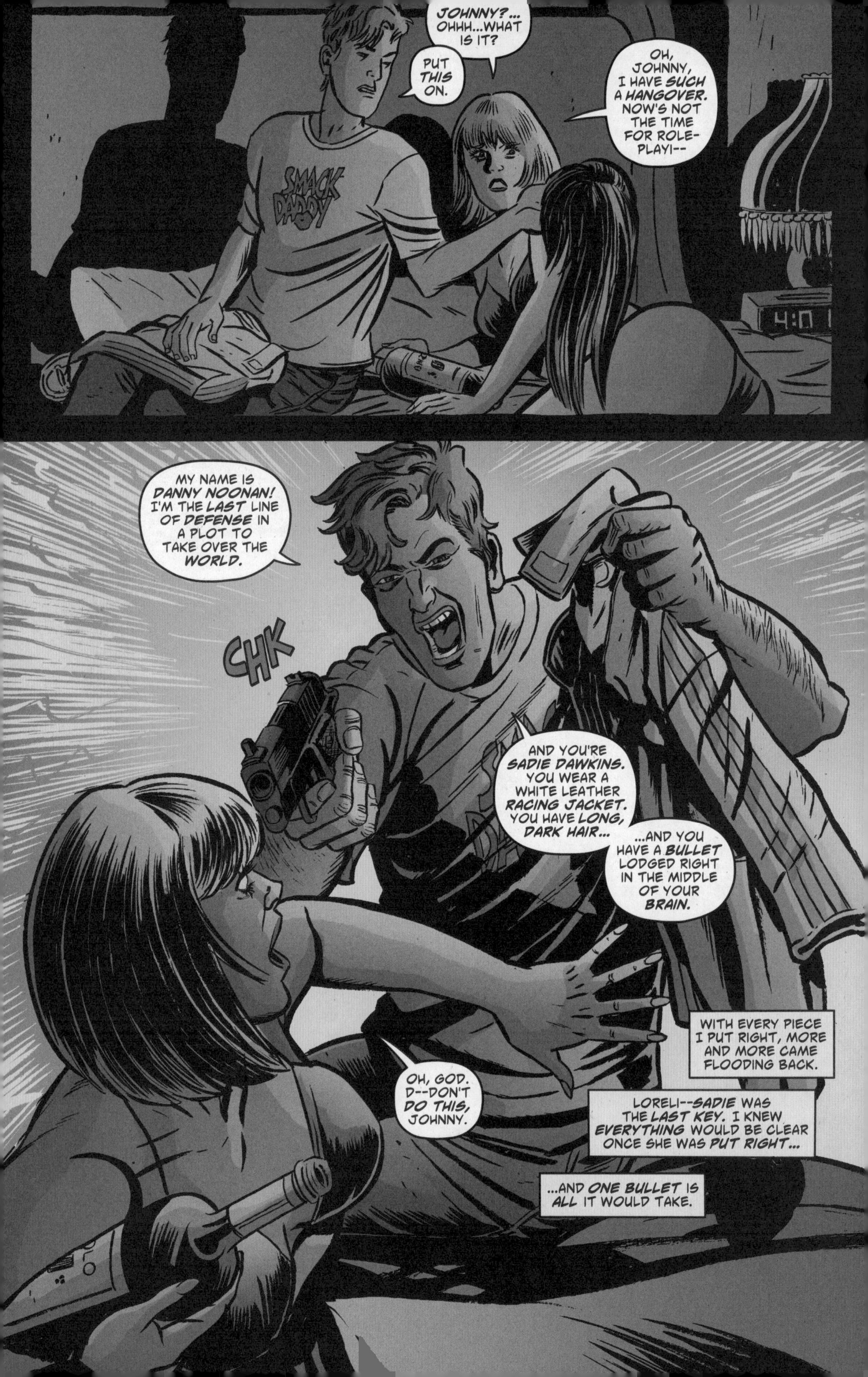
JOHNNY?... OHHH...WHAT IS IT?
PUT THIS ON.
OH, JOHNNY, I HAVE SUCH A HANGOVER. NOW'S NOT THE TIME FOR ROLE-PLAYI--
SMACK DADDY
MY NAME IS DANNY NOONAN! I'M THE LAST LINE OF DEFENSE IN A PLOT TO TAKE OVER THE WORLD.
CHK
AND YOU'RE SADIE DAWKINS. YOU WEAR A WHITE LEATHER RACING JACKET. YOU HAVE LONG, DARK HAIR...
...AND YOU HAVE A BULLET LODGED RIGHT IN THE MIDDLE OF YOUR BRAIN.
WITH EVERY PIECE I PUT RIGHT, MORE AND MORE CAME FLOODING BACK.
OH, GOD. D--DON'T DO THIS, JOHNNY.
LORELI--SADIE WAS THE LAST KEY. I KNEW EVERYTHING WOULD BE CLEAR ONCE SHE WAS PUT RIGHT...
...AND ONE BULLET IS ALL IT WOULD TAKE.

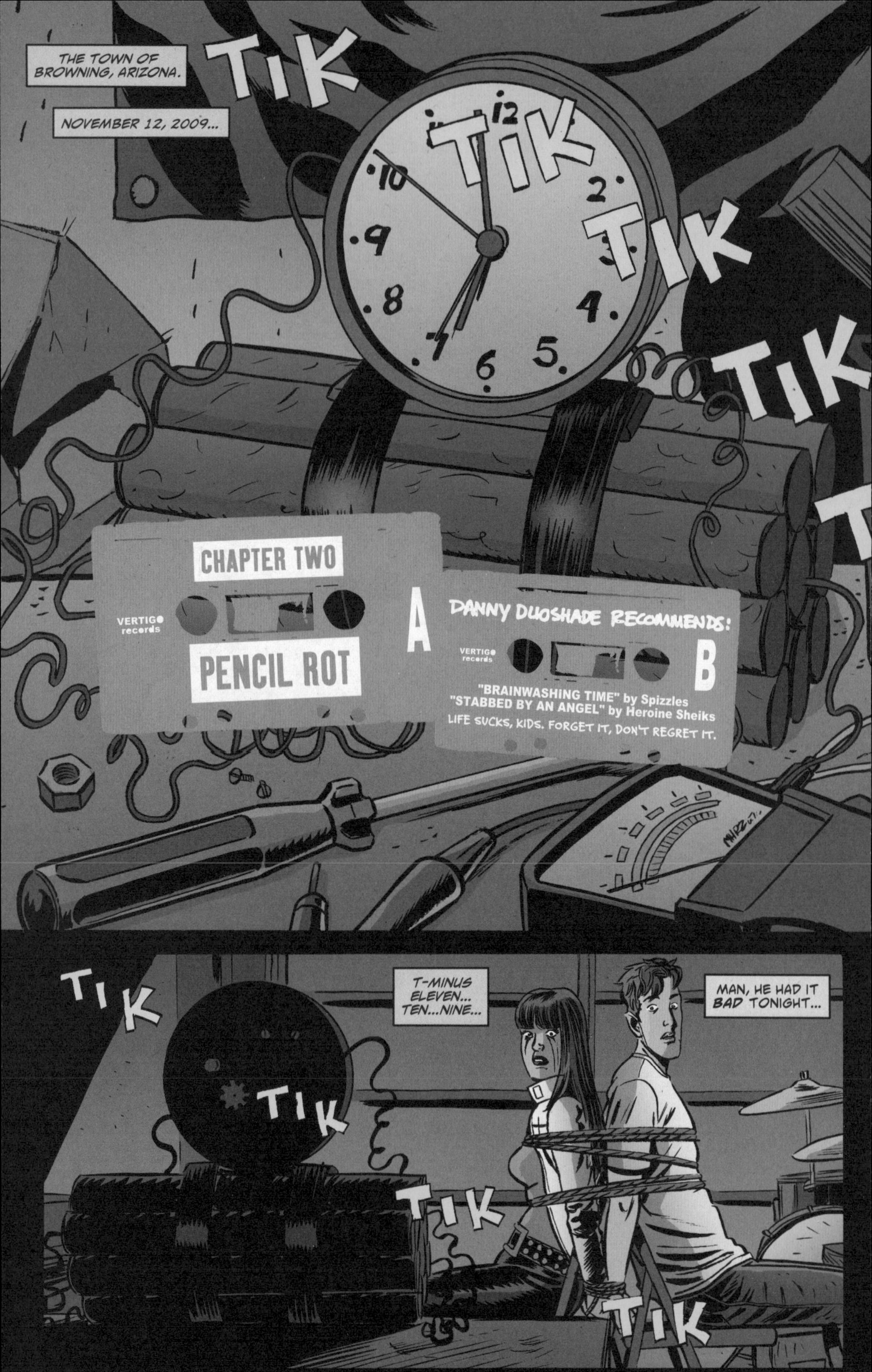
THE TOWN OF BROWNING, ARIZONA.
NOVEMBER 12, 2009...
TIK
TIK
TIK
TIK
CHAPTER TWO
VERTIGO records
A
PENCIL ROT
DANNY DUOSHADE RECOMMENDS:
VERTIGO records
B
"BRAINWASHING TIME" by Spizzles
"STABBED BY AN ANGEL" by Heroine Sheiks
LIFE SUCKS, KIDS. FORGET IT, DON'T REGRET IT.
TIK
T-MINUS ELEVEN... TEN...NINE...
MAN, HE HAD IT BAD TONIGHT...
TIK
TIK
TIK

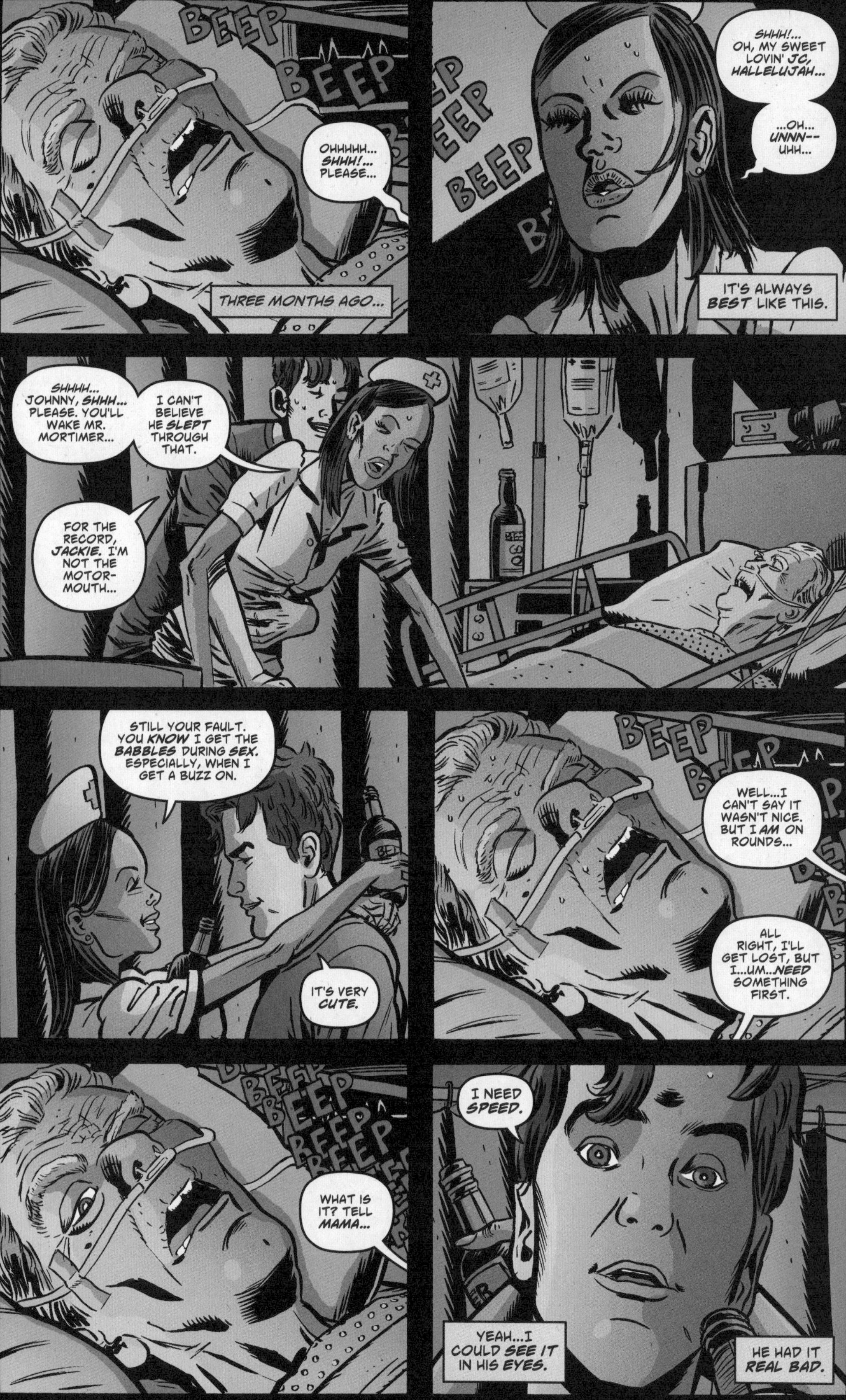
BEEP
BEEP
OHHHHH... SHHH!... PLEASE...
THREE MONTHS AGO...
BEEP
BEEP
BEEP
SHHH!... OH, MY SWEET LOVIN' JC, HALLELUJAH...
...OH... UNNN-- UHH...
IT'S ALWAYS BEST LIKE THIS.
SHHHH... JOHNNY, SHHH... PLEASE. YOU'LL WAKE MR. MORTIMER...
I CAN'T BELIEVE HE SLEPT THROUGH THAT.
FOR THE RECORD, JACKIE. I'M NOT THE MOTOR-MOUTH...
STILL YOUR FAULT. YOU KNOW I GET THE BABBLES DURING SEX. ESPECIALLY, WHEN I GET A BUZZ ON.
IT'S VERY CUTE.
BEEP
WELL...I CAN'T SAY IT WASN'T NICE. BUT I AM ON ROUNDS...
ALL RIGHT, I'LL GET LOST, BUT I...UM...NEED SOMETHING FIRST.
BEEP
WHAT IS IT? TELL MAMA...
I NEED SPEED.
YEAH...I COULD SEE IT IN HIS EYES.
HE HAD IT REAL BAD.

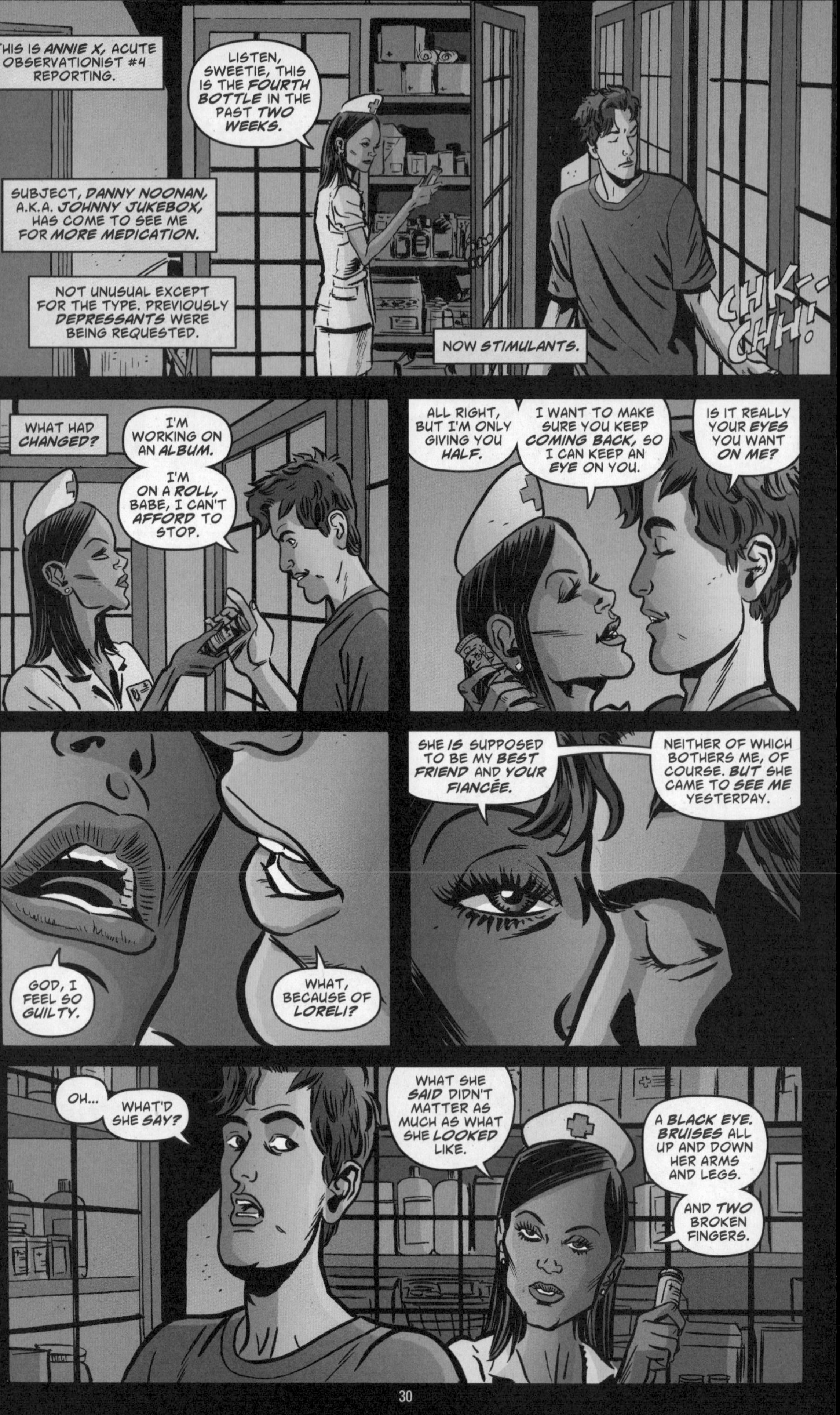
THIS IS ANNIE X, ACUTE OBSERVATIONIST #4 REPORTING.
LISTEN, SWEETIE, THIS IS THE FOURTH BOTTLE IN THE PAST TWO WEEKS.
SUBJECT, DANNY NOONAN, A.K.A. JOHNNY JUKEBOX, HAS COME TO SEE ME FOR MORE MEDICATION.
NOT UNUSUAL EXCEPT FOR THE TYPE. PREVIOUSLY DEPRESSANTS WERE BEING REQUESTED.
NOW STIMULANTS.
CHK-CHH!
WHAT HAD CHANGED?
I'M WORKING ON AN ALBUM.
I'M ON A ROLL, BABE, I CAN'T AFFORD TO STOP.
ALL RIGHT, BUT I'M ONLY GIVING YOU HALF.
I WANT TO MAKE SURE YOU KEEP COMING BACK, SO I CAN KEEP AN EYE ON YOU.
IS IT REALLY YOUR EYES YOU WANT ON ME?
GOD, I FEEL SO GUILTY.
WHAT, BECAUSE OF LORELI?
SHE IS SUPPOSED TO BE MY BEST FRIEND AND YOUR FIANCÉE.
NEITHER OF WHICH BOTHERS ME, OF COURSE. BUT SHE CAME TO SEE ME YESTERDAY.
OH...
WHAT'D SHE SAY?
WHAT SHE SAID DIDN'T MATTER AS MUCH AS WHAT SHE LOOKED LIKE.
A BLACK EYE. BRUISES ALL UP AND DOWN HER ARMS AND LEGS.
AND TWO BROKEN FINGERS.

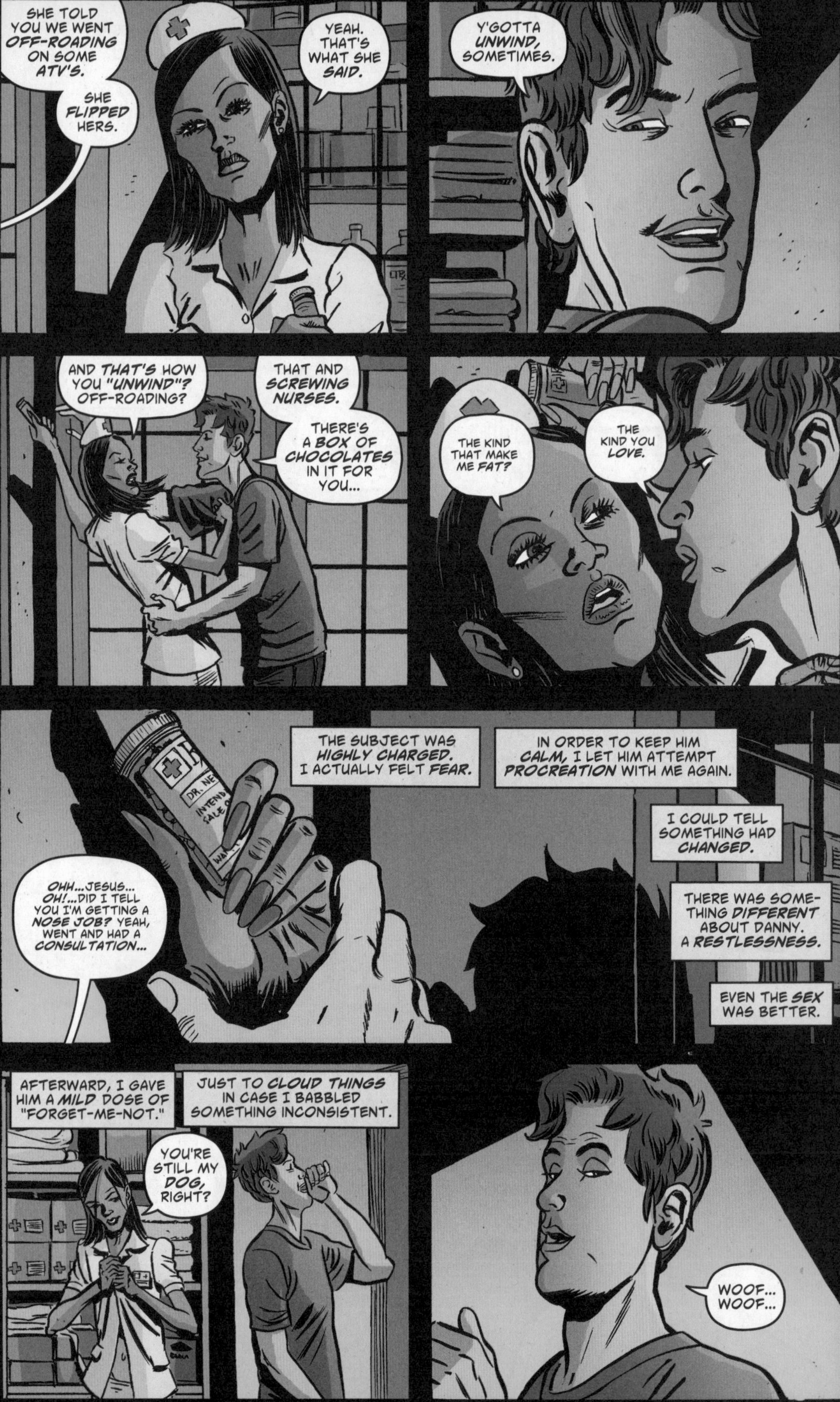
SHE TOLD YOU WE WENT OFF-ROADING ON SOME ATV'S.
SHE FLIPPED HERS.
YEAH. THAT'S WHAT SHE SAID.
Y'GOTTA UNWIND, SOMETIMES.
AND THAT'S HOW YOU "UNWIND"? OFF-ROADING?
THAT AND SCREWING NURSES.
THERE'S A BOX OF CHOCOLATES IN IT FOR YOU...
THE KIND THAT MAKE ME FAT?
THE KIND YOU LOVE.
THE SUBJECT WAS HIGHLY CHARGED. I ACTUALLY FELT FEAR.
IN ORDER TO KEEP HIM CALM, I LET HIM ATTEMPT PROCREATION WITH ME AGAIN.
OHH...JESUS... OH!...DID I TELL YOU I'M GETTING A NOSE JOB? YEAH, WENT AND HAD A CONSULTATION...
I COULD TELL SOMETHING HAD CHANGED.
THERE WAS SOME-THING DIFFERENT ABOUT DANNY. A RESTLESSNESS.
EVEN THE SEX WAS BETTER.
AFTERWARD, I GAVE HIM A MILD DOSE OF "FORGET-ME-NOT."
JUST TO CLOUD THINGS IN CASE I BABBLED SOMETHING INCONSISTENT.
YOU'RE STILL MY DOG, RIGHT?
WOOF... WOOF...

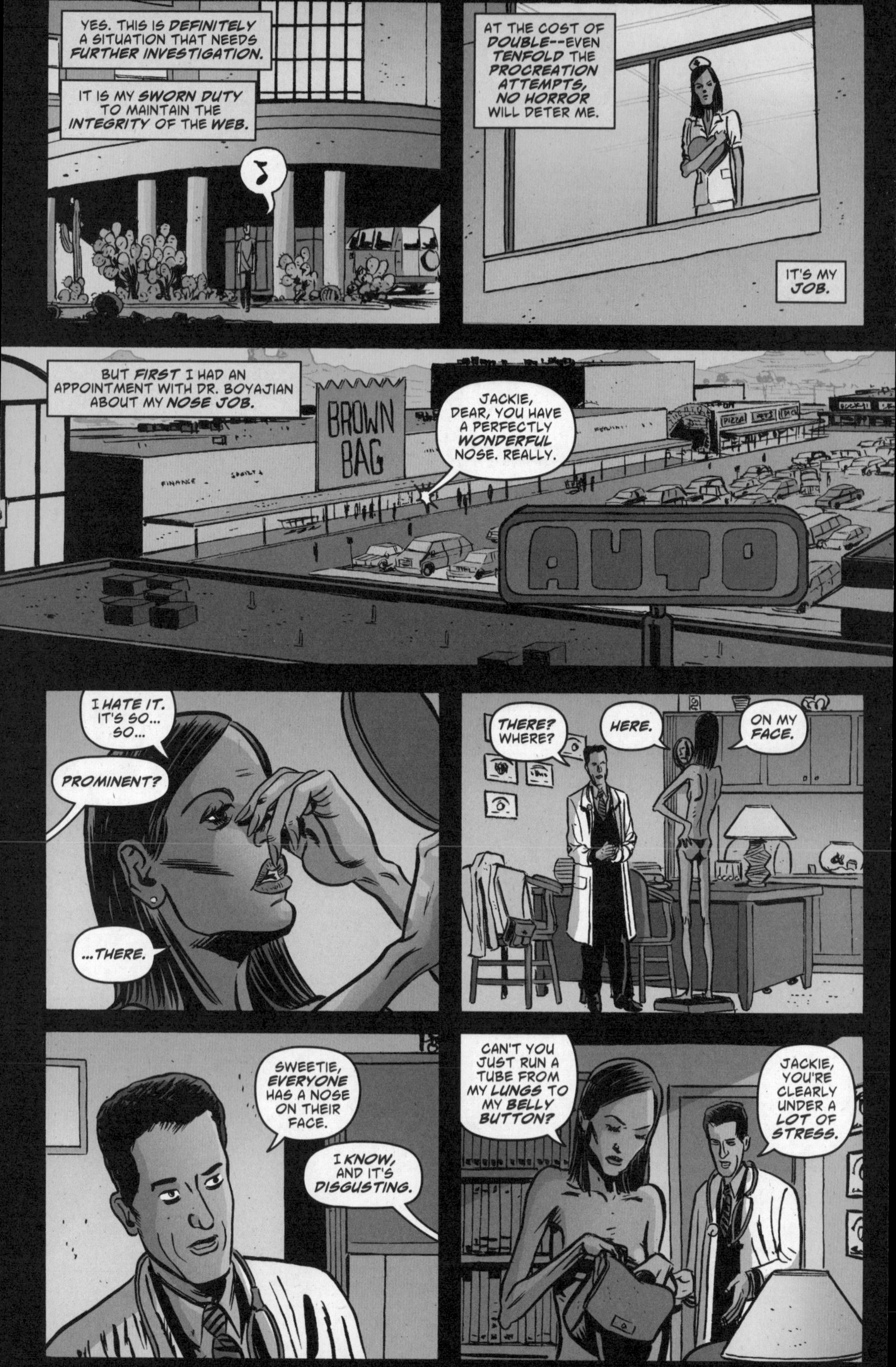
YES. THIS IS *DEFINITELY* A SITUATION THAT NEEDS *FURTHER INVESTIGATION*.
IT IS MY *SWORN DUTY* TO MAINTAIN THE *INTEGRITY* OF THE *WEB*.
AT THE COST OF *DOUBLE*--EVEN *TENFOLD* THE *PROCREATION ATTEMPTS*, *NO HORROR* WILL DETER ME.
IT'S MY *JOB*.
BUT *FIRST* I HAD AN APPOINTMENT WITH DR. BOYAJIAN ABOUT MY *NOSE JOB*.
BROWN BAG
JACKIE, DEAR, YOU HAVE A PERFECTLY *WONDERFUL* NOSE. REALLY.
AUTO
I *HATE* IT. IT'S SO... SO...
PROMINENT?
...THERE.
THERE? WHERE?
HERE.
ON MY *FACE.*
SWEETIE, *EVERYONE* HAS A NOSE ON THEIR FACE.
I *KNOW,* AND IT'S *DISGUSTING.*
CAN'T YOU JUST RUN A TUBE FROM MY *LUNGS* TO MY *BELLY BUTTON?*
JACKIE, YOU'RE CLEARLY UNDER A *LOT OF STRESS.*

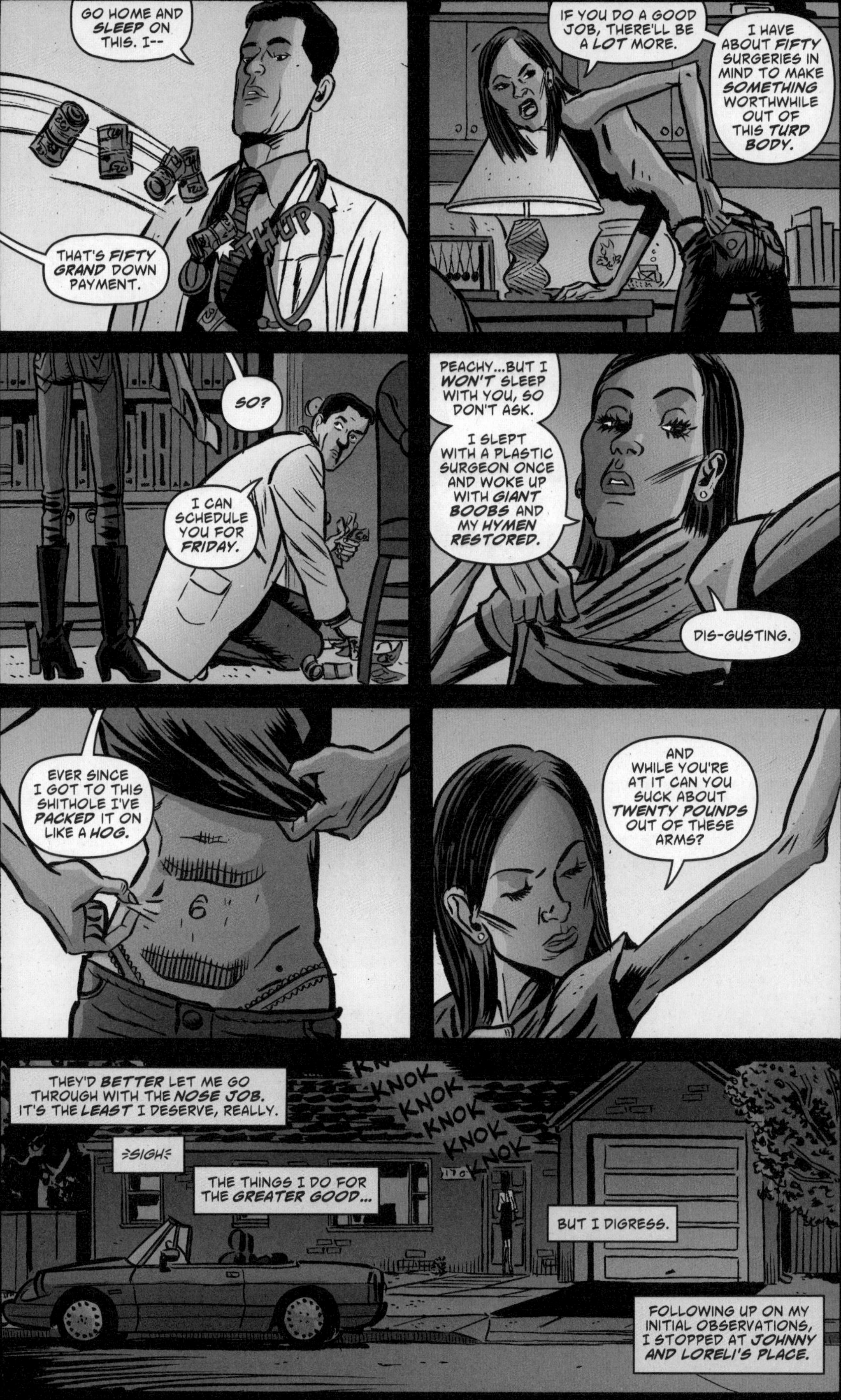
GO HOME AND SLEEP ON THIS. I--
THUP
THAT'S FIFTY GRAND DOWN PAYMENT.
IF YOU DO A GOOD JOB, THERE'LL BE A LOT MORE.
I HAVE ABOUT FIFTY SURGERIES IN MIND TO MAKE SOMETHING WORTHWHILE OUT OF THIS TURD BODY.
SO?
I CAN SCHEDULE YOU FOR FRIDAY.
PEACHY...BUT I WON'T SLEEP WITH YOU, SO DON'T ASK.
I SLEPT WITH A PLASTIC SURGEON ONCE AND WOKE UP WITH GIANT BOOBS AND MY HYMEN RESTORED.
DIS-GUSTING.
EVER SINCE I GOT TO THIS SHITHOLE I'VE PACKED IT ON LIKE A HOG.
AND WHILE YOU'RE AT IT CAN YOU SUCK ABOUT TWENTY POUNDS OUT OF THESE ARMS?
FOLLOWING UP ON MY INITIAL OBSERVATIONS, I STOPPED AT JOHNNY AND LORELI'S PLACE.
BUT I DIGRESS.
KNOK KNOK KNOK KNOK KNOK
THEY'D BETTER LET ME GO THROUGH WITH THE NOSE JOB. IT'S THE LEAST I DESERVE, REALLY.
=SIGH=
THE THINGS I DO FOR THE GREATER GOOD...

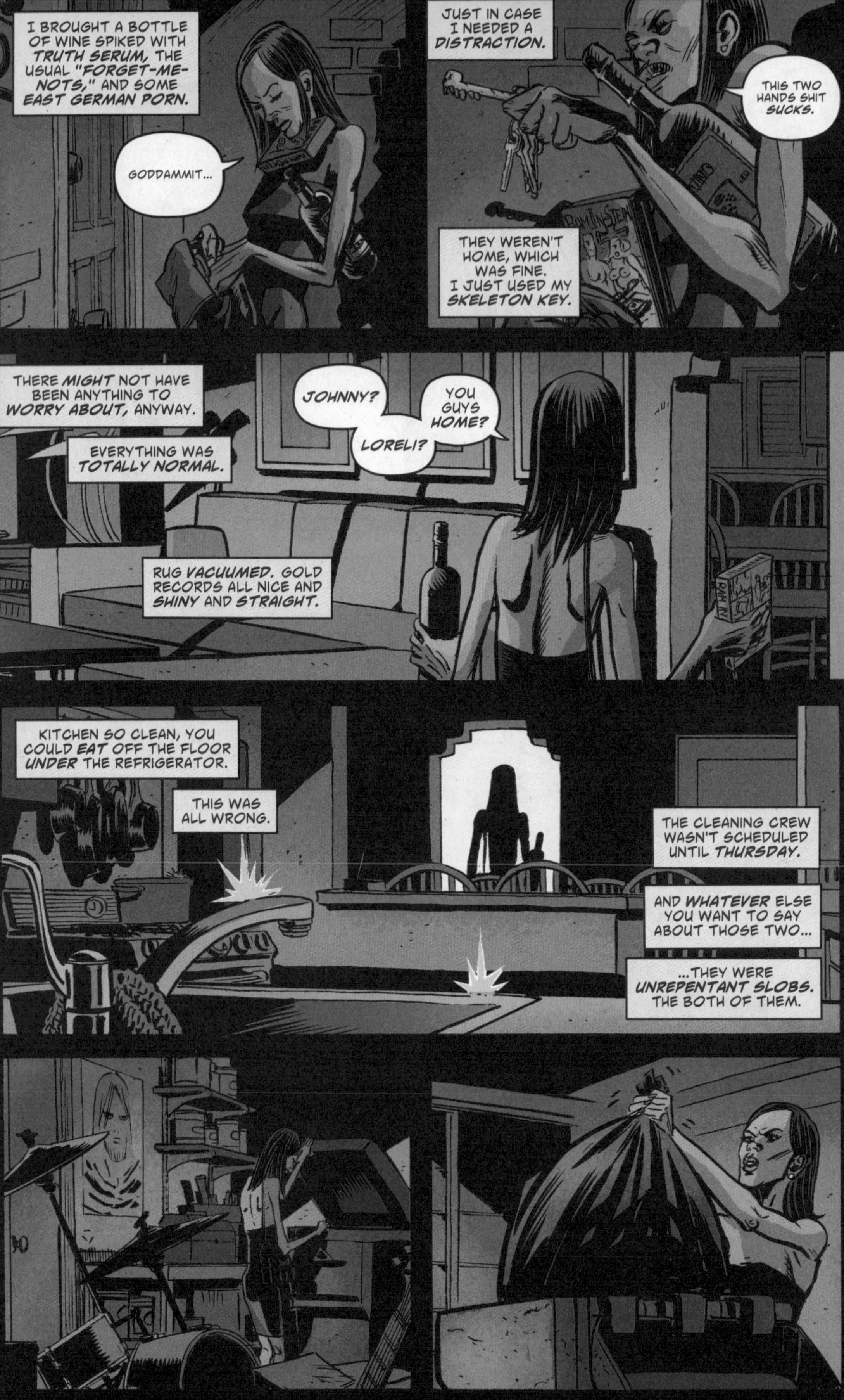
I BROUGHT A BOTTLE OF WINE SPIKED WITH TRUTH SERUM, THE USUAL "FORGET-ME-NOTS," AND SOME EAST GERMAN PORN.
GODDAMMIT...
JUST IN CASE I NEEDED A DISTRACTION.
THIS TWO HANDS SHIT SUCKS.
THEY WEREN'T HOME, WHICH WAS FINE. I JUST USED MY SKELETON KEY.
THERE MIGHT NOT HAVE BEEN ANYTHING TO WORRY ABOUT, ANYWAY.
JOHNNY?
YOU GUYS HOME?
LORELI?
EVERYTHING WAS TOTALLY NORMAL.
RUG VACUUMED. GOLD RECORDS ALL NICE AND SHINY AND STRAIGHT.
KITCHEN SO CLEAN, YOU COULD EAT OFF THE FLOOR UNDER THE REFRIGERATOR.
THIS WAS ALL WRONG.
THE CLEANING CREW WASN'T SCHEDULED UNTIL THURSDAY.
AND WHATEVER ELSE YOU WANT TO SAY ABOUT THOSE TWO...
...THEY WERE UNREPENTANT SLOBS. THE BOTH OF THEM.

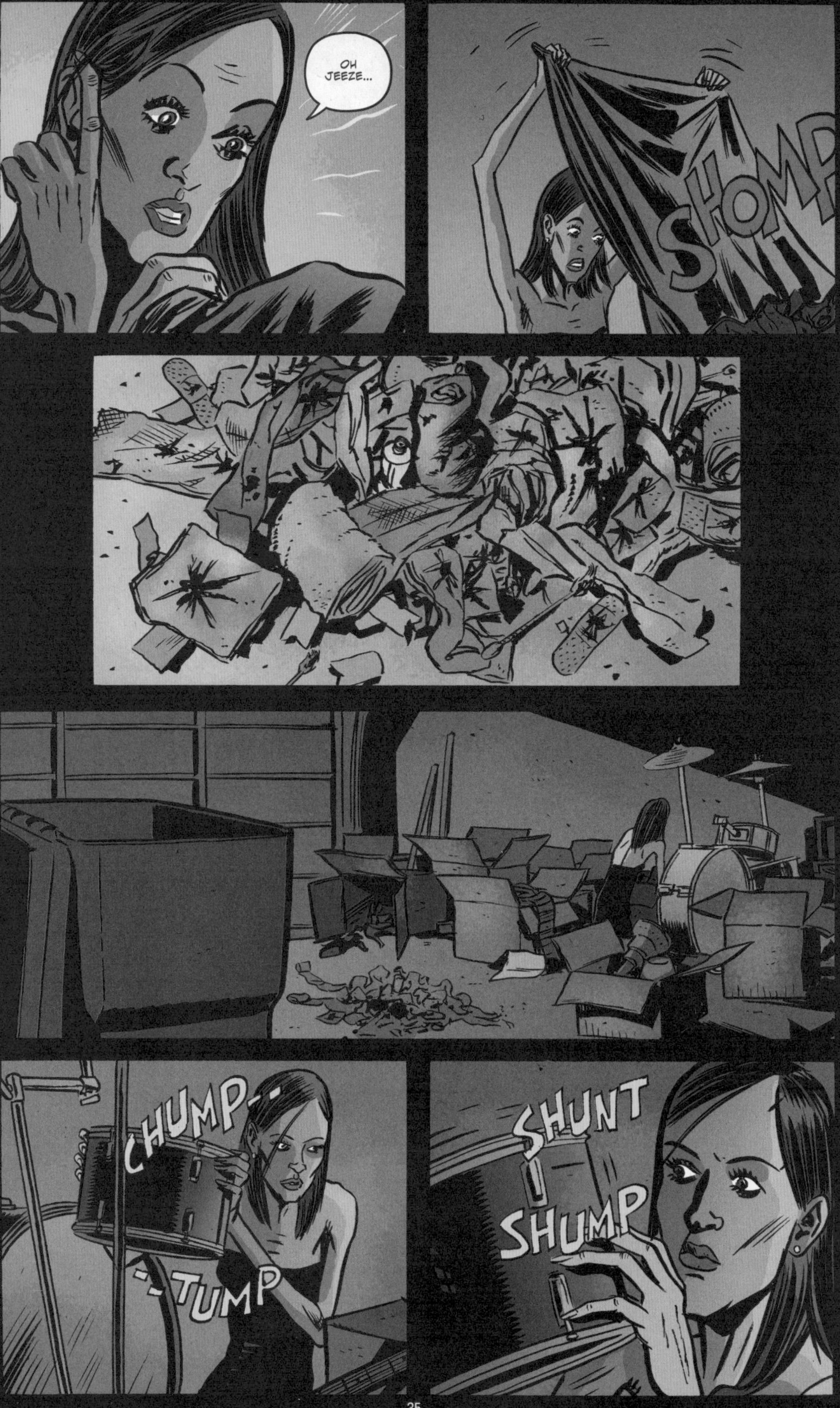
OH JEEZE...
SHOMP
CHUMP--
--TUMP
SHUNT
SHUMP

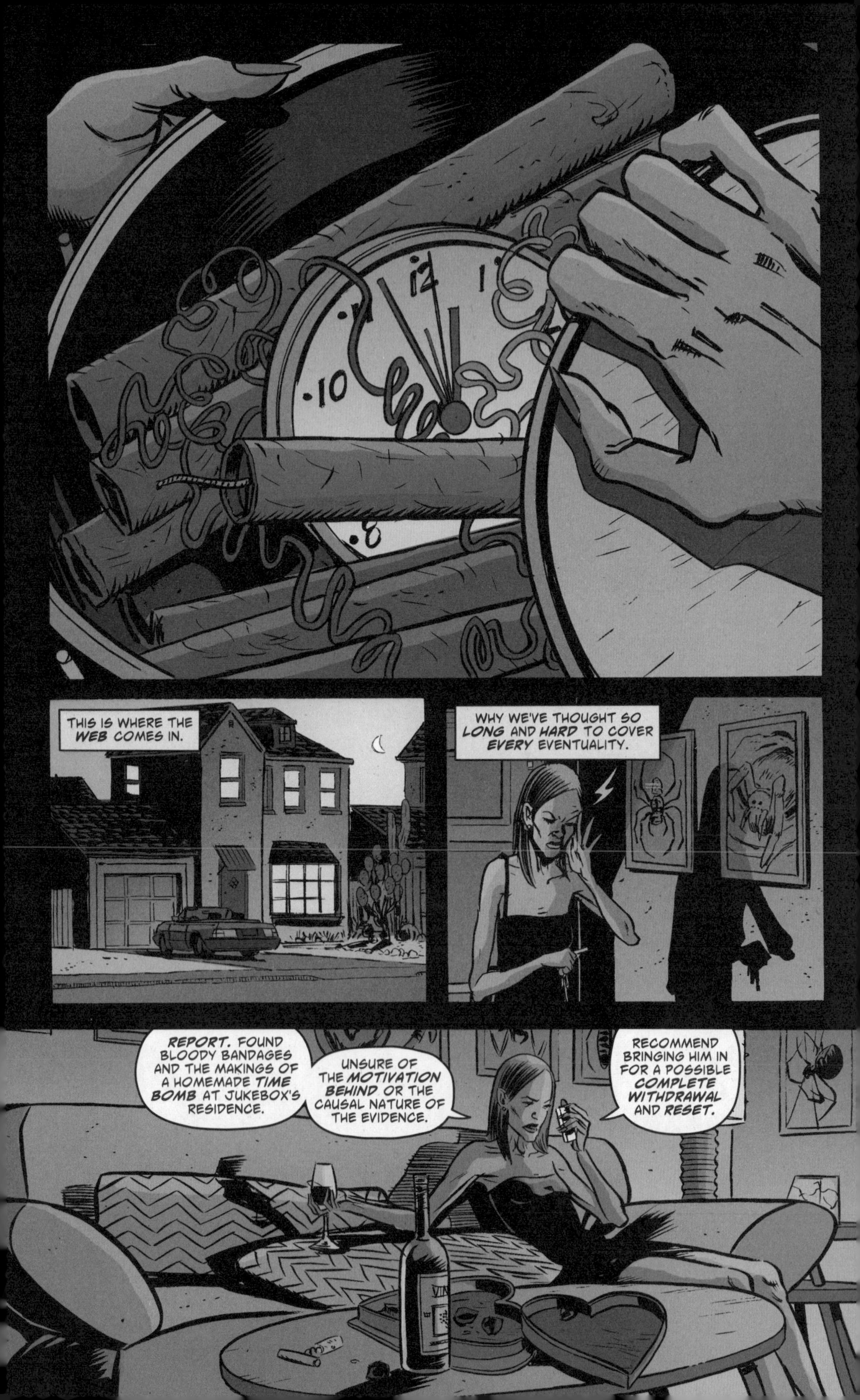
THIS IS WHERE THE *WEB* COMES IN.
WHY WE'VE THOUGHT SO *LONG* AND *HARD* TO COVER *EVERY* EVENTUALITY.
REPORT. FOUND BLOODY BANDAGES AND THE MAKINGS OF A HOMEMADE *TIME BOMB* AT JUKEBOX'S RESIDENCE.
UNSURE OF THE *MOTIVATION BEHIND* OR THE CAUSAL NATURE OF THE EVIDENCE.
RECOMMEND BRINGING HIM IN FOR A POSSIBLE *COMPLETE WITHDRAWAL* AND *RESET.*

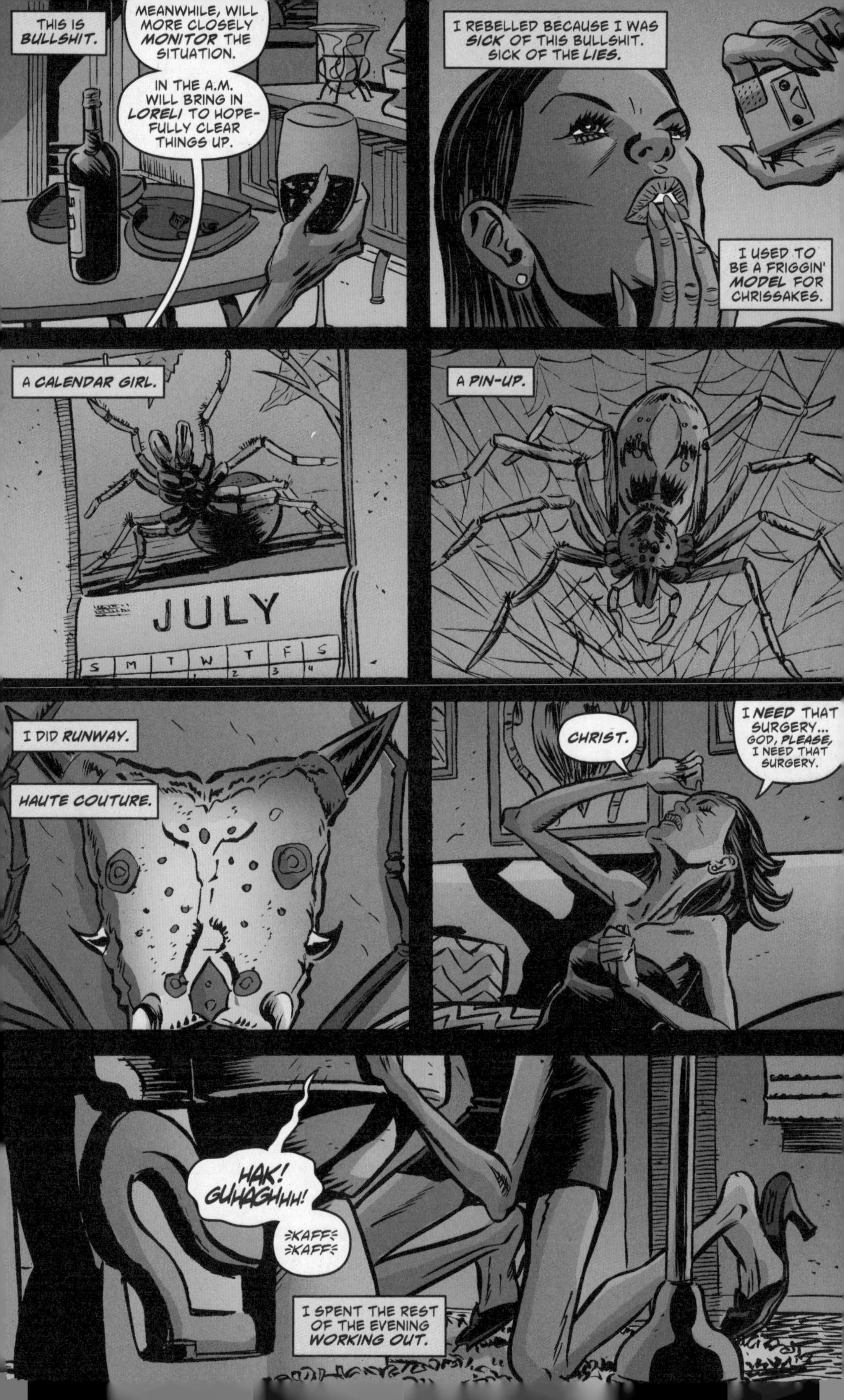

THIS IS *BULLSHIT.*
MEANWHILE, WILL MORE CLOSELY *MONITOR* THE SITUATION.
IN THE A.M. WILL BRING IN *LORELI* TO HOPE-FULLY CLEAR THINGS UP.
I REBELLED BECAUSE I WAS *SICK* OF THIS BULLSHIT. SICK OF THE *LIES.*
I USED TO BE A FRIGGIN' *MODEL* FOR CHRISSAKES.
A *CALENDAR GIRL.*
JULY
S M T W T F S
1 2 3 4
A *PIN-UP.*
I DID *RUNWAY.*
HAUTE COUTURE.
CHRIST.
I *NEED* THAT SURGERY... GOD, *PLEASE,* I NEED THAT SURGERY.
HAK! GUHAGHHH!
KAFF KAFF
I SPENT THE REST OF THE EVENING *WORKING OUT.*

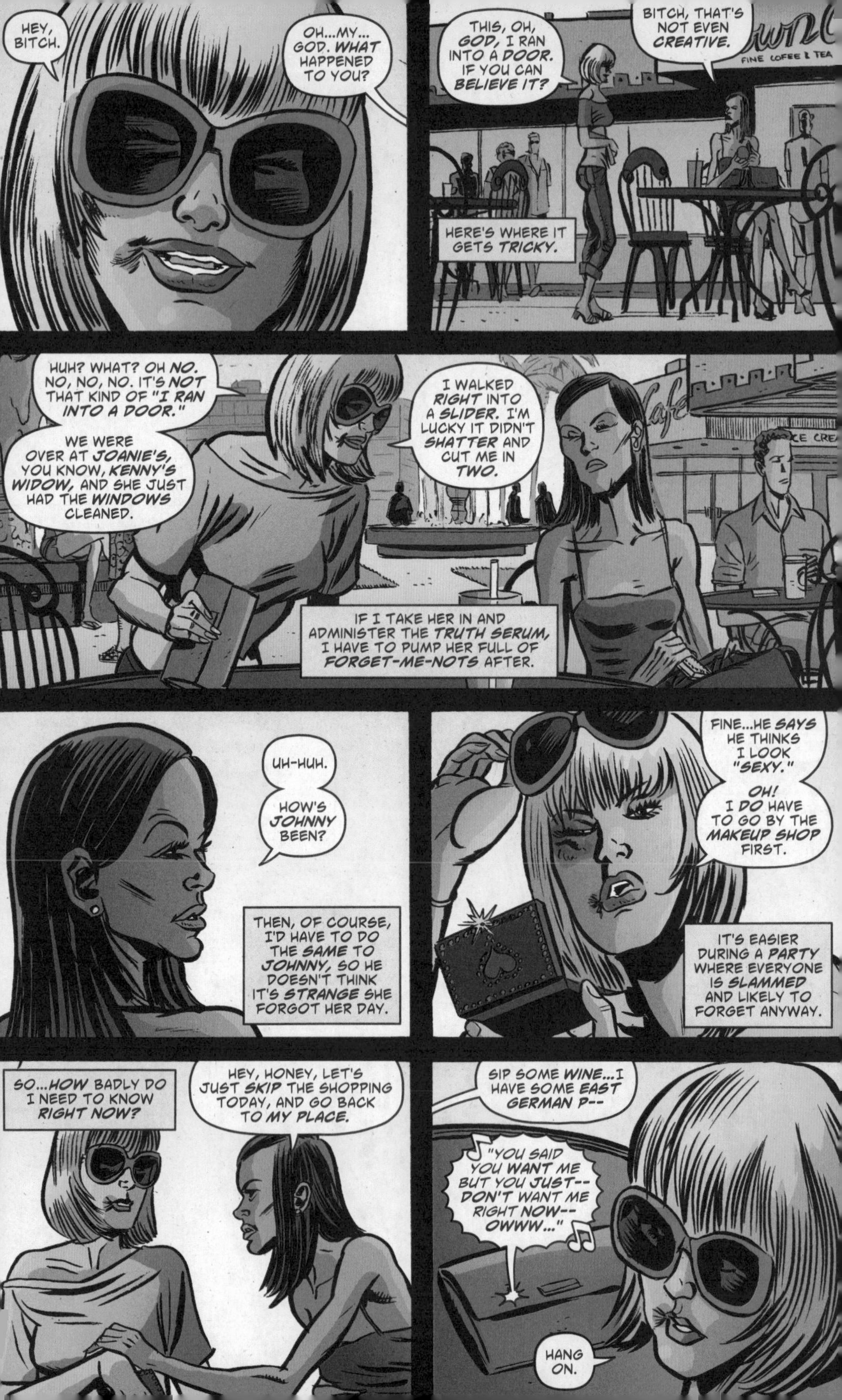
HEY, BITCH.
OH...MY... GOD. WHAT HAPPENED TO YOU?
THIS, OH, GOD, I RAN INTO A DOOR. IF YOU CAN BELIEVE IT?
BITCH, THAT'S NOT EVEN CREATIVE.
FINE COFEE & TEA
HERE'S WHERE IT GETS TRICKY.
HUH? WHAT? OH NO. NO, NO, NO. IT'S NOT THAT KIND OF "I RAN INTO A DOOR."
WE WERE OVER AT JOANIE'S, YOU KNOW, KENNY'S WIDOW, AND SHE JUST HAD THE WINDOWS CLEANED.
I WALKED RIGHT INTO A SLIDER. I'M LUCKY IT DIDN'T SHATTER AND CUT ME IN TWO.
IF I TAKE HER IN AND ADMINISTER THE TRUTH SERUM, I HAVE TO PUMP HER FULL OF FORGET-ME-NOTS AFTER.
UH-HUH.
HOW'S JOHNNY BEEN?
THEN, OF COURSE, I'D HAVE TO DO THE SAME TO JOHNNY, SO HE DOESN'T THINK IT'S STRANGE SHE FORGOT HER DAY.
FINE...HE SAYS HE THINKS I LOOK "SEXY."
OH! I DO HAVE TO GO BY THE MAKEUP SHOP FIRST.
IT'S EASIER DURING A PARTY WHERE EVERYONE IS SLAMMED AND LIKELY TO FORGET ANYWAY.
SO...HOW BADLY DO I NEED TO KNOW RIGHT NOW?
HEY, HONEY, LET'S JUST SKIP THE SHOPPING TODAY, AND GO BACK TO MY PLACE.
SIP SOME WINE...I HAVE SOME EAST GERMAN P--
"YOU SAID YOU WANT ME BUT YOU JUST-- DON'T WANT ME RIGHT NOW-- OWWW..."
HANG ON.

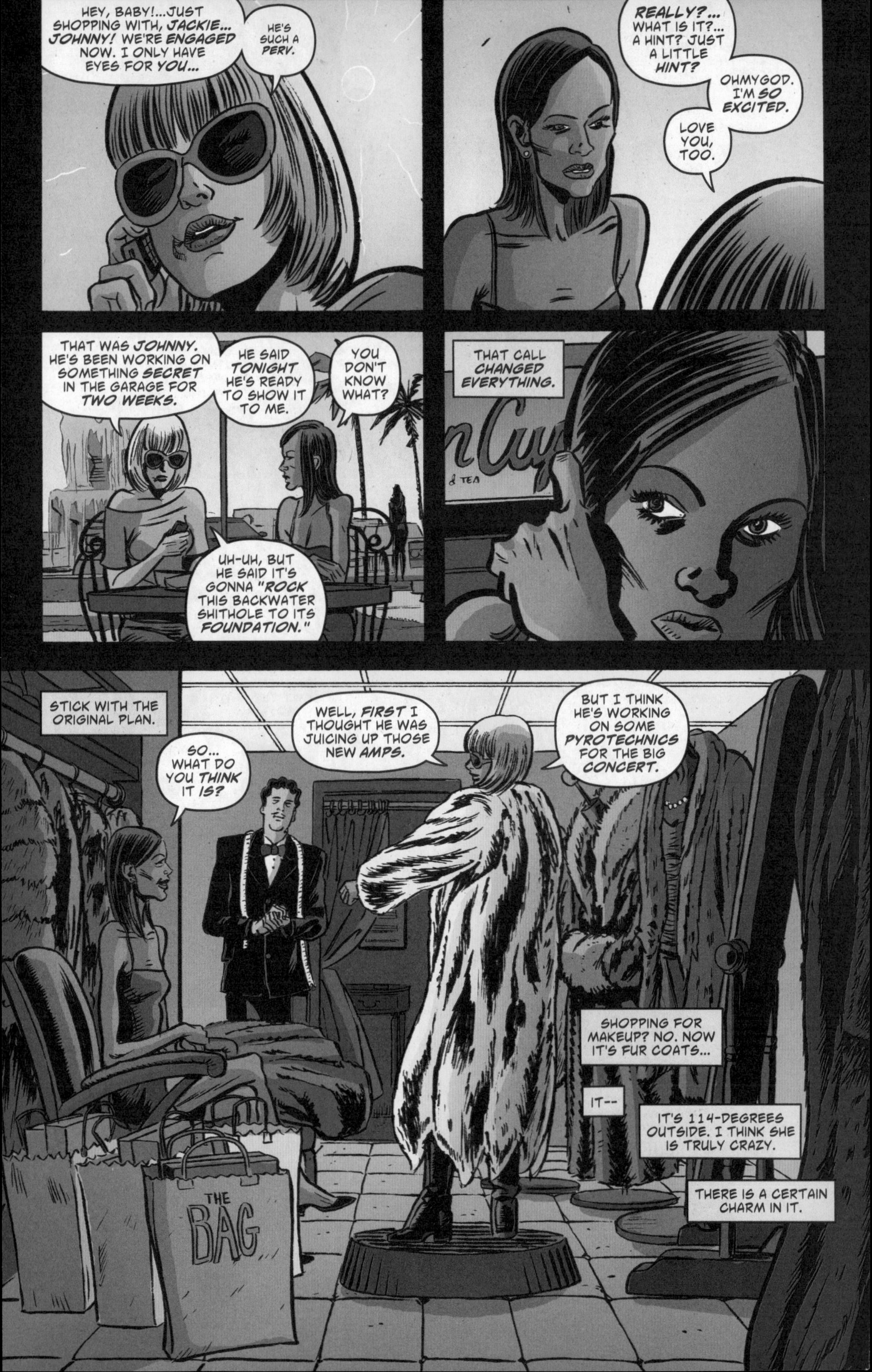

HEY, BABY!...JUST SHOPPING WITH, JACKIE... JOHNNY! WE'RE ENGAGED NOW. I ONLY HAVE EYES FOR YOU...
HE'S SUCH A PERV.
REALLY?... WHAT IS IT?... A HINT? JUST A LITTLE HINT?
OHMYGOD. I'M SO EXCITED.
LOVE YOU, TOO.
THAT WAS JOHNNY. HE'S BEEN WORKING ON SOMETHING SECRET IN THE GARAGE FOR TWO WEEKS.
HE SAID TONIGHT HE'S READY TO SHOW IT TO ME.
YOU DON'T KNOW WHAT?
UH-UH, BUT HE SAID IT'S GONNA "ROCK THIS BACKWATER SHITHOLE TO ITS FOUNDATION."
THAT CALL CHANGED EVERYTHING.
STICK WITH THE ORIGINAL PLAN.
SO... WHAT DO YOU THINK IT IS?
WELL, FIRST I THOUGHT HE WAS JUICING UP THOSE NEW AMPS.
BUT I THINK HE'S WORKING ON SOME PYROTECHNICS FOR THE BIG CONCERT.
SHOPPING FOR MAKEUP? NO. NOW IT'S FUR COATS...
IT--
IT'S 114-DEGREES OUTSIDE. I THINK SHE IS TRULY CRAZY.
THERE IS A CERTAIN CHARM IN IT.
THE BAG

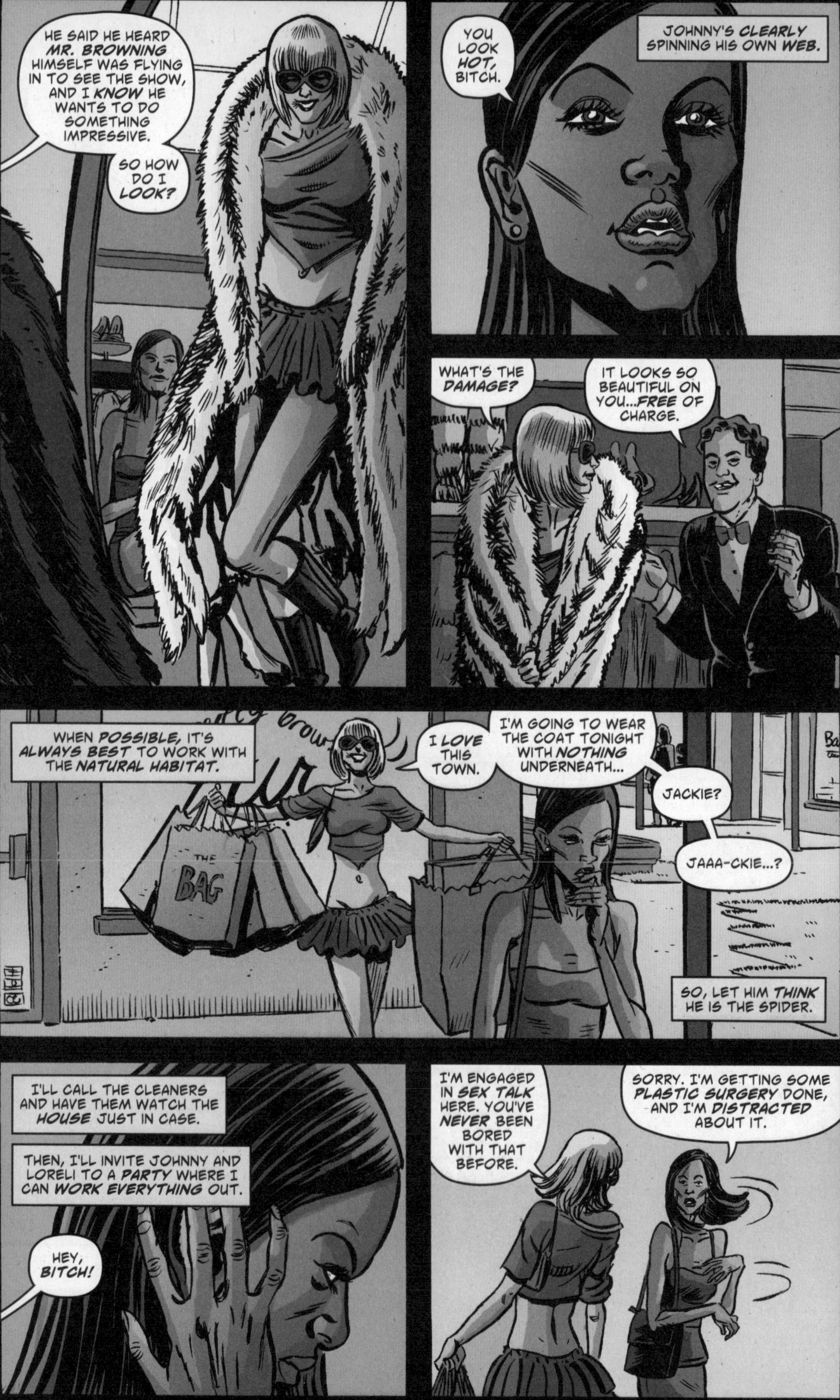

HE SAID HE HEARD MR. BROWNING HIMSELF WAS FLYING IN TO SEE THE SHOW, AND I KNOW HE WANTS TO DO SOMETHING IMPRESSIVE.
SO HOW DO I LOOK?
JOHNNY'S CLEARLY SPINNING HIS OWN WEB.
YOU LOOK HOT, BITCH.
WHAT'S THE DAMAGE?
IT LOOKS SO BEAUTIFUL ON YOU...FREE OF CHARGE.
WHEN POSSIBLE, IT'S ALWAYS BEST TO WORK WITH THE NATURAL HABITAT.
I LOVE THIS TOWN.
I'M GOING TO WEAR THE COAT TONIGHT WITH NOTHING UNDERNEATH...
JACKIE?
JAAA-CKIE...?
SO, LET HIM THINK HE IS THE SPIDER.
I'LL CALL THE CLEANERS AND HAVE THEM WATCH THE HOUSE JUST IN CASE.
THEN, I'LL INVITE JOHNNY AND LORELI TO A PARTY WHERE I CAN WORK EVERYTHING OUT.
HEY, BITCH!
I'M ENGAGED IN SEX TALK HERE. YOU'VE NEVER BEEN BORED WITH THAT BEFORE.
SORRY. I'M GETTING SOME PLASTIC SURGERY DONE, AND I'M DISTRACTED ABOUT IT.

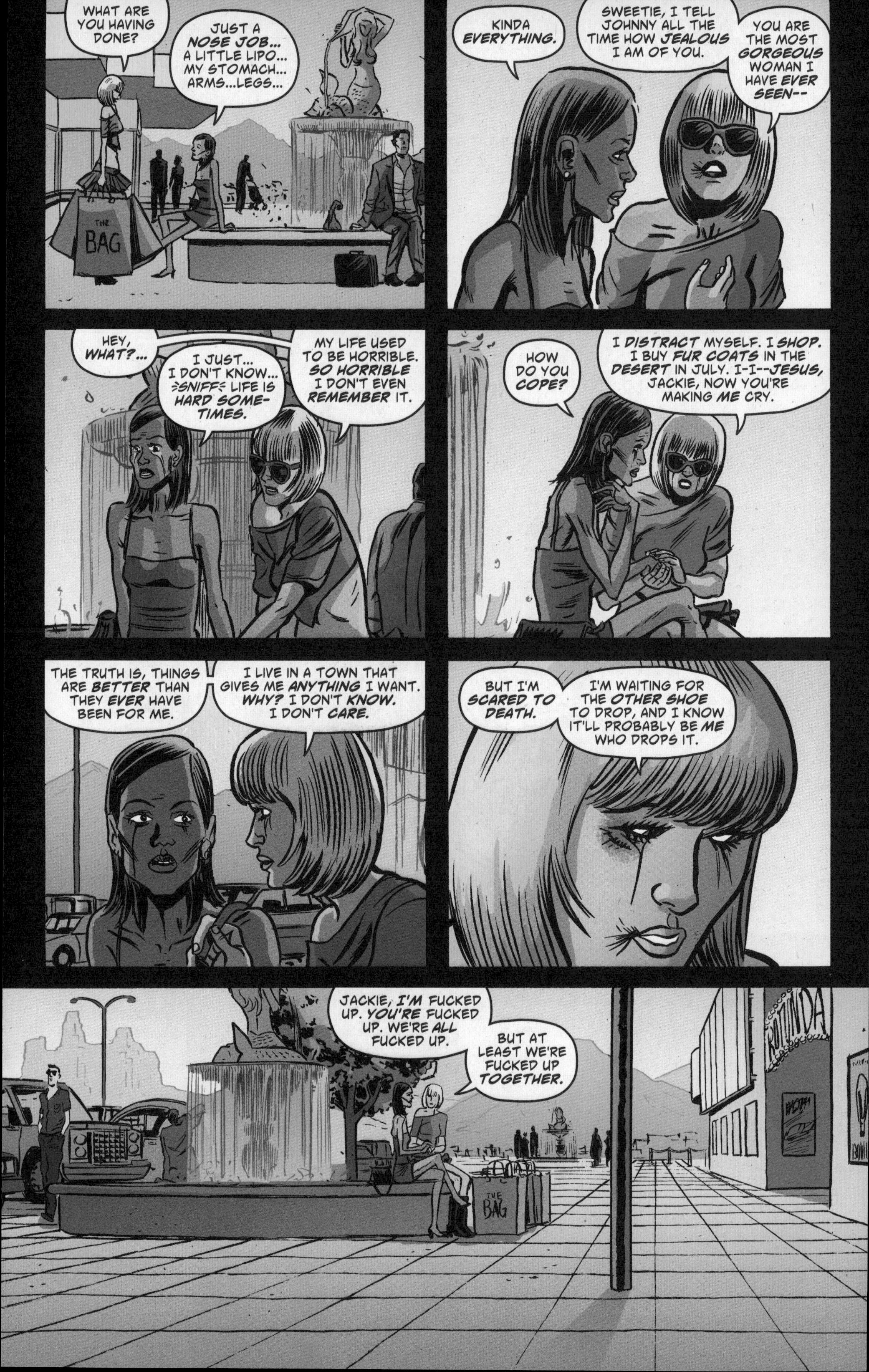
WHAT ARE YOU HAVING DONE?
JUST A NOSE JOB... A LITTLE LIPO... MY STOMACH... ARMS...LEGS...
THE BAG
KINDA EVERYTHING.
SWEETIE, I TELL JOHNNY ALL THE TIME HOW JEALOUS I AM OF YOU.
YOU ARE THE MOST GORGEOUS WOMAN I HAVE EVER SEEN--
HEY, WHAT?...
I JUST... I DON'T KNOW... =SNIFF= LIFE IS HARD SOMETIMES.
MY LIFE USED TO BE HORRIBLE. SO HORRIBLE I DON'T EVEN REMEMBER IT.
HOW DO YOU COPE?
I DISTRACT MYSELF. I SHOP. I BUY FUR COATS IN THE DESERT IN JULY. I-I--JESUS, JACKIE, NOW YOU'RE MAKING ME CRY.
THE TRUTH IS, THINGS ARE BETTER THAN THEY EVER HAVE BEEN FOR ME.
I LIVE IN A TOWN THAT GIVES ME ANYTHING I WANT. WHY? I DON'T KNOW. I DON'T CARE.
BUT I'M SCARED TO DEATH.
I'M WAITING FOR THE OTHER SHOE TO DROP, AND I KNOW IT'LL PROBABLY BE ME WHO DROPS IT.
JACKIE, I'M FUCKED UP. YOU'RE FUCKED UP. WE'RE ALL FUCKED UP.
BUT AT LEAST WE'RE FUCKED UP TOGETHER.
THE BAG
ROTUNDA

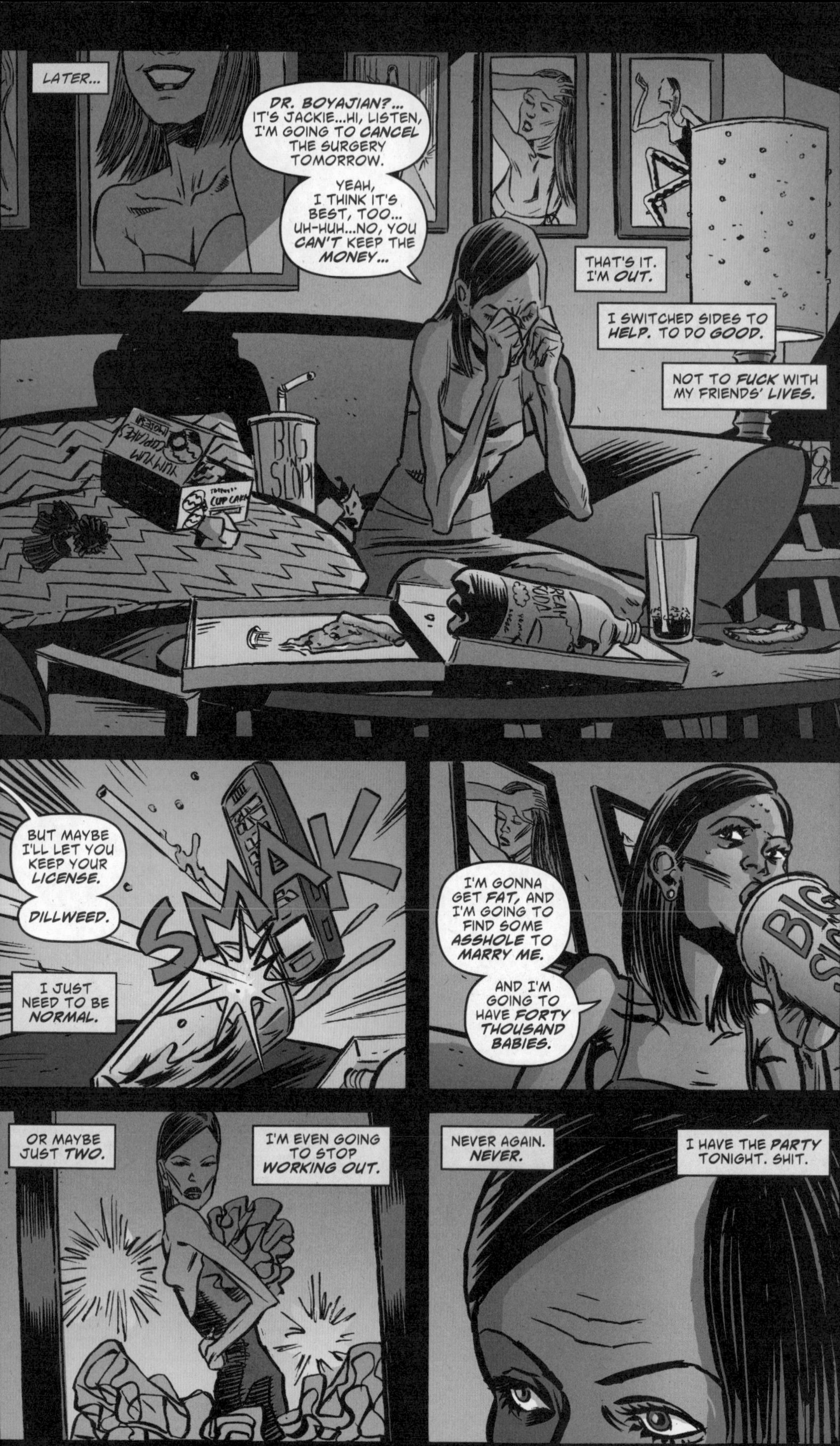
LATER...
DR. BOYAJIAN?... IT'S JACKIE...HI, LISTEN, I'M GOING TO CANCEL THE SURGERY TOMORROW.
YEAH, I THINK IT'S BEST, TOO... UH-HUH...NO, YOU CAN'T KEEP THE MONEY...
THAT'S IT. I'M OUT.
I SWITCHED SIDES TO HELP. TO DO GOOD.
NOT TO FUCK WITH MY FRIENDS' LIVES.
BIG SLOP
YUMYUM CUPCAKES
BUT MAYBE I'LL LET YOU KEEP YOUR LICENSE.
DILLWEED.
SMAK
I JUST NEED TO BE NORMAL.
I'M GONNA GET FAT, AND I'M GOING TO FIND SOME ASSHOLE TO MARRY ME.
AND I'M GOING TO HAVE FORTY THOUSAND BABIES.
OR MAYBE JUST TWO.
I'M EVEN GOING TO STOP WORKING OUT.
NEVER AGAIN. NEVER.
I HAVE THE PARTY TONIGHT. SHIT.

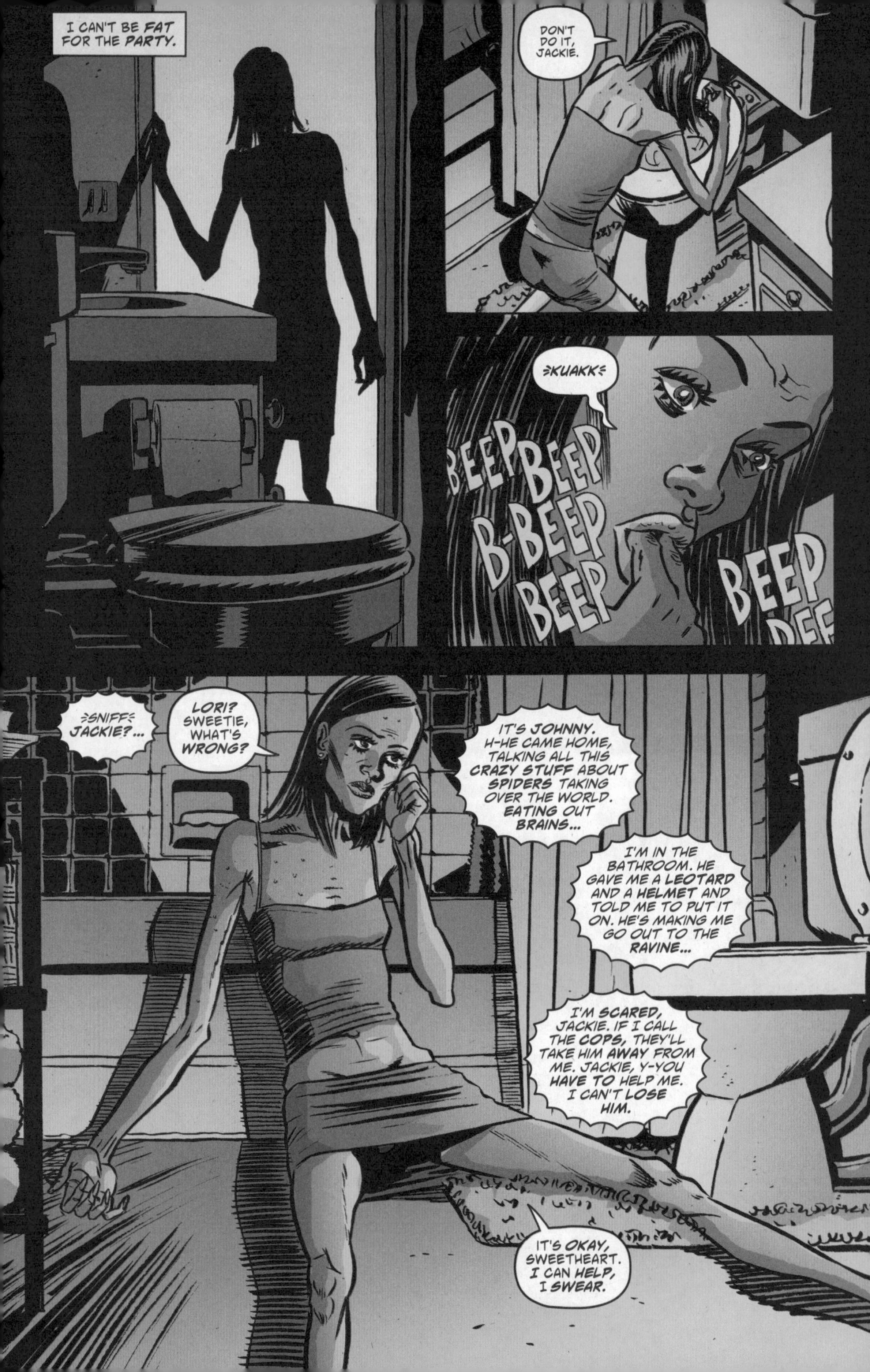
I CAN'T BE *FAT* FOR THE *PARTY*.
DON'T DO IT, JACKIE.
≈KUAKK≈
BEEP BEEP B-BEEP BEEP
BEEP
≈SNIFF≈ JACKIE?...
LORI? SWEETIE, WHAT'S *WRONG?*
IT'S *JOHNNY.* H-HE CAME HOME, TALKING ALL THIS *CRAZY STUFF* ABOUT *SPIDERS* TAKING OVER THE WORLD. *EATING OUT BRAINS...*
I'M IN THE BATHROOM. HE GAVE ME A *LEOTARD* AND A *HELMET* AND TOLD ME TO PUT IT ON. HE'S MAKING ME GO OUT TO THE *RAVINE...*
I'M *SCARED,* JACKIE. IF I CALL THE *COPS,* THEY'LL TAKE HIM *AWAY* FROM ME. JACKIE, Y-YOU *HAVE* TO *HELP* ME. I CAN'T *LOSE HIM.*
IT'S *OKAY,* SWEETHEART. I CAN *HELP,* I *SWEAR.*

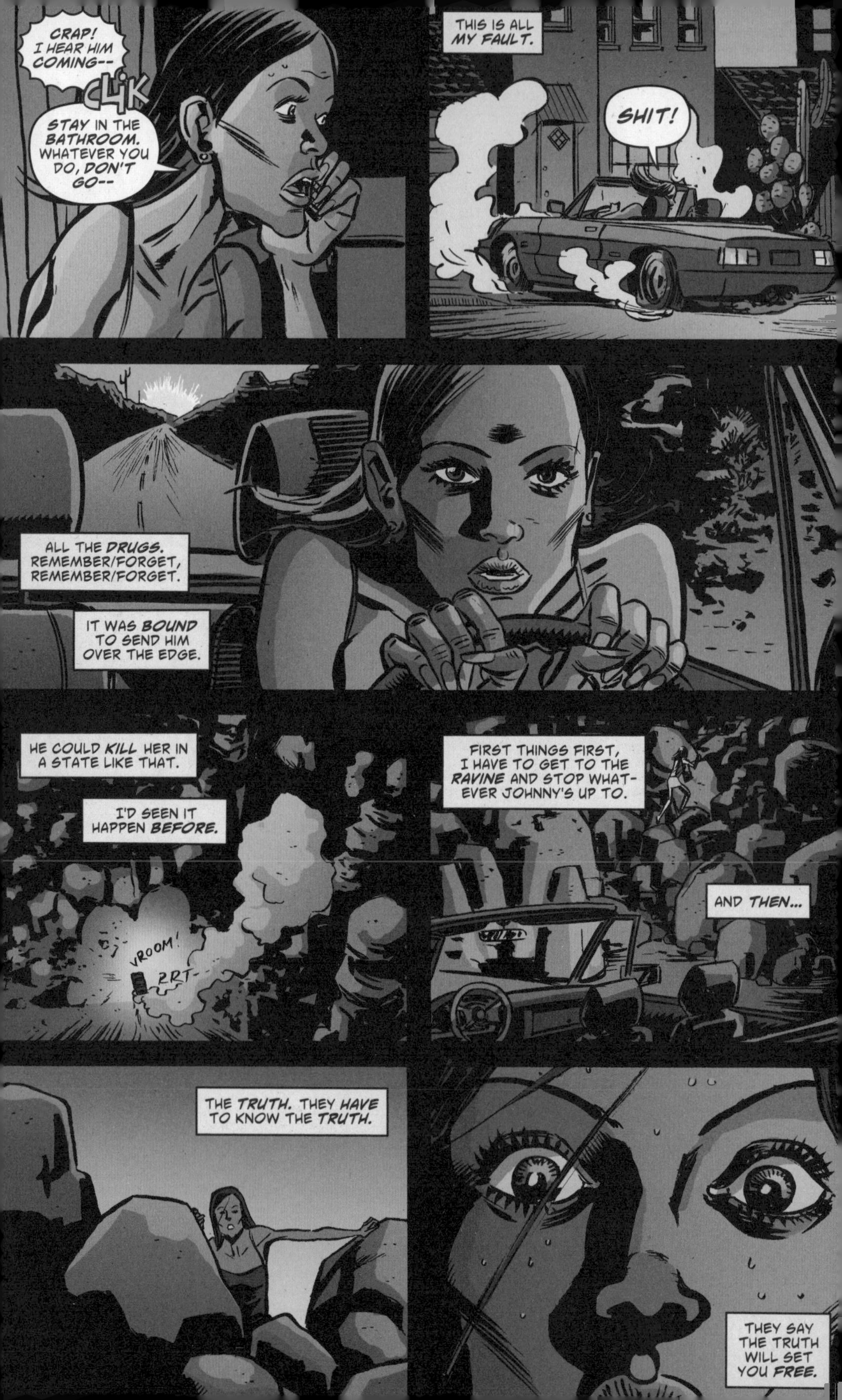
CRAP! I HEAR HIM COMING--
CLIK
STAY IN THE BATHROOM. WHATEVER YOU DO, DON'T GO--
THIS IS ALL MY FAULT.
SHIT!
ALL THE DRUGS. REMEMBER/FORGET, REMEMBER/FORGET.
IT WAS BOUND TO SEND HIM OVER THE EDGE.
HE COULD KILL HER IN A STATE LIKE THAT.
I'D SEEN IT HAPPEN BEFORE.
VROOM!
ZRT--
FIRST THINGS FIRST, I HAVE TO GET TO THE RAVINE AND STOP WHATEVER JOHNNY'S UP TO.
AND THEN...
THE TRUTH. THEY HAVE TO KNOW THE TRUTH.
THEY SAY THE TRUTH WILL SET YOU FREE.

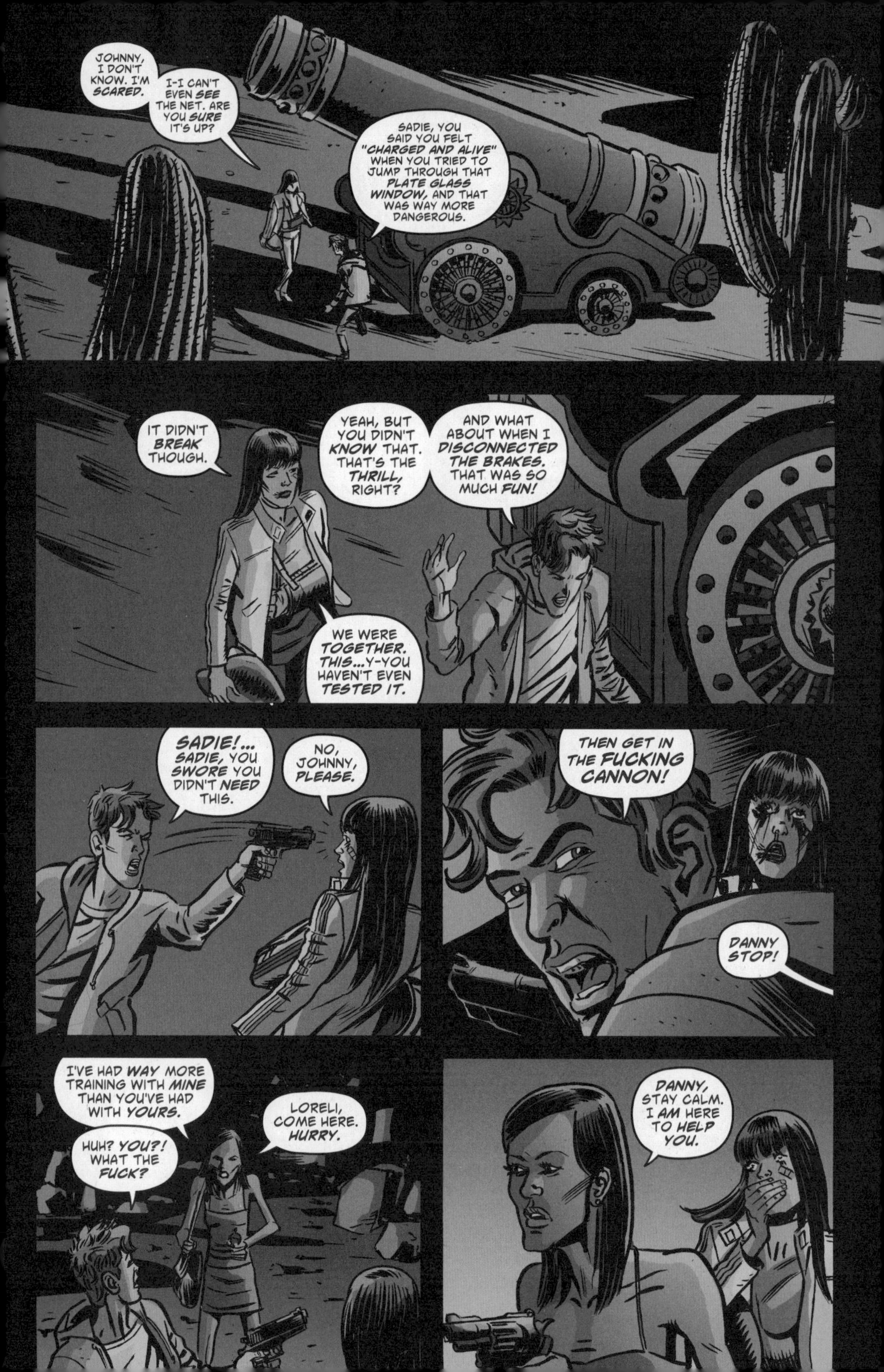
JOHNNY, I DON'T KNOW. I'M SCARED.
I-I CAN'T EVEN SEE THE NET. ARE YOU SURE IT'S UP?
SADIE, YOU SAID YOU FELT "CHARGED AND ALIVE" WHEN YOU TRIED TO JUMP THROUGH THAT PLATE GLASS WINDOW, AND THAT WAS WAY MORE DANGEROUS.
IT DIDN'T BREAK THOUGH.
YEAH, BUT YOU DIDN'T KNOW THAT. THAT'S THE THRILL, RIGHT?
AND WHAT ABOUT WHEN I DISCONNECTED THE BRAKES. THAT WAS SO MUCH FUN!
WE WERE TOGETHER. THIS...Y-YOU HAVEN'T EVEN TESTED IT.
SADIE!... SADIE, YOU SWORE YOU DIDN'T NEED THIS.
NO, JOHNNY, PLEASE.
THEN GET IN THE FUCKING CANNON!
DANNY STOP!
I'VE HAD WAY MORE TRAINING WITH MINE THAN YOU'VE HAD WITH YOURS.
HUH? YOU?! WHAT THE FUCK?
LORELI, COME HERE. HURRY.
DANNY, STAY CALM. I AM HERE TO HELP YOU.

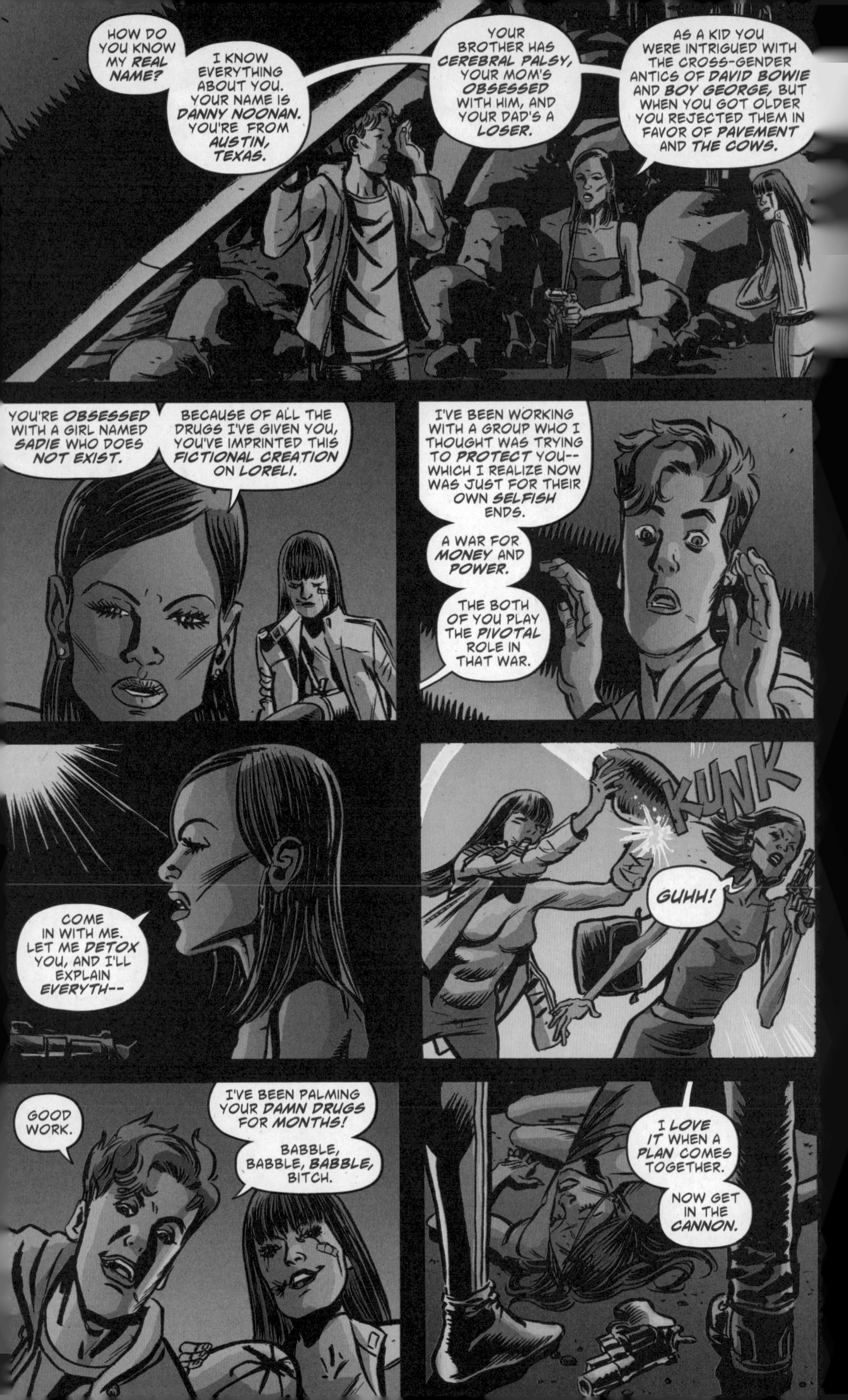
HOW DO YOU KNOW MY *REAL NAME?*
I KNOW EVERYTHING ABOUT YOU. YOUR NAME IS *DANNY NOONAN.* YOU'RE FROM *AUSTIN, TEXAS.*
YOUR BROTHER HAS *CEREBRAL PALSY,* YOUR MOM'S *OBSESSED* WITH HIM, AND YOUR DAD'S A *LOSER.*
AS A KID YOU WERE INTRIGUED WITH THE CROSS-GENDER ANTICS OF *DAVID BOWIE* AND *BOY GEORGE,* BUT WHEN YOU GOT OLDER YOU REJECTED THEM IN FAVOR OF *PAVEMENT* AND *THE COWS.*
YOU'RE *OBSESSED* WITH A GIRL NAMED *SADIE* WHO DOES *NOT EXIST.*
BECAUSE OF ALL THE DRUGS I'VE GIVEN YOU, YOU'VE IMPRINTED THIS *FICTIONAL CREATION* ON *LORELI.*
I'VE BEEN WORKING WITH A GROUP WHO I THOUGHT WAS TRYING TO *PROTECT* YOU-- WHICH I REALIZE NOW WAS JUST FOR THEIR OWN *SELFISH* ENDS.
A WAR FOR *MONEY* AND *POWER.*
THE BOTH OF YOU PLAY THE *PIVOTAL* ROLE IN THAT WAR.
COME IN WITH ME. LET ME *DETOX* YOU, AND I'LL EXPLAIN *EVERYTH--*
KUNK
GUHH!
GOOD WORK.
I'VE BEEN PALMING YOUR *DAMN DRUGS* FOR *MONTHS!*
BABBLE, BABBLE, *BABBLE,* BITCH.
I *LOVE IT* WHEN A *PLAN* COMES TOGETHER.
NOW GET IN THE *CANNON.*

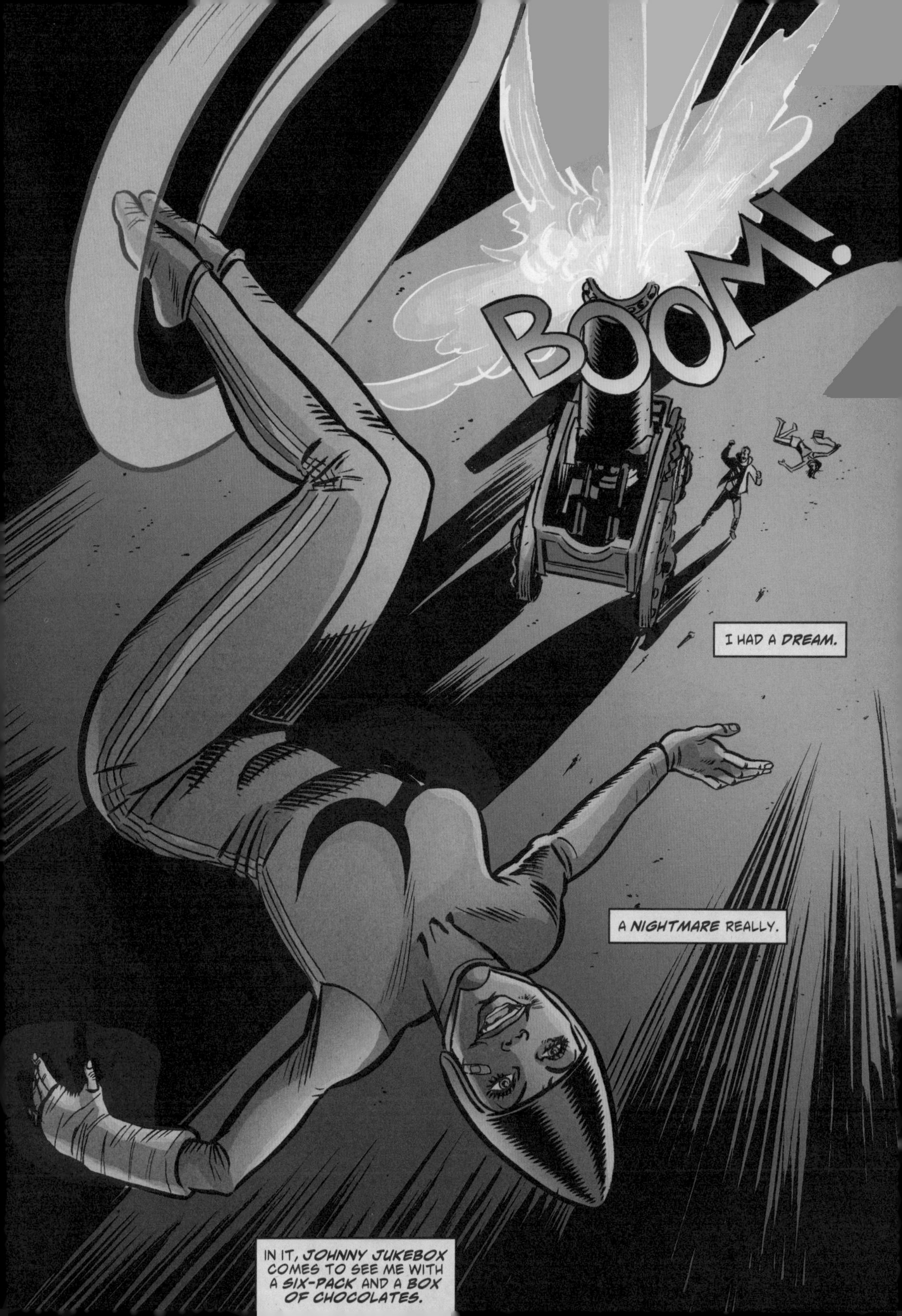
BOOM!
I HAD A *DREAM.*
A *NIGHTMARE* REALLY.
IN IT, *JOHNNY JUKEBOX* COMES TO SEE ME WITH A *SIX-PACK* AND A *BOX OF CHOCOLATES.*

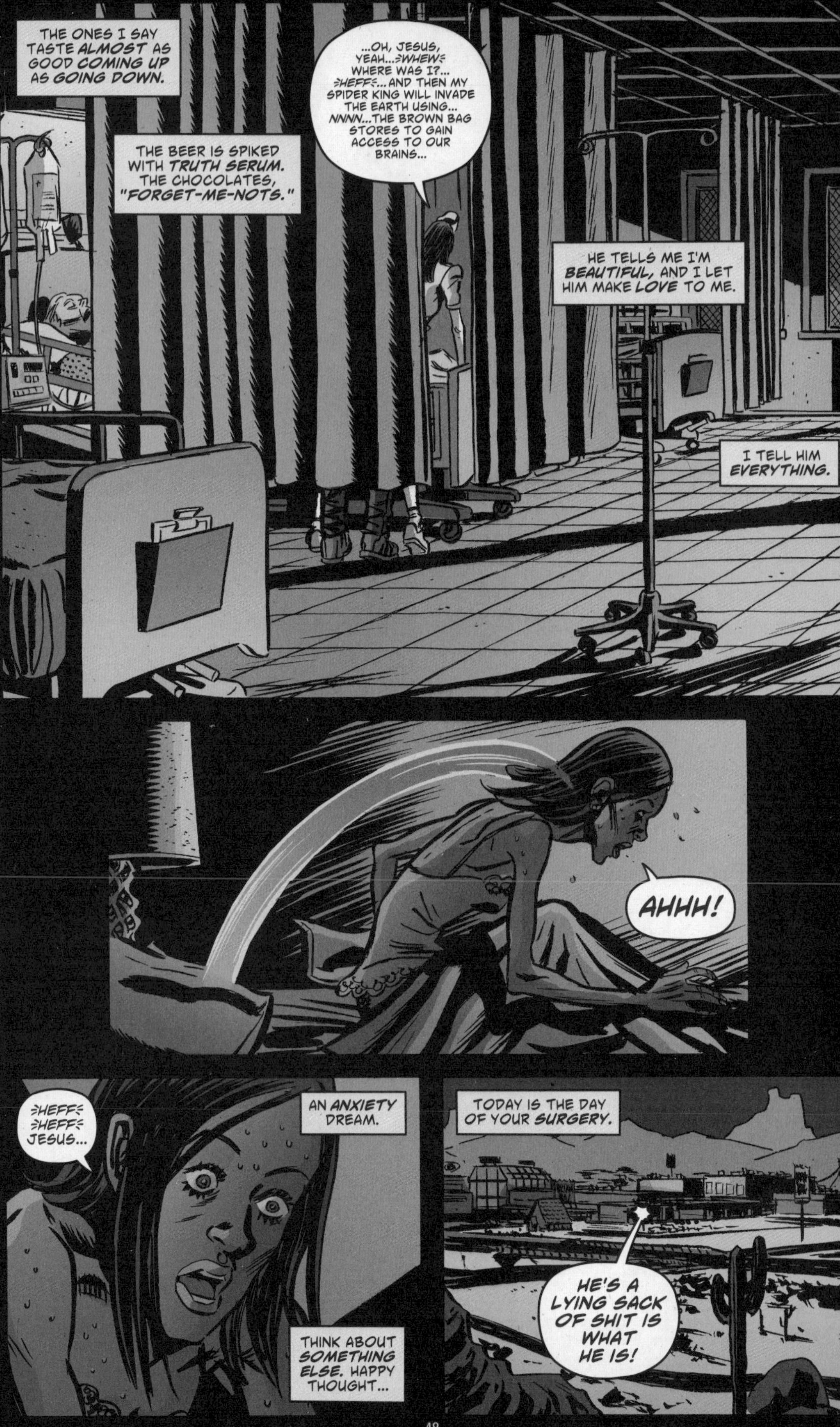
THE ONES I SAY TASTE ALMOST AS GOOD COMING UP AS GOING DOWN.
THE BEER IS SPIKED WITH TRUTH SERUM. THE CHOCOLATES, "FORGET-ME-NOTS."
...OH, JESUS, YEAH... ≶WHEW≶ WHERE WAS I?... ≶HEFF≶ ...AND THEN MY SPIDER KING WILL INVADE THE EARTH USING... NNNN... THE BROWN BAG STORES TO GAIN ACCESS TO OUR BRAINS...
HE TELLS ME I'M BEAUTIFUL, AND I LET HIM MAKE LOVE TO ME.
I TELL HIM EVERYTHING.
AHHH!
≶HEFF≶ ≶HEFF≶ JESUS...
AN ANXIETY DREAM.
THINK ABOUT SOMETHING ELSE. HAPPY THOUGHT...
TODAY IS THE DAY OF YOUR SURGERY.
HE'S A LYING SACK OF SHIT IS WHAT HE IS!

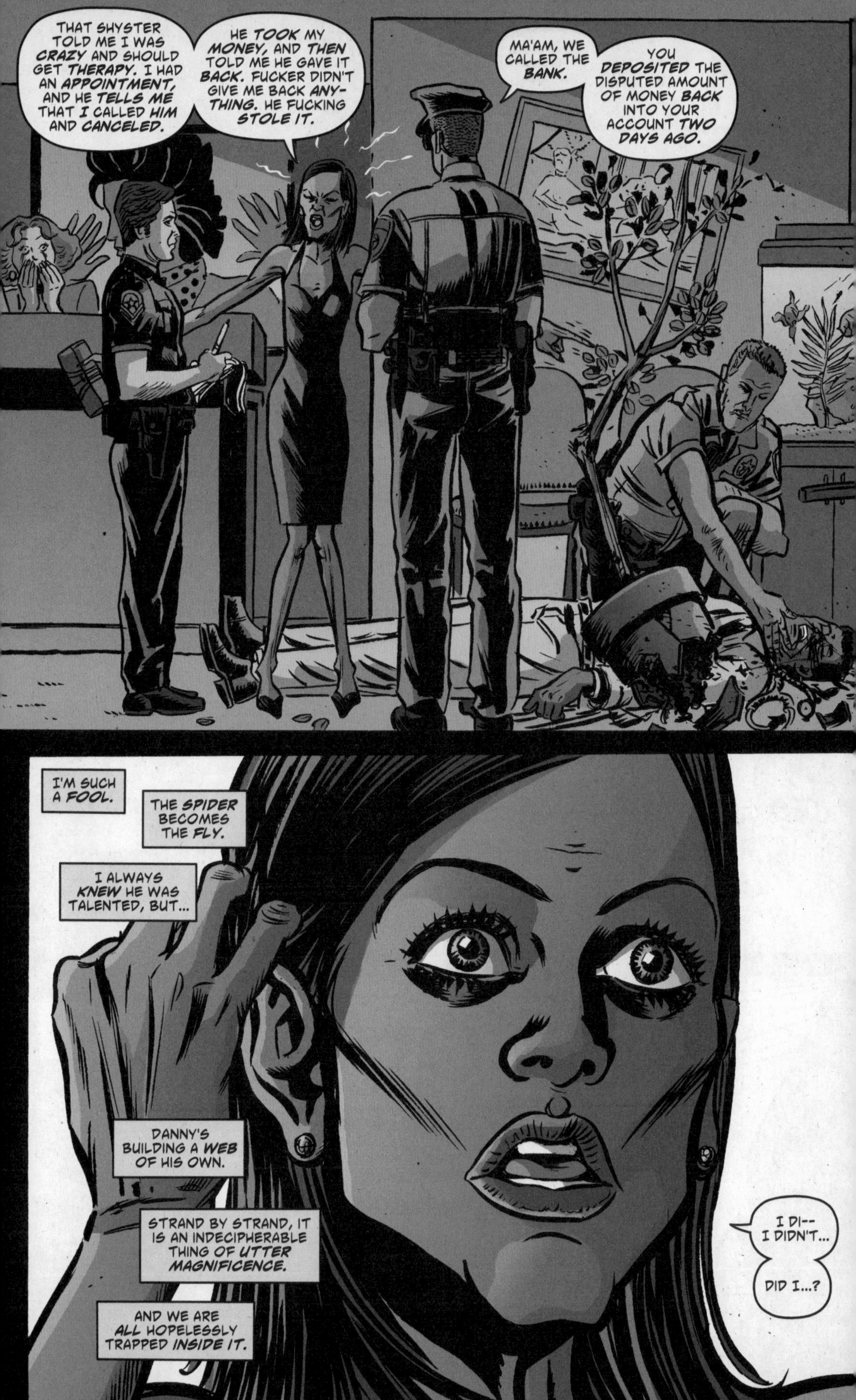
THAT SHYSTER TOLD ME I WAS CRAZY AND SHOULD GET THERAPY. I HAD AN APPOINTMENT, AND HE TELLS ME THAT I CALLED HIM AND CANCELED.
HE TOOK MY MONEY, AND THEN TOLD ME HE GAVE IT BACK. FUCKER DIDN'T GIVE ME BACK ANYTHING. HE FUCKING STOLE IT.
MA'AM, WE CALLED THE BANK.
YOU DEPOSITED THE DISPUTED AMOUNT OF MONEY BACK INTO YOUR ACCOUNT TWO DAYS AGO.
I'M SUCH A FOOL.
THE SPIDER BECOMES THE FLY.
I ALWAYS KNEW HE WAS TALENTED, BUT...
DANNY'S BUILDING A WEB OF HIS OWN.
STRAND BY STRAND, IT IS AN INDECIPHERABLE THING OF UTTER MAGNIFICENCE.
AND WE ARE ALL HOPELESSLY TRAPPED INSIDE IT.
I DI-- I DIDN'T...
DID I...?

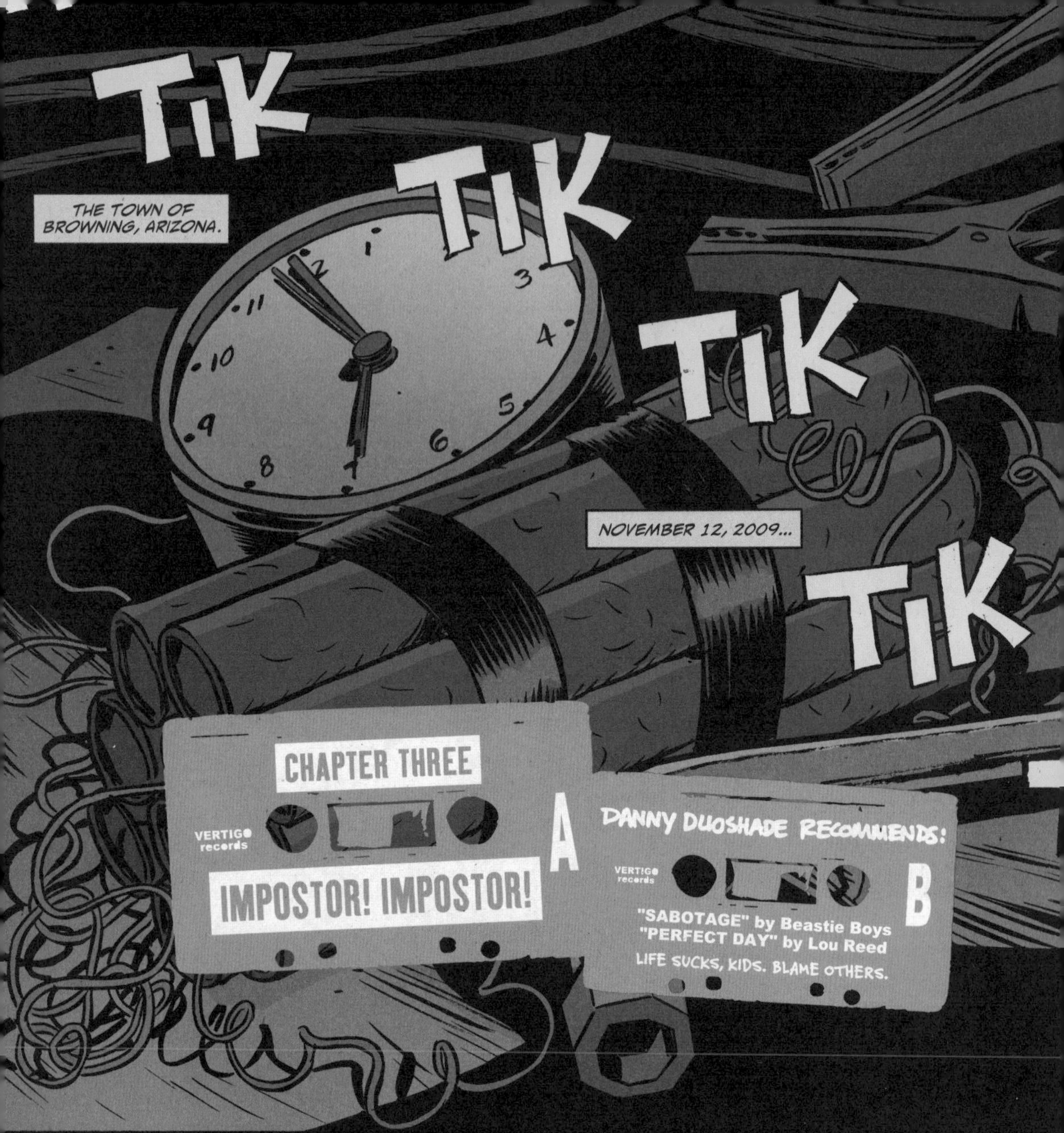
TIK
THE TOWN OF BROWNING, ARIZONA.
TIK
TIK
NOVEMBER 12, 2009...
TIK
CHAPTER THREE
VERTIGO records
A
IMPOSTOR! IMPOSTOR!
DANNY DUOSHADE RECOMMENDS:
VERTIGO records
B
"SABOTAGE" by Beastie Boys
"PERFECT DAY" by Lou Reed
LIFE SUCKS, KIDS. BLAME OTHERS.

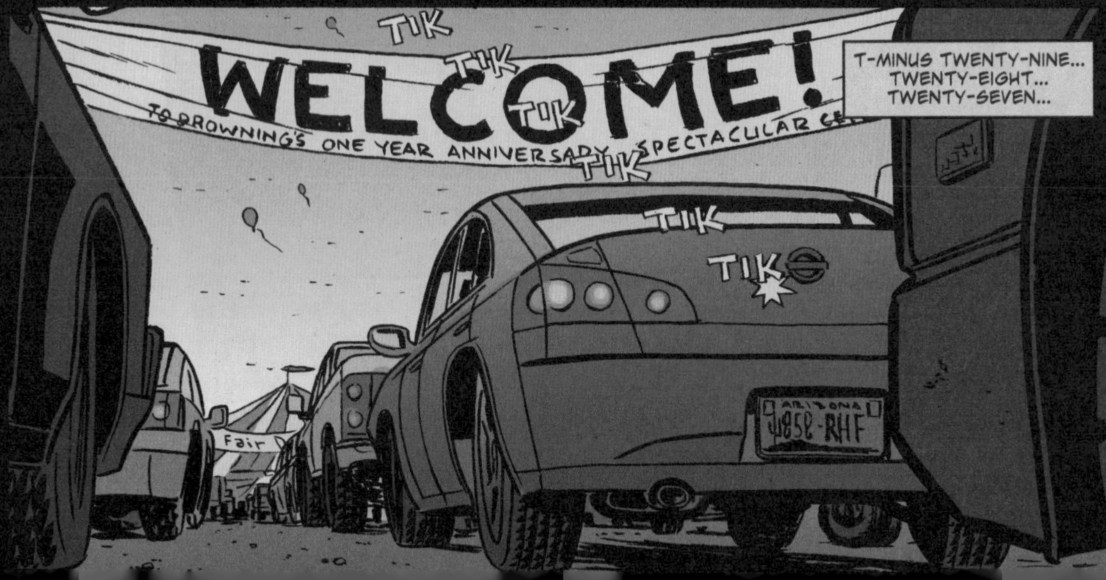
TIK
TIK
WELCOME!
TIK
TO BROWNING'S ONE YEAR ANNIVERSARY SPECTACULAR
TIK
T-MINUS TWENTY-NINE...
TWENTY-EIGHT...
TWENTY-SEVEN...
TIK
TIK
ARIZONA
J858-RHF
Fair

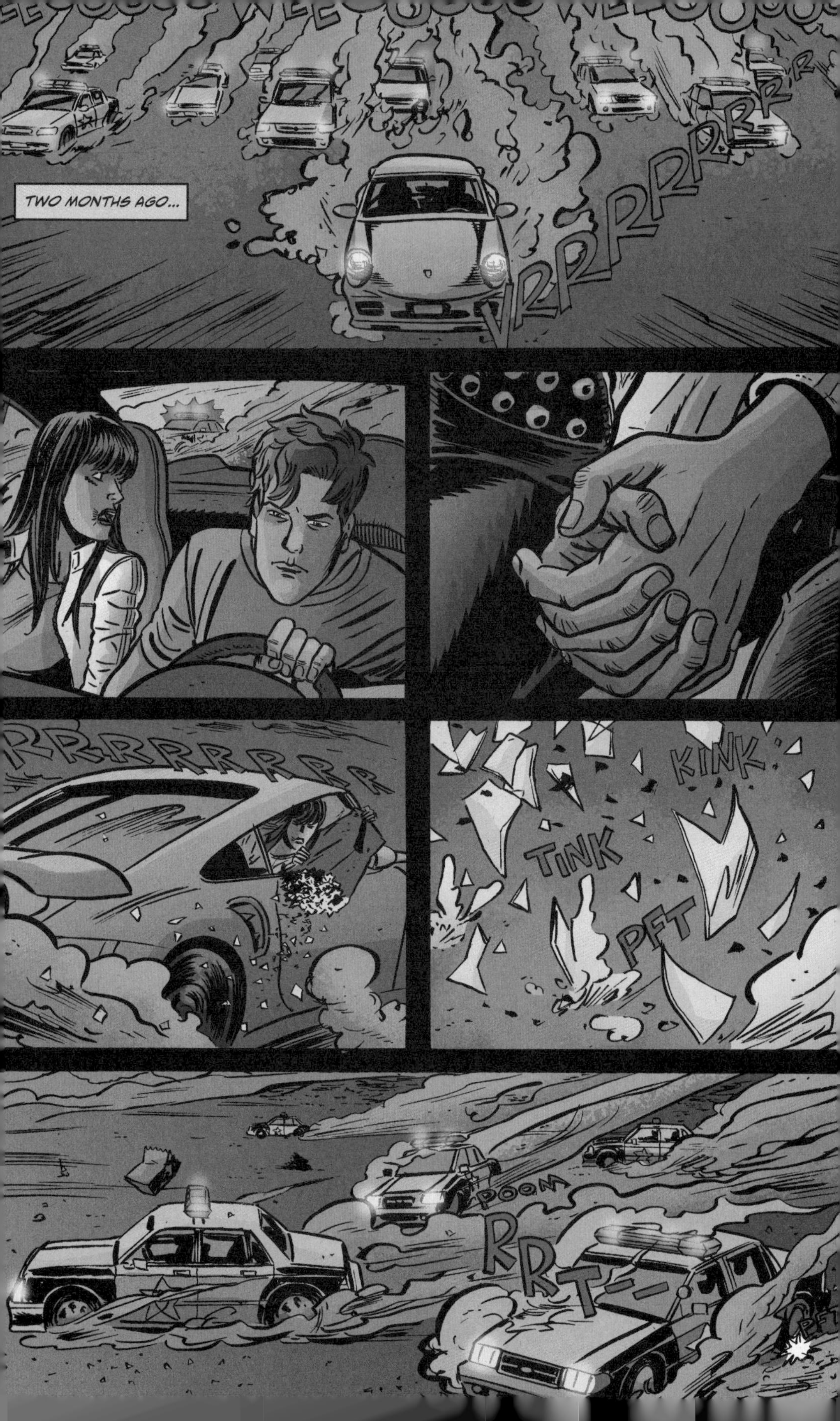
TWO MONTHS AGO...
VRRRRRRRRRR
RRRRRRRRRR
KINK
TINK
PFT
POOM
RRT--
PFT

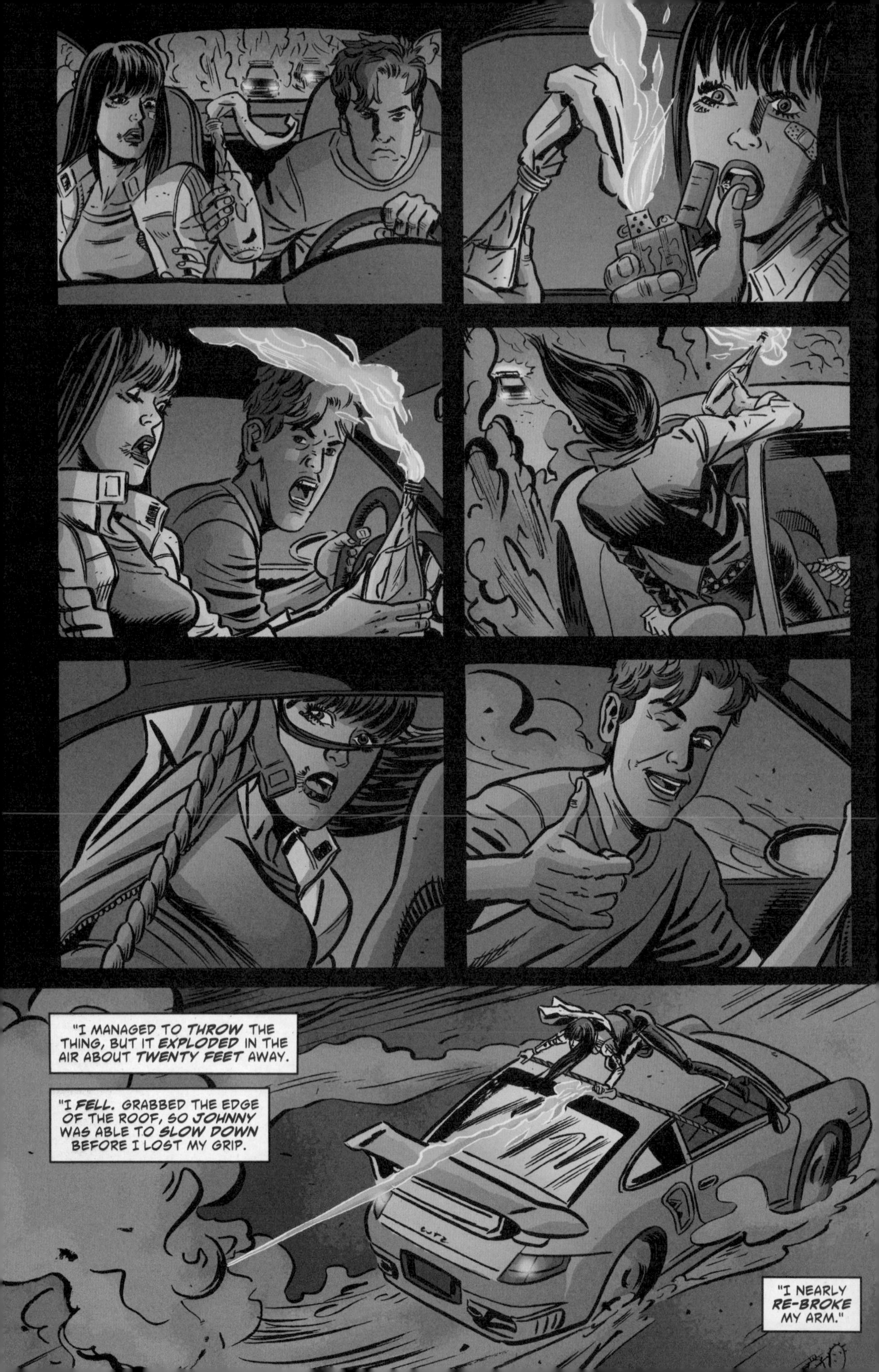
"I MANAGED TO THROW THE THING, BUT IT EXPLODED IN THE AIR ABOUT TWENTY FEET AWAY.
"I FELL. GRABBED THE EDGE OF THE ROOF, SO JOHNNY WAS ABLE TO SLOW DOWN BEFORE I LOST MY GRIP.
"I NEARLY RE-BROKE MY ARM."

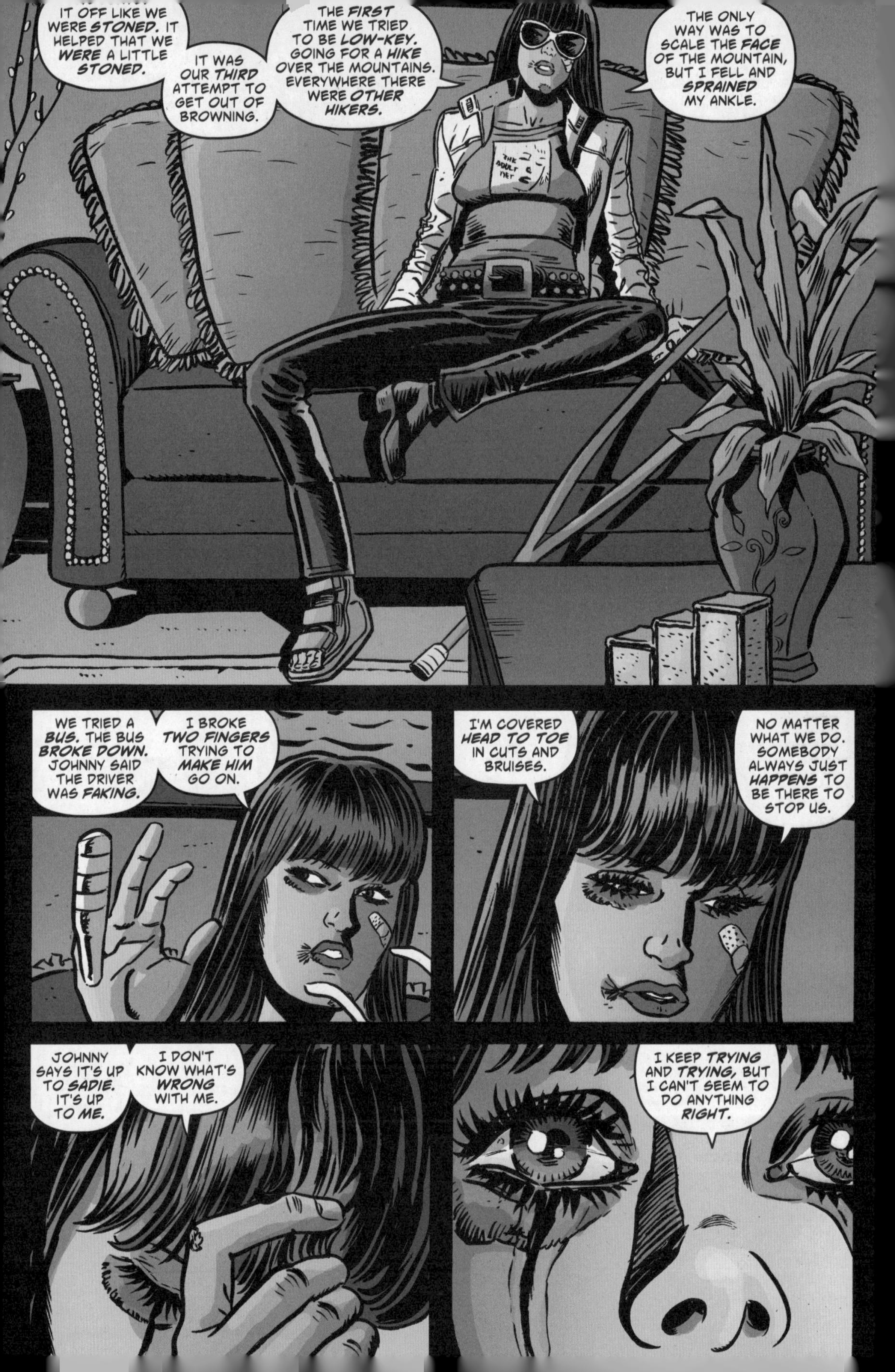
IT OFF LIKE WE WERE STONED. IT HELPED THAT WE WERE A LITTLE STONED.
IT WAS OUR THIRD ATTEMPT TO GET OUT OF BROWNING.
THE FIRST TIME WE TRIED TO BE LOW-KEY. GOING FOR A HIKE OVER THE MOUNTAINS. EVERYWHERE THERE WERE OTHER HIKERS.
THE ONLY WAY WAS TO SCALE THE FACE OF THE MOUNTAIN, BUT I FELL AND SPRAINED MY ANKLE.
THE ADULT YET
WE TRIED A BUS. THE BUS BROKE DOWN. JOHNNY SAID THE DRIVER WAS FAKING.
I BROKE TWO FINGERS TRYING TO MAKE HIM GO ON.
I'M COVERED HEAD TO TOE IN CUTS AND BRUISES.
NO MATTER WHAT WE DO. SOMEBODY ALWAYS JUST HAPPENS TO BE THERE TO STOP US.
JOHNNY SAYS IT'S UP TO SADIE. IT'S UP TO ME.
I DON'T KNOW WHAT'S WRONG WITH ME.
I KEEP TRYING AND TRYING, BUT I CAN'T SEEM TO DO ANYTHING RIGHT.

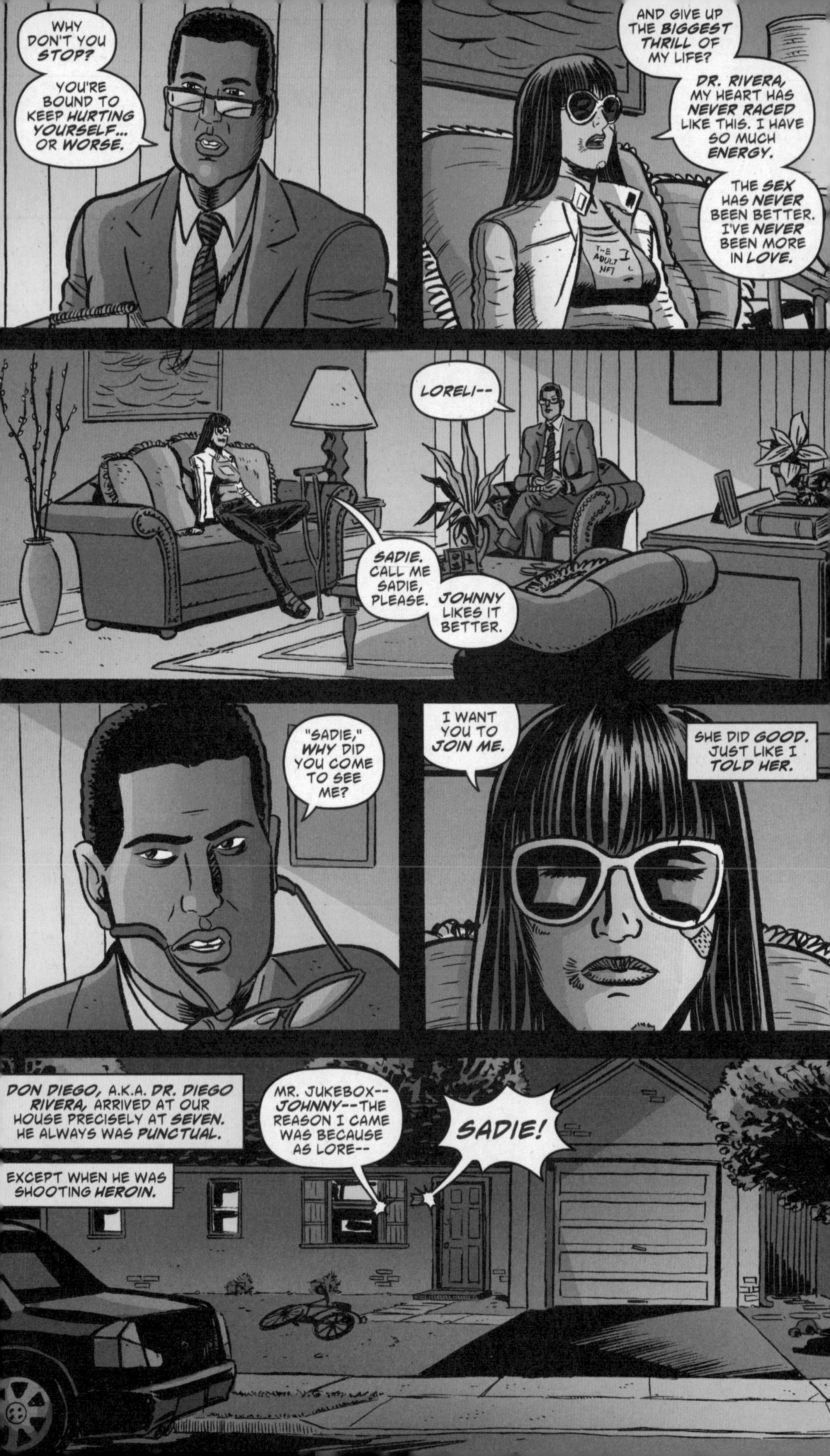
WHY DON'T YOU STOP?
YOU'RE BOUND TO KEEP HURTING YOURSELF... OR WORSE.
AND GIVE UP THE BIGGEST THRILL OF MY LIFE?
DR. RIVERA, MY HEART HAS NEVER RACED LIKE THIS. I HAVE SO MUCH ENERGY.
THE SEX HAS NEVER BEEN BETTER. I'VE NEVER BEEN MORE IN LOVE.
THE ADULT NFT
LORELI--
SADIE. CALL ME SADIE, PLEASE.
JOHNNY LIKES IT BETTER.
"SADIE," WHY DID YOU COME TO SEE ME?
I WANT YOU TO JOIN ME.
SHE DID GOOD. JUST LIKE I TOLD HER.
DON DIEGO, A.K.A. DR. DIEGO RIVERA, ARRIVED AT OUR HOUSE PRECISELY AT SEVEN. HE ALWAYS WAS PUNCTUAL.
EXCEPT WHEN HE WAS SHOOTING HEROIN.
MR. JUKEBOX-- JOHNNY--THE REASON I CAME WAS BECAUSE AS LORE--
SADIE!

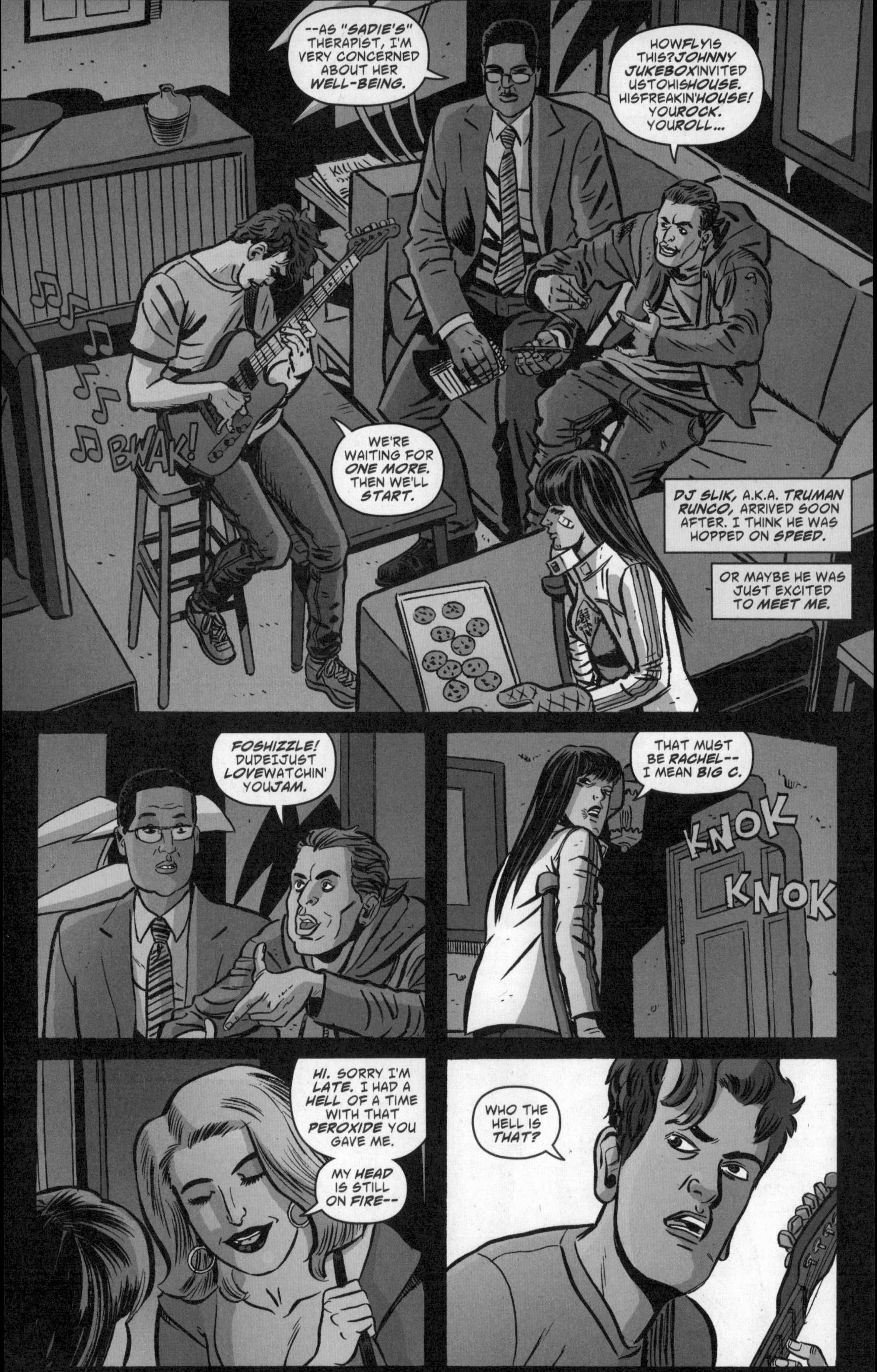
--AS "SADIE'S" THERAPIST, I'M VERY CONCERNED ABOUT HER WELL-BEING.
HOWFLYIS THIS?JOHNNY JUKEBOXINVITED USTOHISHOUSE. HISFREAKIN'HOUSE! YOUROCK. YOUROLL...
BWAK!
WE'RE WAITING FOR ONE MORE. THEN WE'LL START.
DJ SLIK, A.K.A. TRUMAN RUNCO, ARRIVED SOON AFTER. I THINK HE WAS HOPPED ON SPEED.
OR MAYBE HE WAS JUST EXCITED TO MEET ME.
FOSHIZZLE! DUDEIJUST LOVEWATCHIN' YOUJAM.
THAT MUST BE RACHEL-- I MEAN BIG C.
KNOK
KNOK
HI. SORRY I'M LATE. I HAD A HELL OF A TIME WITH THAT PEROXIDE YOU GAVE ME.
MY HEAD IS STILL ON FIRE--
WHO THE HELL IS THAT?

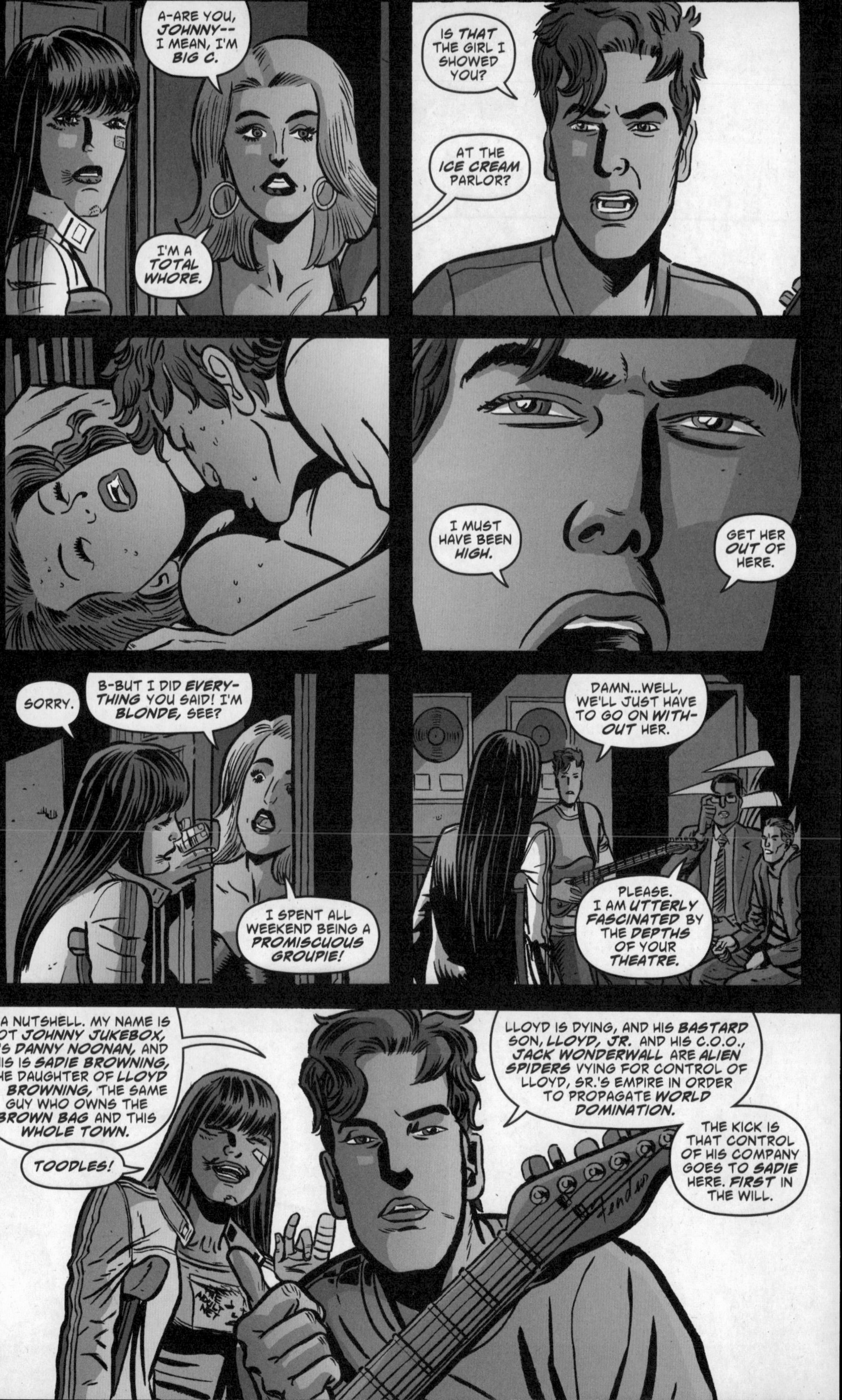
A-ARE YOU, JOHNNY-- I MEAN, I'M BIG C.
I'M A TOTAL WHORE.
IS THAT THE GIRL I SHOWED YOU?
AT THE ICE CREAM PARLOR?
I MUST HAVE BEEN HIGH.
GET HER OUT OF HERE.
SORRY.
B-BUT I DID EVERY-THING YOU SAID! I'M BLONDE, SEE?
I SPENT ALL WEEKEND BEING A PROMISCUOUS GROUPIE!
DAMN...WELL, WE'LL JUST HAVE TO GO ON WITH-OUT HER.
PLEASE. I AM UTTERLY FASCINATED BY THE DEPTHS OF YOUR THEATRE.
IN A NUTSHELL. MY NAME IS NOT JOHNNY JUKEBOX, IT'S DANNY NOONAN, AND THIS IS SADIE BROWNING, THE DAUGHTER OF LLOYD T. BROWNING, THE SAME GUY WHO OWNS THE BROWN BAG AND THIS WHOLE TOWN.
TOODLES!
LLOYD IS DYING, AND HIS BASTARD SON, LLOYD, JR. AND HIS C.O.O., JACK WONDERWALL ARE ALIEN SPIDERS VYING FOR CONTROL OF LLOYD, SR.'S EMPIRE IN ORDER TO PROPAGATE WORLD DOMINATION.
THE KICK IS THAT CONTROL OF HIS COMPANY GOES TO SADIE HERE. FIRST IN THE WILL.

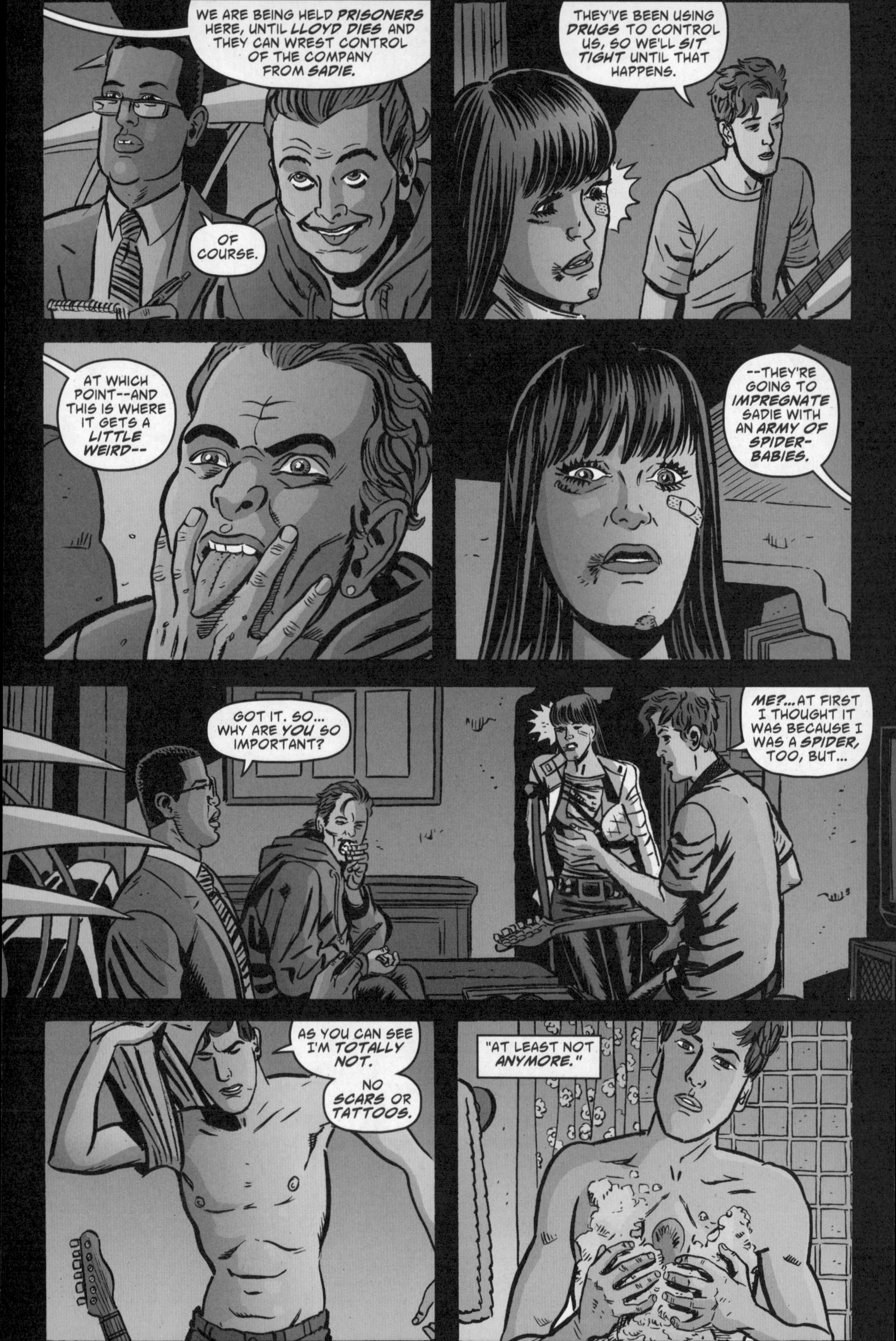
WE ARE BEING HELD *PRISONERS* HERE, UNTIL *LLOYD DIES* AND THEY CAN WREST CONTROL OF THE COMPANY FROM *SADIE*.
OF COURSE.
THEY'VE BEEN USING *DRUGS* TO CONTROL US, SO WE'LL *SIT TIGHT* UNTIL THAT HAPPENS.
AT WHICH POINT--AND THIS IS WHERE IT GETS A *LITTLE WEIRD*--
--THEY'RE GOING TO *IMPREGNATE* SADIE WITH AN *ARMY OF SPIDER-BABIES*.
GOT IT. SO... WHY ARE *YOU* SO IMPORTANT?
ME?...AT FIRST I THOUGHT IT WAS BECAUSE I WAS A *SPIDER*, TOO, BUT...
AS YOU CAN SEE I'M *TOTALLY NOT*.
NO *SCARS* OR *TATTOOS*.
"AT LEAST NOT *ANYMORE*."

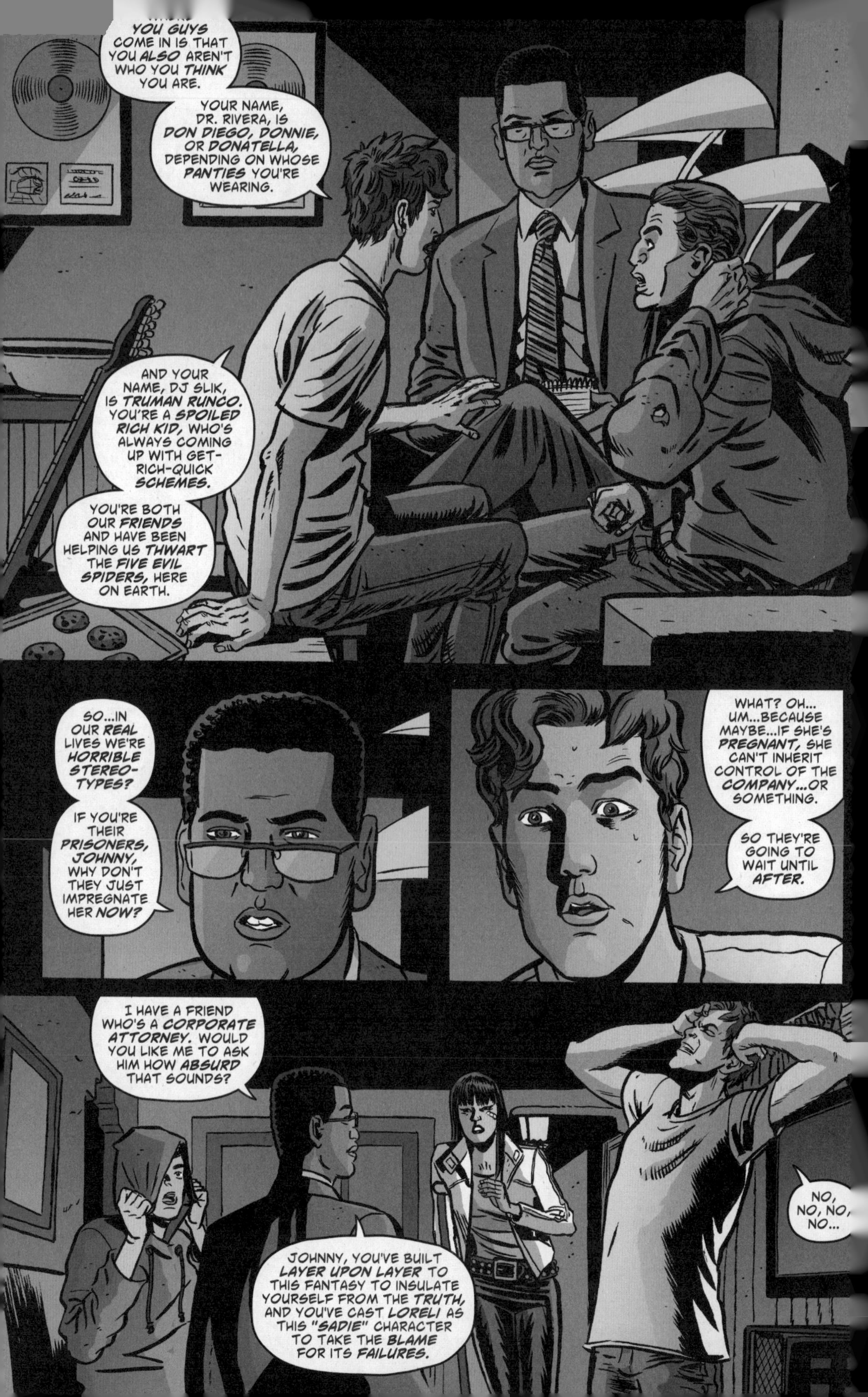
YOU GUYS COME IN IS THAT YOU ALSO AREN'T WHO YOU THINK YOU ARE.
YOUR NAME, DR. RIVERA, IS DON DIEGO, DONNIE, OR DONATELLA, DEPENDING ON WHOSE PANTIES YOU'RE WEARING.
AND YOUR NAME, DJ SLIK, IS TRUMAN RUNCO. YOU'RE A SPOILED RICH KID, WHO'S ALWAYS COMING UP WITH GET-RICH-QUICK SCHEMES.
YOU'RE BOTH OUR FRIENDS AND HAVE BEEN HELPING US THWART THE FIVE EVIL SPIDERS, HERE ON EARTH.
SO...IN OUR REAL LIVES WE'RE HORRIBLE STEREO-TYPES?
IF YOU'RE THEIR PRISONERS, JOHNNY, WHY DON'T THEY JUST IMPREGNATE HER NOW?
WHAT? OH... UM...BECAUSE MAYBE...IF SHE'S PREGNANT, SHE CAN'T INHERIT CONTROL OF THE COMPANY...OR SOMETHING.
SO THEY'RE GOING TO WAIT UNTIL AFTER.
I HAVE A FRIEND WHO'S A CORPORATE ATTORNEY. WOULD YOU LIKE ME TO ASK HIM HOW ABSURD THAT SOUNDS?
JOHNNY, YOU'VE BUILT LAYER UPON LAYER TO THIS FANTASY TO INSULATE YOURSELF FROM THE TRUTH, AND YOU'VE CAST LORELI AS THIS "SADIE" CHARACTER TO TAKE THE BLAME FOR ITS FAILURES.
NO, NO, NO, NO...

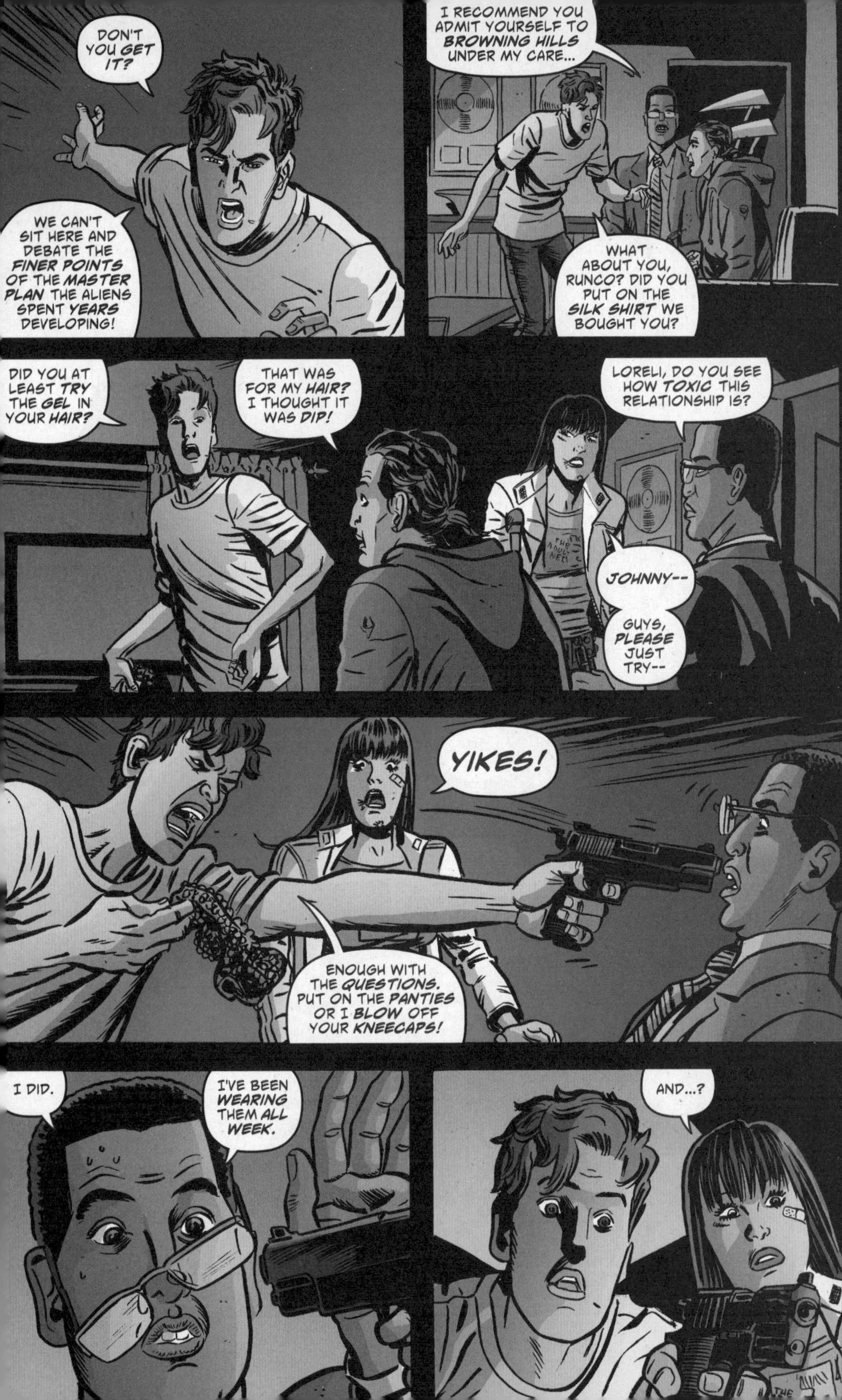
DON'T YOU GET IT?
WE CAN'T SIT HERE AND DEBATE THE FINER POINTS OF THE MASTER PLAN THE ALIENS SPENT YEARS DEVELOPING!
I RECOMMEND YOU ADMIT YOURSELF TO BROWNING HILLS UNDER MY CARE...
WHAT ABOUT YOU, RUNCO? DID YOU PUT ON THE SILK SHIRT WE BOUGHT YOU?
DID YOU AT LEAST TRY THE GEL IN YOUR HAIR?
THAT WAS FOR MY HAIR? I THOUGHT IT WAS DIP!
LORELI, DO YOU SEE HOW TOXIC THIS RELATIONSHIP IS?
JOHNNY--
GUYS, PLEASE JUST TRY--
YIKES!
ENOUGH WITH THE QUESTIONS. PUT ON THE PANTIES OR I BLOW OFF YOUR KNEECAPS!
I DID.
I'VE BEEN WEARING THEM ALL WEEK.
AND...?

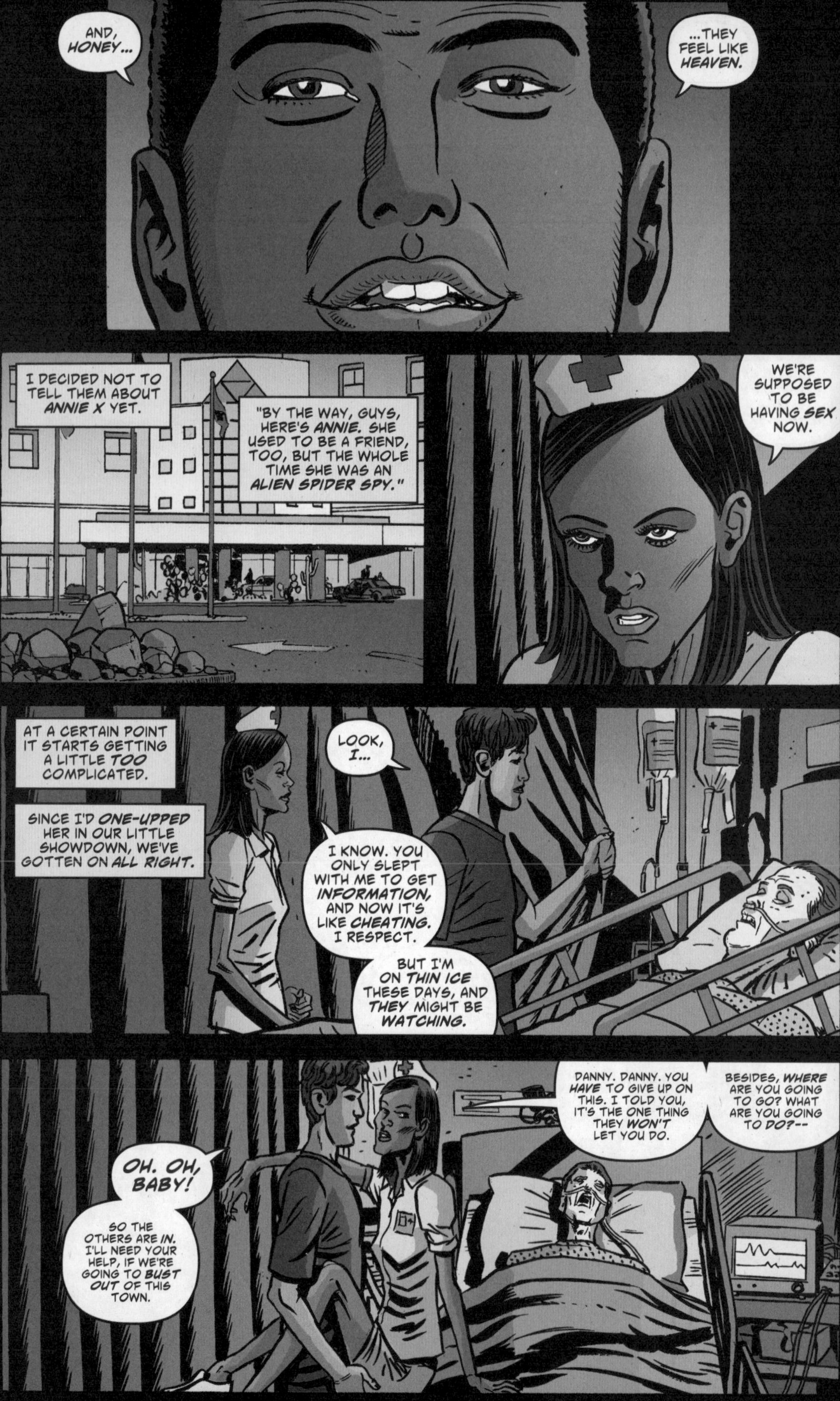
AND, HONEY...
...THEY FEEL LIKE HEAVEN.
I DECIDED NOT TO TELL THEM ABOUT ANNIE X YET.
"BY THE WAY, GUYS, HERE'S ANNIE. SHE USED TO BE A FRIEND, TOO, BUT THE WHOLE TIME SHE WAS AN ALIEN SPIDER SPY."
WE'RE SUPPOSED TO BE HAVING SEX NOW.
AT A CERTAIN POINT IT STARTS GETTING A LITTLE TOO COMPLICATED.
SINCE I'D ONE-UPPED HER IN OUR LITTLE SHOWDOWN, WE'VE GOTTEN ON ALL RIGHT.
LOOK, I...
I KNOW. YOU ONLY SLEPT WITH ME TO GET INFORMATION, AND NOW IT'S LIKE CHEATING. I RESPECT.
BUT I'M ON THIN ICE THESE DAYS, AND THEY MIGHT BE WATCHING.
DANNY. DANNY. YOU HAVE TO GIVE UP ON THIS. I TOLD YOU, IT'S THE ONE THING THEY WON'T LET YOU DO.
BESIDES, WHERE ARE YOU GOING TO GO? WHAT ARE YOU GOING TO DO?--
OH. OH, BABY!
SO THE OTHERS ARE IN. I'LL NEED YOUR HELP, IF WE'RE GOING TO BUST OUT OF THIS TOWN.

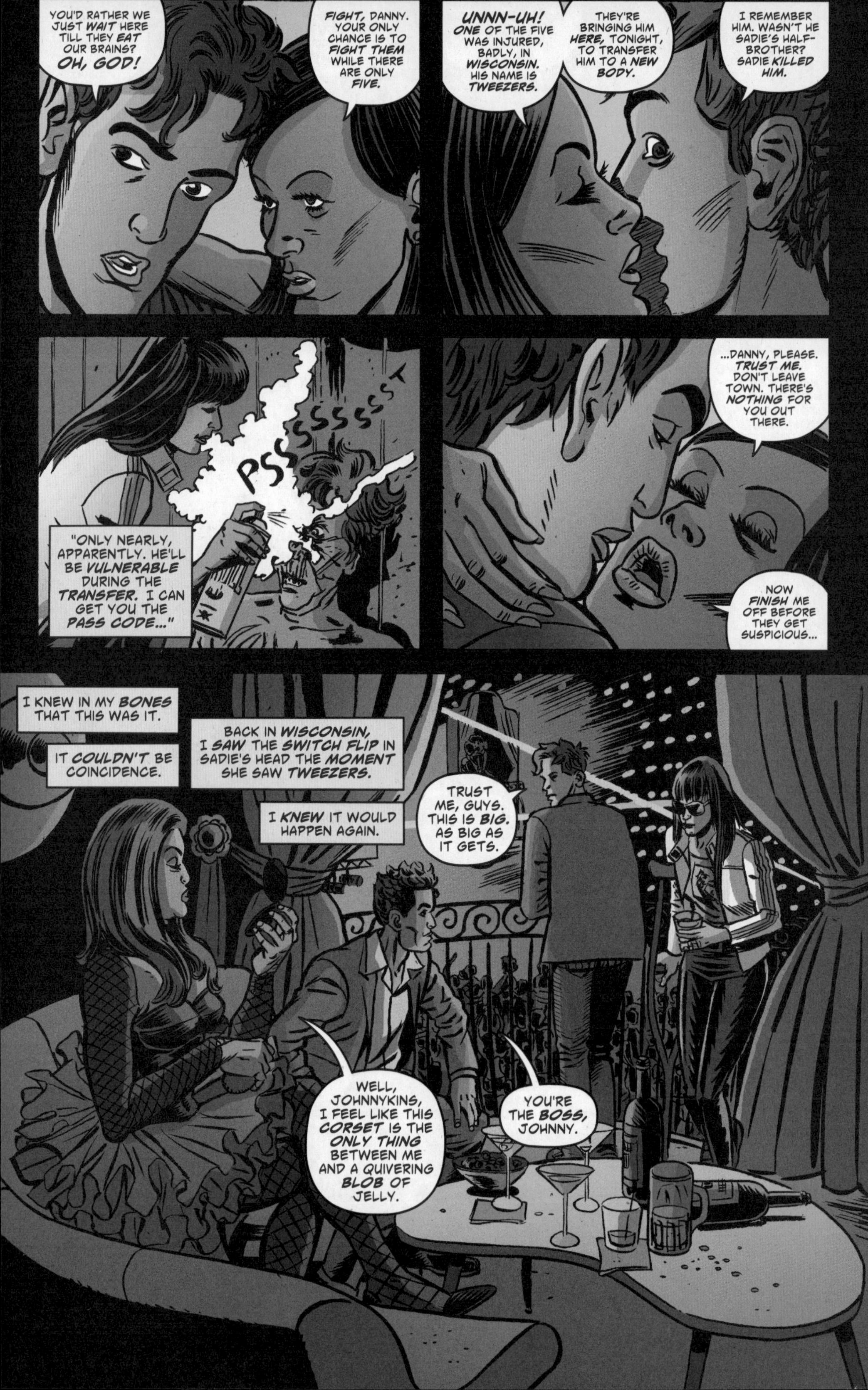
YOU'D RATHER WE JUST WAIT HERE TILL THEY EAT OUR BRAINS? OH, GOD!
FIGHT, DANNY. YOUR ONLY CHANCE IS TO FIGHT THEM WHILE THERE ARE ONLY FIVE.
UNNN-UH! ONE OF THE FIVE WAS INJURED, BADLY, IN WISCONSIN. HIS NAME IS TWEEZERS.
THEY'RE BRINGING HIM HERE, TONIGHT, TO TRANSFER HIM TO A NEW BODY.
I REMEMBER HIM. WASN'T HE SADIE'S HALF-BROTHER? SADIE KILLED HIM.
PSSSSSSSSST
"ONLY NEARLY, APPARENTLY. HE'LL BE VULNERABLE DURING THE TRANSFER. I CAN GET YOU THE PASS CODE..."
...DANNY, PLEASE. TRUST ME. DON'T LEAVE TOWN. THERE'S NOTHING FOR YOU OUT THERE.
NOW FINISH ME OFF BEFORE THEY GET SUSPICIOUS...
I KNEW IN MY BONES THAT THIS WAS IT.
IT COULDN'T BE COINCIDENCE.
BACK IN WISCONSIN, I SAW THE SWITCH FLIP IN SADIE'S HEAD THE MOMENT SHE SAW TWEEZERS.
I KNEW IT WOULD HAPPEN AGAIN.
TRUST ME, GUYS. THIS IS BIG. AS BIG AS IT GETS.
WELL, JOHNNYKINS, I FEEL LIKE THIS CORSET IS THE ONLY THING BETWEEN ME AND A QUIVERING BLOB OF JELLY.
YOU'RE THE BOSS, JOHNNY.

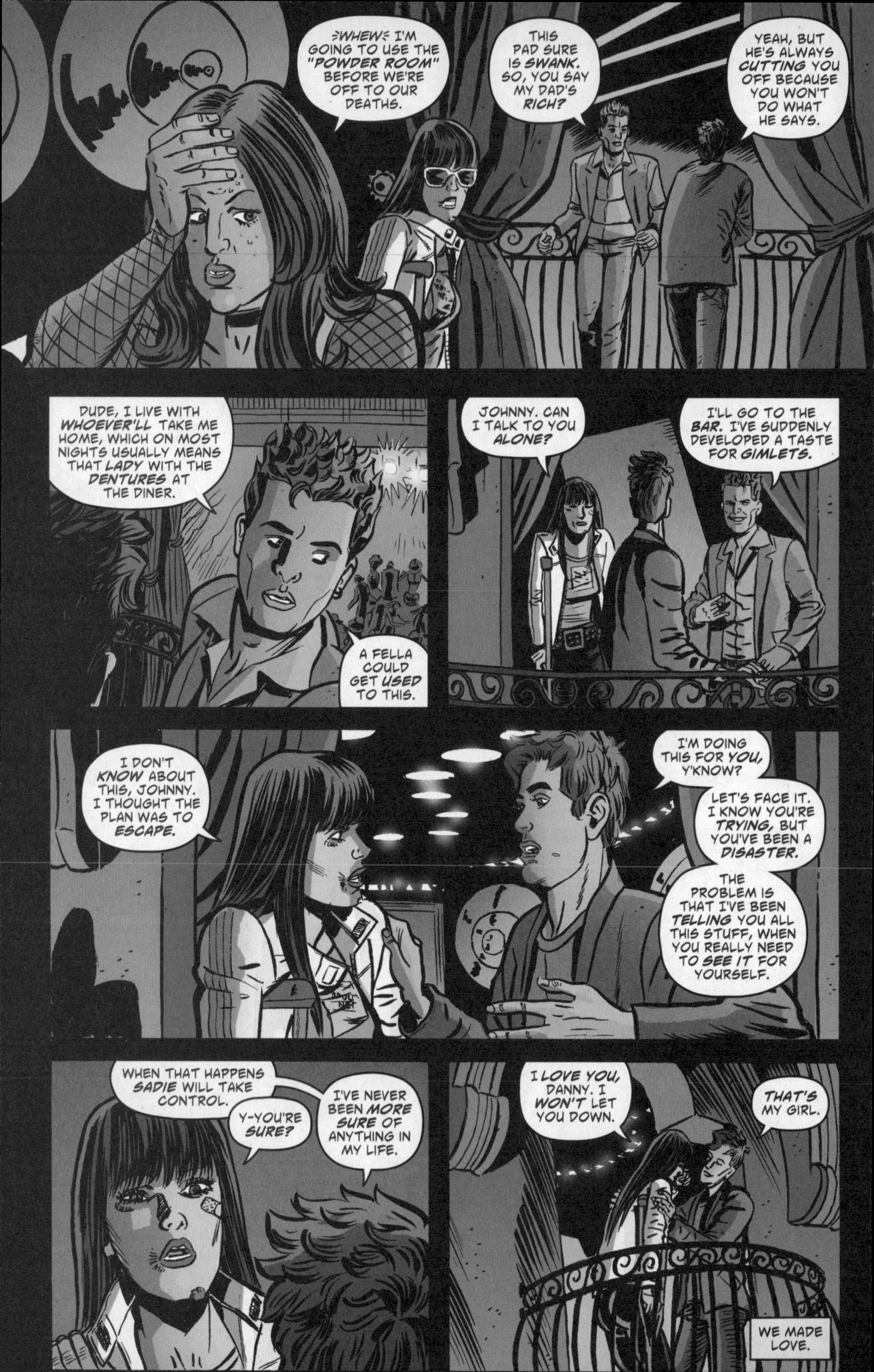
=WHEW= I'M GOING TO USE THE "POWDER ROOM" BEFORE WE'RE OFF TO OUR DEATHS.
THIS PAD SURE IS SWANK. SO, YOU SAY MY DAD'S RICH?
YEAH, BUT HE'S ALWAYS CUTTING YOU OFF BECAUSE YOU WON'T DO WHAT HE SAYS.
DUDE, I LIVE WITH WHOEVER'LL TAKE ME HOME, WHICH ON MOST NIGHTS USUALLY MEANS THAT LADY WITH THE DENTURES AT THE DINER.
A FELLA COULD GET USED TO THIS.
JOHNNY. CAN I TALK TO YOU ALONE?
I'LL GO TO THE BAR. I'VE SUDDENLY DEVELOPED A TASTE FOR GIMLETS.
I DON'T KNOW ABOUT THIS, JOHNNY. I THOUGHT THE PLAN WAS TO ESCAPE.
I'M DOING THIS FOR YOU, Y'KNOW?
LET'S FACE IT. I KNOW YOU'RE TRYING, BUT YOU'VE BEEN A DISASTER.
THE PROBLEM IS THAT I'VE BEEN TELLING YOU ALL THIS STUFF, WHEN YOU REALLY NEED TO SEE IT FOR YOURSELF.
WHEN THAT HAPPENS SADIE WILL TAKE CONTROL.
Y-YOU'RE SURE?
I'VE NEVER BEEN MORE SURE OF ANYTHING IN MY LIFE.
I LOVE YOU, DANNY. I WON'T LET YOU DOWN.
THAT'S MY GIRL.
WE MADE LOVE.

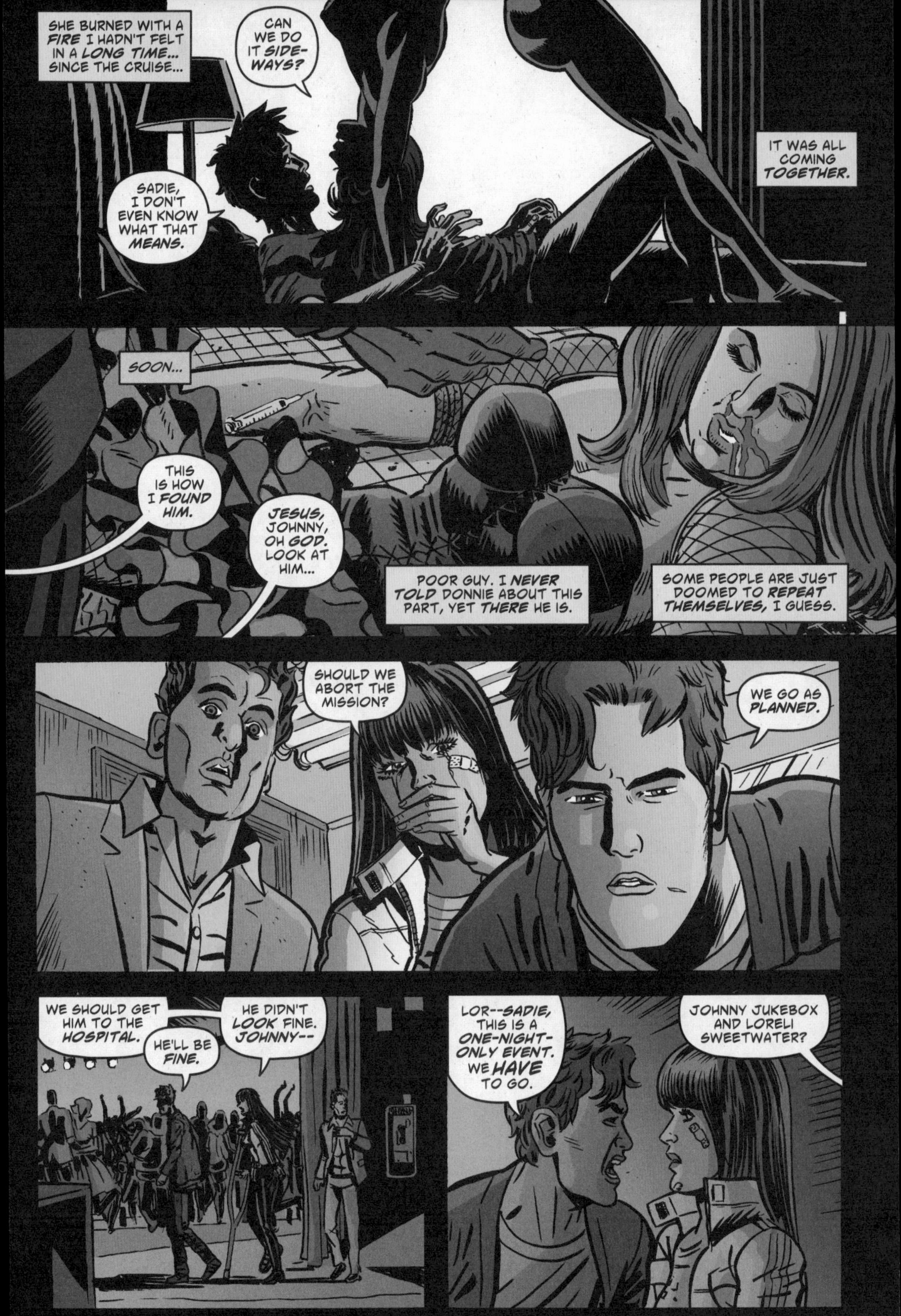
SHE BURNED WITH A *FIRE* I HADN'T FELT IN A *LONG TIME*... SINCE THE CRUISE...
CAN WE DO IT *SIDE-WAYS?*
SADIE, I DON'T EVEN KNOW WHAT THAT *MEANS.*
IT WAS ALL COMING *TOGETHER.*
SOON...
THIS IS HOW I *FOUND HIM.*
JESUS, JOHNNY, OH *GOD.* LOOK AT HIM...
POOR GUY. I *NEVER TOLD* DONNIE ABOUT THIS PART, YET *THERE* HE IS.
SOME PEOPLE ARE JUST DOOMED TO *REPEAT THEMSELVES,* I GUESS.
SHOULD WE ABORT THE MISSION?
WE GO AS *PLANNED.*
WE SHOULD GET HIM TO THE *HOSPITAL.*
HE'LL BE *FINE.*
HE DIDN'T *LOOK* FINE. *JOHNNY--*
LOR--*SADIE,* THIS IS A *ONE-NIGHT-ONLY EVENT.* WE *HAVE* TO GO.
JOHNNY JUKEBOX AND LORELI SWEETWATER?

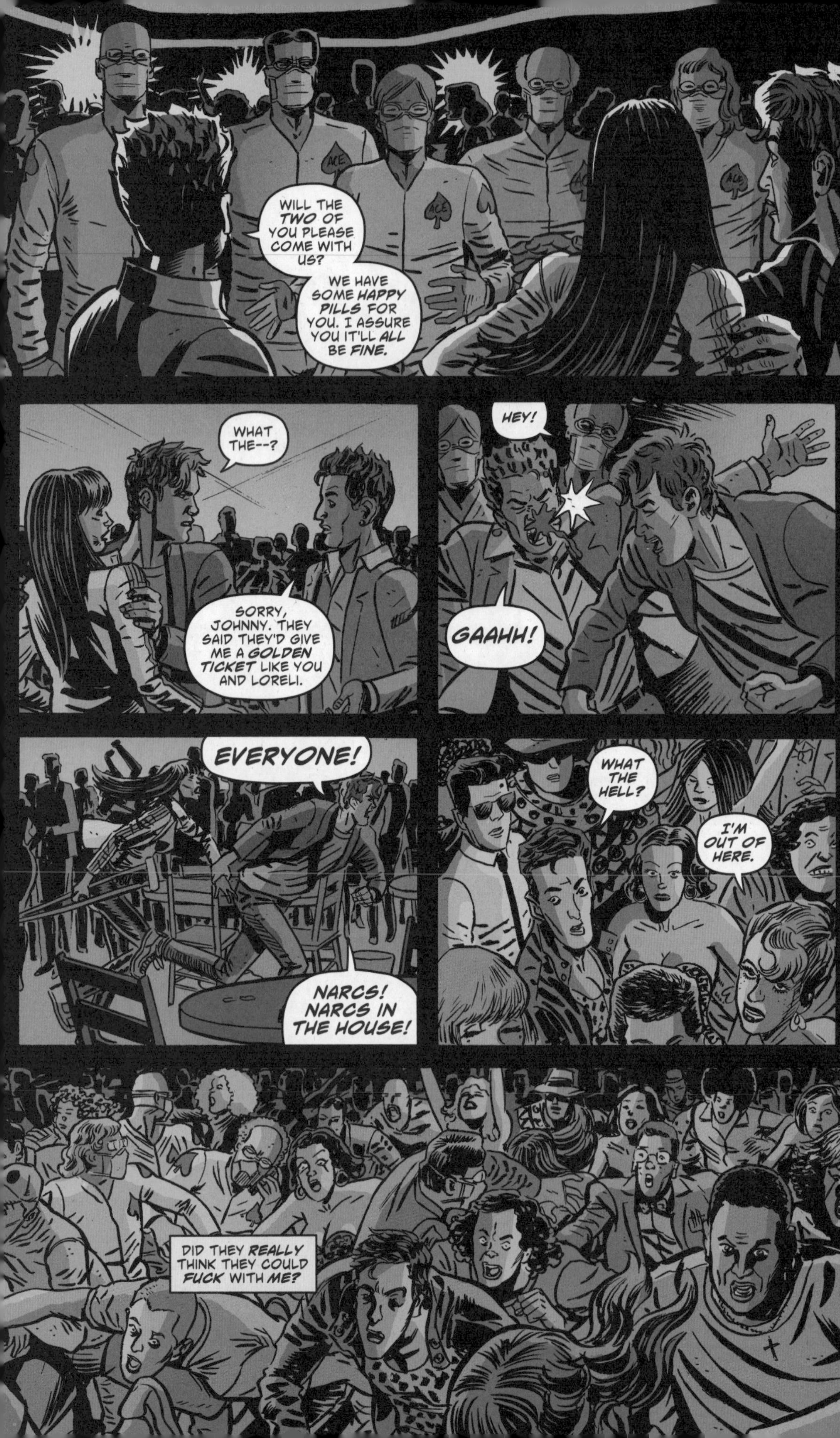
WILL THE TWO OF YOU PLEASE COME WITH US?
WE HAVE SOME HAPPY PILLS FOR YOU. I ASSURE YOU IT'LL ALL BE FINE.
WHAT THE--?
SORRY, JOHNNY. THEY SAID THEY'D GIVE ME A GOLDEN TICKET LIKE YOU AND LORELI.
HEY!
GAAHH!
EVERYONE!
NARCS! NARCS IN THE HOUSE!
WHAT THE HELL?
I'M OUT OF HERE.
DID THEY REALLY THINK THEY COULD FUCK WITH ME?

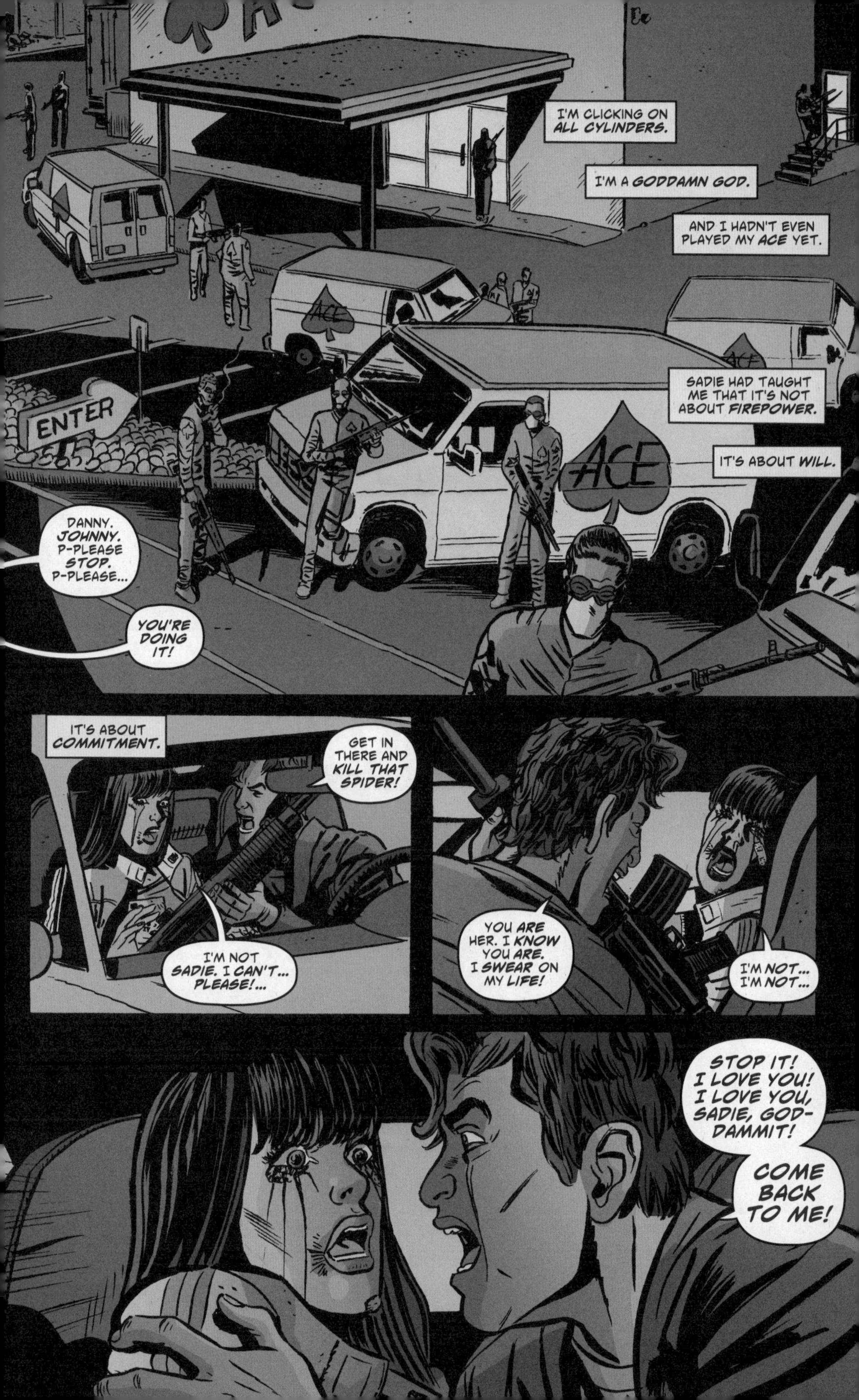
I'M CLICKING ON ALL CYLINDERS.
I'M A GODDAMN GOD.
AND I HADN'T EVEN PLAYED MY ACE YET.
ACE
ENTER
SADIE HAD TAUGHT ME THAT IT'S NOT ABOUT FIREPOWER.
IT'S ABOUT WILL.
DANNY. JOHNNY. P-PLEASE STOP. P-PLEASE...
YOU'RE DOING IT!
IT'S ABOUT COMMITMENT.
GET IN THERE AND KILL THAT SPIDER!
I'M NOT SADIE. I CAN'T... PLEASE!...
YOU ARE HER. I KNOW YOU ARE. I SWEAR ON MY LIFE!
I'M NOT... I'M NOT...
STOP IT! I LOVE YOU! I LOVE YOU, SADIE, GOD-DAMMIT!
COME BACK TO ME!

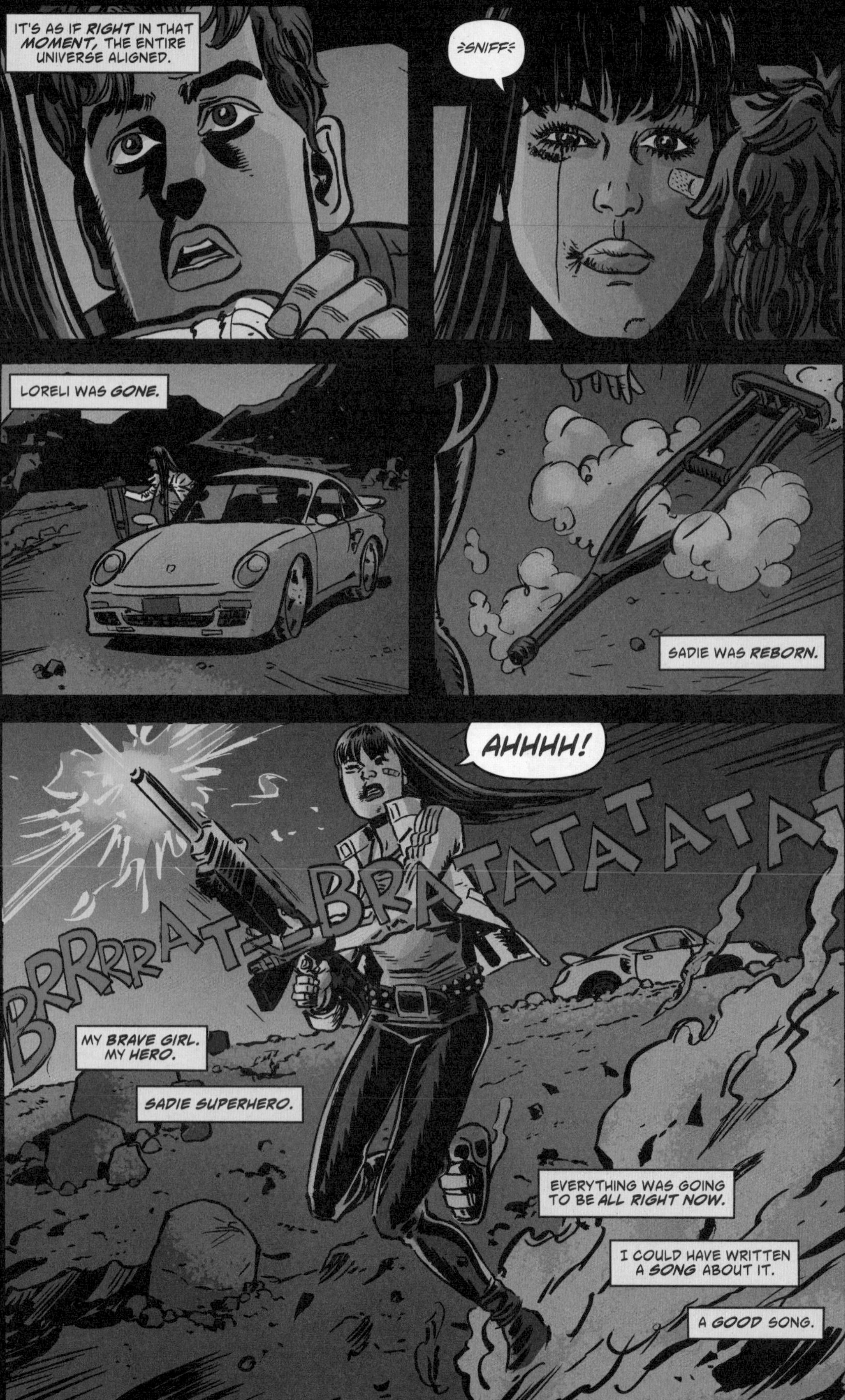
IT'S AS IF RIGHT IN THAT MOMENT, THE ENTIRE UNIVERSE ALIGNED.
≈SNIFF≈
LORELI WAS GONE.
SADIE WAS REBORN.
AHHHH!
BRRRRATE—BRATATATATAT
MY BRAVE GIRL. MY HERO.
SADIE SUPERHERO.
EVERYTHING WAS GOING TO BE ALL RIGHT NOW.
I COULD HAVE WRITTEN A SONG ABOUT IT.
A GOOD SONG.

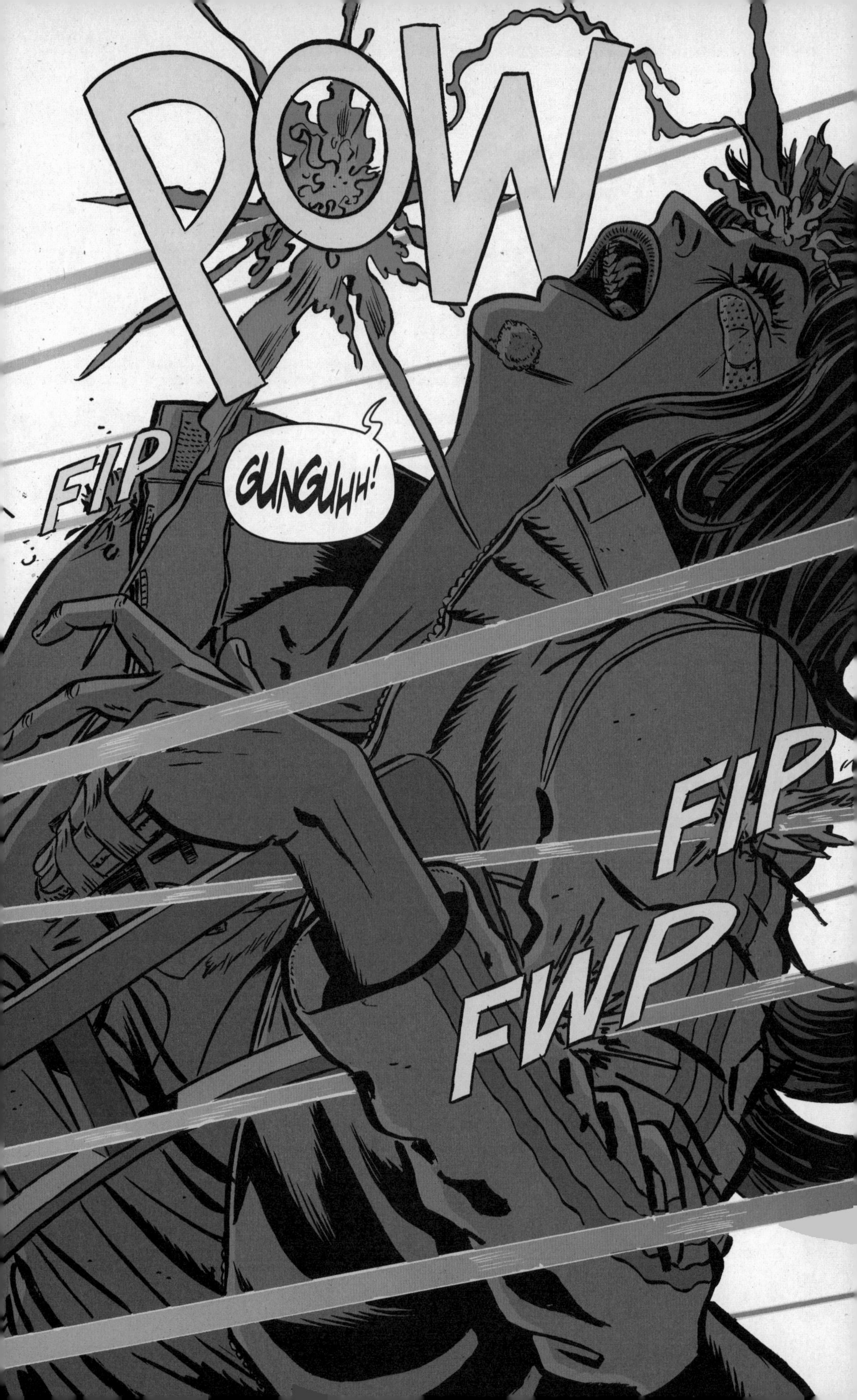
POW
FIP
GUNGUHH!
FIP
FWP

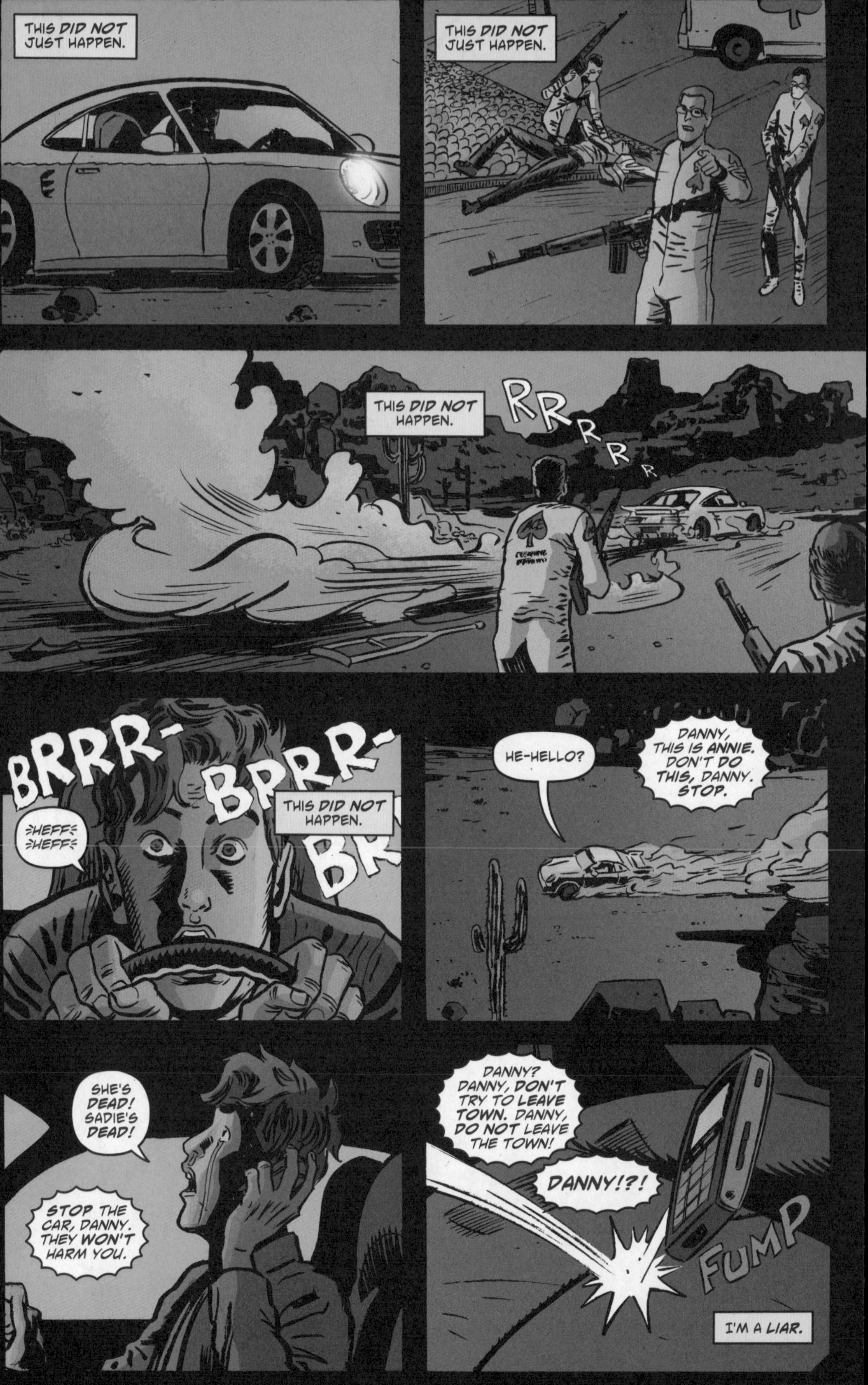
THIS DID NOT JUST HAPPEN.
THIS DID NOT JUST HAPPEN.
THIS DID NOT HAPPEN.
RRRRRR
BRRR-
BRRR-
BR
THIS DID NOT HAPPEN.
HEFF HEFF
HE-HELLO?
DANNY, THIS IS ANNIE. DON'T DO THIS, DANNY. STOP.
SHE'S DEAD! SADIE'S DEAD!
STOP THE CAR, DANNY. THEY WON'T HARM YOU.
DANNY? DANNY, DON'T TRY TO LEAVE TOWN. DANNY, DO NOT LEAVE THE TOWN!
DANNY!?!
FUMP
I'M A LIAR.

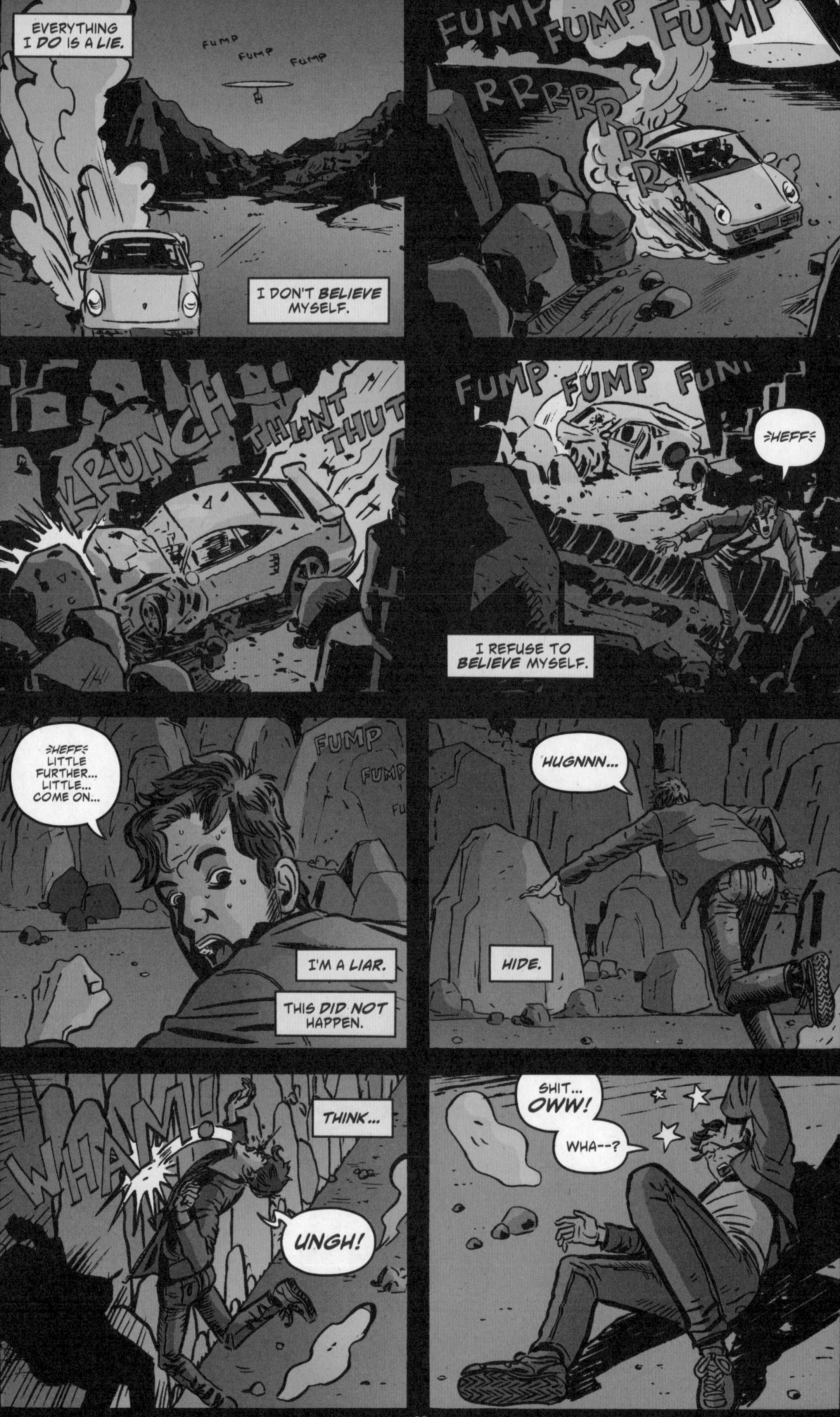
EVERYTHING I DO IS A LIE.
FUMP
FUMP
FUMP
I DON'T BELIEVE MYSELF.
FUMP FUMP FUMP
RRRRRRRR
KRUNCH
THUNT THUT
FUMP FUMP FUM
≈HEFF≈
I REFUSE TO BELIEVE MYSELF.
≈HEFF≈ LITTLE FURTHER... LITTLE... COME ON...
FUMP
FUMP
I'M A LIAR.
THIS DID NOT HAPPEN.
HUGNNN...
HIDE.
WHAM!
THINK...
UNGH!
SHIT... OWW!
WHA--?

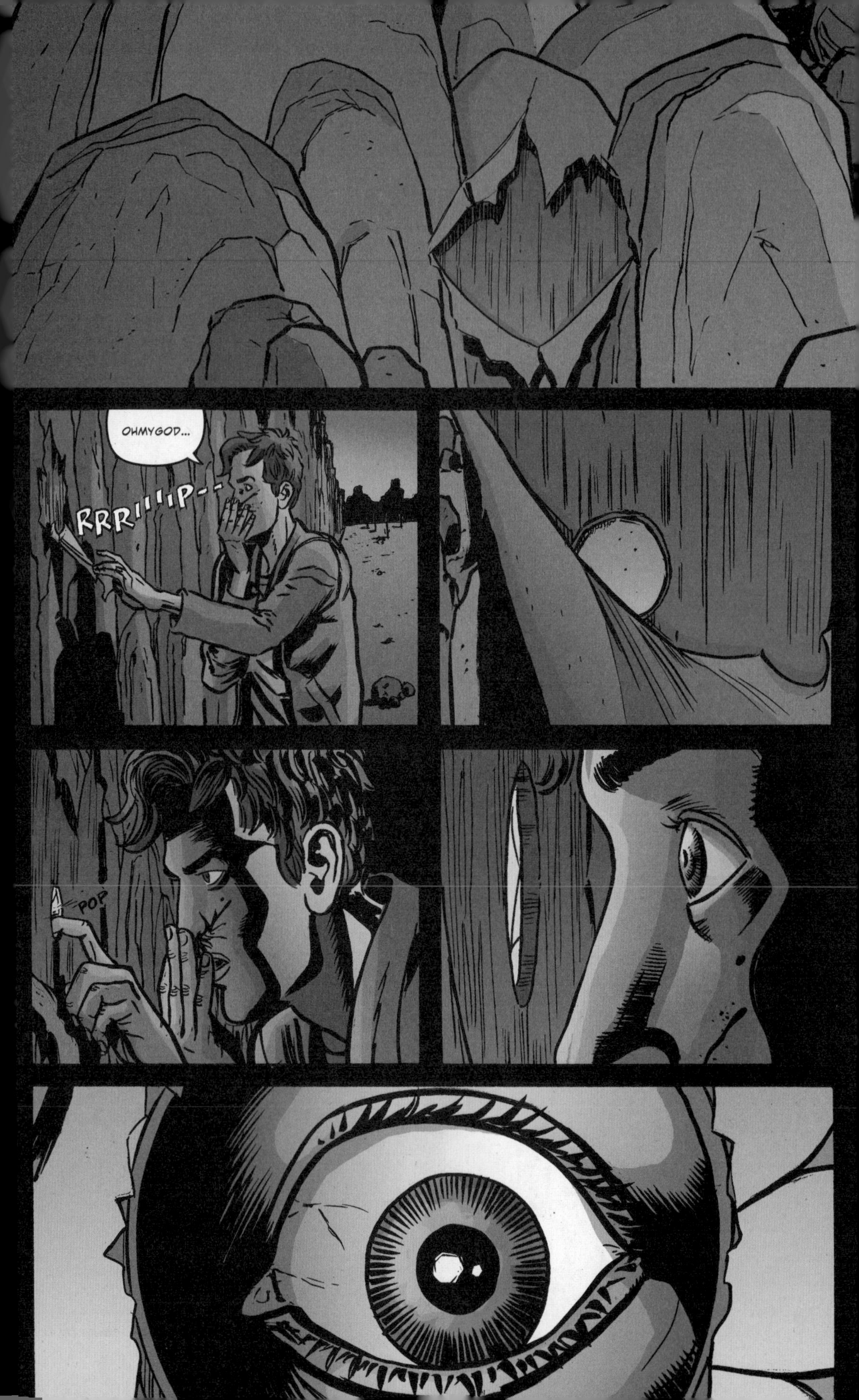
OHMYGOD...
RRRIIIIP--
POP

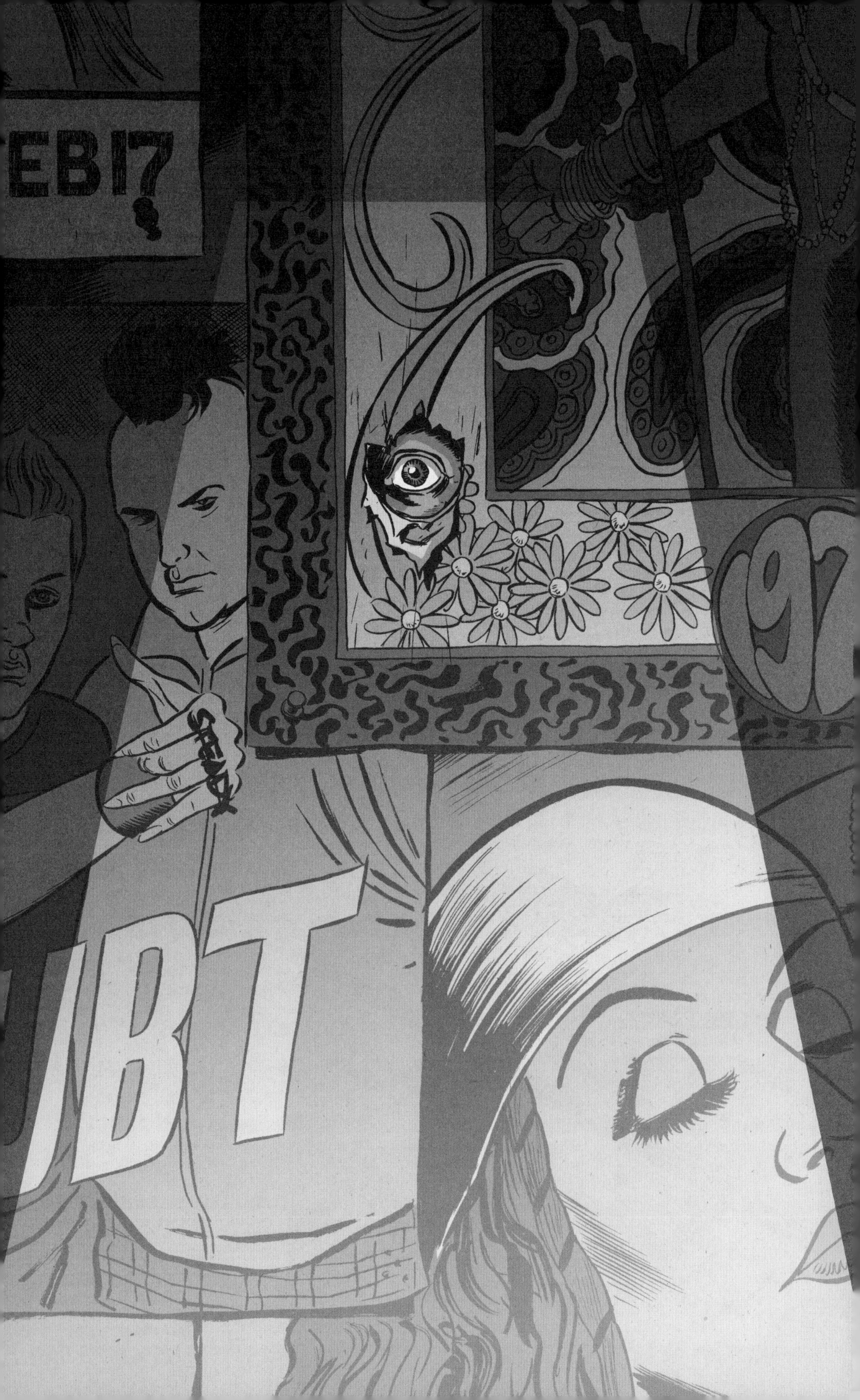

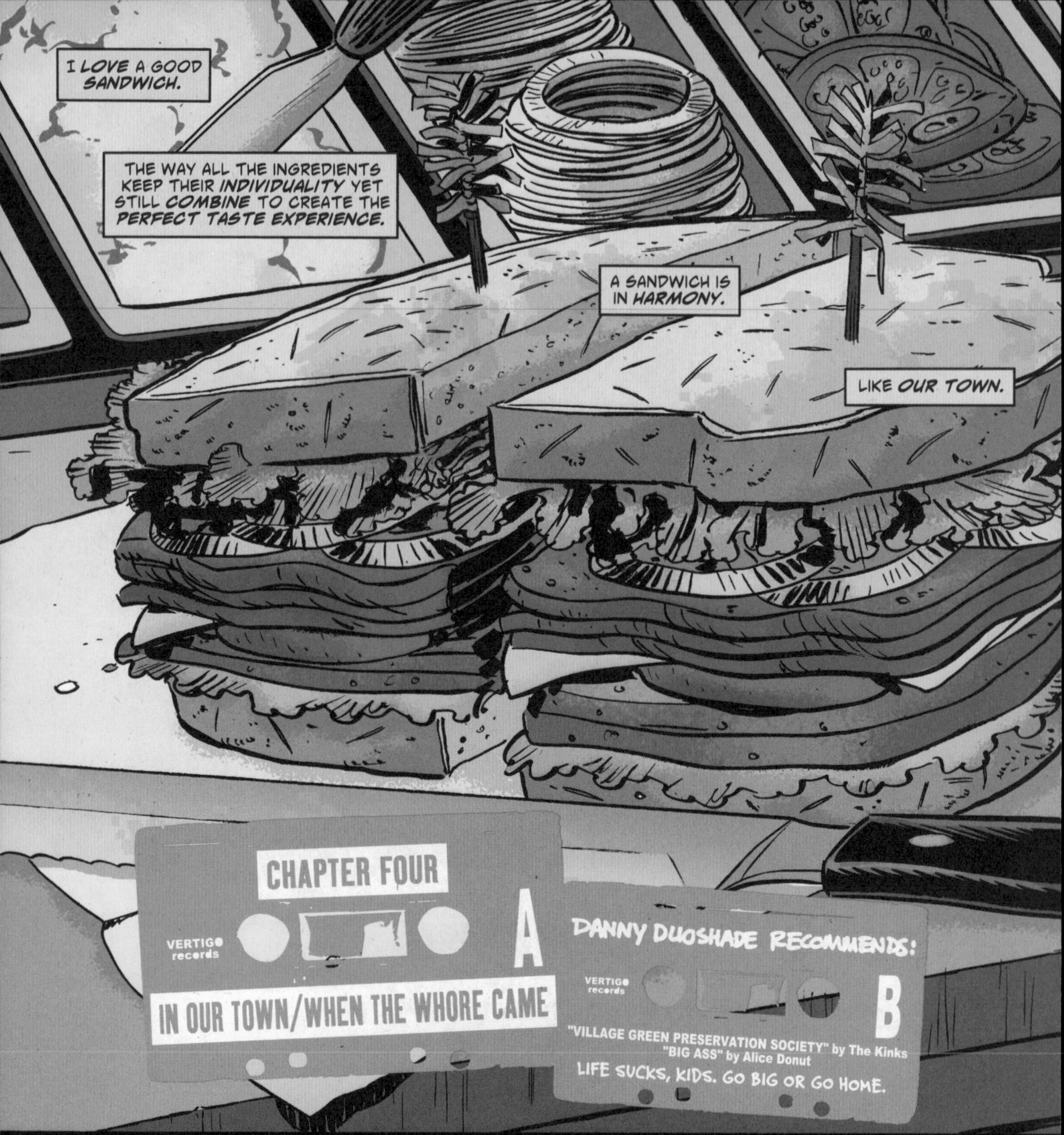
I LOVE A GOOD SANDWICH.
THE WAY ALL THE INGREDIENTS KEEP THEIR INDIVIDUALITY YET STILL COMBINE TO CREATE THE PERFECT TASTE EXPERIENCE.
A SANDWICH IS IN HARMONY.
LIKE OUR TOWN.
CHAPTER FOUR
VERTIGO records
A
IN OUR TOWN/WHEN THE WHORE CAME
DANNY DUOSHADE RECOMMENDS:
VERTIGO records
B
"VILLAGE GREEN PRESERVATION SOCIETY" by The Kinks
"BIG ASS" by Alice Donut
LIFE SUCKS, KIDS. GO BIG OR GO HOME.

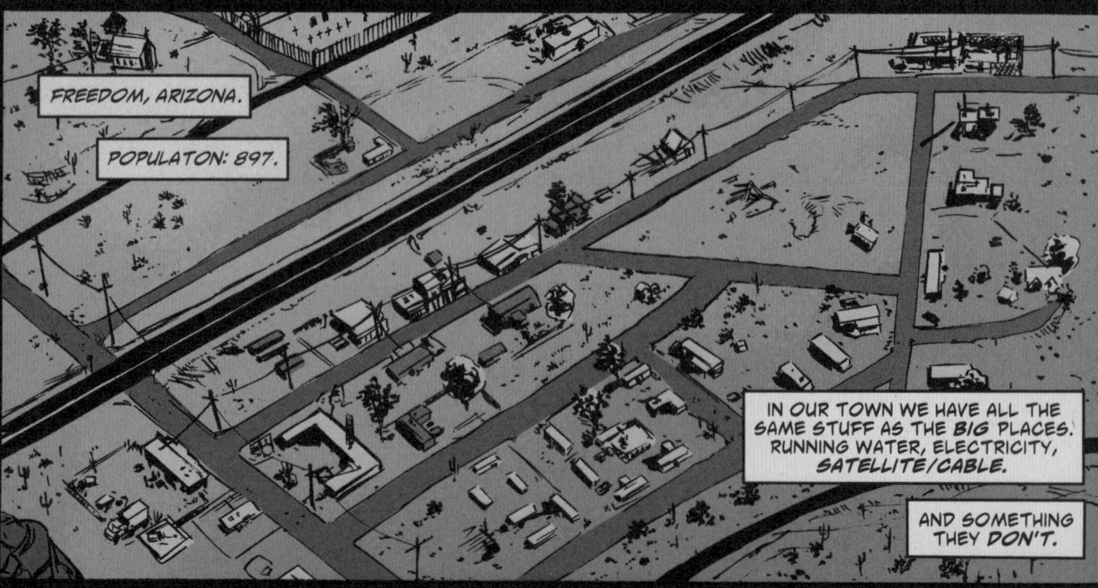
FREEDOM, ARIZONA.
POPULATON: 897.
IN OUR TOWN WE HAVE ALL THE SAME STUFF AS THE BIG PLACES. RUNNING WATER, ELECTRICITY, SATELLITE/CABLE.
AND SOMETHING THEY DON'T.

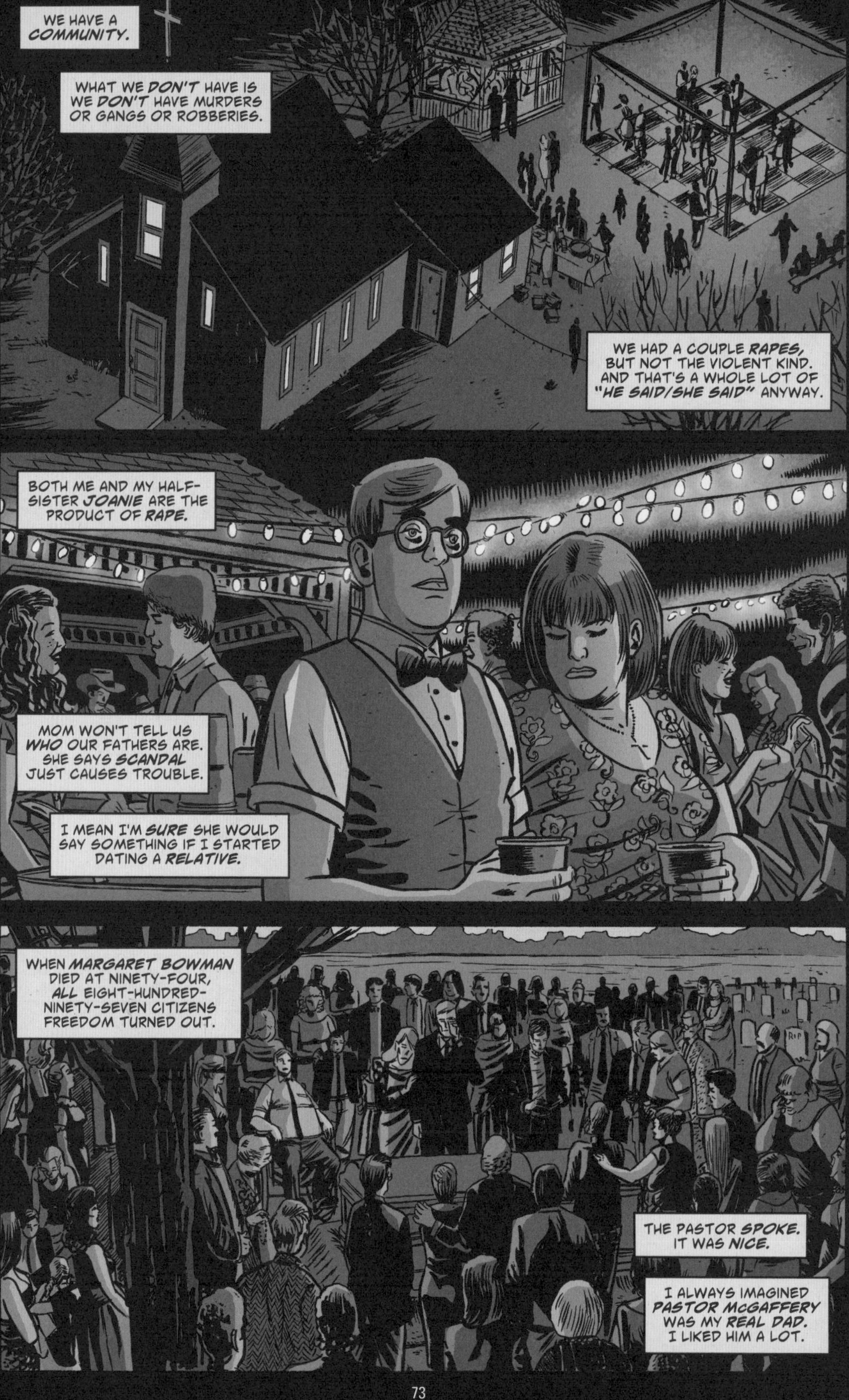
WE HAVE A COMMUNITY.
WHAT WE DON'T HAVE IS WE DON'T HAVE MURDERS OR GANGS OR ROBBERIES.
WE HAD A COUPLE RAPES, BUT NOT THE VIOLENT KIND. AND THAT'S A WHOLE LOT OF "HE SAID/SHE SAID" ANYWAY.
BOTH ME AND MY HALF-SISTER JOANIE ARE THE PRODUCT OF RAPE.
MOM WON'T TELL US WHO OUR FATHERS ARE. SHE SAYS SCANDAL JUST CAUSES TROUBLE.
I MEAN I'M SURE SHE WOULD SAY SOMETHING IF I STARTED DATING A RELATIVE.
WHEN MARGARET BOWMAN DIED AT NINETY-FOUR, ALL EIGHT-HUNDRED-NINETY-SEVEN CITIZENS FREEDOM TURNED OUT.
RIP
THE PASTOR SPOKE. IT WAS NICE.
I ALWAYS IMAGINED PASTOR McGAFFERY WAS MY REAL DAD. I LIKED HIM A LOT.

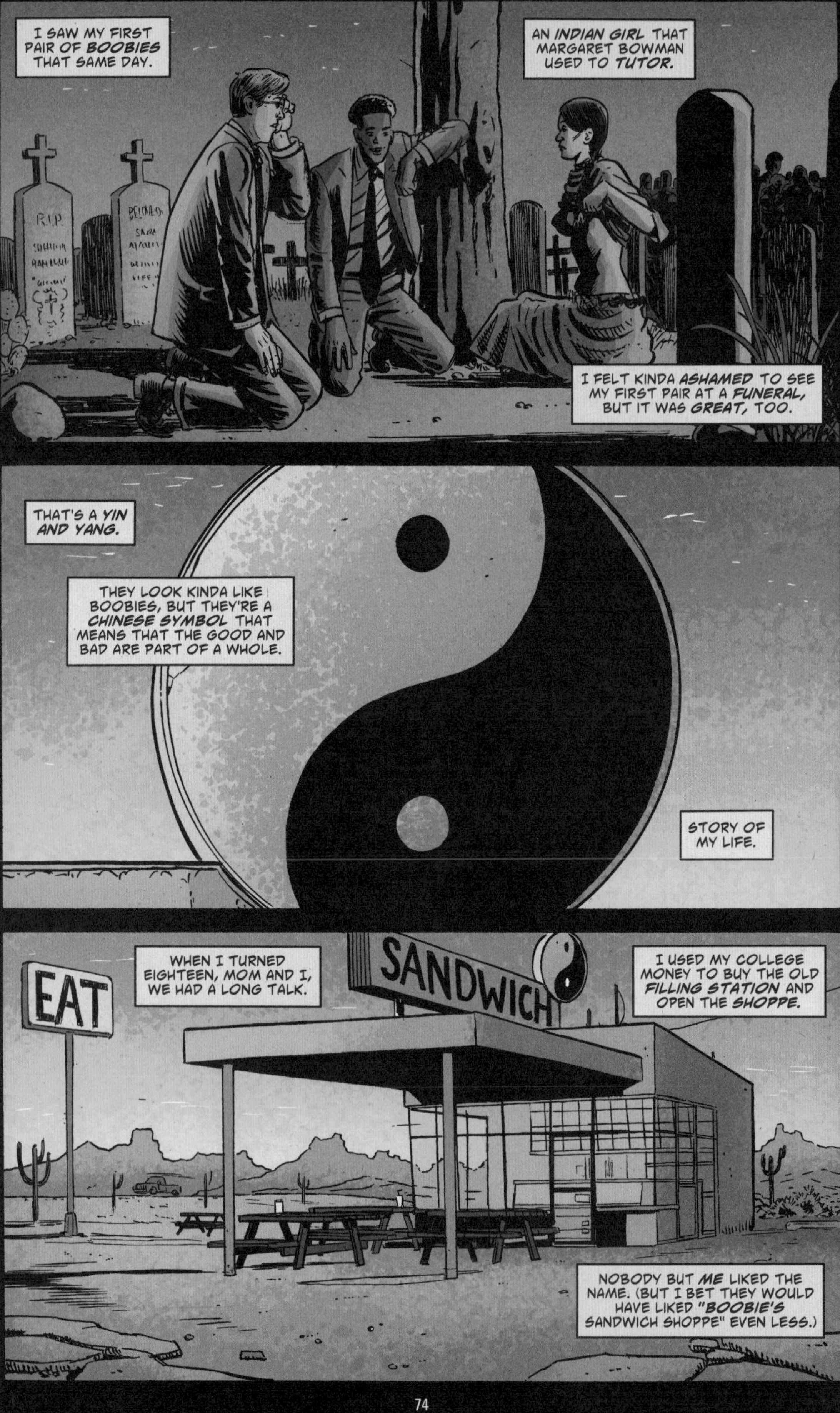
I SAW MY FIRST PAIR OF *BOOBIES* THAT SAME DAY.
AN *INDIAN GIRL* THAT MARGARET BOWMAN USED TO *TUTOR.*
I FELT KINDA *ASHAMED* TO SEE MY FIRST PAIR AT A *FUNERAL,* BUT IT WAS *GREAT,* TOO.
THAT'S A *YIN AND YANG.*
THEY LOOK KINDA LIKE BOOBIES, BUT THEY'RE A *CHINESE SYMBOL* THAT MEANS THAT THE GOOD AND BAD ARE PART OF A WHOLE.
STORY OF MY LIFE.
EAT
WHEN I TURNED EIGHTEEN, MOM AND I, WE HAD A LONG TALK.
SANDWICH
I USED MY COLLEGE MONEY TO BUY THE OLD *FILLING STATION* AND OPEN THE *SHOPPE.*
NOBODY BUT *ME* LIKED THE NAME. (BUT I BET THEY WOULD HAVE LIKED "*BOOBIE'S* SANDWICH SHOPPE" EVEN LESS.)

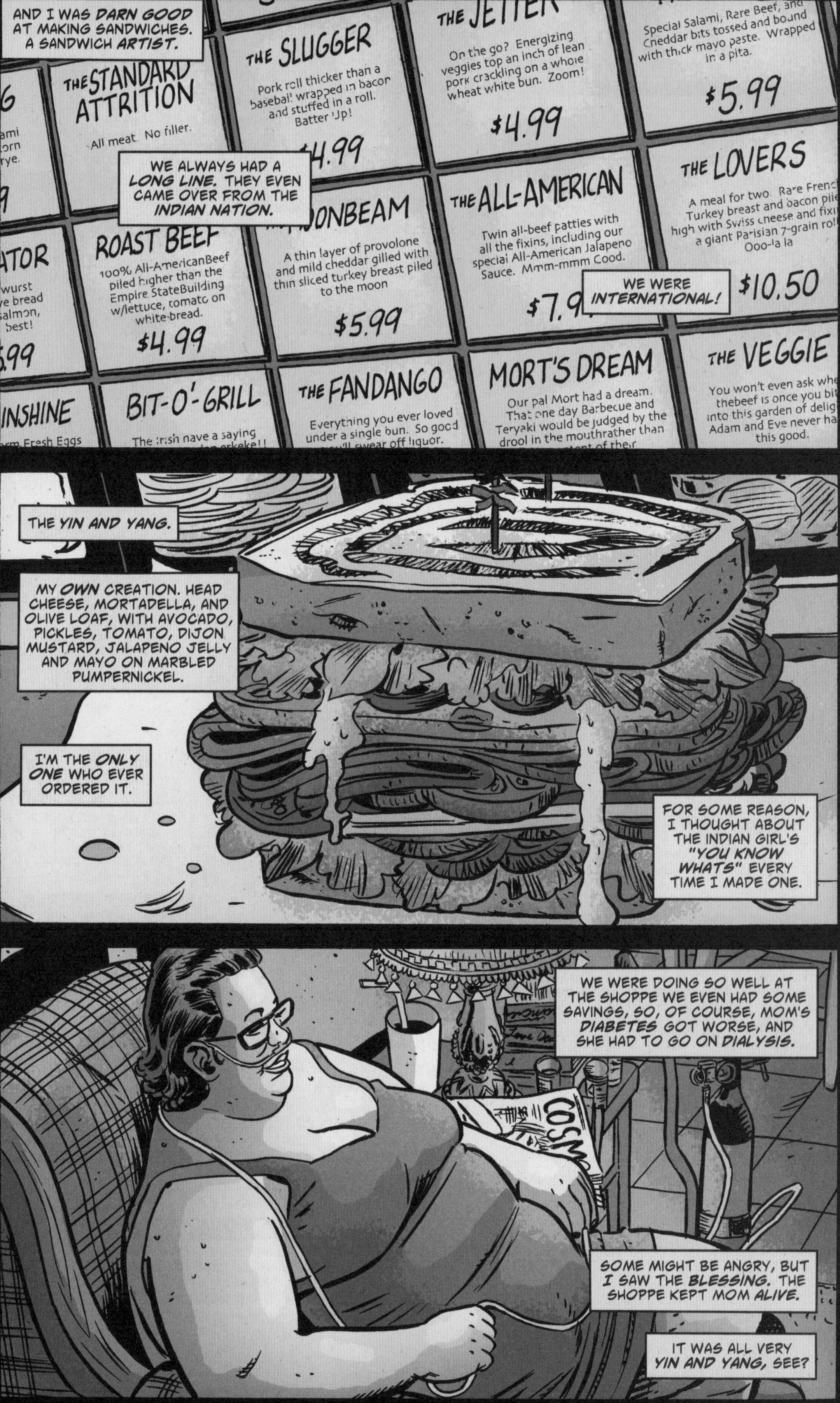
AND I WAS DARN GOOD AT MAKING SANDWICHES. A SANDWICH ARTIST.
THE SLUGGER
Pork roll thicker than a baseball wrapped in bacon and stuffed in a roll. Batter Up!
THE JETTER
On the go? Energizing veggies top an inch of lean pork crackling on a whole wheat white bun. Zoom!
$4.99
Special Salami, Rare Beef, and Cheddar bits tossed and bound with thick mayo paste. Wrapped in a pita.
$5.99
THE STANDARD ATTRITION
All meat. No filler.
WE ALWAYS HAD A LONG LINE. THEY EVEN CAME OVER FROM THE INDIAN NATION.
THE ALL-AMERICAN
Twin all-beef patties with all the fixins, including our special All-American Jalapeno Sauce. Mmm-mmm Good.
THE LOVERS
ROAST BEEF
100% All-AmericanBeef piled higher than the Empire StateBuilding w/lettuce, tomato on white-bread.
$4.99
A thin layer of provolone and mild cheddar gilled with thin sliced turkey breast piled to the moon
$5.99
WE WERE INTERNATIONAL!
$10.50
BIT-O'-GRILL
THE FANDANGO
Everything you ever loved under a single bun. So good
MORT'S DREAM
Our pal Mort had a dream. That one day Barbecue and Teryaki would be judged by the drool in the mouthrather than
THE VEGGIE
this good.
THE YIN AND YANG.
MY OWN CREATION. HEAD CHEESE, MORTADELLA, AND OLIVE LOAF, WITH AVOCADO, PICKLES, TOMATO, DIJON MUSTARD, JALAPENO JELLY AND MAYO ON MARBLED PUMPERNICKEL.
I'M THE ONLY ONE WHO EVER ORDERED IT.
FOR SOME REASON, I THOUGHT ABOUT THE INDIAN GIRL'S "YOU KNOW WHATS" EVERY TIME I MADE ONE.
WE WERE DOING SO WELL AT THE SHOPPE WE EVEN HAD SOME SAVINGS, SO, OF COURSE, MOM'S DIABETES GOT WORSE, AND SHE HAD TO GO ON DIALYSIS.
SOME MIGHT BE ANGRY, BUT I SAW THE BLESSING. THE SHOPPE KEPT MOM ALIVE.
IT WAS ALL VERY YIN AND YANG, SEE?

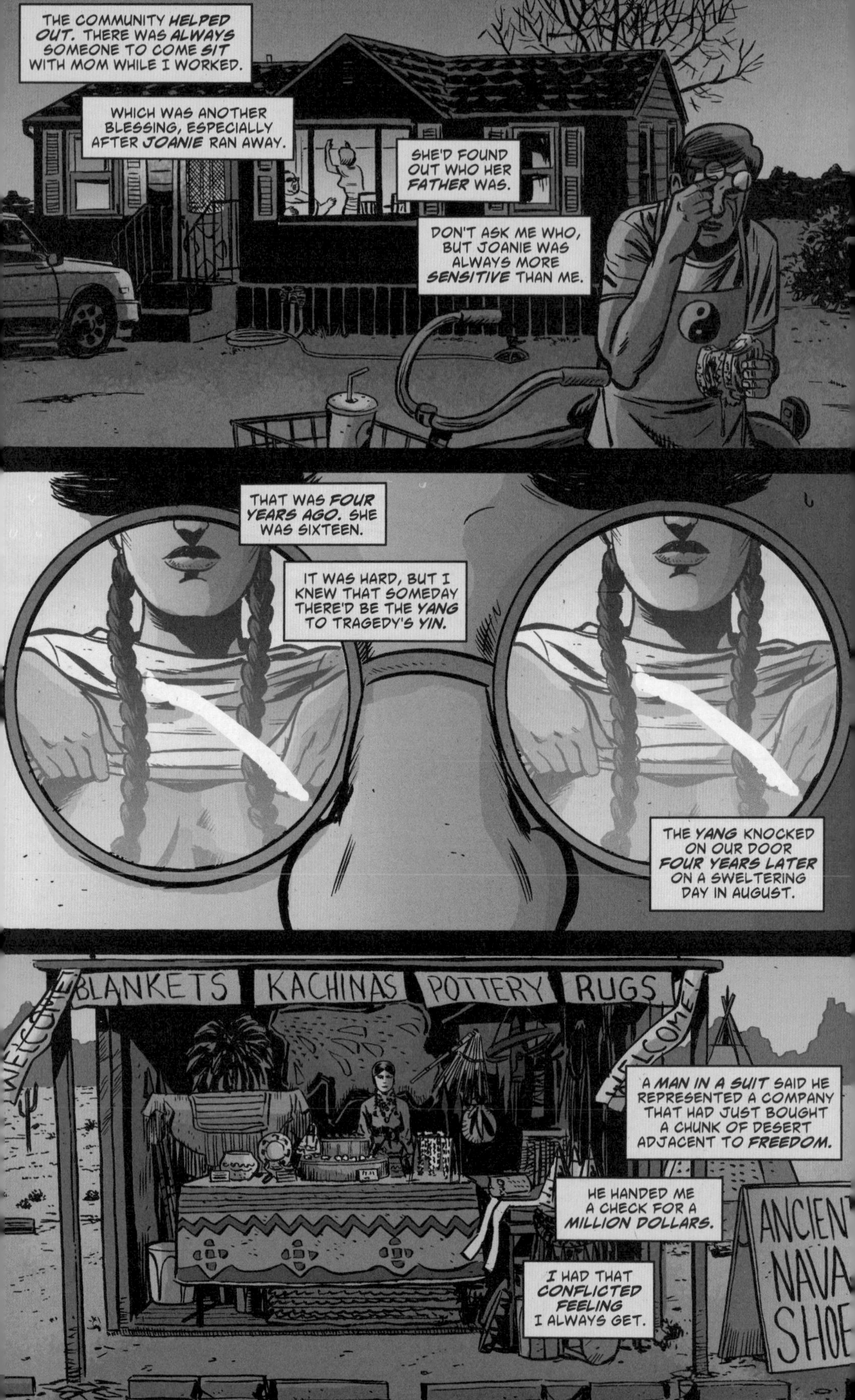
THE COMMUNITY HELPED OUT. THERE WAS ALWAYS SOMEONE TO COME SIT WITH MOM WHILE I WORKED.
WHICH WAS ANOTHER BLESSING, ESPECIALLY AFTER JOANIE RAN AWAY.
SHE'D FOUND OUT WHO HER FATHER WAS.
DON'T ASK ME WHO, BUT JOANIE WAS ALWAYS MORE SENSITIVE THAN ME.
THAT WAS FOUR YEARS AGO. SHE WAS SIXTEEN.
IT WAS HARD, BUT I KNEW THAT SOMEDAY THERE'D BE THE YANG TO TRAGEDY'S YIN.
THE YANG KNOCKED ON OUR DOOR FOUR YEARS LATER ON A SWELTERING DAY IN AUGUST.
BLANKETS
KACHINAS
POTTERY
RUGS
WELCOME
WELCOME!
A MAN IN A SUIT SAID HE REPRESENTED A COMPANY THAT HAD JUST BOUGHT A CHUNK OF DESERT ADJACENT TO FREEDOM.
HE HANDED ME A CHECK FOR A MILLION DOLLARS.
ANCIEN NAVA SHOE
I HAD THAT CONFLICTED FEELING I ALWAYS GET.

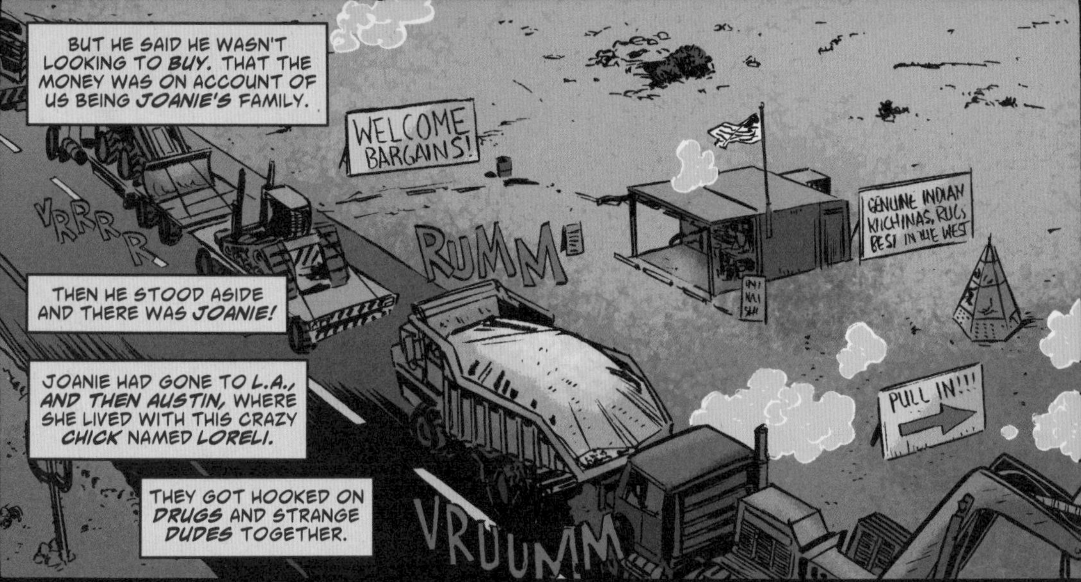
BUT HE SAID HE WASN'T LOOKING TO BUY. THAT THE MONEY WAS ON ACCOUNT OF US BEING JOANIE'S FAMILY.
WELCOME BARGAINS!
GENUINE INDIAN KACHINAS, RUGS BEST IN THE WEST
VRRRRR
RUMM
THEN HE STOOD ASIDE AND THERE WAS JOANIE!
JOANIE HAD GONE TO L.A., AND THEN AUSTIN, WHERE SHE LIVED WITH THIS CRAZY CHICK NAMED LORELI.
PULL IN!!!
THEY GOT HOOKED ON DRUGS AND STRANGE DUDES TOGETHER.
VRUUMM

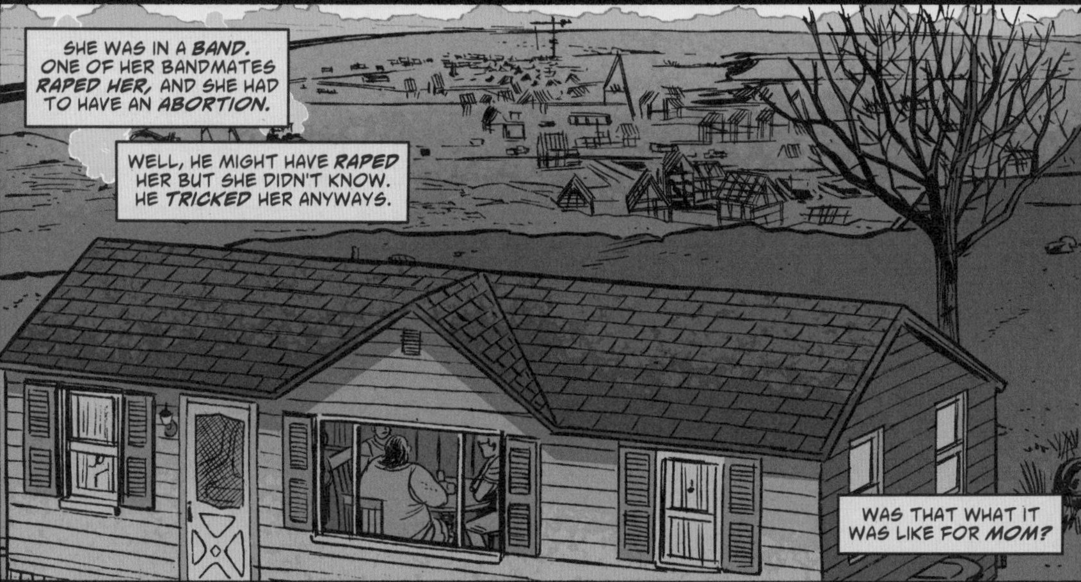
SHE WAS IN A BAND. ONE OF HER BANDMATES RAPED HER, AND SHE HAD TO HAVE AN ABORTION.
WELL, HE MIGHT HAVE RAPED HER BUT SHE DIDN'T KNOW. HE TRICKED HER ANYWAYS.
WAS THAT WHAT IT WAS LIKE FOR MOM?

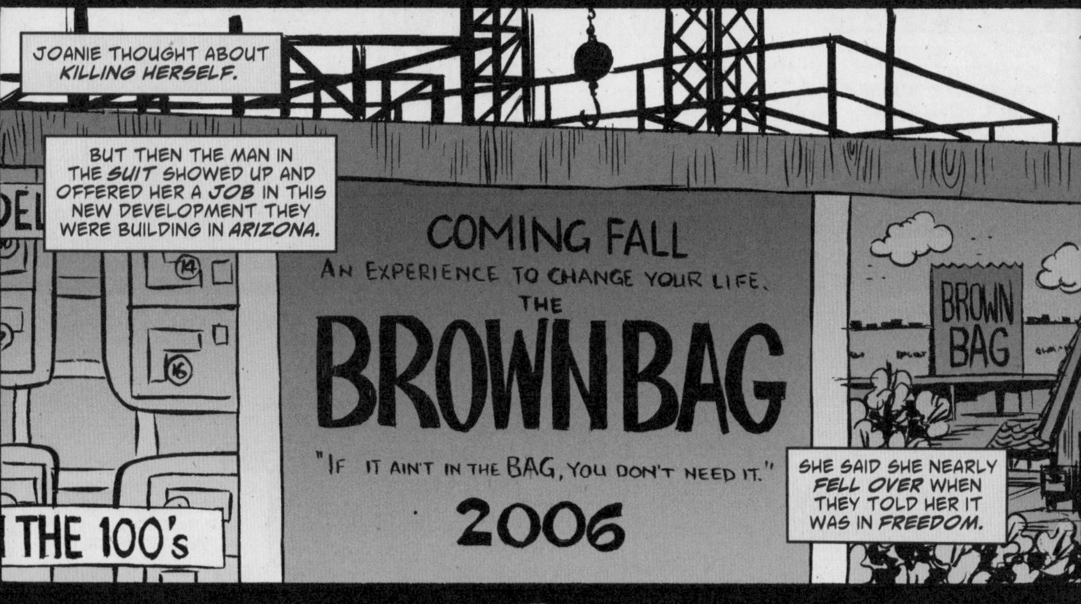
JOANIE THOUGHT ABOUT KILLING HERSELF.
BUT THEN THE MAN IN THE SUIT SHOWED UP AND OFFERED HER A JOB IN THIS NEW DEVELOPMENT THEY WERE BUILDING IN ARIZONA.
COMING FALL
AN EXPERIENCE TO CHANGE YOUR LIFE.
THE
BROWN BAG
"IF IT AIN'T IN THE BAG, YOU DON'T NEED IT."
2006
BROWN BAG
THE 100's
SHE SAID SHE NEARLY FELL OVER WHEN THEY TOLD HER IT WAS IN FREEDOM.

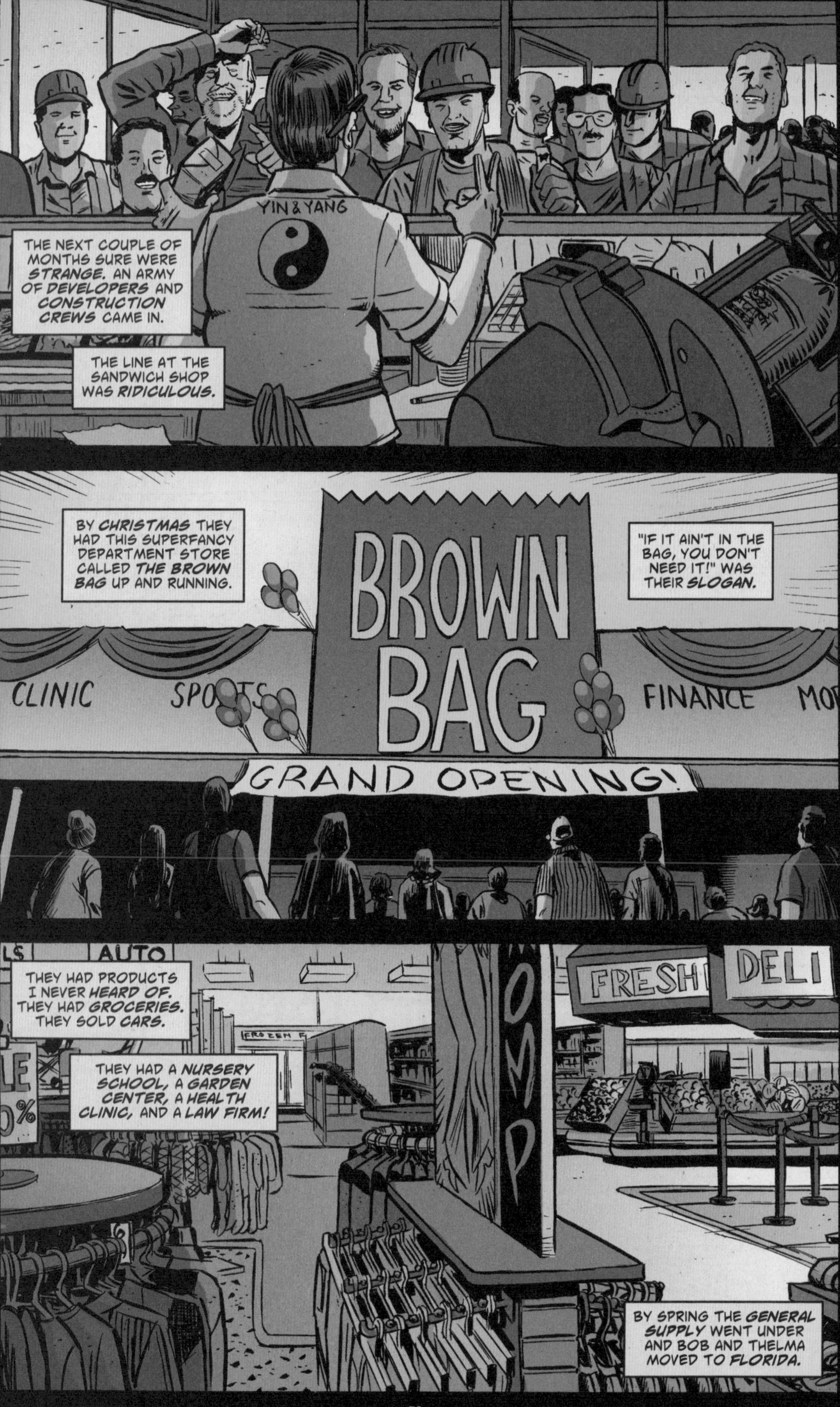
YIN & YANG
THE NEXT COUPLE OF MONTHS SURE WERE *STRANGE*. AN ARMY OF *DEVELOPERS* AND *CONSTRUCTION CREWS* CAME IN.
THE LINE AT THE SANDWICH SHOP WAS *RIDICULOUS*.
BY *CHRISTMAS* THEY HAD THIS SUPERFANCY DEPARTMENT STORE CALLED *THE BROWN BAG* UP AND RUNNING.
BROWN BAG
"IF IT AIN'T IN THE BAG, YOU DON'T NEED IT!" WAS THEIR *SLOGAN*.
CLINIC
FINANCE
GRAND OPENING!
AUTO
THEY HAD PRODUCTS I NEVER *HEARD OF*. THEY HAD *GROCERIES*. THEY SOLD *CARS*.
FRESH
DELI
THEY HAD A *NURSERY SCHOOL*, A *GARDEN CENTER*, A *HEALTH CLINIC*, AND A *LAW FIRM!*
BY SPRING THE *GENERAL SUPPLY* WENT UNDER AND BOB AND THELMA MOVED TO *FLORIDA*.

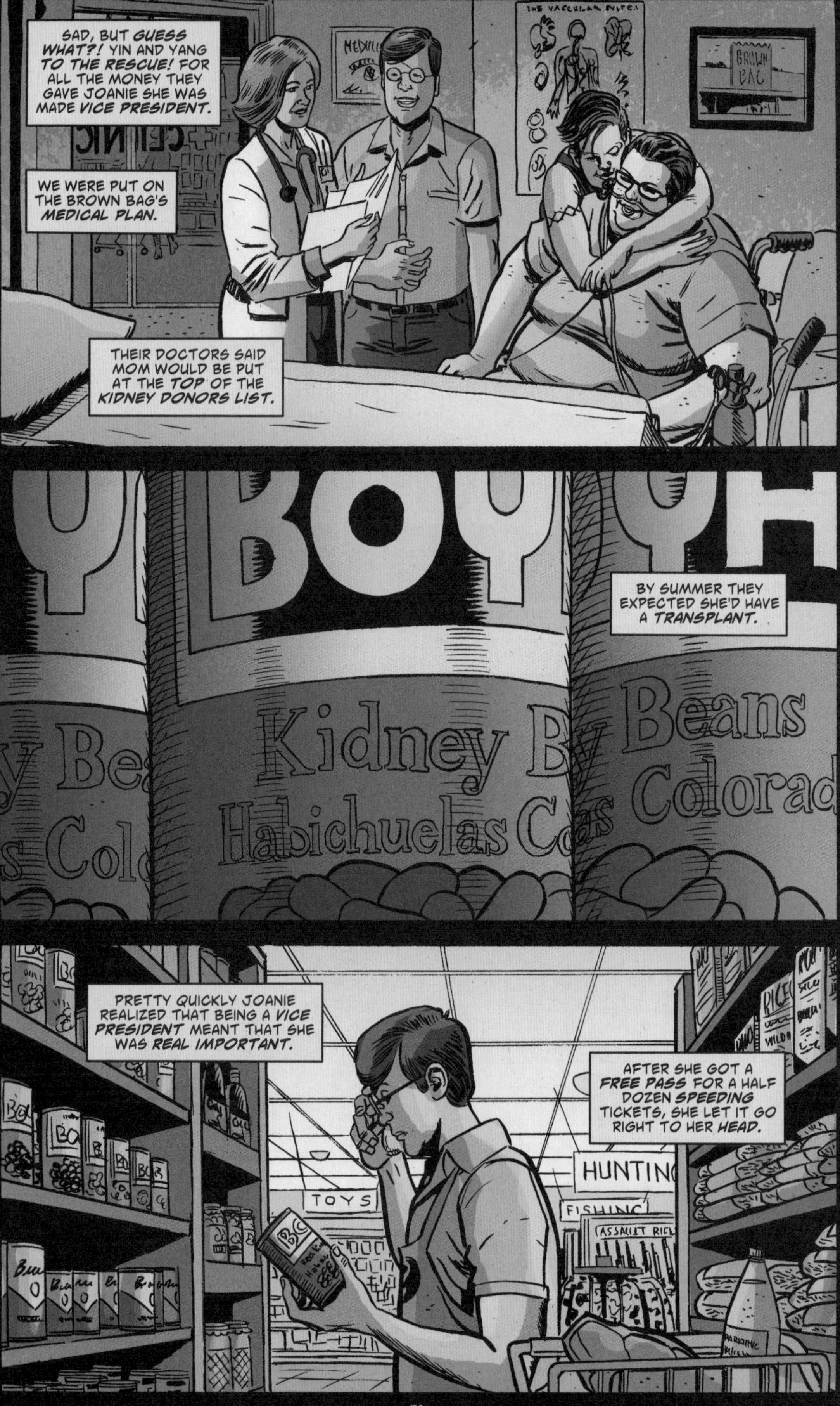
SAD, BUT GUESS WHAT?! YIN AND YANG TO THE RESCUE! FOR ALL THE MONEY THEY GAVE JOANIE SHE WAS MADE VICE PRESIDENT.
WE WERE PUT ON THE BROWN BAG'S MEDICAL PLAN.
THEIR DOCTORS SAID MOM WOULD BE PUT AT THE TOP OF THE KIDNEY DONORS LIST.
BY SUMMER THEY EXPECTED SHE'D HAVE A TRANSPLANT.
BOY
Kidney Beans
Habichuelas Coloradas
PRETTY QUICKLY JOANIE REALIZED THAT BEING A VICE PRESIDENT MEANT THAT SHE WAS REAL IMPORTANT.
AFTER SHE GOT A FREE PASS FOR A HALF DOZEN SPEEDING TICKETS, SHE LET IT GO RIGHT TO HER HEAD.
HUNTING
TOYS
FISHING
ASSAULT RIFL

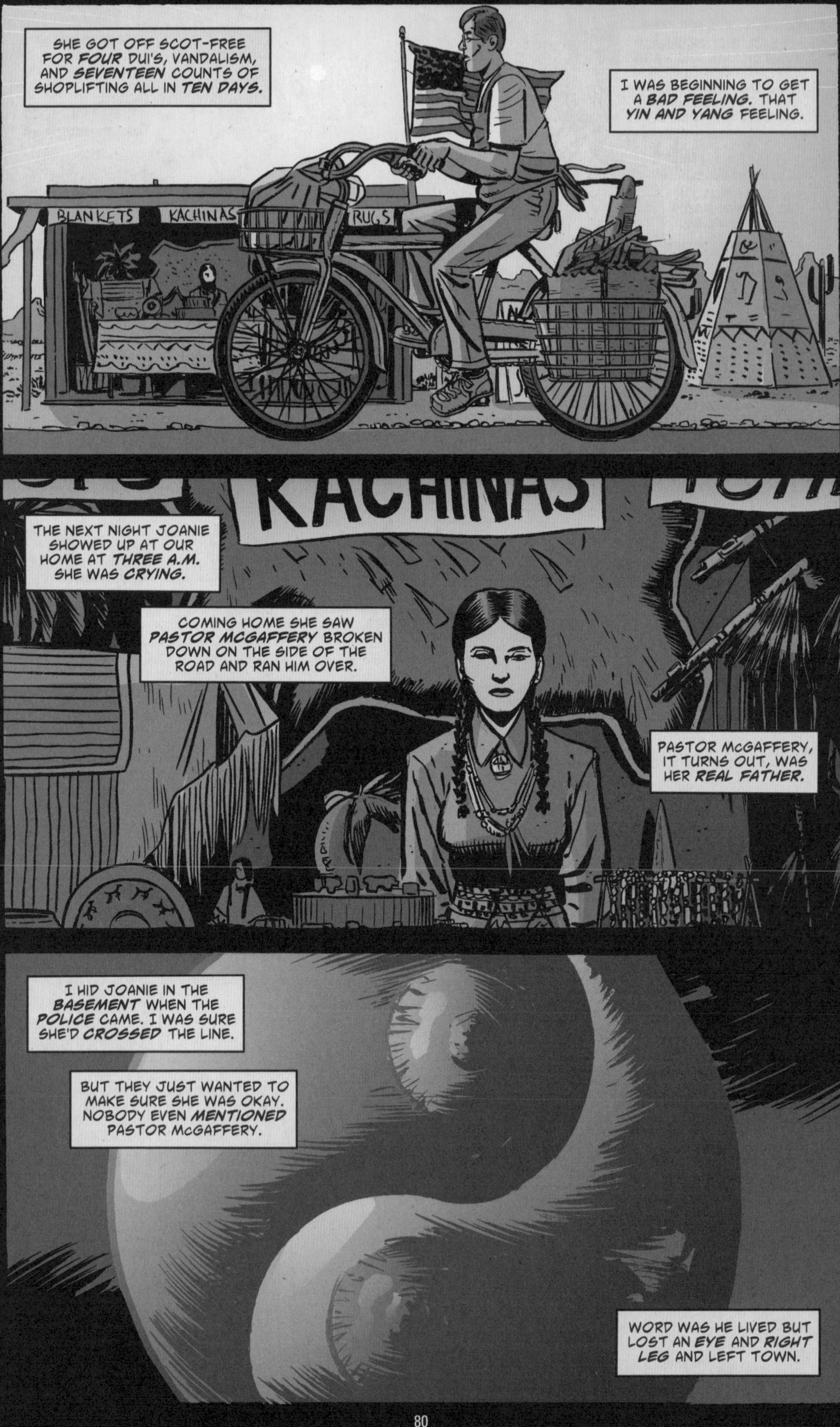
SHE GOT OFF SCOT-FREE FOR FOUR DUI'S, VANDALISM, AND SEVENTEEN COUNTS OF SHOPLIFTING ALL IN TEN DAYS.
I WAS BEGINNING TO GET A BAD FEELING. THAT YIN AND YANG FEELING.
BLANKETS
KACHINAS
RUGS
KACHINAS
THE NEXT NIGHT JOANIE SHOWED UP AT OUR HOME AT THREE A.M. SHE WAS CRYING.
COMING HOME SHE SAW PASTOR MCGAFFERY BROKEN DOWN ON THE SIDE OF THE ROAD AND RAN HIM OVER.
PASTOR MCGAFFERY, IT TURNS OUT, WAS HER REAL FATHER.
I HID JOANIE IN THE BASEMENT WHEN THE POLICE CAME. I WAS SURE SHE'D CROSSED THE LINE.
BUT THEY JUST WANTED TO MAKE SURE SHE WAS OKAY. NOBODY EVEN MENTIONED PASTOR McGAFFERY.
WORD WAS HE LIVED BUT LOST AN EYE AND RIGHT LEG AND LEFT TOWN.

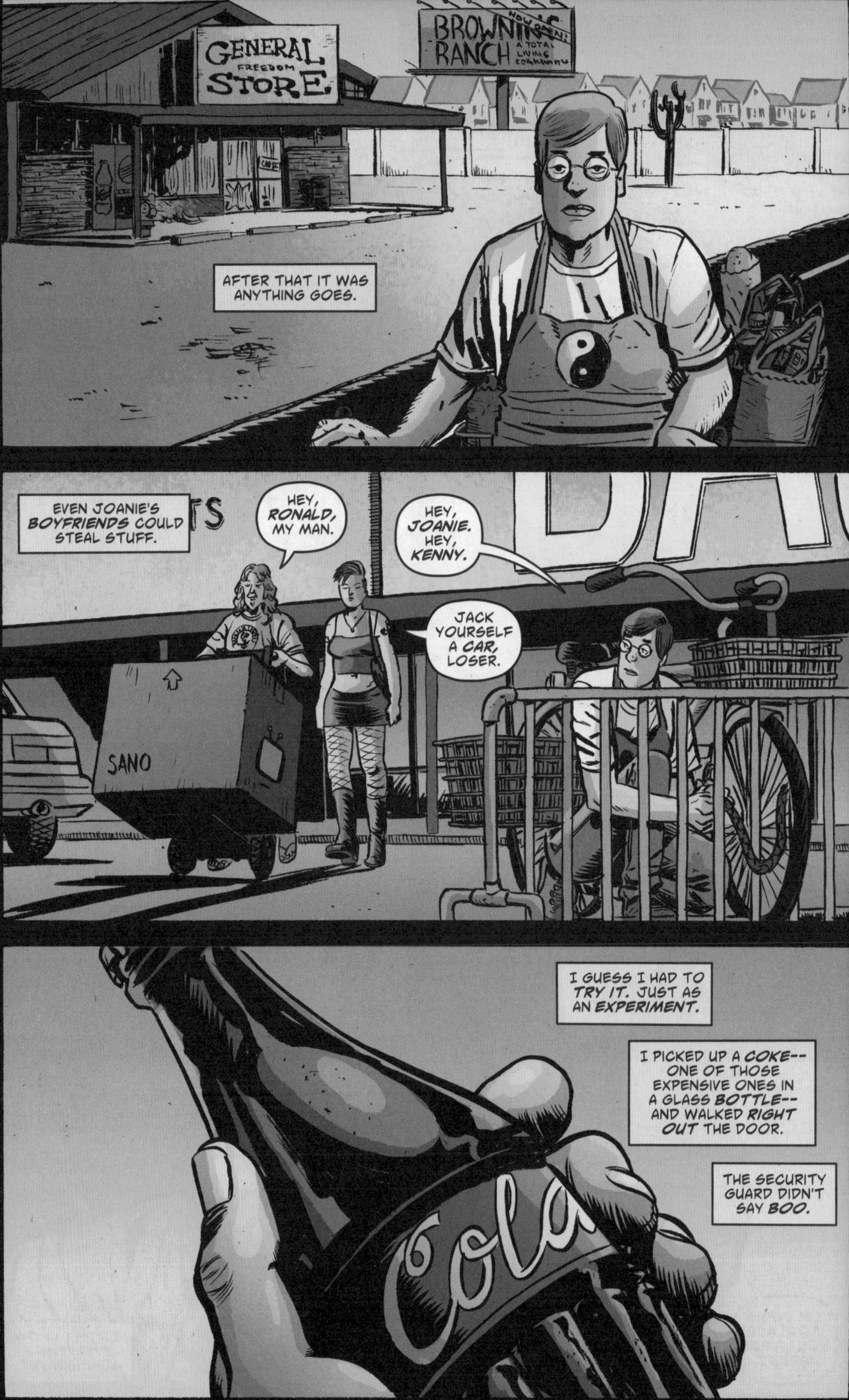
GENERAL FREEDOM STORE
BROWNING'S RANCH A TOTAL LIVING COMMUNITY
NOW OPEN!
AFTER THAT IT WAS ANYTHING GOES.
EVEN JOANIE'S BOYFRIENDS COULD STEAL STUFF.
HEY, RONALD, MY MAN.
HEY, JOANIE. HEY, KENNY.
JACK YOURSELF A CAR, LOSER.
SANO
I GUESS I HAD TO TRY IT. JUST AS AN EXPERIMENT.
I PICKED UP A COKE-- ONE OF THOSE EXPENSIVE ONES IN A GLASS BOTTLE-- AND WALKED RIGHT OUT THE DOOR.
THE SECURITY GUARD DIDN'T SAY BOO.
Cola

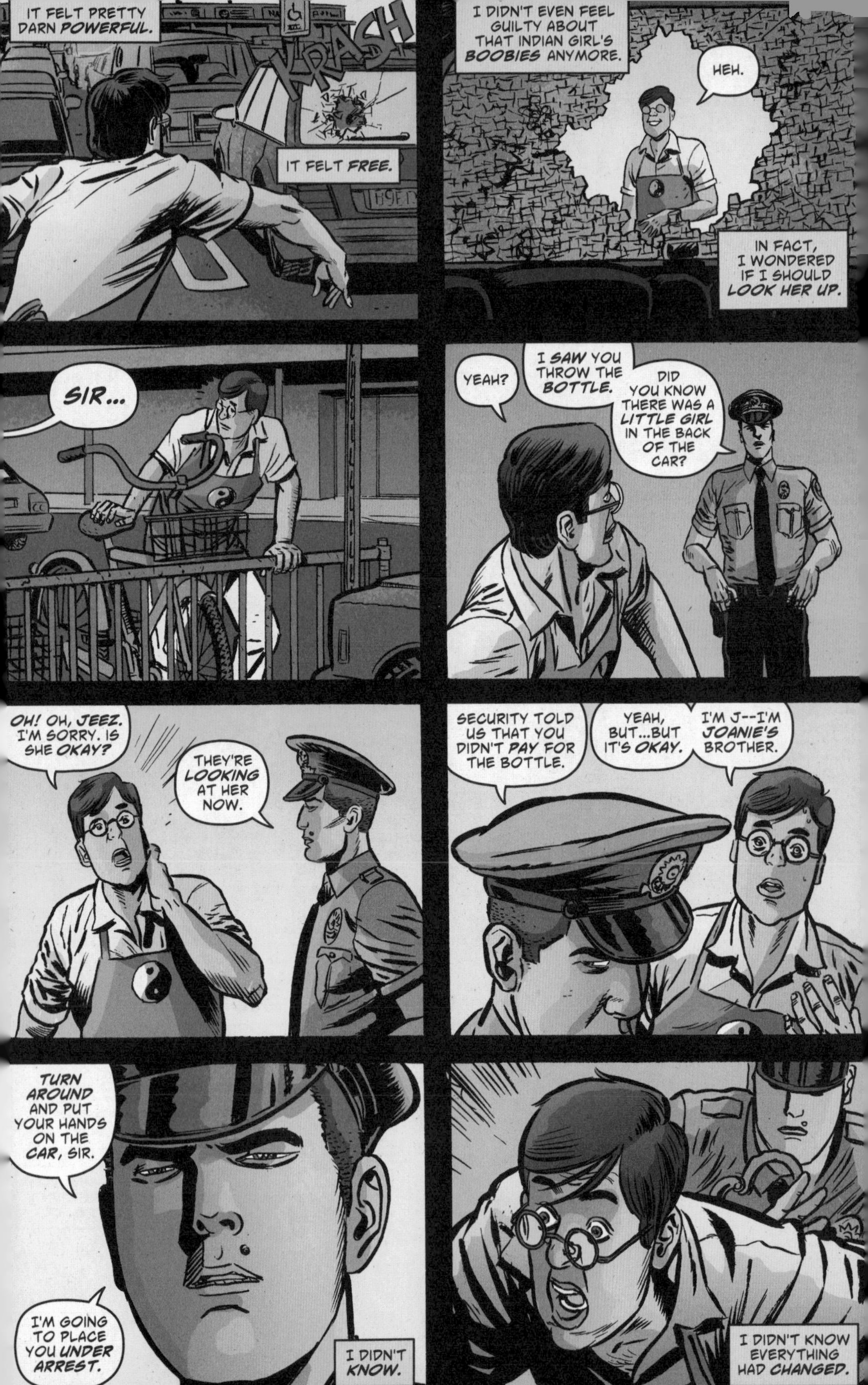
IT FELT PRETTY DARN *POWERFUL*.
KRASH
IT FELT *FREE*.
I DIDN'T EVEN FEEL GUILTY ABOUT THAT INDIAN GIRL'S *BOOBIES* ANYMORE.
HEH.
IN FACT, I WONDERED IF I SHOULD *LOOK HER UP*.
SIR...
YEAH?
I *SAW* YOU THROW THE *BOTTLE*.
DID YOU KNOW THERE WAS A *LITTLE GIRL* IN THE BACK OF THE CAR?
OH! OH, *JEEZ*. I'M SORRY. IS SHE *OKAY?*
THEY'RE *LOOKING* AT HER NOW.
SECURITY TOLD US THAT YOU DIDN'T *PAY* FOR THE BOTTLE.
YEAH, BUT...BUT IT'S *OKAY*.
I'M J--I'M *JOANIE'S* BROTHER.
TURN AROUND AND PUT YOUR HANDS ON THE *CAR*, SIR.
I'M GOING TO PLACE YOU *UNDER ARREST*.
I DIDN'T *KNOW*.
I DIDN'T KNOW EVERYTHING HAD *CHANGED*.

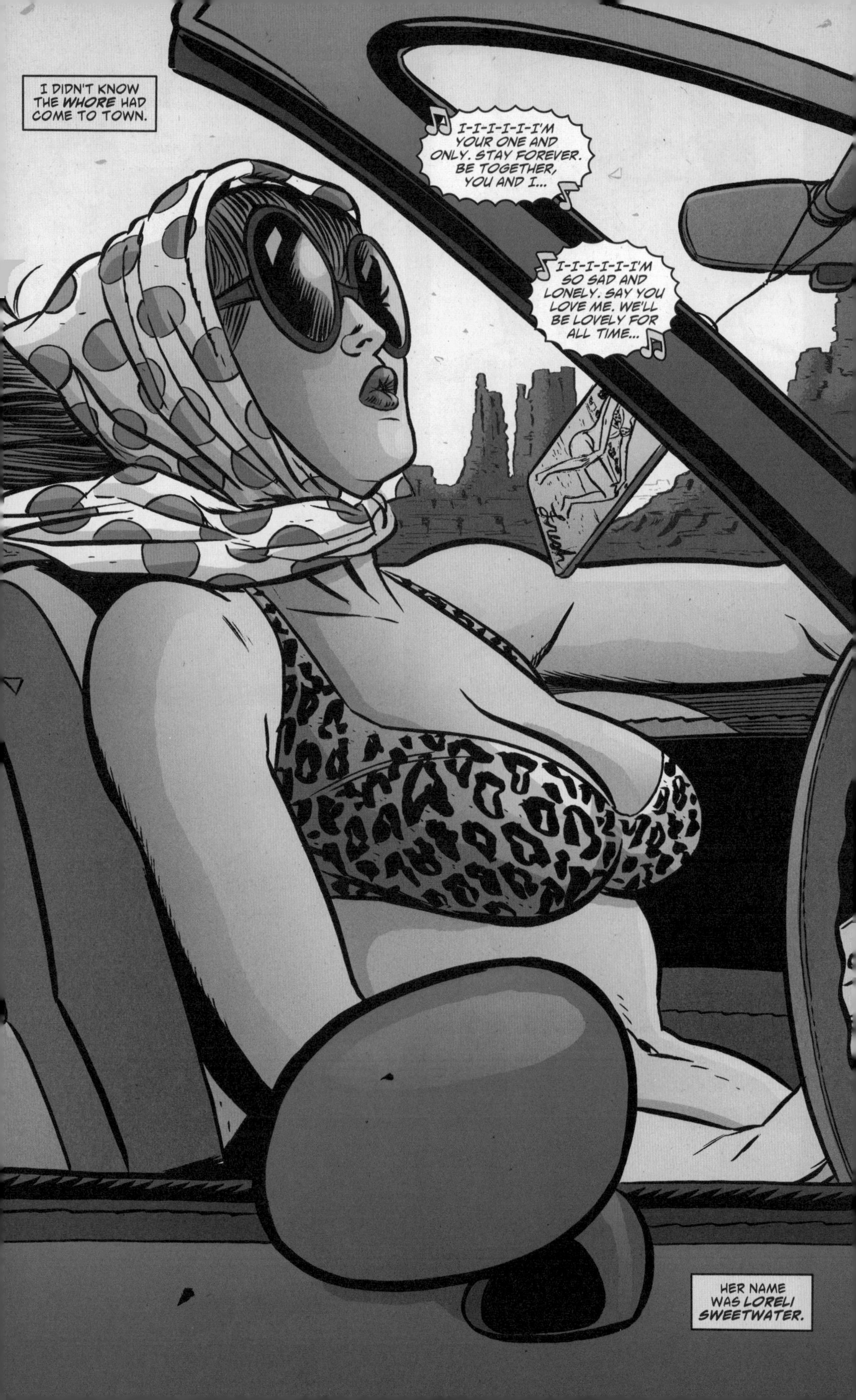
I DIDN'T KNOW THE WHORE HAD COME TO TOWN.
I-I-I-I-I-I'M YOUR ONE AND ONLY. STAY FOREVER. BE TOGETHER, YOU AND I...
I-I-I-I-I-I'M SO SAD AND LONELY. SAY YOU LOVE ME. WE'LL BE LOVELY FOR ALL TIME...
HER NAME WAS LORELI SWEETWATER.

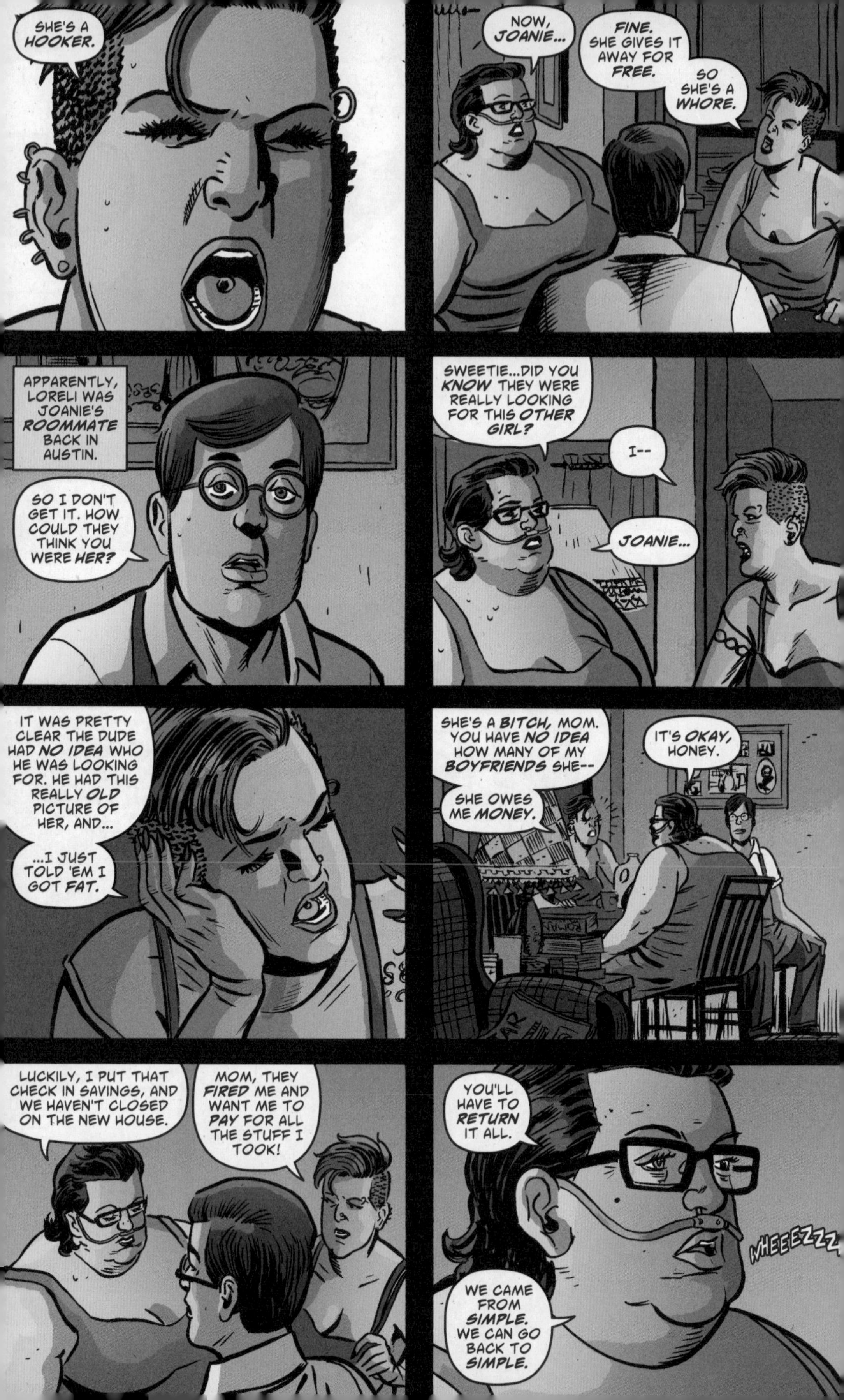
SHE'S A *HOOKER.*
NOW, *JOANIE...*
FINE. SHE GIVES IT AWAY FOR *FREE.*
SO SHE'S A *WHORE.*
APPARENTLY, LORELI WAS JOANIE'S *ROOMMATE* BACK IN AUSTIN.
SO I DON'T GET IT. HOW COULD THEY THINK YOU WERE *HER?*
SWEETIE...DID YOU *KNOW* THEY WERE REALLY LOOKING FOR THIS *OTHER GIRL?*
I--
JOANIE...
IT WAS PRETTY CLEAR THE DUDE HAD *NO IDEA* WHO HE WAS LOOKING FOR. HE HAD THIS REALLY *OLD* PICTURE OF HER, AND...
...I JUST TOLD 'EM I GOT *FAT.*
SHE'S A *BITCH,* MOM. YOU HAVE *NO IDEA* HOW MANY OF MY *BOYFRIENDS* SHE--
IT'S *OKAY,* HONEY.
SHE OWES ME *MONEY.*
LUCKILY, I PUT THAT CHECK IN SAVINGS, AND WE HAVEN'T CLOSED ON THE NEW HOUSE.
MOM, THEY *FIRED* ME AND WANT ME TO *PAY* FOR ALL THE STUFF I TOOK!
YOU'LL HAVE TO *RETURN* IT ALL.
WHEEEZZZ
WE CAME FROM *SIMPLE.* WE CAN GO BACK TO *SIMPLE.*

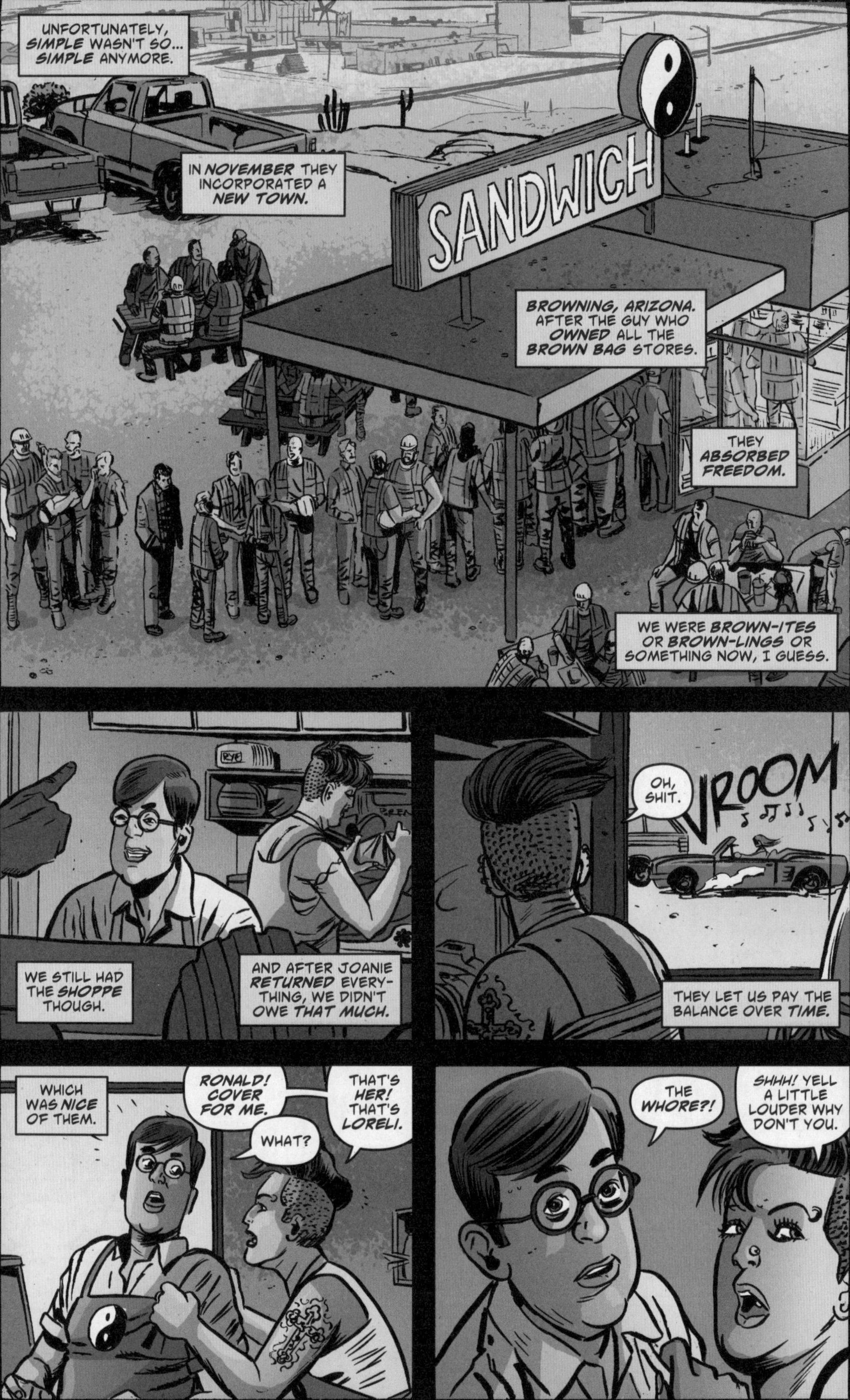

UNFORTUNATELY, SIMPLE WASN'T SO... SIMPLE ANYMORE.
IN NOVEMBER THEY INCORPORATED A NEW TOWN.
SANDWICH
BROWNING, ARIZONA. AFTER THE GUY WHO OWNED ALL THE BROWN BAG STORES.
THEY ABSORBED FREEDOM.
WE WERE BROWN-ITES OR BROWN-LINGS OR SOMETHING NOW, I GUESS.
WE STILL HAD THE SHOPPE THOUGH.
AND AFTER JOANIE RETURNED EVERY-THING, WE DIDN'T OWE THAT MUCH.
OH, SHIT.
VROOM
THEY LET US PAY THE BALANCE OVER TIME.
WHICH WAS NICE OF THEM.
RONALD! COVER FOR ME.
WHAT?
THAT'S HER! THAT'S LORELI.
THE WHORE?!
SHHH! YELL A LITTLE LOUDER WHY DON'T YOU.

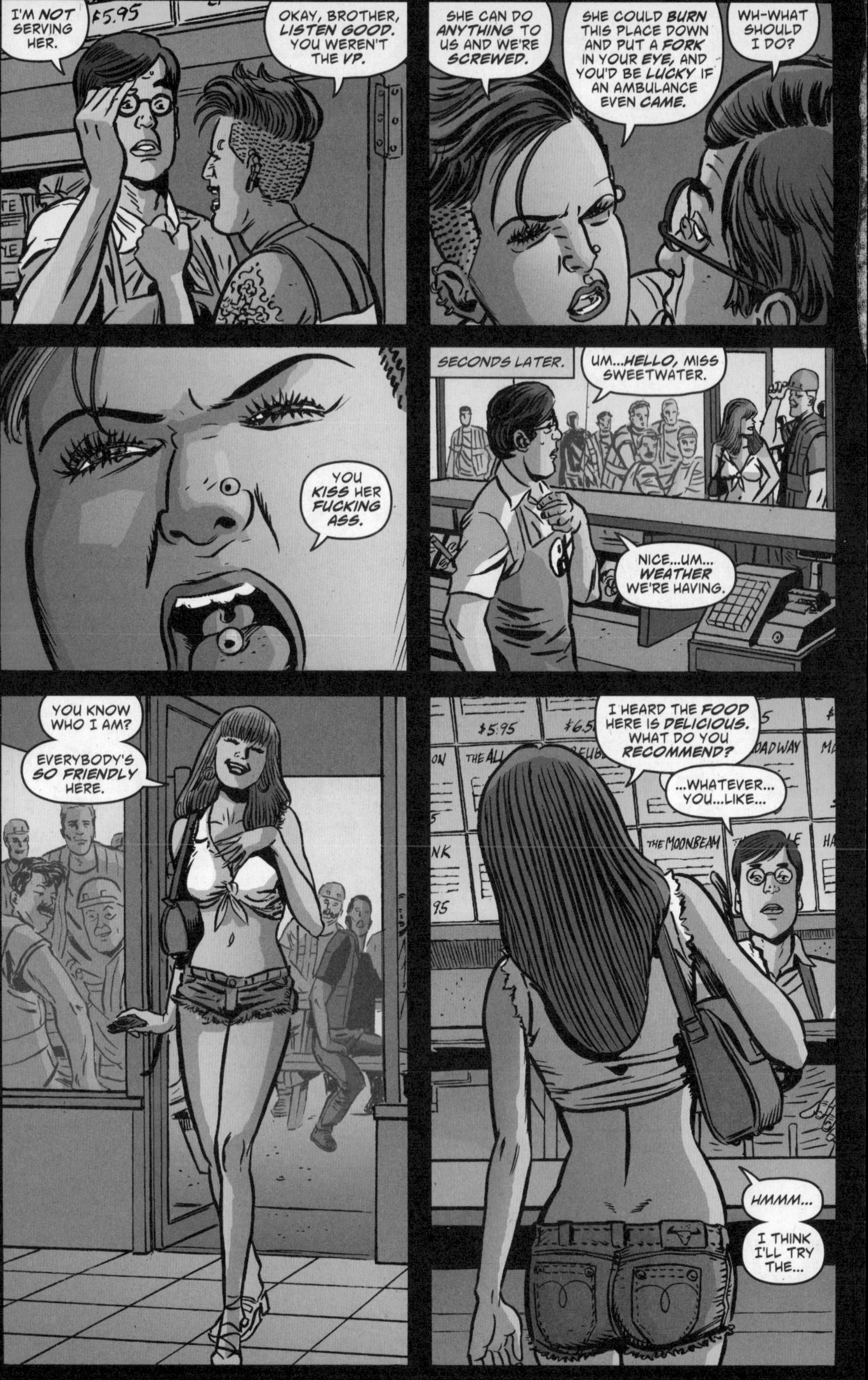
I'M **NOT** SERVING HER.
$5.95
OKAY, BROTHER, **LISTEN GOOD.** YOU WEREN'T THE **VP.**
SHE CAN DO **ANYTHING** TO US AND WE'RE **SCREWED.**
SHE COULD **BURN** THIS PLACE DOWN AND PUT A **FORK** IN YOUR **EYE,** AND YOU'D BE **LUCKY** IF AN AMBULANCE EVEN **CAME.**
WH-WHAT SHOULD I DO?
YOU **KISS** HER **FUCKING ASS.**
SECONDS LATER.
UM...**HELLO,** MISS SWEETWATER.
NICE...UM... **WEATHER** WE'RE HAVING.
YOU KNOW WHO I AM?
EVERYBODY'S **SO FRIENDLY** HERE.
I HEARD THE **FOOD** HERE IS **DELICIOUS.** WHAT DO YOU **RECOMMEND?**
...WHATEVER... YOU...LIKE...
THE MOONBEAM
HMMM...
I THINK I'LL TRY THE...

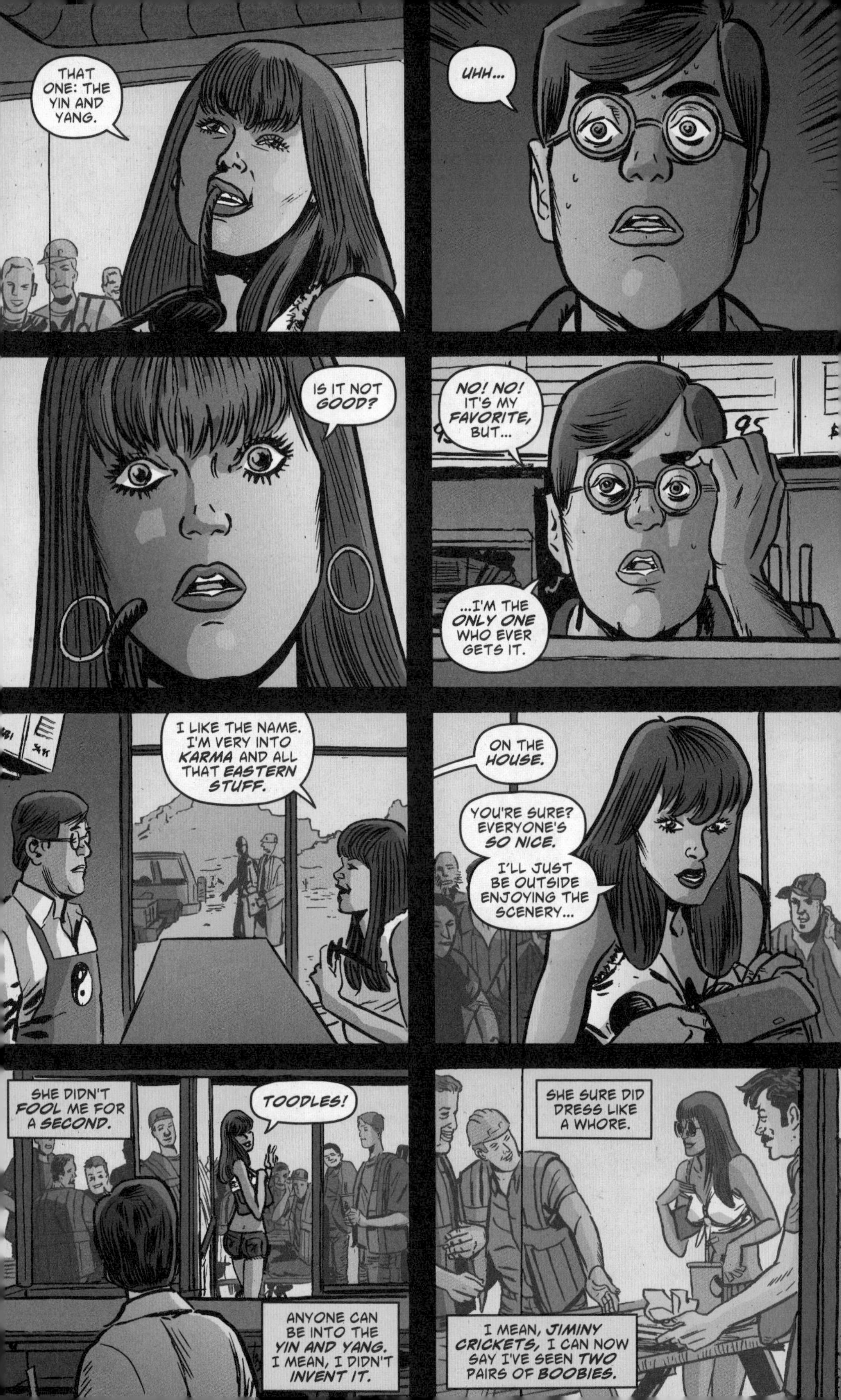
THAT ONE: THE YIN AND YANG.
UHH...
IS IT NOT *GOOD?*
NO! NO! IT'S MY *FAVORITE,* BUT...
...I'M THE *ONLY ONE* WHO EVER GETS IT.
I LIKE THE NAME. I'M VERY INTO *KARMA* AND ALL THAT *EASTERN STUFF.*
ON THE *HOUSE.*
YOU'RE SURE? EVERYONE'S *SO NICE.*
I'LL JUST BE OUTSIDE ENJOYING THE SCENERY...
SHE DIDN'T *FOOL* ME FOR A *SECOND.*
TOODLES!
ANYONE CAN BE INTO THE *YIN AND YANG.* I MEAN, I DIDN'T *INVENT* IT.
SHE SURE DID DRESS LIKE A WHORE.
I MEAN, *JIMINY CRICKETS,* I CAN NOW SAY I'VE SEEN *TWO* PAIRS OF *BOOBIES.*

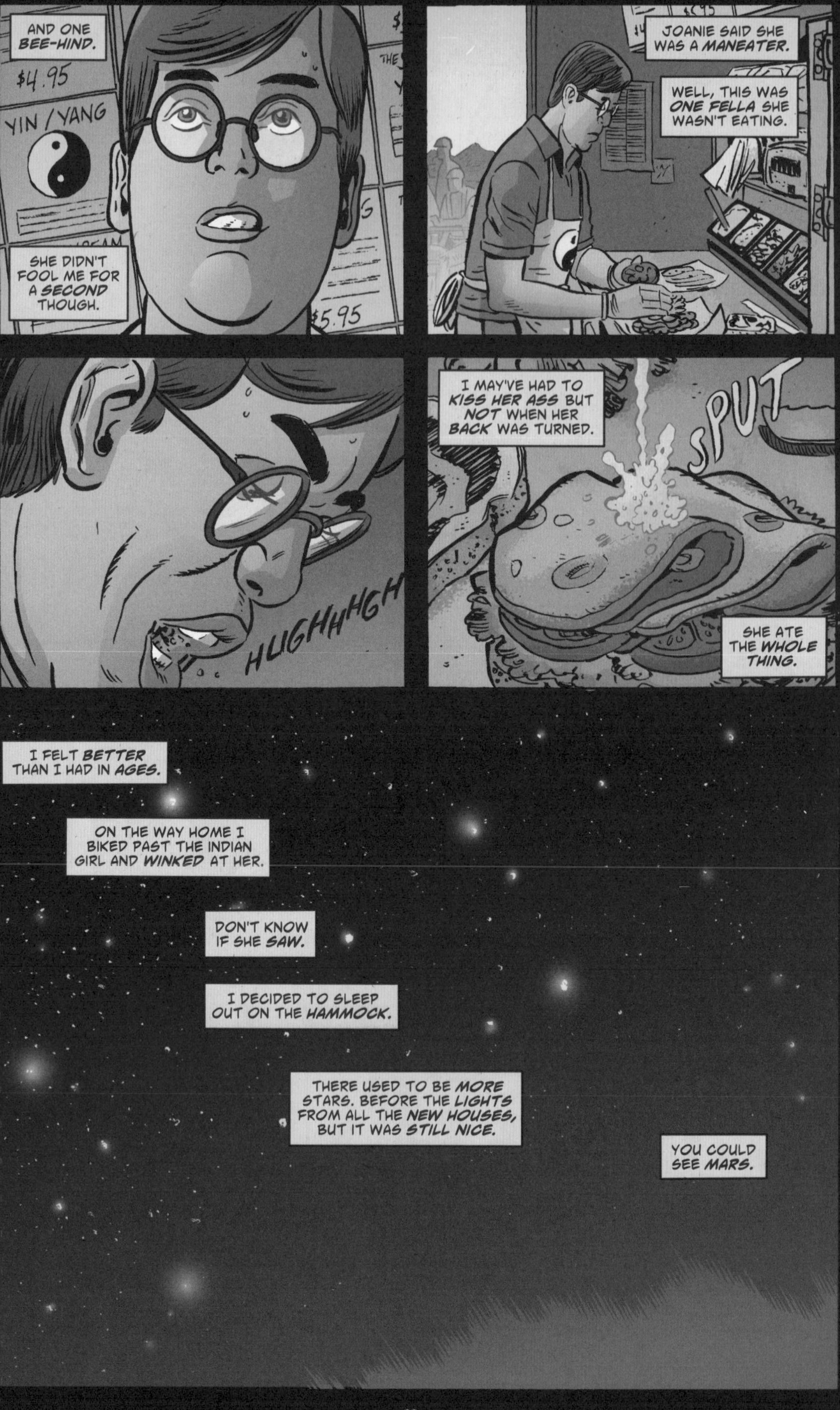
AND ONE *BEE-HIND.*
$4.95
YIN / YANG
SHE DIDN'T FOOL ME FOR A *SECOND* THOUGH.
$5.95
JOANIE SAID SHE WAS A *MANEATER.*
WELL, THIS WAS *ONE FELLA* SHE WASN'T EATING.
HUGHHHGH
I MAY'VE HAD TO *KISS HER ASS* BUT *NOT* WHEN HER *BACK* WAS TURNED.
SPUT
SHE ATE THE *WHOLE THING.*
I FELT *BETTER* THAN I HAD IN *AGES.*
ON THE WAY HOME I BIKED PAST THE INDIAN GIRL AND *WINKED* AT HER.
DON'T KNOW IF SHE *SAW.*
I DECIDED TO SLEEP OUT ON THE *HAMMOCK.*
THERE USED TO BE *MORE* STARS. BEFORE THE *LIGHTS* FROM ALL THE *NEW HOUSES,* BUT IT WAS *STILL NICE.*
YOU COULD SEE *MARS.*

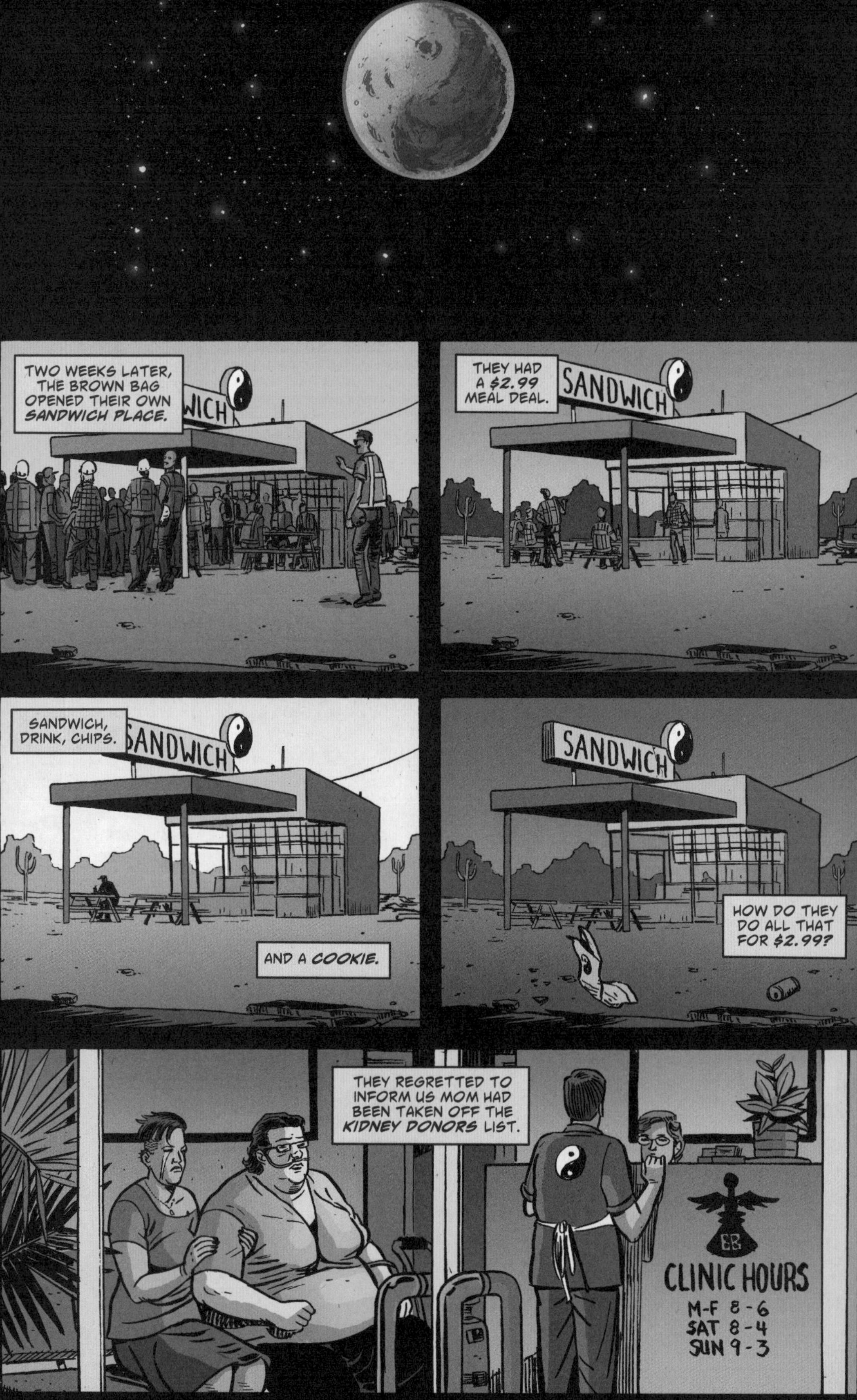
TWO WEEKS LATER, THE BROWN BAG OPENED THEIR OWN *SANDWICH PLACE.*
WICH
THEY HAD A *$2.99* MEAL DEAL.
SANDWICH
SANDWICH, DRINK, CHIPS.
SANDWICH
AND A *COOKIE.*
SANDWICH
HOW DO THEY DO ALL THAT FOR $2.99?
THEY REGRETTED TO INFORM US MOM HAD BEEN TAKEN OFF THE *KIDNEY DONORS* LIST.
CLINIC HOURS
M-F 8-6
SAT 8-4
SUN 9-3

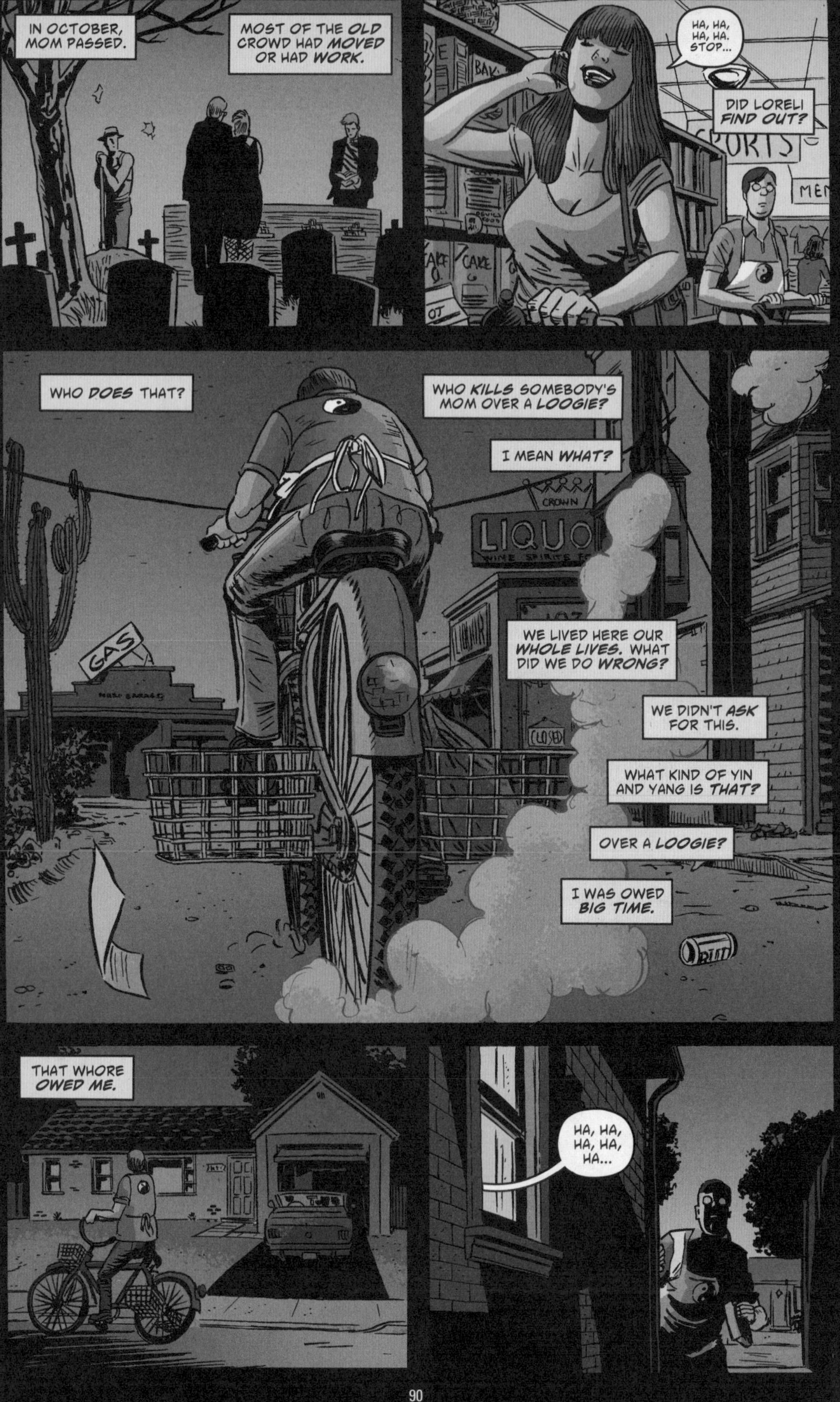
IN OCTOBER, MOM PASSED.
MOST OF THE *OLD* CROWD HAD *MOVED* OR HAD *WORK*.
HA, HA, HA, HA. STOP...
DID LORELI *FIND OUT?*
WHO *DOES* THAT?
WHO *KILLS* SOMEBODY'S MOM OVER A *LOOGIE?*
I MEAN *WHAT?*
CROWN
LIQUO
WE LIVED HERE OUR *WHOLE LIVES.* WHAT DID WE DO *WRONG?*
CLOSED
WE DIDN'T *ASK* FOR THIS.
WHAT KIND OF YIN AND YANG IS *THAT?*
GAS
OVER A *LOOGIE?*
I WAS OWED *BIG TIME.*
THAT WHORE *OWED ME.*
HA, HA, HA, HA, HA...

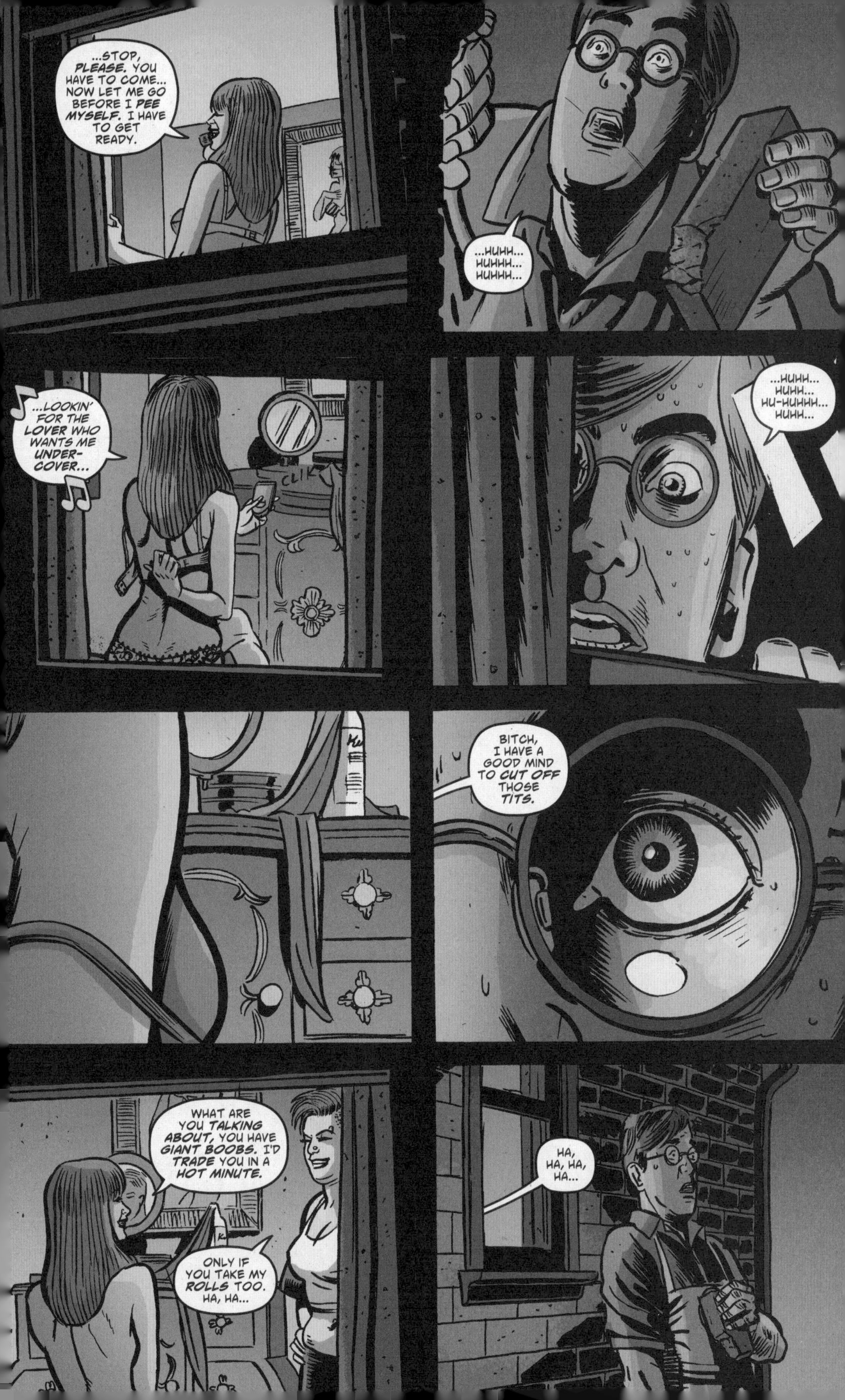
...STOP, PLEASE. YOU HAVE TO COME... NOW LET ME GO BEFORE I PEE MYSELF. I HAVE TO GET READY.
...HUHH... HUHHH... HUHHH...
...LOOKIN' FOR THE LOVER WHO WANTS ME UNDER-COVER...
CLIK
...HUHH... HUHH... HU-HUHHH... HUHH...
BITCH, I HAVE A GOOD MIND TO CUT OFF THOSE TITS.
WHAT ARE YOU TALKING ABOUT, YOU HAVE GIANT BOOBS. I'D TRADE YOU IN A HOT MINUTE.
ONLY IF YOU TAKE MY ROLLS TOO. HA, HA...
HA, HA, HA, HA...

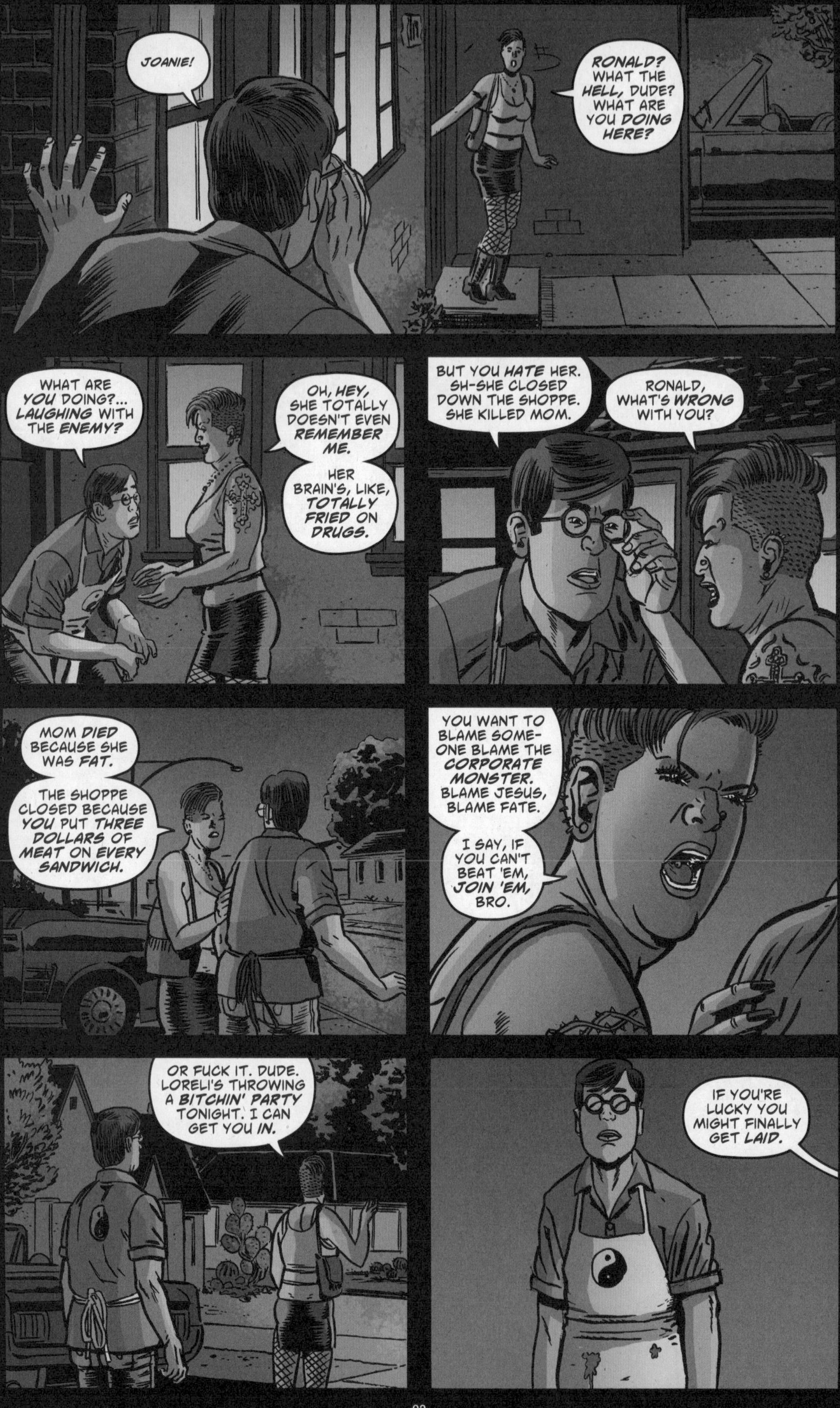
JOANIE!
RONALD? WHAT THE HELL, DUDE? WHAT ARE YOU DOING HERE?
WHAT ARE YOU DOING?... LAUGHING WITH THE ENEMY?
OH, HEY, SHE TOTALLY DOESN'T EVEN REMEMBER ME.
HER BRAIN'S, LIKE, TOTALLY FRIED ON DRUGS.
BUT YOU HATE HER. SH-SHE CLOSED DOWN THE SHOPPE. SHE KILLED MOM.
RONALD, WHAT'S WRONG WITH YOU?
MOM DIED BECAUSE SHE WAS FAT.
THE SHOPPE CLOSED BECAUSE YOU PUT THREE DOLLARS OF MEAT ON EVERY SANDWICH.
YOU WANT TO BLAME SOME-ONE BLAME THE CORPORATE MONSTER. BLAME JESUS, BLAME FATE.
I SAY, IF YOU CAN'T BEAT 'EM, JOIN 'EM, BRO.
OR FUCK IT. DUDE. LORELI'S THROWING A BITCHIN' PARTY TONIGHT. I CAN GET YOU IN.
IF YOU'RE LUCKY YOU MIGHT FINALLY GET LAID.

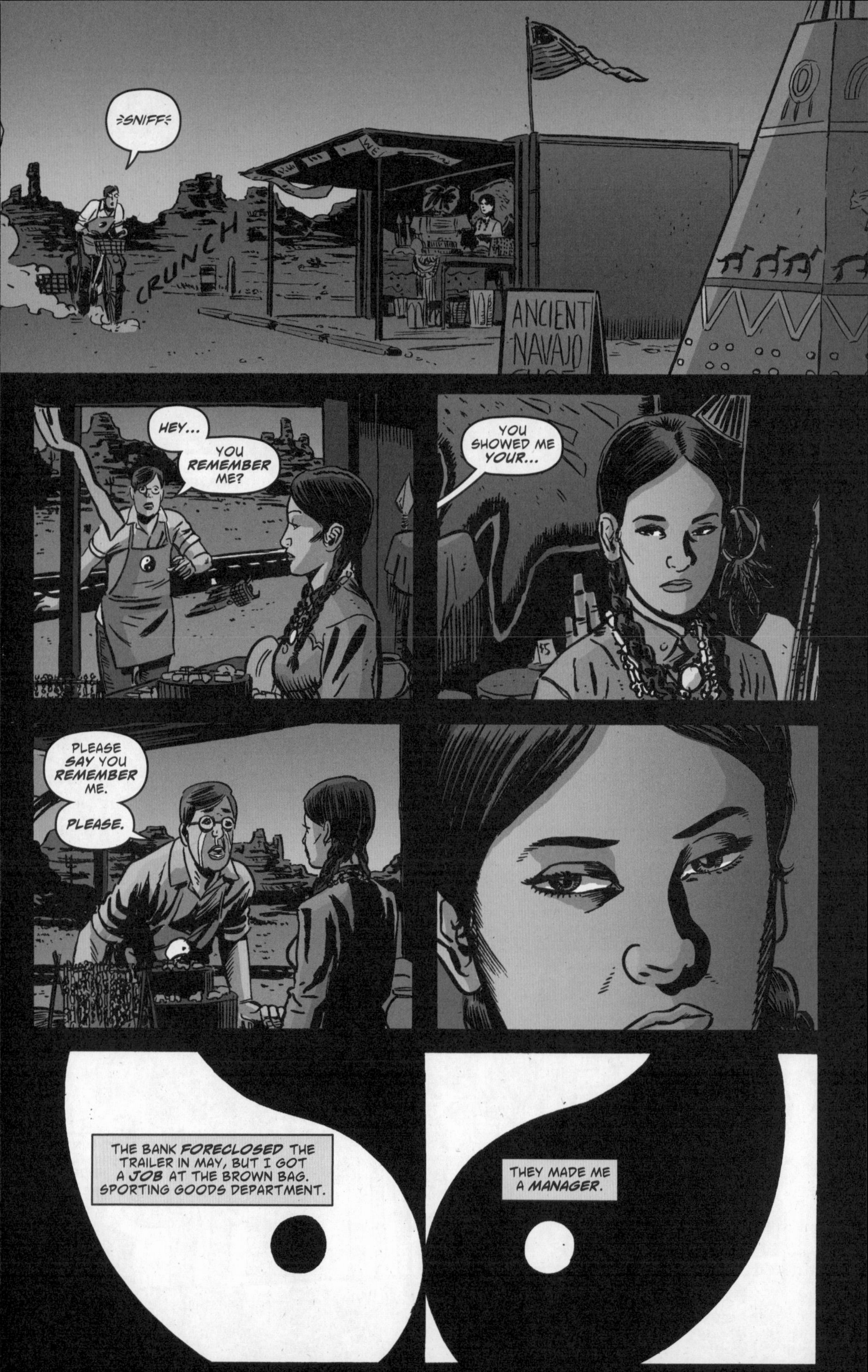
SNIFF
CRUNCH
ANCIENT NAVAJO
HEY...
YOU REMEMBER ME?
YOU SHOWED ME YOUR...
PLEASE SAY YOU REMEMBER ME.
PLEASE.
THE BANK FORECLOSED THE TRAILER IN MAY, BUT I GOT A JOB AT THE BROWN BAG. SPORTING GOODS DEPARTMENT.
THEY MADE ME A MANAGER.

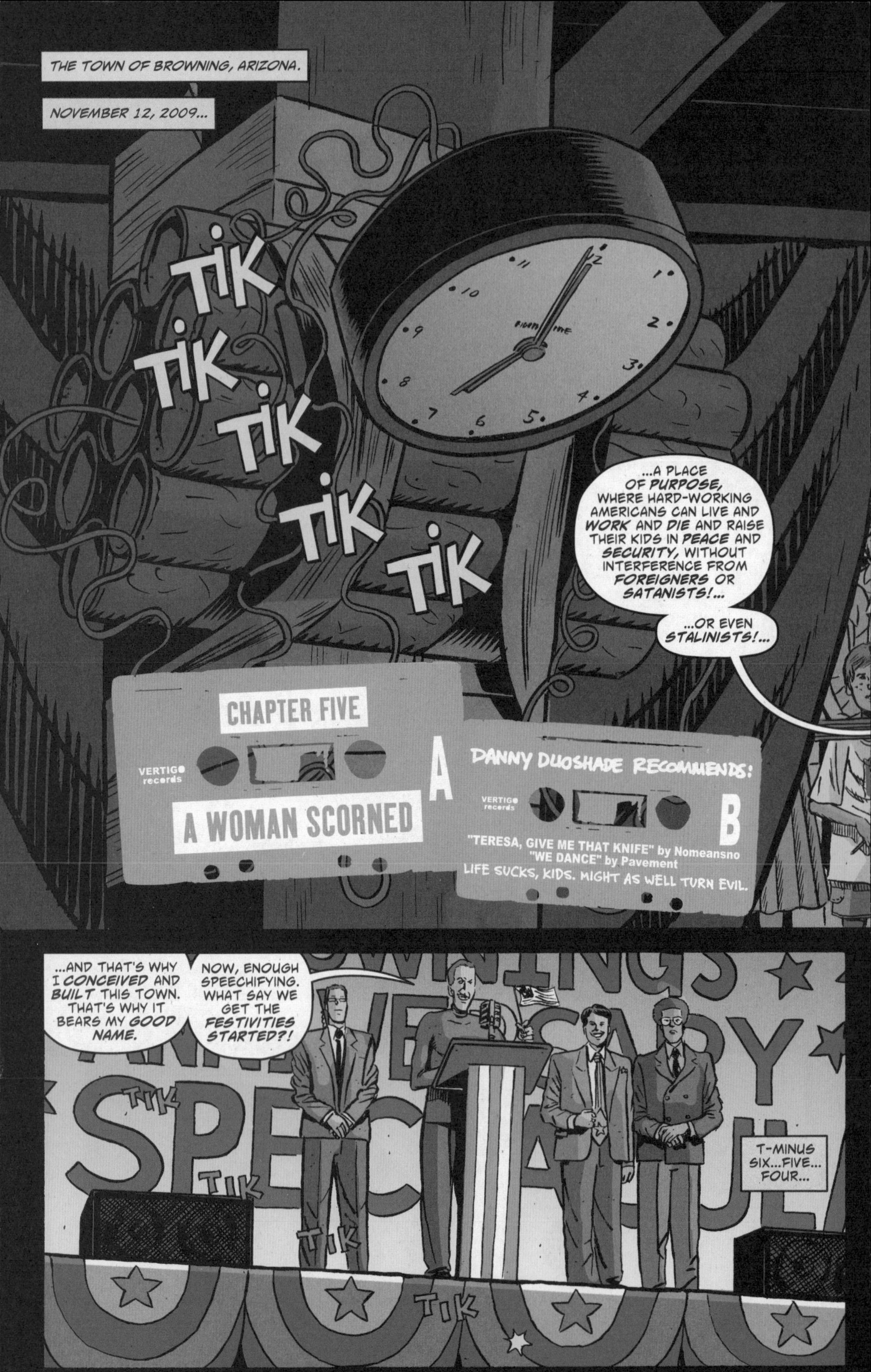
THE TOWN OF BROWNING, ARIZONA.
NOVEMBER 12, 2009...
TIK TIK TIK TIK TIK
...A PLACE OF PURPOSE, WHERE HARD-WORKING AMERICANS CAN LIVE AND WORK AND DIE AND RAISE THEIR KIDS IN PEACE AND SECURITY, WITHOUT INTERFERENCE FROM FOREIGNERS OR SATANISTS!...
...OR EVEN STALINISTS!...
CHAPTER FIVE
VERTIGO records
A
A WOMAN SCORNED
DANNY DUOSHADE RECOMMENDS:
VERTIGO records
B
"TERESA, GIVE ME THAT KNIFE" by Nomeansno
"WE DANCE" by Pavement
LIFE SUCKS, KIDS. MIGHT AS WELL TURN EVIL.
...AND THAT'S WHY I CONCEIVED AND BUILT THIS TOWN. THAT'S WHY IT BEARS MY GOOD NAME.
NOW, ENOUGH SPEECHIFYING. WHAT SAY WE GET THE FESTIVITIES STARTED?!
TIK TIK TIK TIK
T-MINUS SIX...FIVE... FOUR...

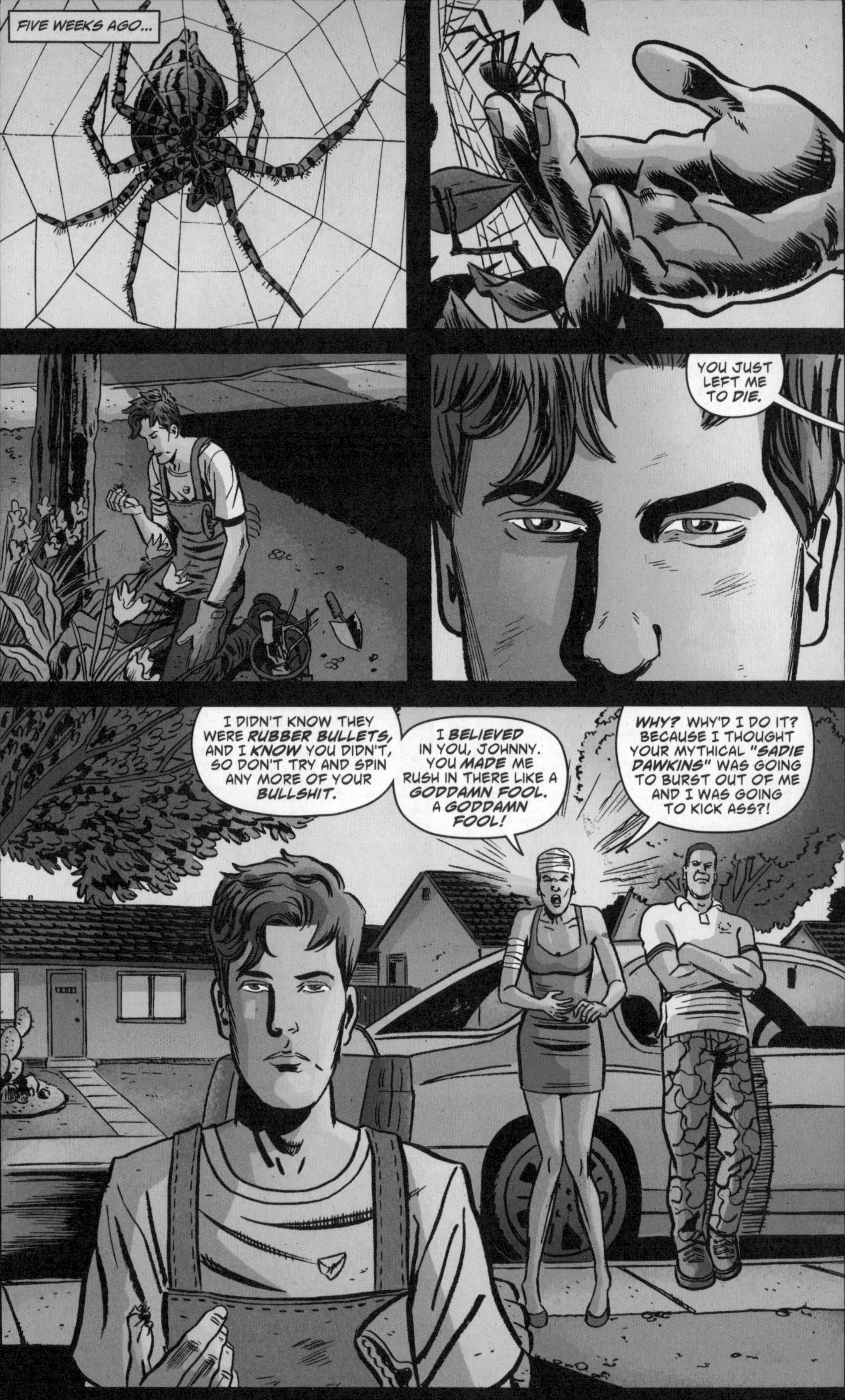
FIVE WEEKS AGO...
YOU JUST LEFT ME TO DIE.
I DIDN'T KNOW THEY WERE RUBBER BULLETS, AND I KNOW YOU DIDN'T, SO DON'T TRY AND SPIN ANY MORE OF YOUR BULLSHIT.
I BELIEVED IN YOU, JOHNNY. YOU MADE ME RUSH IN THERE LIKE A GODDAMN FOOL. A GODDAMN FOOL!
WHY? WHY'D I DO IT? BECAUSE I THOUGHT YOUR MYTHICAL "SADIE DAWKINS" WAS GOING TO BURST OUT OF ME AND I WAS GOING TO KICK ASS?!

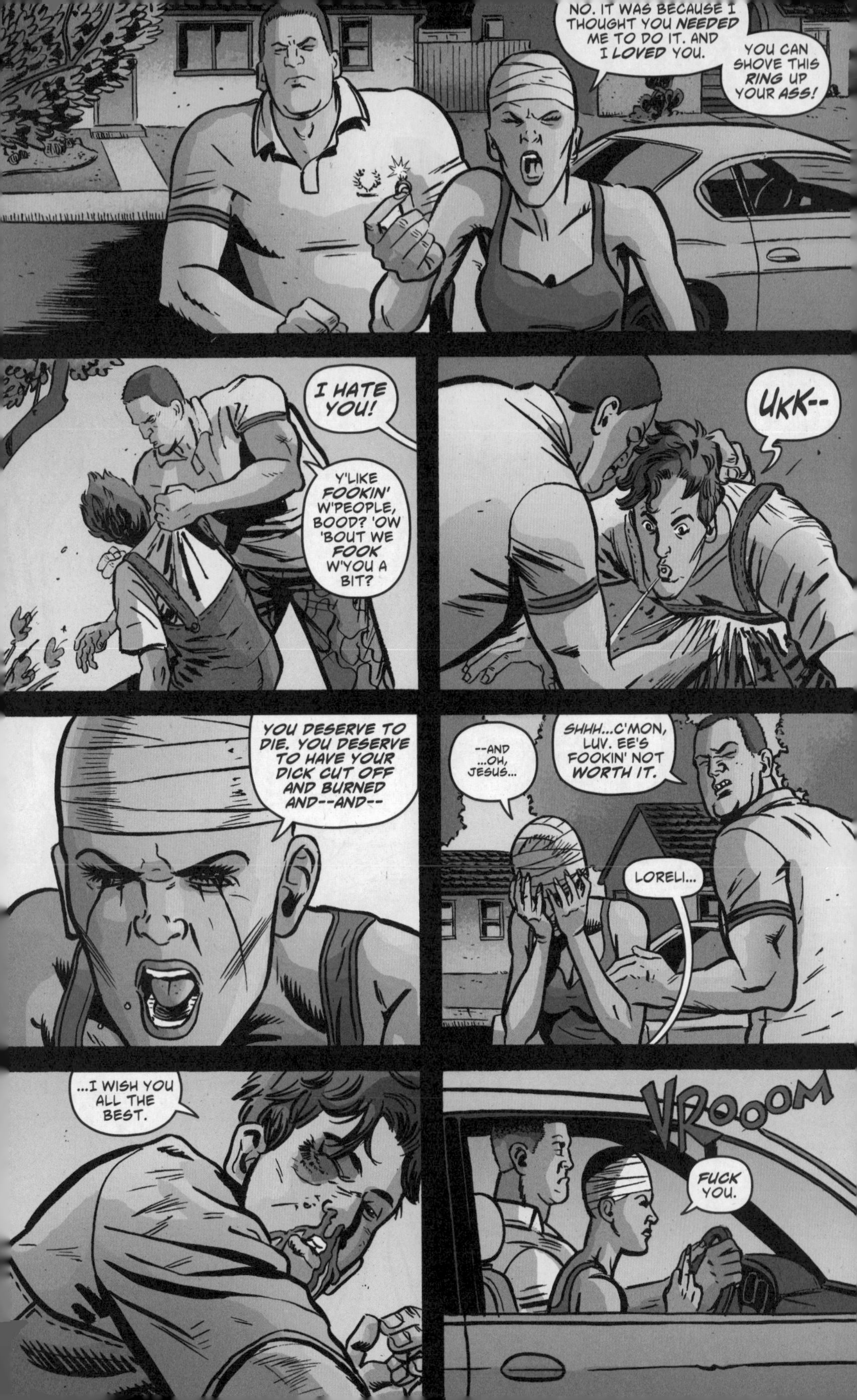

NO. IT WAS BECAUSE I THOUGHT YOU NEEDED ME TO DO IT. AND I LOVED YOU.
YOU CAN SHOVE THIS RING UP YOUR ASS!
I HATE YOU!
Y'LIKE FOOKIN' W'PEOPLE, BOOD? 'OW 'BOUT WE FOOK W'YOU A BIT?
UKK--
YOU DESERVE TO DIE. YOU DESERVE TO HAVE YOUR DICK CUT OFF AND BURNED AND--AND--
--AND ...OH, JESUS...
SHHH...C'MON, LUV. EE'S FOOKIN' NOT WORTH IT.
LORELI...
...I WISH YOU ALL THE BEST.
VROOOM
FUCK YOU.

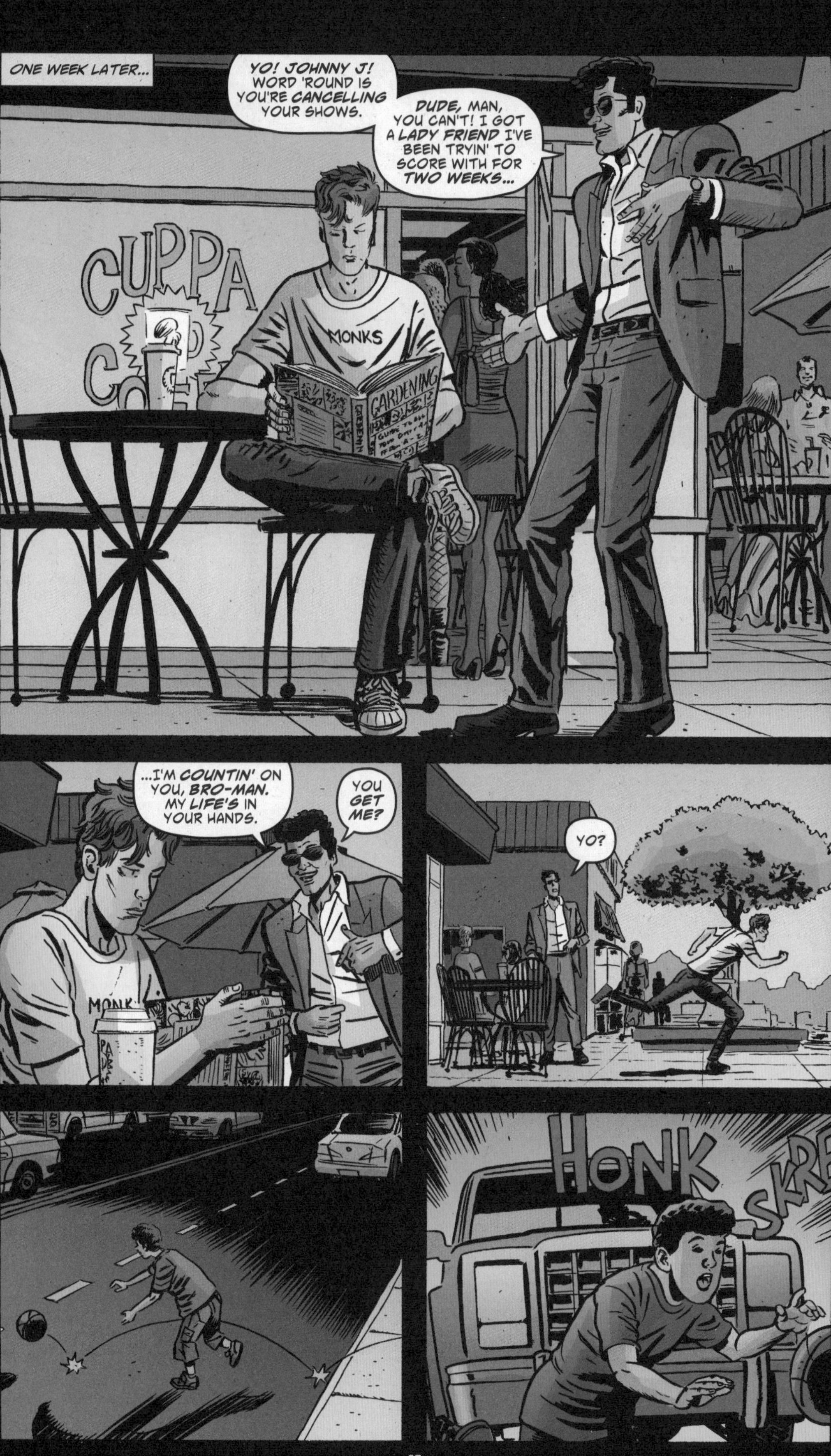
ONE WEEK LATER...
YO! JOHNNY J! WORD 'ROUND IS YOU'RE CANCELLING YOUR SHOWS.
DUDE, MAN, YOU CAN'T! I GOT A LADY FRIEND I'VE BEEN TRYIN' TO SCORE WITH FOR TWO WEEKS...
CUPPA
MONKS
GARDENING
...I'M COUNTIN' ON YOU, BRO-MAN. MY LIFE'S IN YOUR HANDS.
YOU GET ME?
YO?
HONK
SKRE

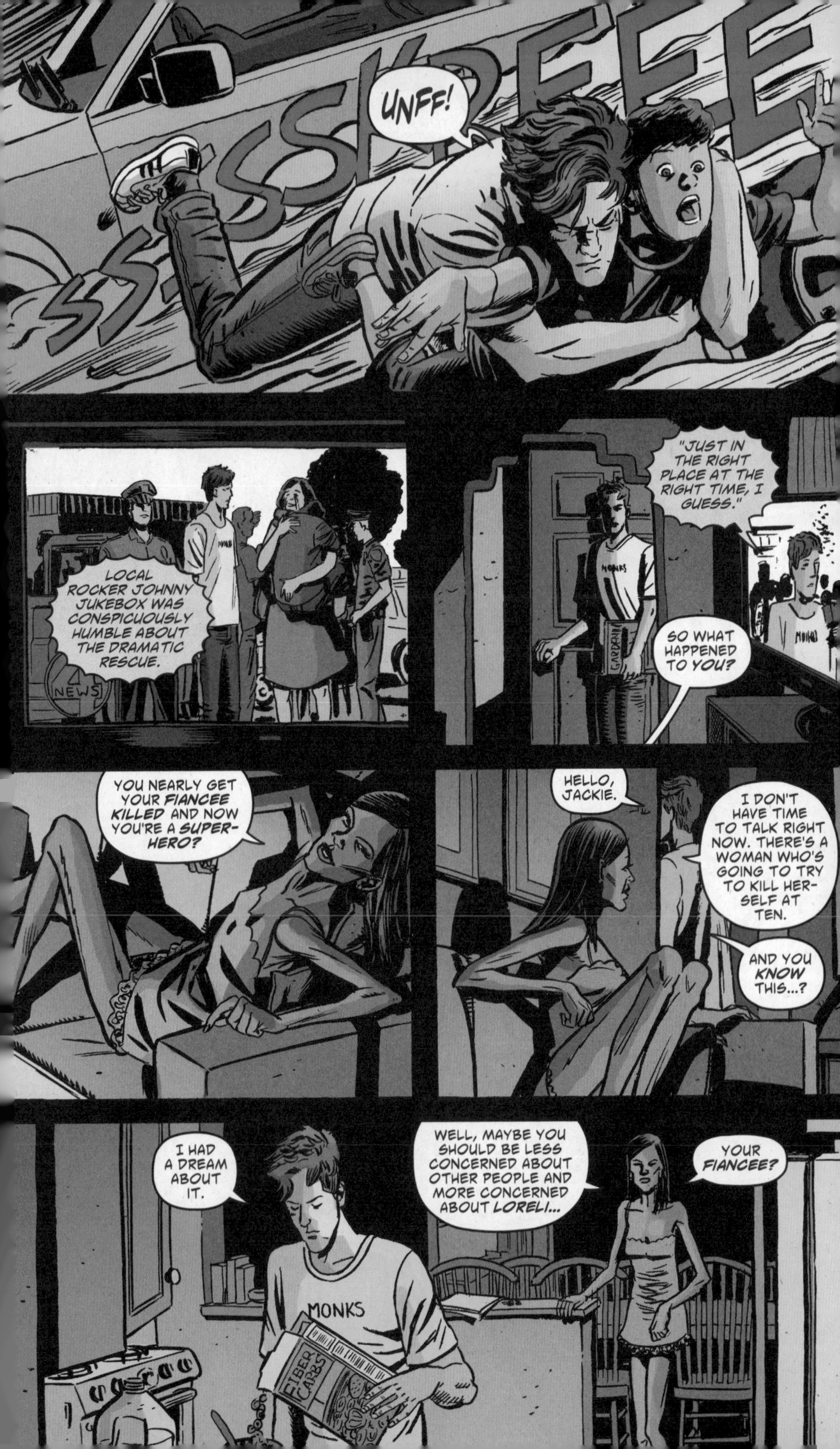
UNFF!
SSSKREEEE
LOCAL ROCKER JOHNNY JUKEBOX WAS CONSPICUOUSLY HUMBLE ABOUT THE DRAMATIC RESCUE.
NEWS
"JUST IN THE RIGHT PLACE AT THE RIGHT TIME, I GUESS."
MONKS
GARDEN
SO WHAT HAPPENED TO YOU?
YOU NEARLY GET YOUR FIANCEE KILLED AND NOW YOU'RE A SUPER-HERO?
HELLO, JACKIE.
I DON'T HAVE TIME TO TALK RIGHT NOW. THERE'S A WOMAN WHO'S GOING TO TRY TO KILL HER-SELF AT TEN.
AND YOU KNOW THIS...?
I HAD A DREAM ABOUT IT.
WELL, MAYBE YOU SHOULD BE LESS CONCERNED ABOUT OTHER PEOPLE AND MORE CONCERNED ABOUT LORELI...
YOUR FIANCEE?
MONKS
FIBER CARBS

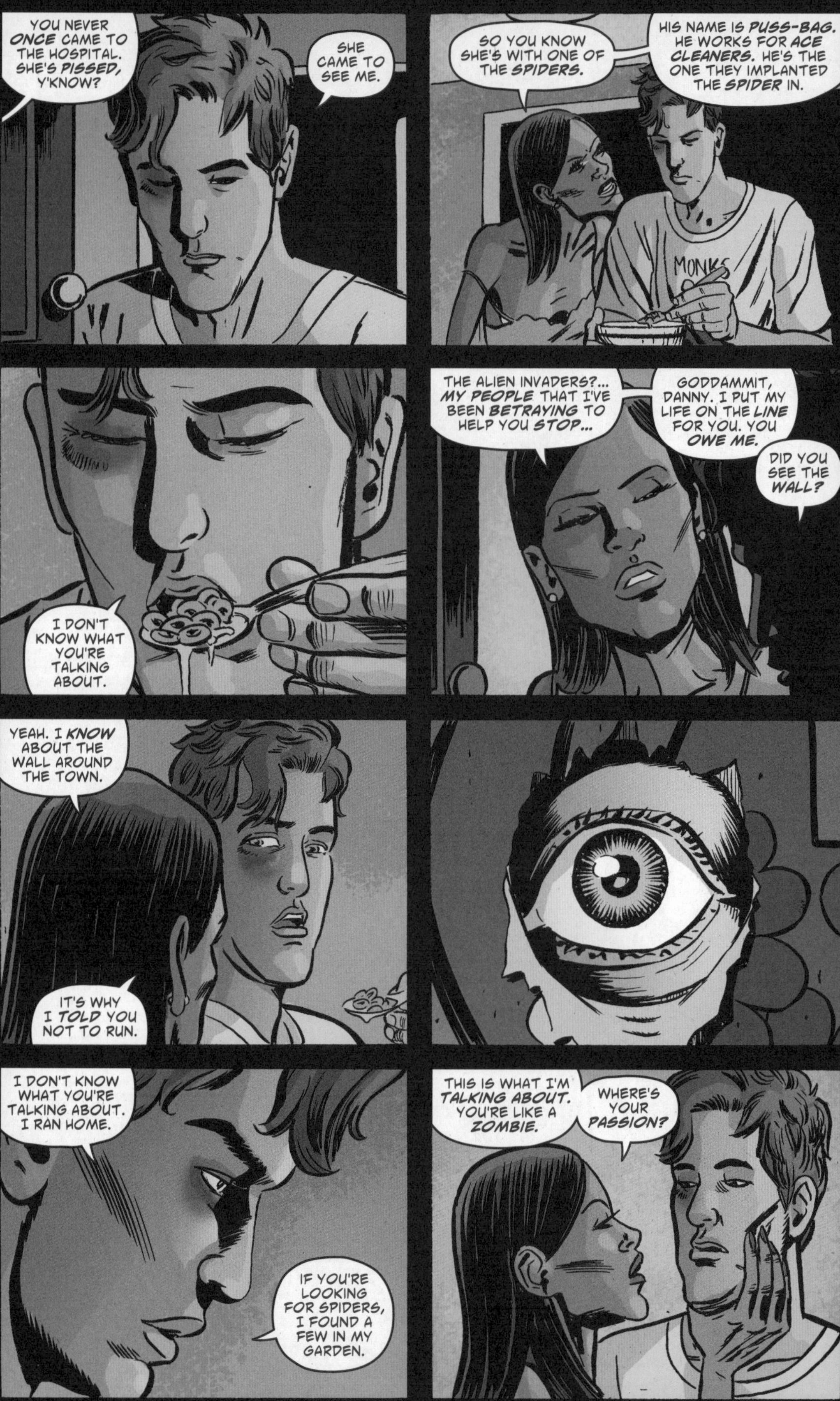
YOU NEVER *ONCE* CAME TO THE HOSPITAL. SHE'S *PISSED*, Y'KNOW?
SHE CAME TO SEE ME.
SO YOU KNOW SHE'S WITH ONE OF THE *SPIDERS*.
HIS NAME IS *PUSS-BAG*. HE WORKS FOR *ACE CLEANERS*. HE'S THE ONE THEY IMPLANTED THE *SPIDER* IN.
MONKS
I DON'T KNOW WHAT YOU'RE TALKING ABOUT.
THE ALIEN INVADERS?... *MY PEOPLE* THAT I'VE BEEN *BETRAYING* TO HELP YOU *STOP*...
GODDAMMIT, DANNY. I PUT MY LIFE ON THE *LINE* FOR YOU. YOU *OWE ME*.
DID YOU SEE THE *WALL?*
YEAH. I *KNOW* ABOUT THE WALL AROUND THE TOWN.
IT'S WHY I *TOLD* YOU NOT TO RUN.
I DON'T KNOW WHAT YOU'RE TALKING ABOUT. I RAN HOME.
IF YOU'RE LOOKING FOR SPIDERS, I FOUND A FEW IN MY GARDEN.
THIS IS WHAT I'M *TALKING ABOUT*. YOU'RE LIKE A *ZOMBIE*.
WHERE'S YOUR *PASSION?*

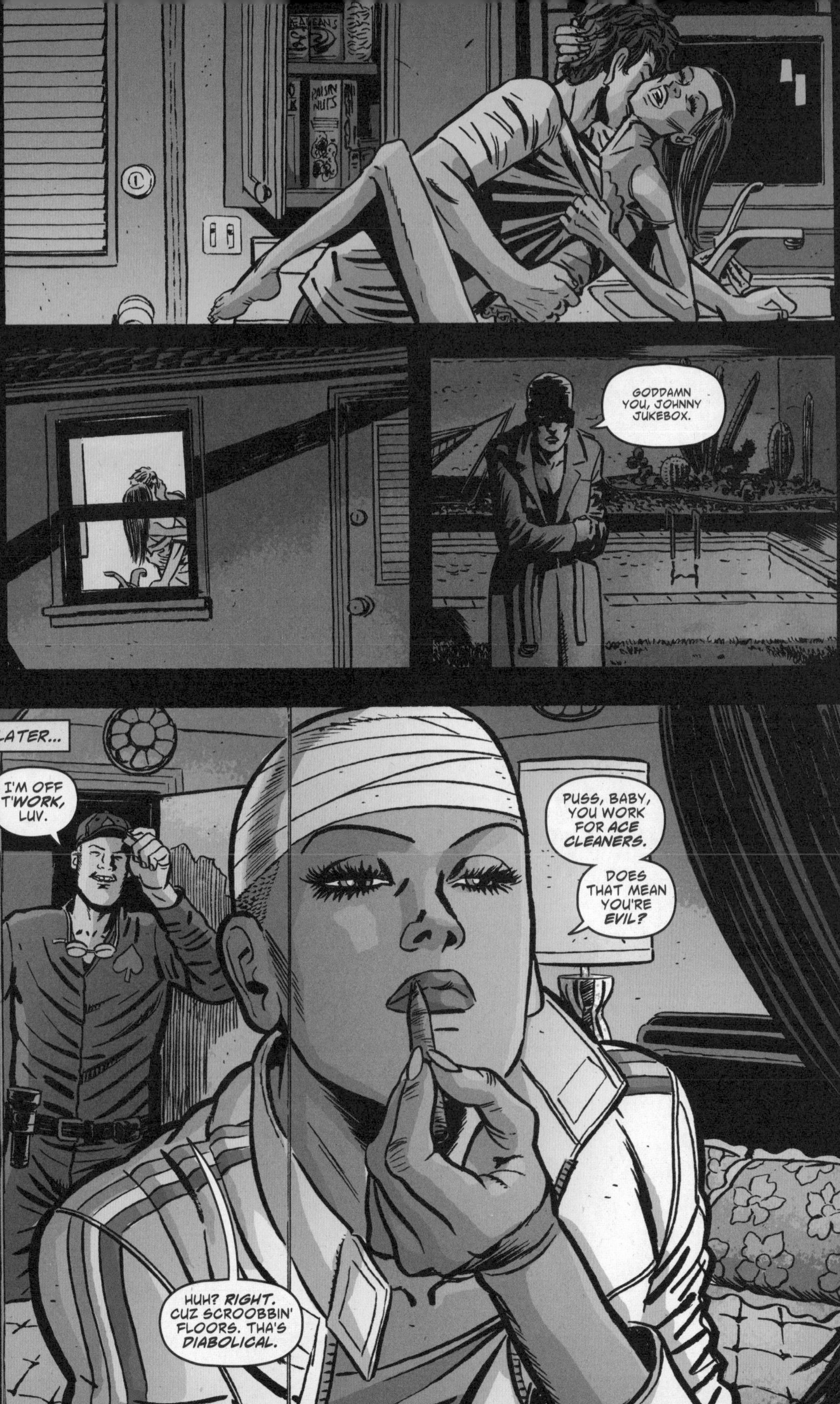
GODDAMN YOU, JOHNNY JUKEBOX.
LATER...
I'M OFF T'WORK, LUV.
PUSS, BABY, YOU WORK FOR ACE CLEANERS.
DOES THAT MEAN YOU'RE EVIL?
HUH? RIGHT. CUZ SCROOBBIN' FLOORS. THA'S DIABOLICAL.

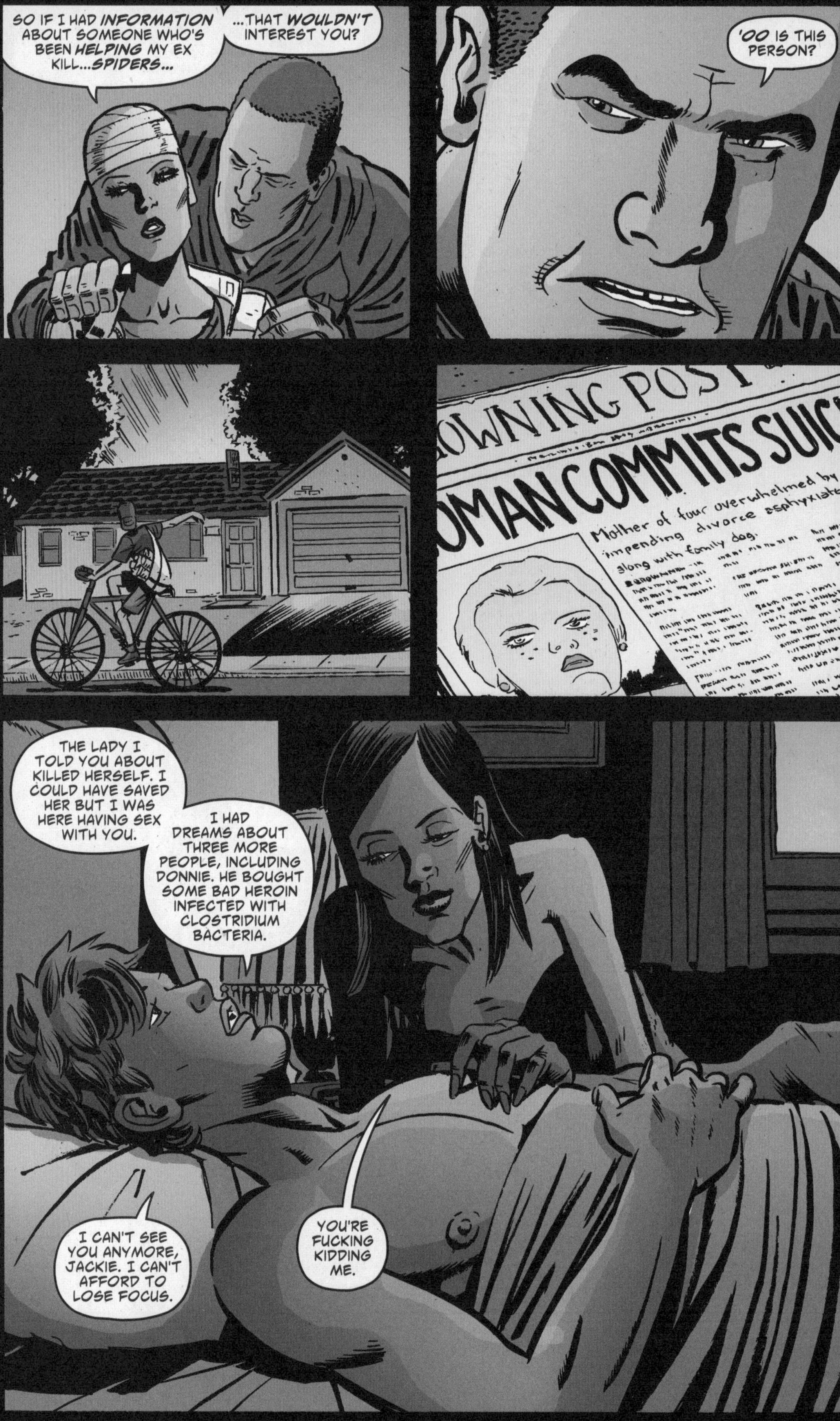
SO IF I HAD *INFORMATION* ABOUT SOMEONE WHO'S BEEN *HELPING* MY EX KILL...*SPIDERS*...
...THAT *WOULDN'T* INTEREST YOU?
'*OO* IS THIS PERSON?
OWNING POST
OMAN COMMITS SUIC
Mother of four overwhelmed by impending divorce asphyxiates along with family dog.
THE LADY I TOLD YOU ABOUT KILLED HERSELF. I COULD HAVE SAVED HER BUT I WAS HERE HAVING SEX WITH YOU.
I HAD DREAMS ABOUT THREE MORE PEOPLE, INCLUDING DONNIE. HE BOUGHT SOME BAD HEROIN INFECTED WITH CLOSTRIDIUM BACTERIA.
I CAN'T SEE YOU ANYMORE, JACKIE. I CAN'T AFFORD TO LOSE FOCUS.
YOU'RE FUCKING KIDDING ME.

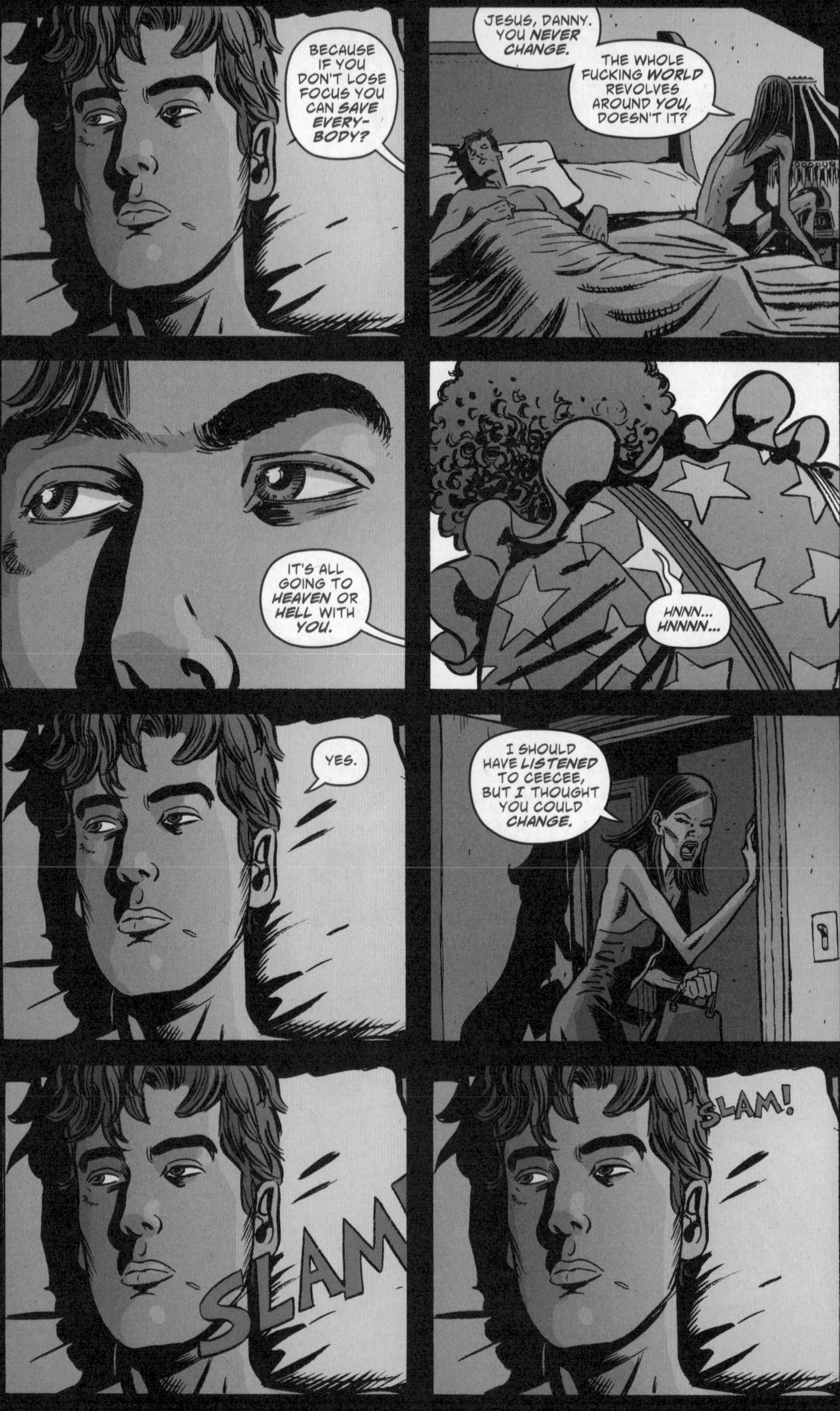
BECAUSE IF YOU DON'T LOSE FOCUS YOU CAN *SAVE EVERY-BODY?*
JESUS, DANNY. YOU *NEVER CHANGE.*
THE WHOLE FUCKING *WORLD* REVOLVES AROUND *YOU,* DOESN'T IT?
IT'S ALL GOING TO *HEAVEN* OR *HELL* WITH *YOU.*
HNNN... HNNNN...
YES.
I SHOULD HAVE *LISTENED* TO CEECEE, BUT I THOUGHT YOU COULD *CHANGE.*
SLAM
SLAM!

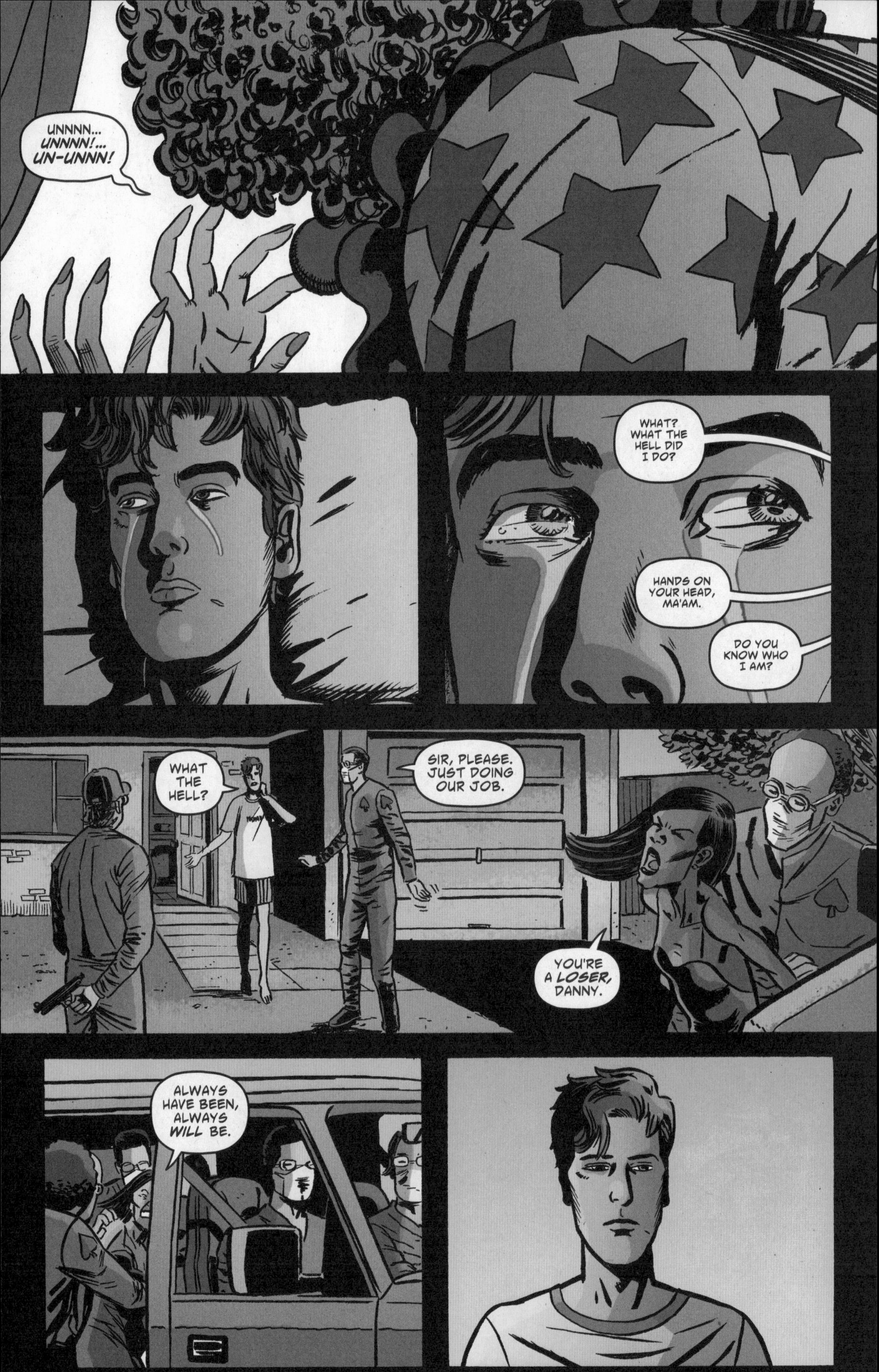
UNNNN... UNNNN!... UN-UNNN!
WHAT? WHAT THE HELL DID I DO?
HANDS ON YOUR HEAD, MA'AM.
DO YOU KNOW WHO I AM?
WHAT THE HELL?
SIR, PLEASE. JUST DOING OUR JOB.
YOU'RE A LOSER, DANNY.
ALWAYS HAVE BEEN, ALWAYS WILL BE.

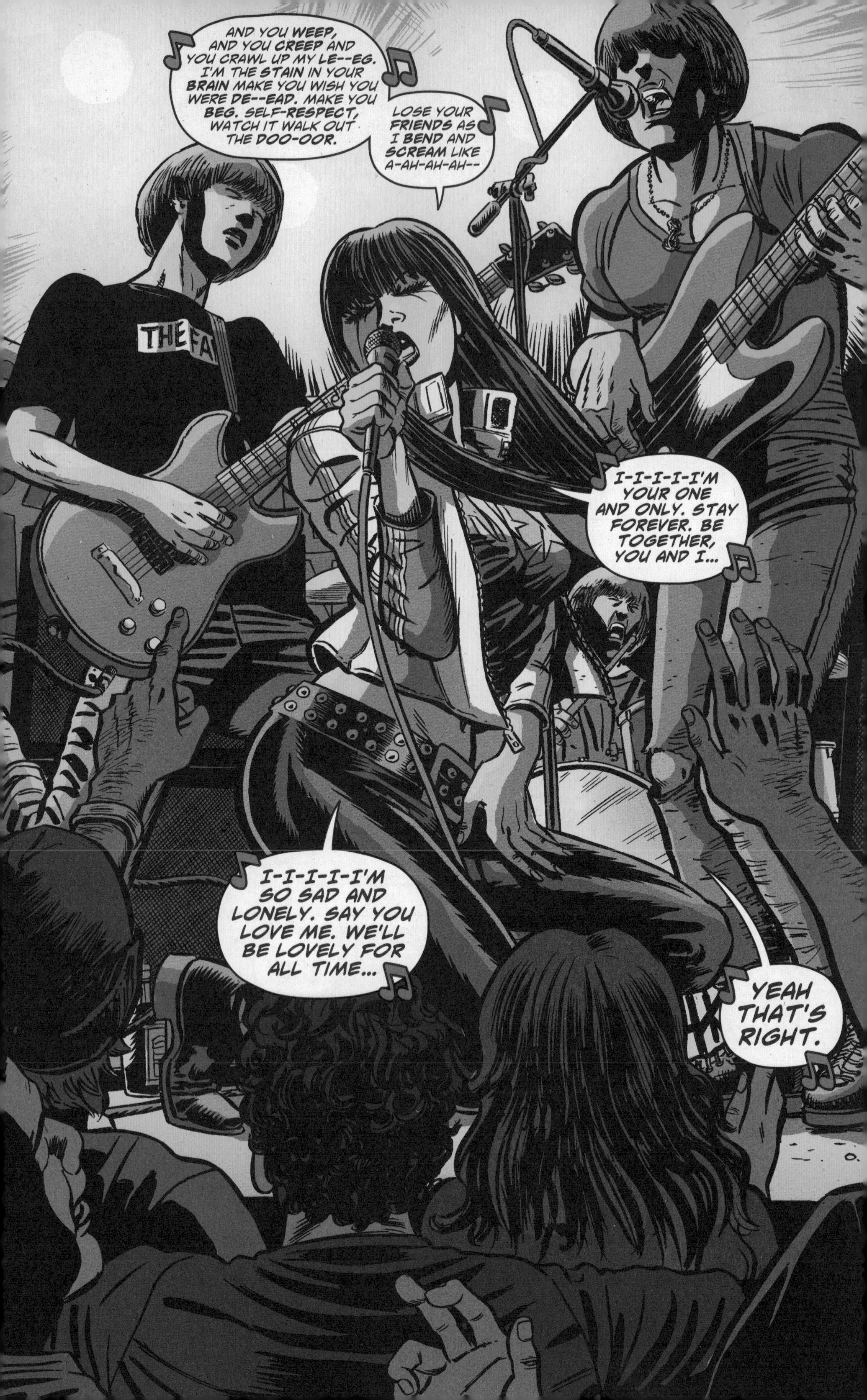
AND YOU WEEP, AND YOU CREEP AND YOU CRAWL UP MY LE--EG. I'M THE STAIN IN YOUR BRAIN MAKE YOU WISH YOU WERE DE--EAD. MAKE YOU BEG. SELF-RESPECT, WATCH IT WALK OUT THE DOO-OOR.
LOSE YOUR FRIENDS AS I BEND AND SCREAM LIKE A-AH-AH-AH--
THE FA
I-I-I-I-I'M YOUR ONE AND ONLY. STAY FOREVER. BE TOGETHER, YOU AND I...
I-I-I-I-I'M SO SAD AND LONELY. SAY YOU LOVE ME. WE'LL BE LOVELY FOR ALL TIME...
YEAH THAT'S RIGHT.

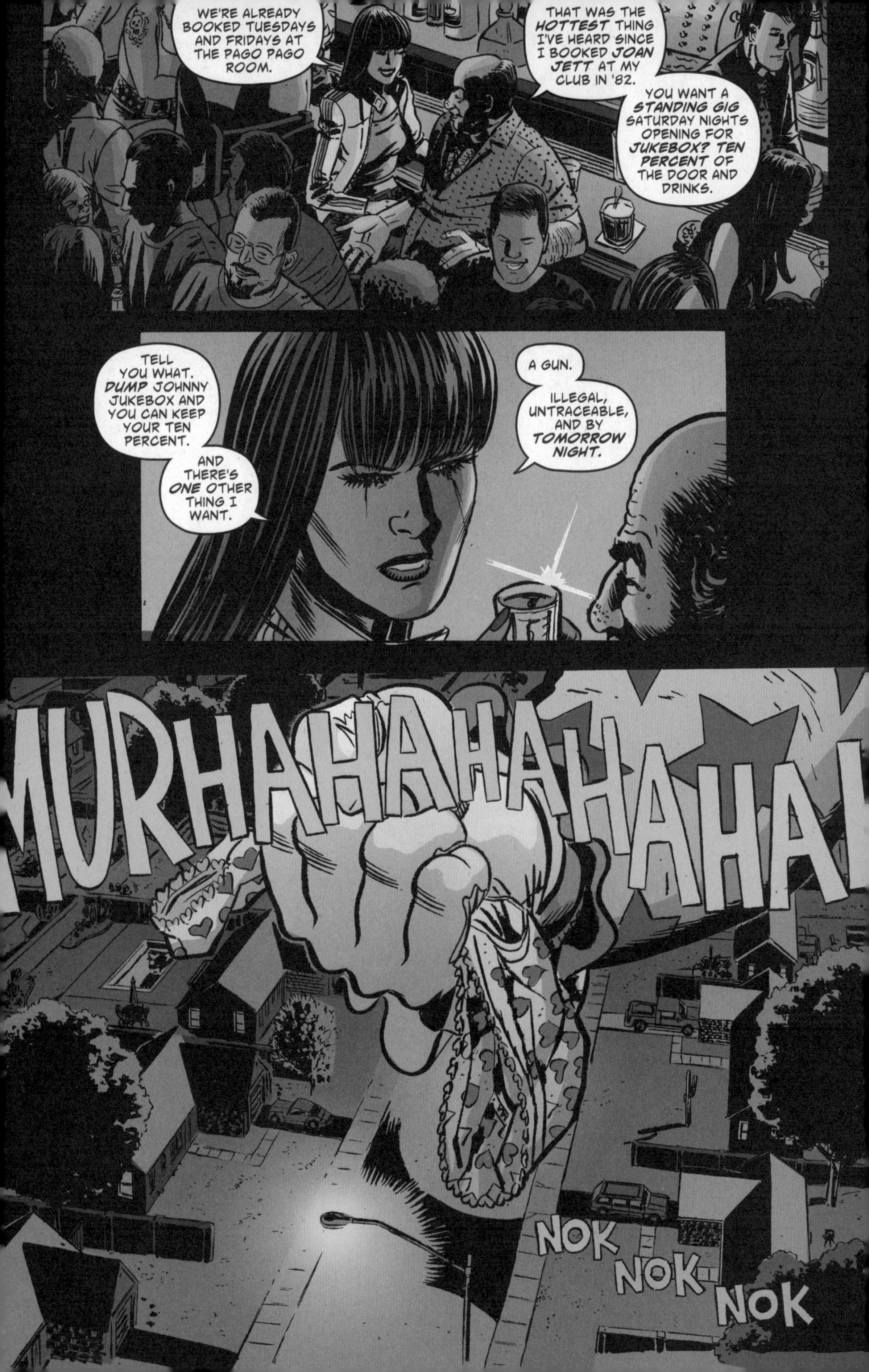
WE'RE ALREADY BOOKED TUESDAYS AND FRIDAYS AT THE PAGO PAGO ROOM.
THAT WAS THE **HOTTEST** THING I'VE HEARD SINCE I BOOKED **JOAN JETT** AT MY CLUB IN '82.
YOU WANT A **STANDING GIG** SATURDAY NIGHTS OPENING FOR **JUKEBOX? TEN PERCENT** OF THE DOOR AND DRINKS.
TELL YOU WHAT. **DUMP** JOHNNY JUKEBOX AND YOU CAN KEEP YOUR TEN PERCENT.
AND THERE'S **ONE** OTHER THING I WANT.
A GUN.
ILLEGAL, UNTRACEABLE, AND BY **TOMORROW NIGHT.**
MURHAHAHAHAHAHAHA
NOK
NOK
NOK

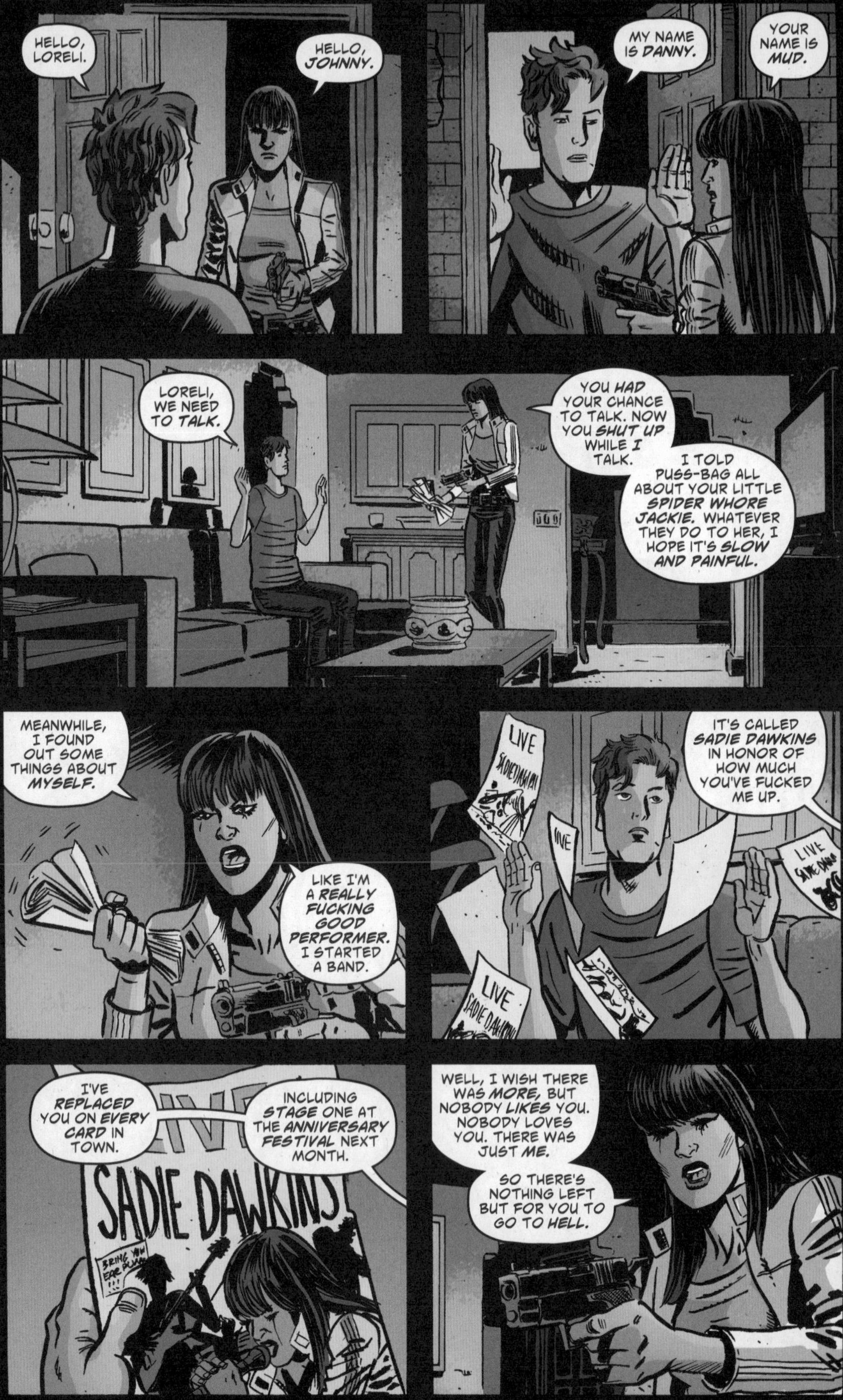
HELLO, LORELI.
HELLO, JOHNNY.
MY NAME IS DANNY.
YOUR NAME IS MUD.
LORELI, WE NEED TO TALK.
YOU HAD YOUR CHANCE TO TALK. NOW YOU SHUT UP WHILE I TALK.
I TOLD PUSS-BAG ALL ABOUT YOUR LITTLE SPIDER WHORE JACKIE. WHATEVER THEY DO TO HER, I HOPE IT'S SLOW AND PAINFUL.
MEANWHILE, I FOUND OUT SOME THINGS ABOUT MYSELF.
LIKE I'M A REALLY FUCKING GOOD PERFORMER. I STARTED A BAND.
IT'S CALLED SADIE DAWKINS IN HONOR OF HOW MUCH YOU'VE FUCKED ME UP.
LIVE
I'VE REPLACED YOU ON EVERY CARD IN TOWN.
INCLUDING STAGE ONE AT THE ANNIVERSARY FESTIVAL NEXT MONTH.
SADIE DAWKINS
WELL, I WISH THERE WAS MORE, BUT NOBODY LIKES YOU. NOBODY LOVES YOU. THERE WAS JUST ME.
SO THERE'S NOTHING LEFT BUT FOR YOU TO GO TO HELL.

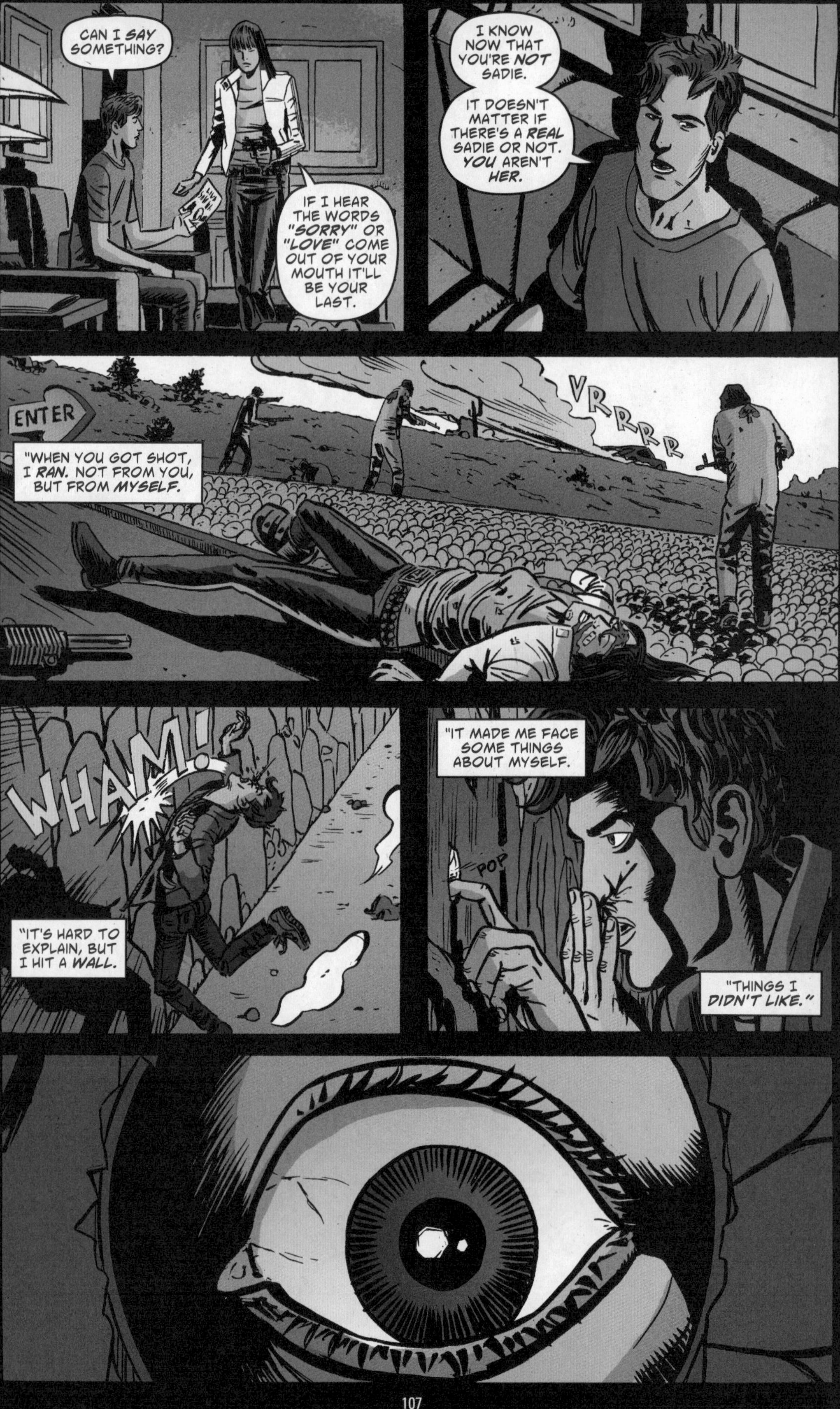
CAN I *SAY* SOMETHING?
IF I HEAR THE WORDS "*SORRY*" OR "*LOVE*" COME OUT OF YOUR MOUTH IT'LL BE YOUR LAST.
I KNOW NOW THAT YOU'RE *NOT* SADIE.
IT DOESN'T MATTER IF THERE'S A *REAL* SADIE OR NOT. *YOU* AREN'T *HER*.
ENTER
VRRRRR
"WHEN YOU GOT SHOT, I *RAN*. NOT FROM YOU, BUT FROM *MYSELF*.
WHAM!
"IT'S HARD TO EXPLAIN, BUT I HIT A *WALL*.
"IT MADE ME FACE SOME THINGS ABOUT MYSELF.
POP
"THINGS I *DIDN'T LIKE*."

EEN
G IN
OF
SE
FOR
PLE
EKS.

I EVEN DOWNED A BOTTLE OF JACKIE'S FORGET-ME-NOTS PILLS.

BUT WHAT I SAW KEEPS BLEEDING BACK THROUGH LIKE MOLD THROUGH FRESH PAINT.

I HAD TO ACCEPT THE TRUTH.

D T'S T?

UNRRRRR! RRRR!

RRR-RRRR-- RRRRRRR!

AHH!
NUU NUU
OD...STOP...
STOP...

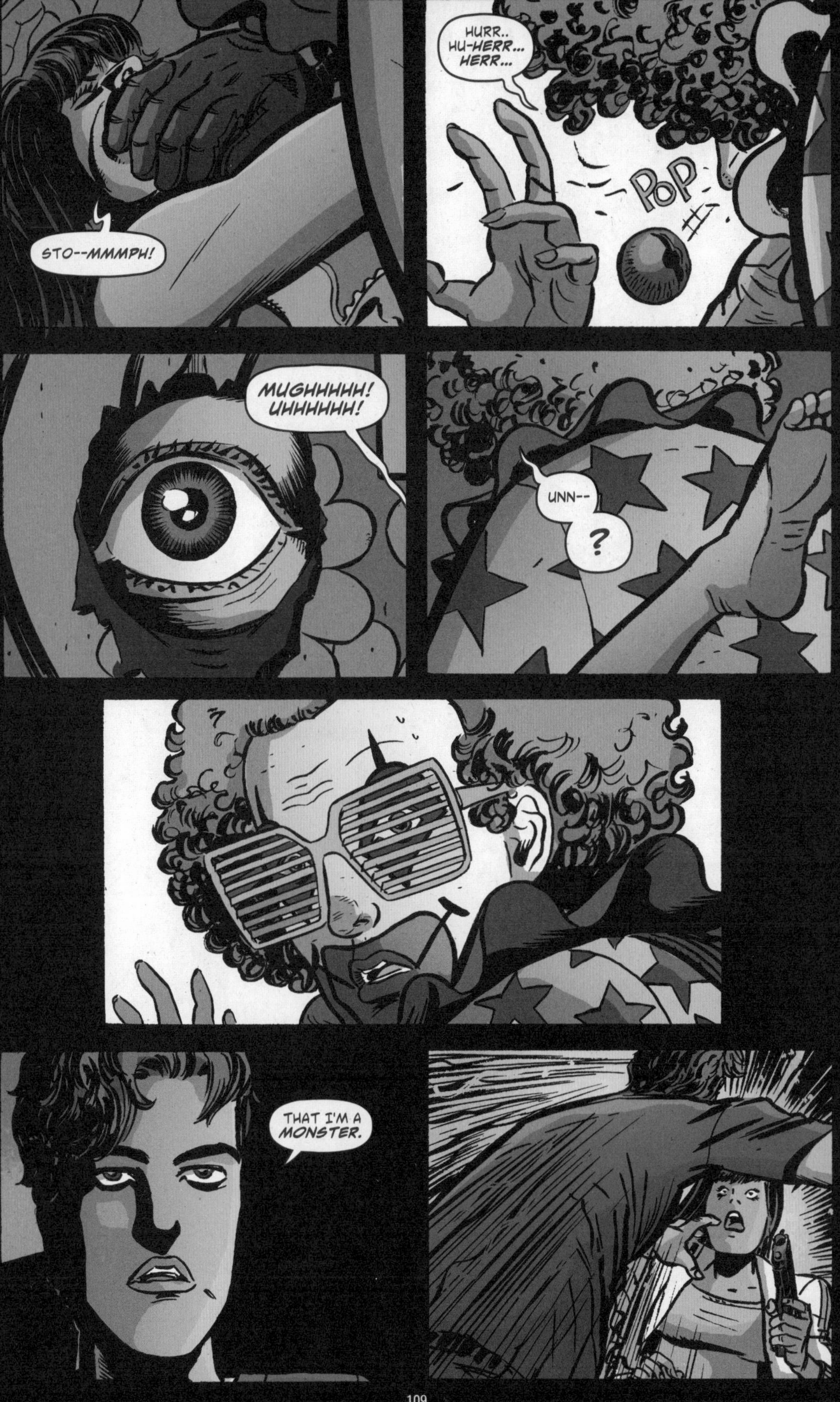
STO--MMMPH!
HURR.. HU-HERR... HERR...
POP
MUGHHHHH! UHHHHHH!
UNN--
?
THAT I'M A MONSTER.

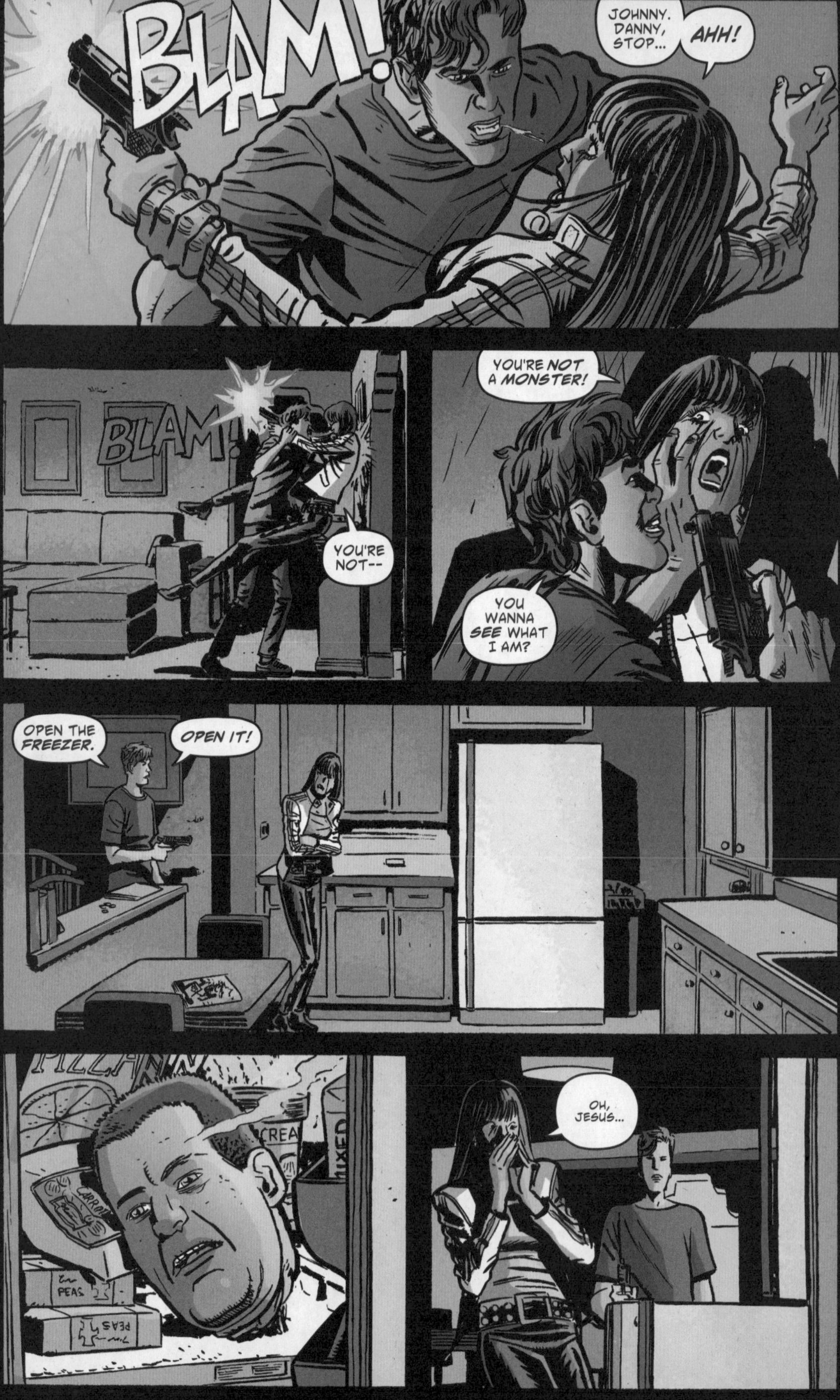
BLAM!
JOHNNY. DANNY, STOP...
AHH!
BLAM!
YOU'RE NOT--
YOU'RE NOT A MONSTER!
YOU WANNA SEE WHAT I AM?
OPEN THE FREEZER.
OPEN IT!
PEAS
PEAS
OH, JESUS...

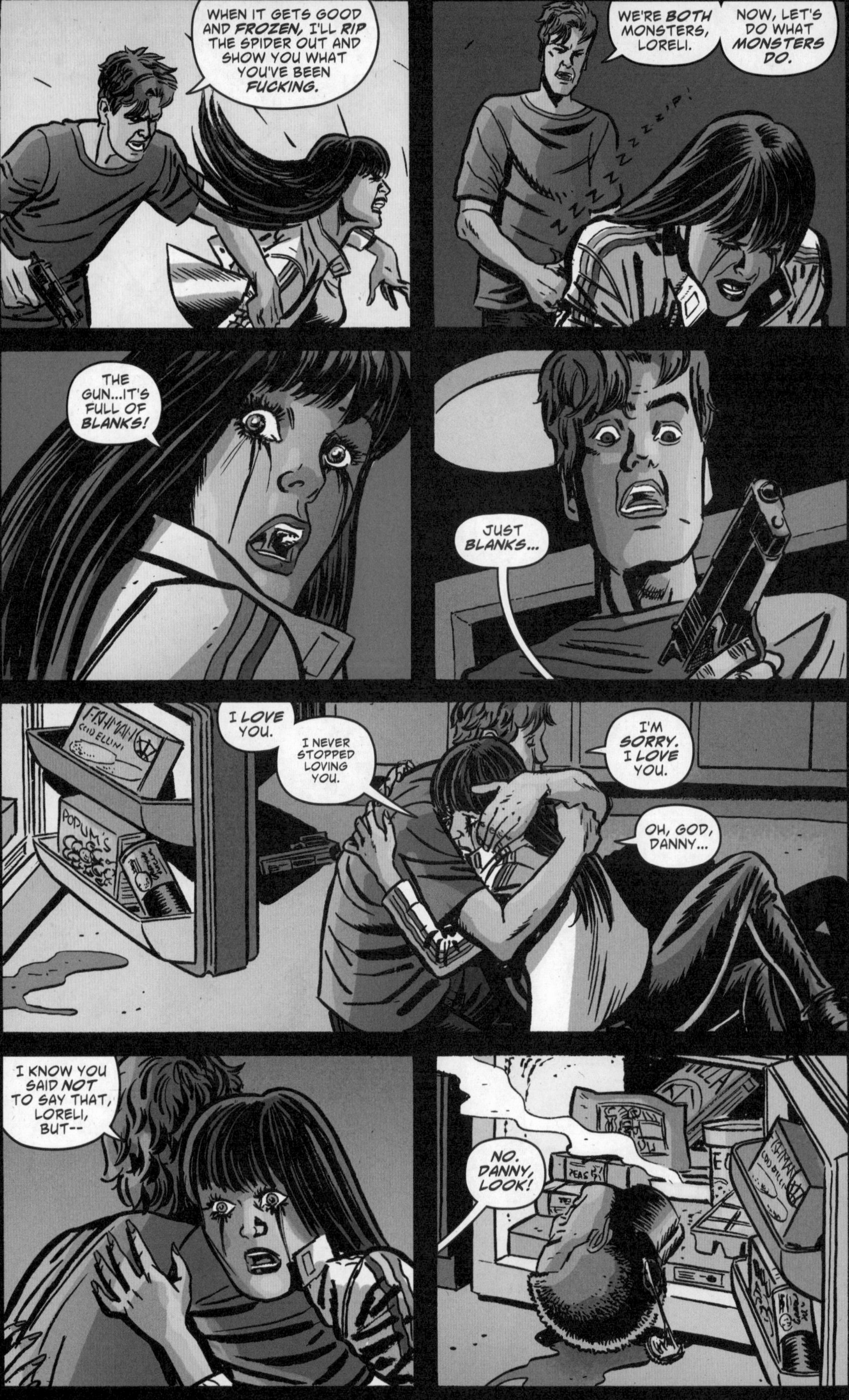
WHEN IT GETS GOOD AND FROZEN, I'LL RIP THE SPIDER OUT AND SHOW YOU WHAT YOU'VE BEEN FUCKING.
WE'RE BOTH MONSTERS, LORELI.
NOW, LET'S DO WHAT MONSTERS DO.
ZZZZZIP!
THE GUN...IT'S FULL OF BLANKS!
JUST BLANKS...
I LOVE YOU.
I NEVER STOPPED LOVING YOU.
I'M SORRY. I LOVE YOU.
OH, GOD, DANNY...
POPUM'S
I KNOW YOU SAID NOT TO SAY THAT, LORELI, BUT--
NO. DANNY, LOOK!
PEAS

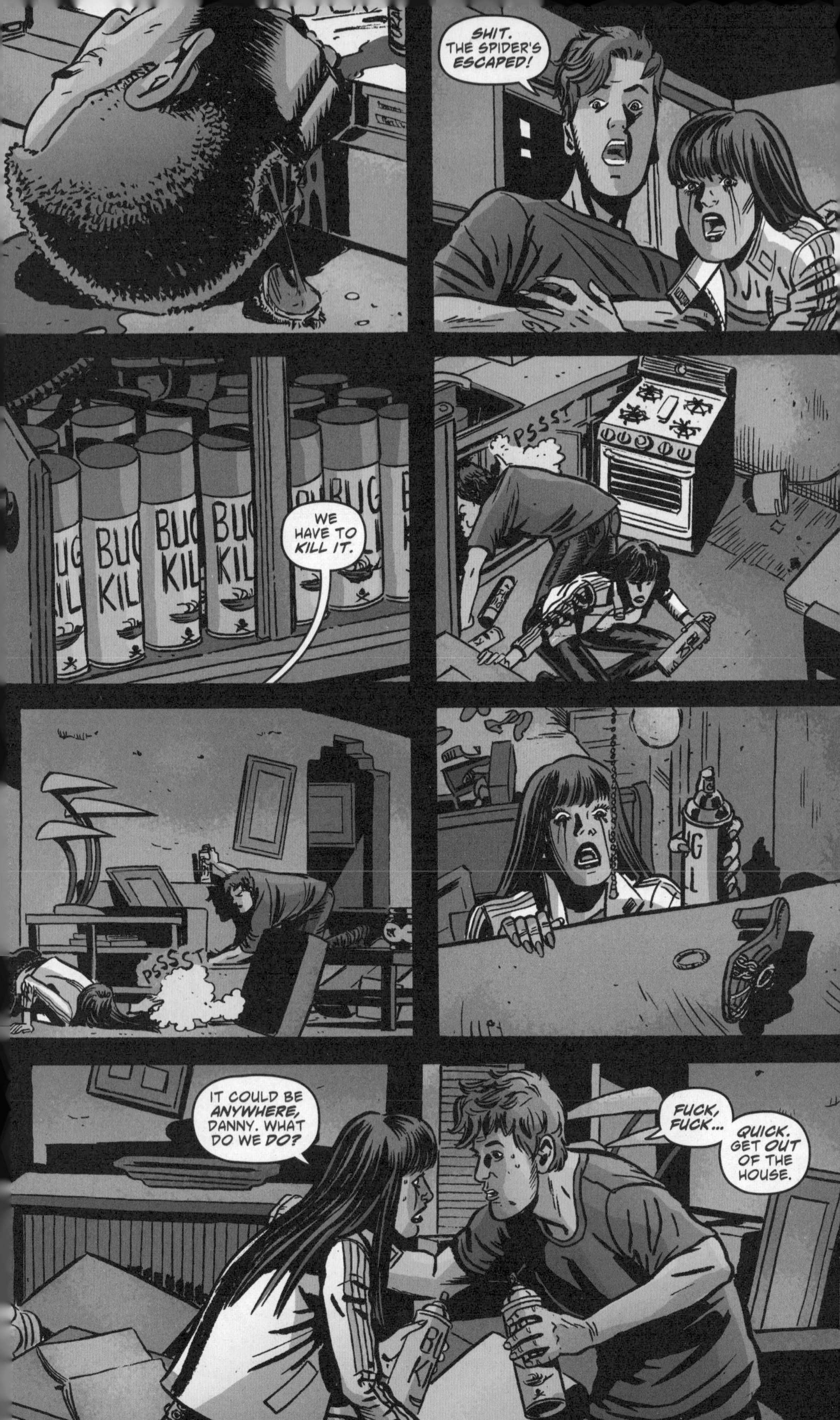
SHIT. THE SPIDER'S ESCAPED!
BUG KILL
WE HAVE TO KILL IT.
PSSST
PSSSST
IT COULD BE ANYWHERE, DANNY. WHAT DO WE DO?
FUCK, FUCK...
QUICK. GET OUT OF THE HOUSE.

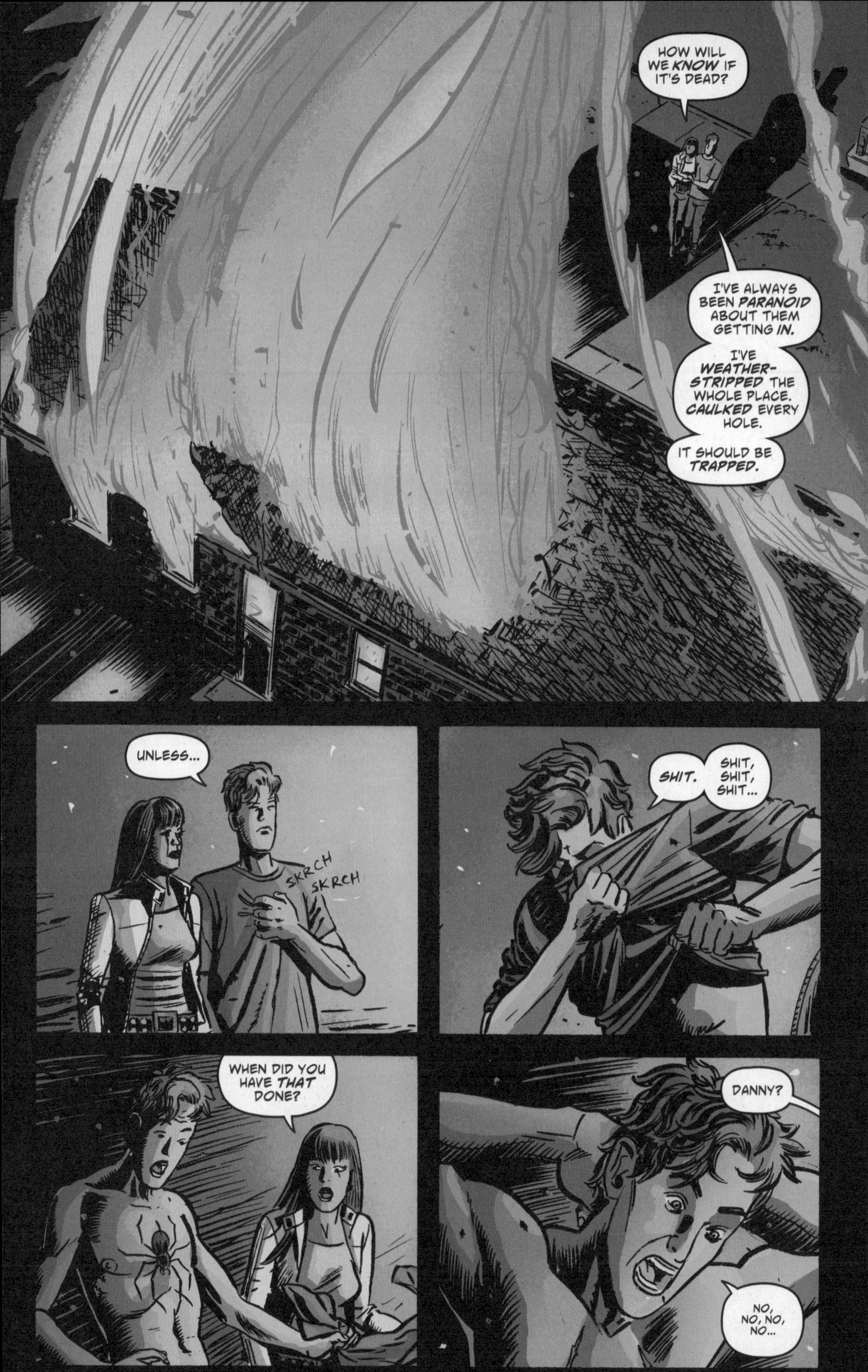
HOW WILL WE *KNOW* IF IT'S DEAD?
I'VE ALWAYS BEEN *PARANOID* ABOUT THEM GETTING *IN.*
I'VE *WEATHER-STRIPPED* THE WHOLE PLACE. *CAULKED* EVERY HOLE.
IT SHOULD BE *TRAPPED.*
UNLESS...
SKRCH SKRCH
SHIT.
SHIT, SHIT, SHIT...
WHEN DID YOU HAVE *THAT* DONE?
DANNY?
NO, NO, NO, NO...

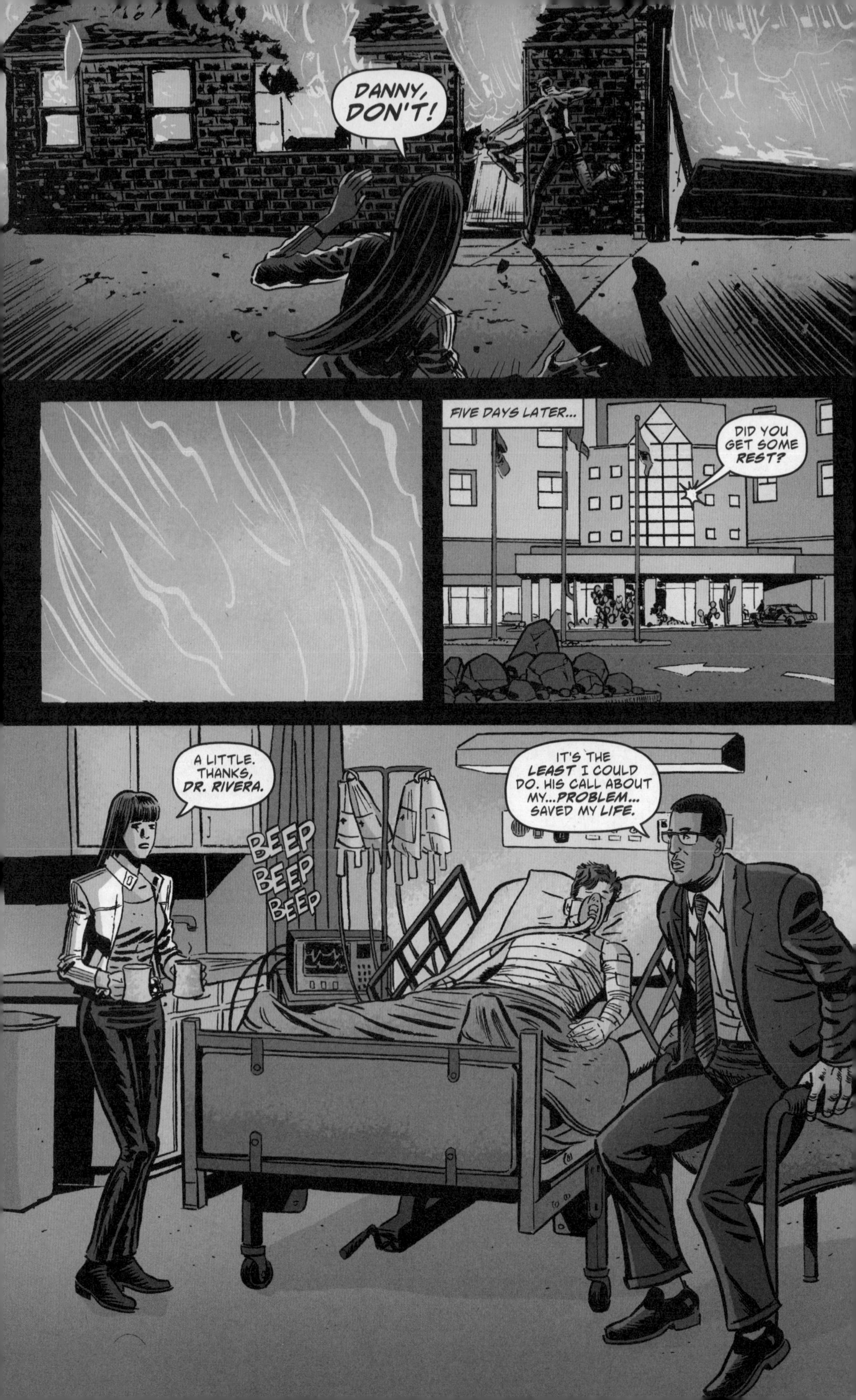
DANNY, DON'T!
FIVE DAYS LATER...
DID YOU GET SOME REST?
A LITTLE. THANKS, DR. RIVERA.
BEEP
BEEP
BEEP
IT'S THE LEAST I COULD DO. HIS CALL ABOUT MY...PROBLEM... SAVED MY LIFE.

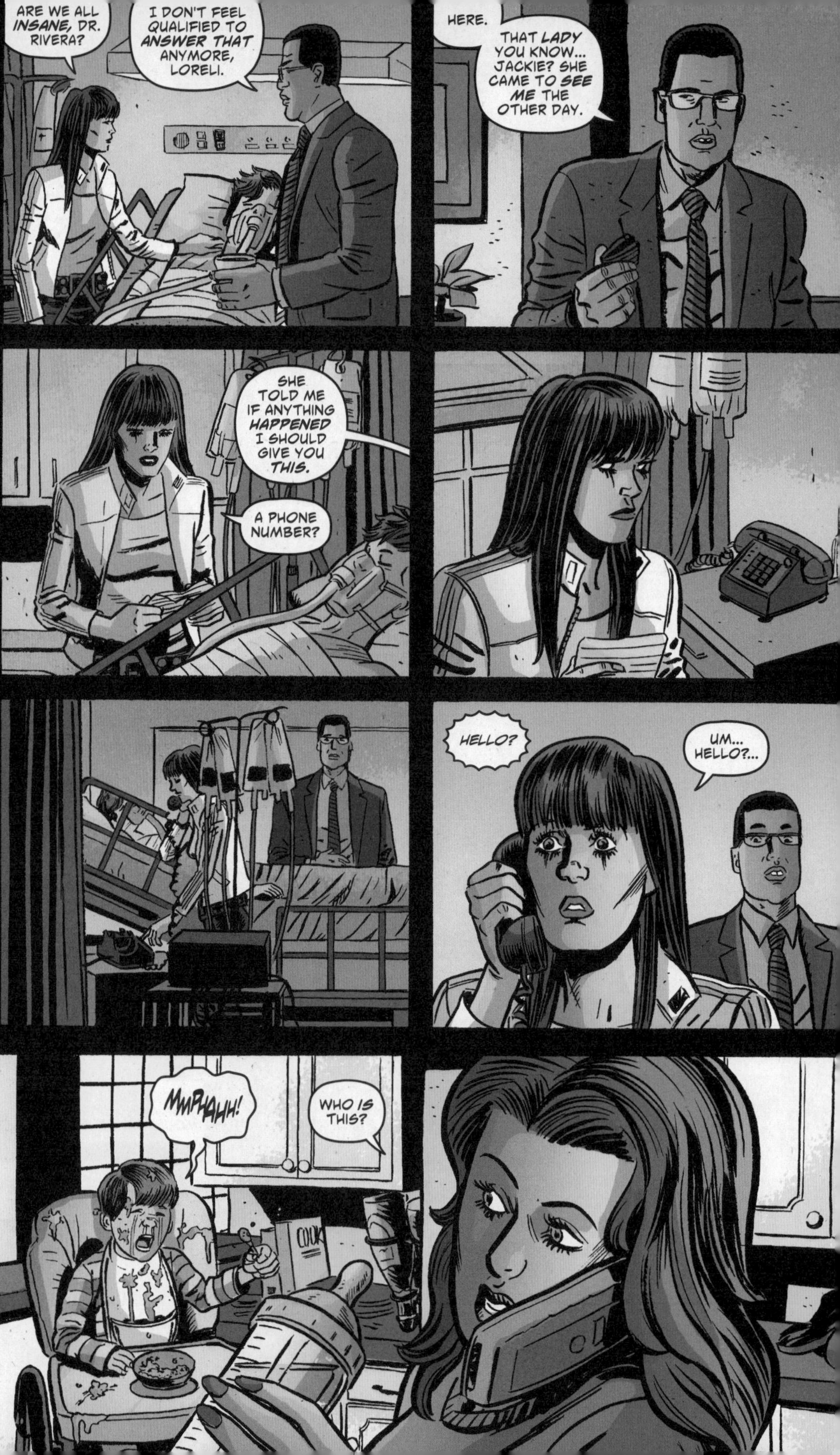
ARE WE ALL INSANE, DR. RIVERA?
I DON'T FEEL QUALIFIED TO ANSWER THAT ANYMORE, LORELI.
HERE.
THAT LADY YOU KNOW... JACKIE? SHE CAME TO SEE ME THE OTHER DAY.
SHE TOLD ME IF ANYTHING HAPPENED I SHOULD GIVE YOU THIS.
A PHONE NUMBER?
HELLO?
UM... HELLO?...
MMPHAHH!
WHO IS THIS?

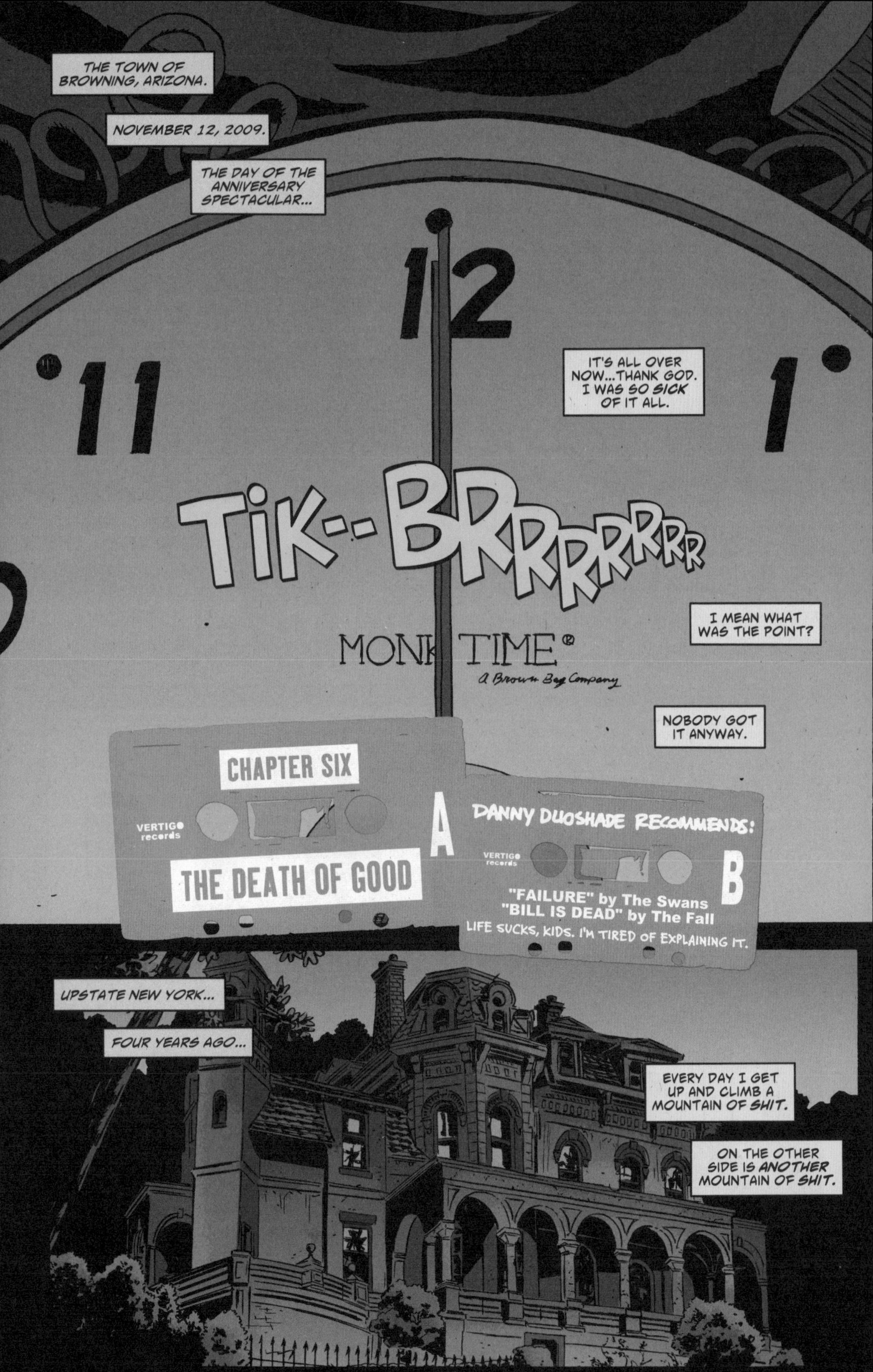
THE TOWN OF BROWNING, ARIZONA.
NOVEMBER 12, 2009.
THE DAY OF THE ANNIVERSARY SPECTACULAR...
12
11
1
IT'S ALL OVER NOW...THANK GOD. I WAS SO *SICK* OF IT ALL.
TIK-- BRRRRRRR
I MEAN WHAT WAS THE POINT?
MONK TIME®
A Brown Bag Company
NOBODY GOT IT ANYWAY.
CHAPTER SIX
VERTIGO records
A
THE DEATH OF GOOD
DANNY DUOSHADE RECOMMENDS:
VERTIGO records
B
"FAILURE" by The Swans
"BILL IS DEAD" by The Fall
LIFE SUCKS, KIDS. I'M TIRED OF EXPLAINING IT.
UPSTATE NEW YORK...
FOUR YEARS AGO...
EVERY DAY I GET UP AND CLIMB A MOUNTAIN OF *SHIT*.
ON THE OTHER SIDE IS *ANOTHER* MOUNTAIN OF *SHIT*.

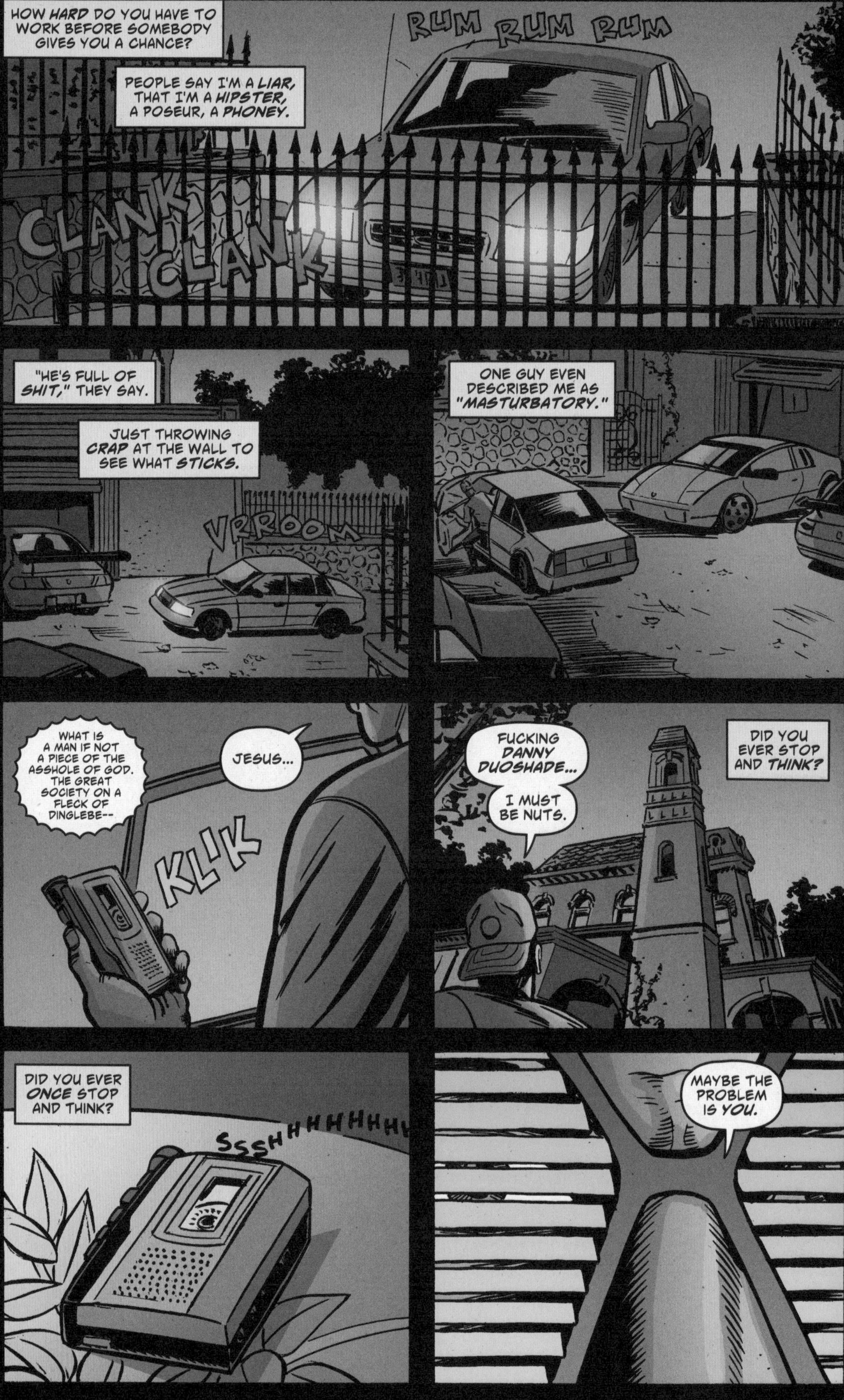

HOW HARD DO YOU HAVE TO WORK BEFORE SOMEBODY GIVES YOU A CHANCE?
RUM RUM RUM
PEOPLE SAY I'M A LIAR, THAT I'M A HIPSTER, A POSEUR, A PHONEY.
CLANK CLANK
"HE'S FULL OF SHIT," THEY SAY.
JUST THROWING CRAP AT THE WALL TO SEE WHAT STICKS.
VRROOM
ONE GUY EVEN DESCRIBED ME AS "MASTURBATORY."
WHAT IS A MAN IF NOT A PIECE OF THE ASSHOLE OF GOD. THE GREAT SOCIETY ON A FLECK OF DINGLEBE--
JESUS...
KLIK
FUCKING DANNY DUOSHADE...
I MUST BE NUTS.
DID YOU EVER STOP AND THINK?
DID YOU EVER ONCE STOP AND THINK?
SSSHHHHHHHH
MAYBE THE PROBLEM IS YOU.

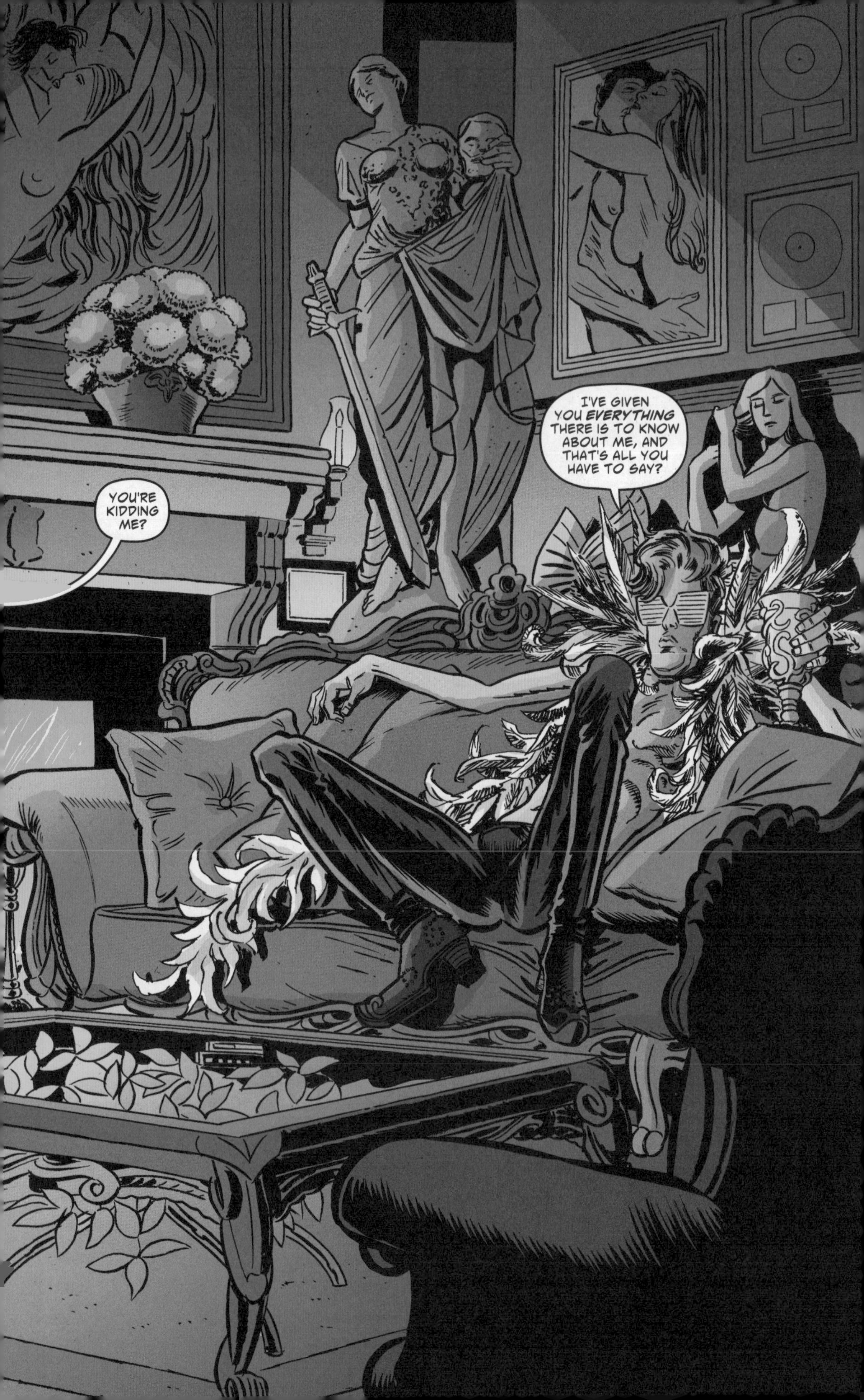
YOU'RE KIDDING ME?
I'VE GIVEN YOU *EVERYTHING* THERE IS TO KNOW ABOUT ME, AND THAT'S ALL YOU HAVE TO SAY?

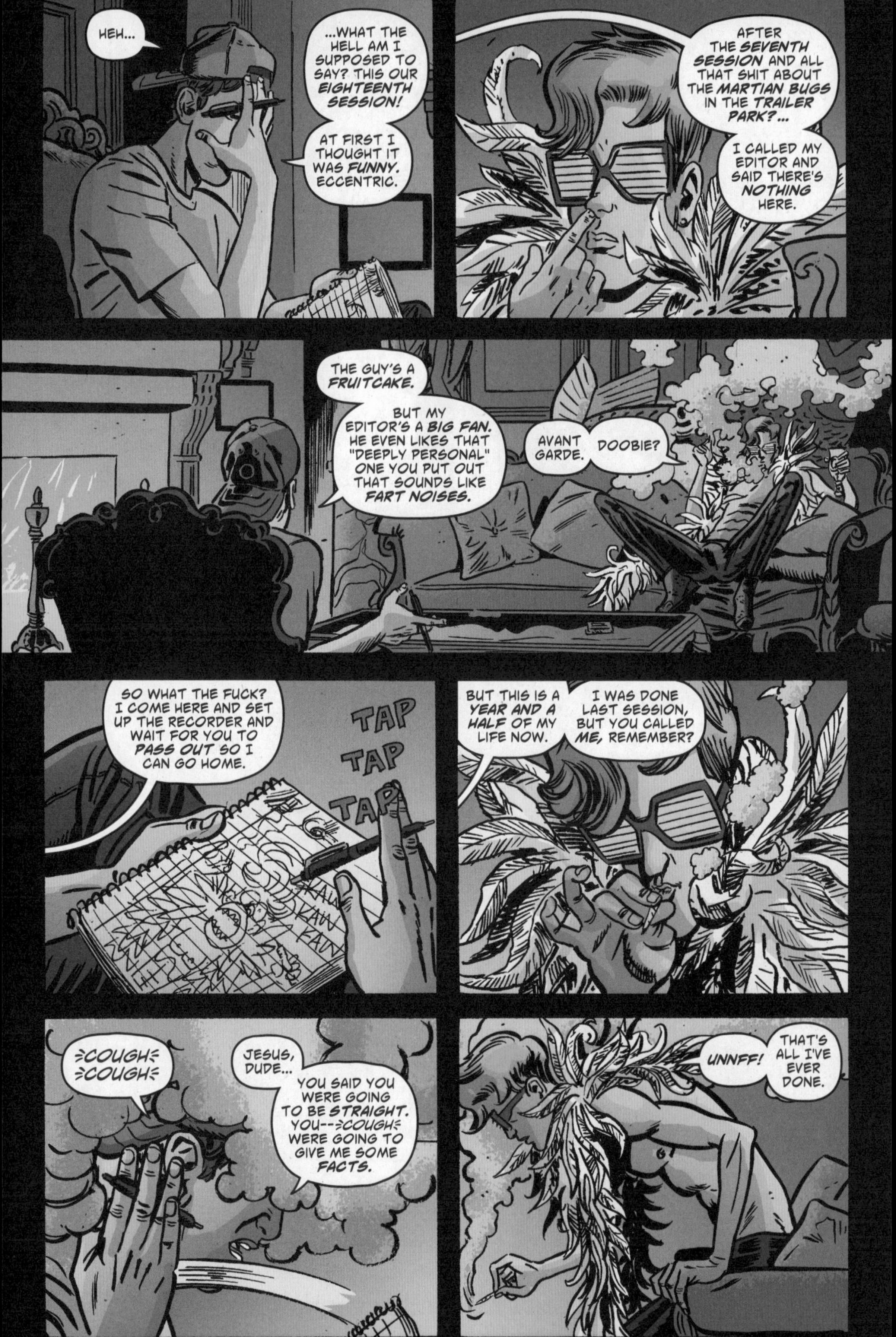
HEH...
...WHAT THE HELL AM I SUPPOSED TO SAY? THIS OUR EIGHTEENTH SESSION!
AT FIRST I THOUGHT IT WAS FUNNY. ECCENTRIC.
AFTER THE SEVENTH SESSION AND ALL THAT SHIT ABOUT THE MARTIAN BUGS IN THE TRAILER PARK?...
I CALLED MY EDITOR AND SAID THERE'S NOTHING HERE.
THE GUY'S A FRUITCAKE.
BUT MY EDITOR'S A BIG FAN. HE EVEN LIKES THAT "DEEPLY PERSONAL" ONE YOU PUT OUT THAT SOUNDS LIKE FART NOISES.
AVANT GARDE.
DOOBIE?
SO WHAT THE FUCK? I COME HERE AND SET UP THE RECORDER AND WAIT FOR YOU TO PASS OUT SO I CAN GO HOME.
TAP
TAP
TAP
KAW
KAW
KAW
BUT THIS IS A YEAR AND A HALF OF MY LIFE NOW.
I WAS DONE LAST SESSION, BUT YOU CALLED ME, REMEMBER?
≈COUGH≈ ≈COUGH≈
JESUS, DUDE...
YOU SAID YOU WERE GOING TO BE STRAIGHT. YOU--≈COUGH≈ WERE GOING TO GIVE ME SOME FACTS.
UNNFF!
THAT'S ALL I'VE EVER DONE.

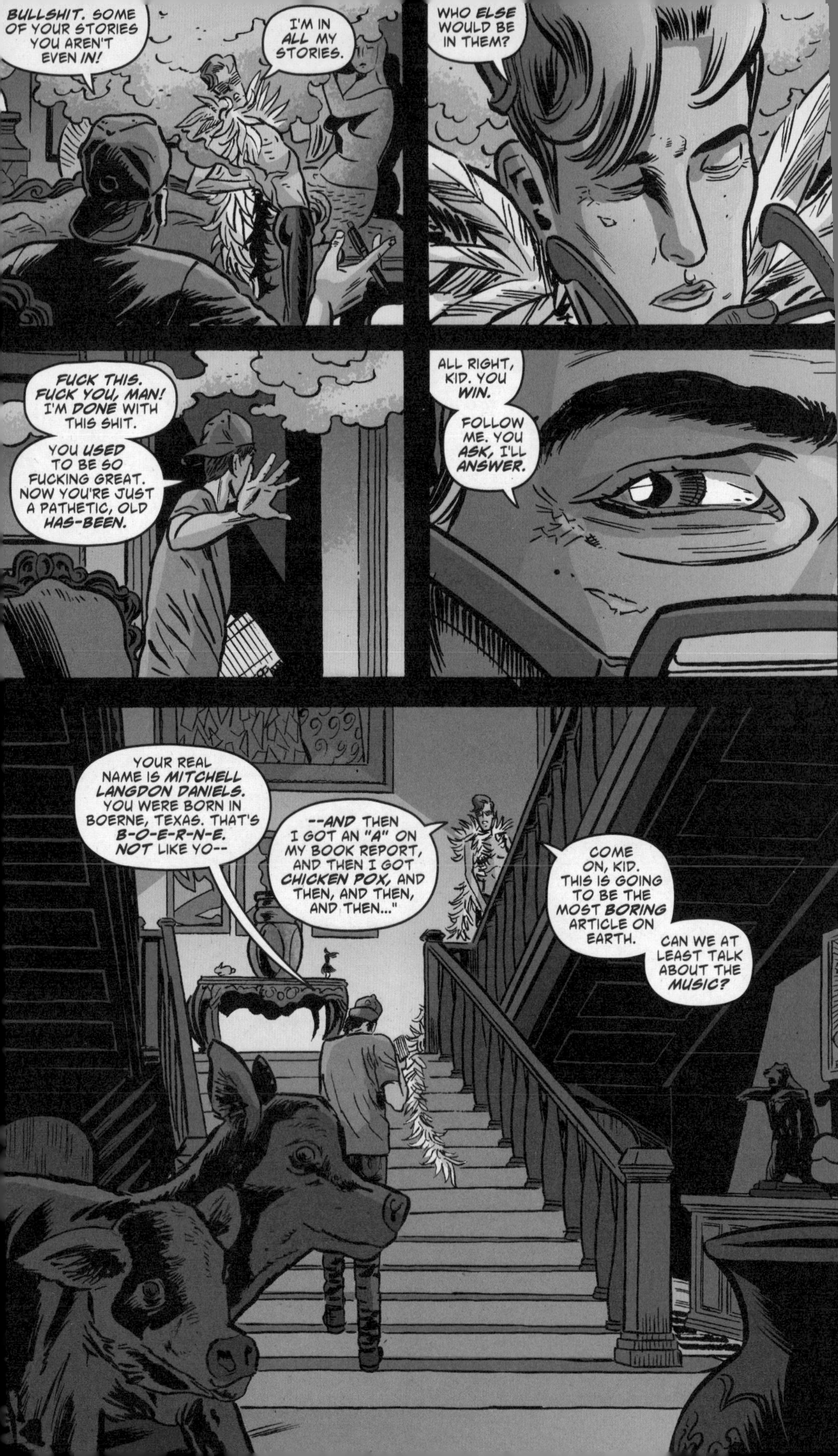

BULLSHIT. SOME OF YOUR STORIES YOU AREN'T EVEN IN!
I'M IN ALL MY STORIES.
WHO ELSE WOULD BE IN THEM?
FUCK THIS. FUCK YOU, MAN! I'M DONE WITH THIS SHIT.
YOU USED TO BE SO FUCKING GREAT. NOW YOU'RE JUST A PATHETIC, OLD HAS-BEEN.
ALL RIGHT, KID. YOU WIN.
FOLLOW ME. YOU ASK, I'LL ANSWER.
YOUR REAL NAME IS MITCHELL LANGDON DANIELS. YOU WERE BORN IN BOERNE, TEXAS. THAT'S B-O-E-R-N-E. NOT LIKE YO--
--AND THEN I GOT AN "A" ON MY BOOK REPORT, AND THEN I GOT CHICKEN POX, AND THEN, AND THEN, AND THEN..."
COME ON, KID. THIS IS GOING TO BE THE MOST BORING ARTICLE ON EARTH.
CAN WE AT LEAST TALK ABOUT THE MUSIC?

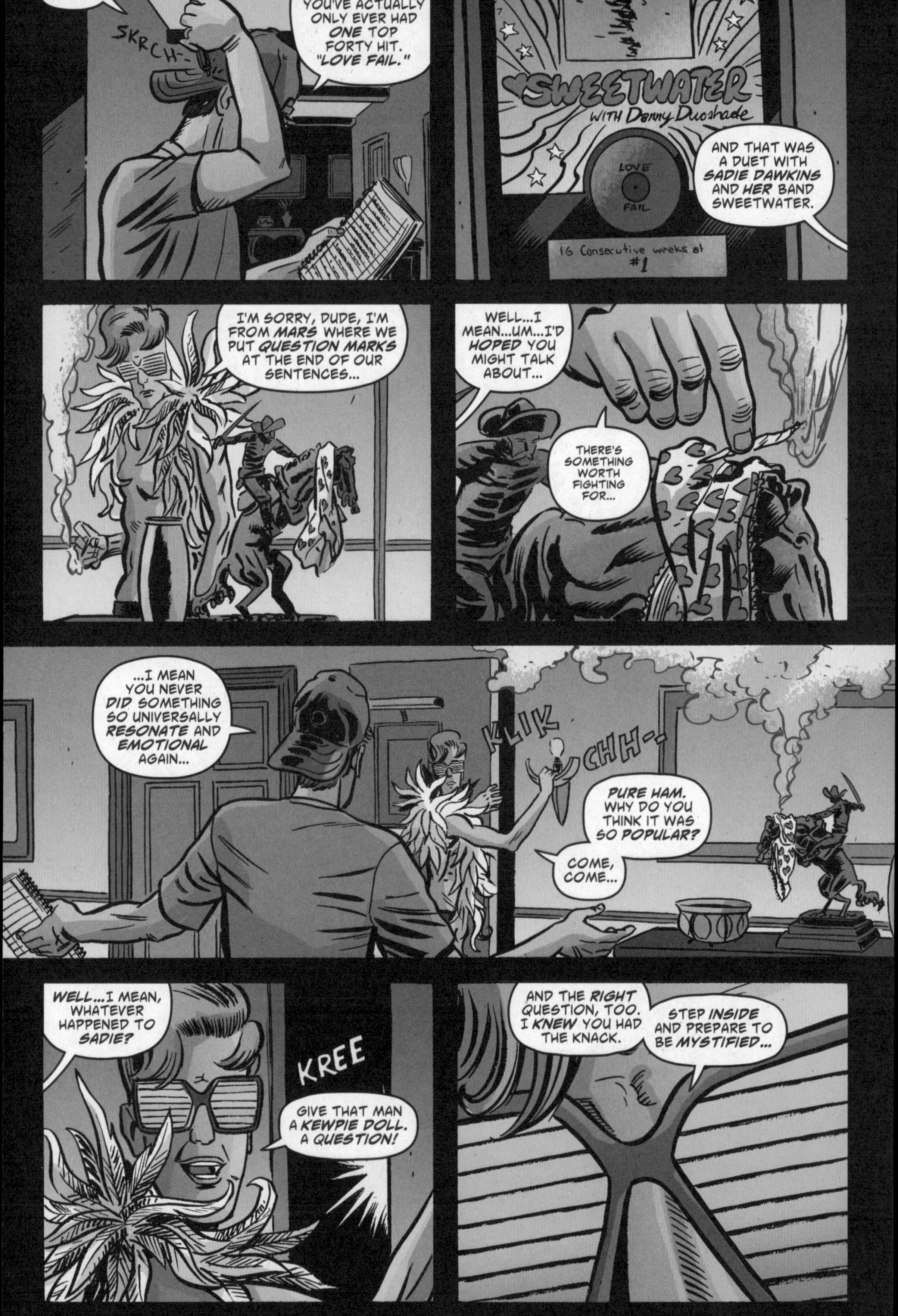

…FINE. FOR ALL YOUR CELEBRITY, YOU'VE ACTUALLY ONLY EVER HAD ONE TOP FORTY HIT. "LOVE FAIL."
SKRCH-
≈SIGH≈
SWEETWATER
WITH Danny Duoshade
LOVE FAIL
16 Consecutive weeks at #1
AND THAT WAS A DUET WITH SADIE DAWKINS AND HER BAND SWEETWATER.
I'M SORRY, DUDE, I'M FROM MARS WHERE WE PUT QUESTION MARKS AT THE END OF OUR SENTENCES…
WELL…I MEAN…UM…I'D HOPED YOU MIGHT TALK ABOUT…
THERE'S SOMETHING WORTH FIGHTING FOR…
…I MEAN YOU NEVER DID SOMETHING SO UNIVERSALLY RESONATE AND EMOTIONAL AGAIN…
KLIK
CHH-
PURE HAM. WHY DO YOU THINK IT WAS SO POPULAR?
COME, COME…
WELL…I MEAN, WHATEVER HAPPENED TO SADIE?
KREE
GIVE THAT MAN A KEWPIE DOLL. A QUESTION!
AND THE RIGHT QUESTION, TOO. I KNEW YOU HAD THE KNACK.
STEP INSIDE AND PREPARE TO BE MYSTIFIED…

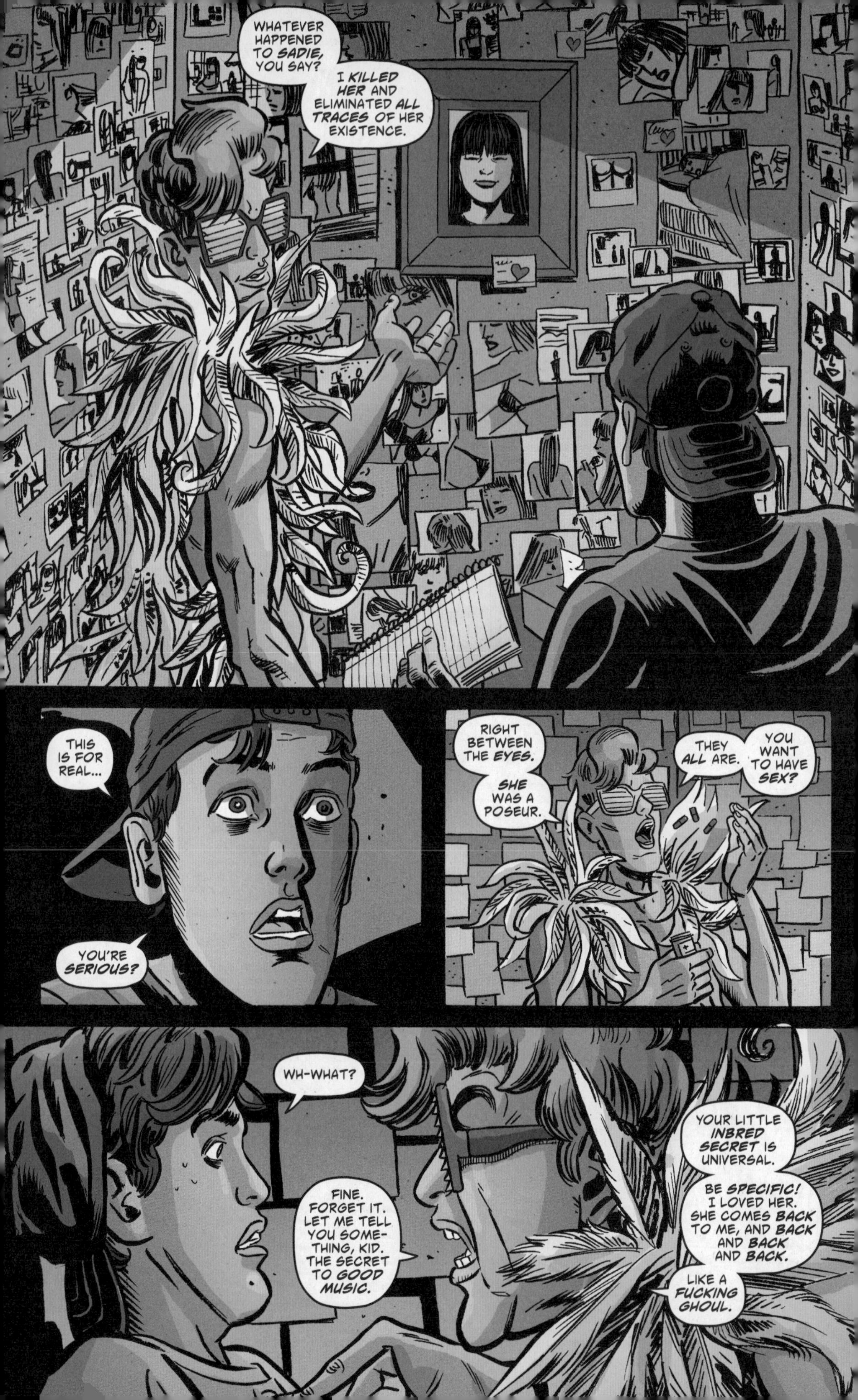
WHATEVER HAPPENED TO SADIE, YOU SAY?
I KILLED HER AND ELIMINATED ALL TRACES OF HER EXISTENCE.
THIS IS FOR REAL...
YOU'RE SERIOUS?
RIGHT BETWEEN THE EYES.
SHE WAS A POSEUR.
THEY ALL ARE.
YOU WANT TO HAVE SEX?
WH-WHAT?
FINE. FORGET IT. LET ME TELL YOU SOME-THING, KID. THE SECRET TO GOOD MUSIC.
YOUR LITTLE INBRED SECRET IS UNIVERSAL.
BE SPECIFIC! I LOVED HER. SHE COMES BACK TO ME, AND BACK AND BACK AND BACK.
LIKE A FUCKING GHOUL.

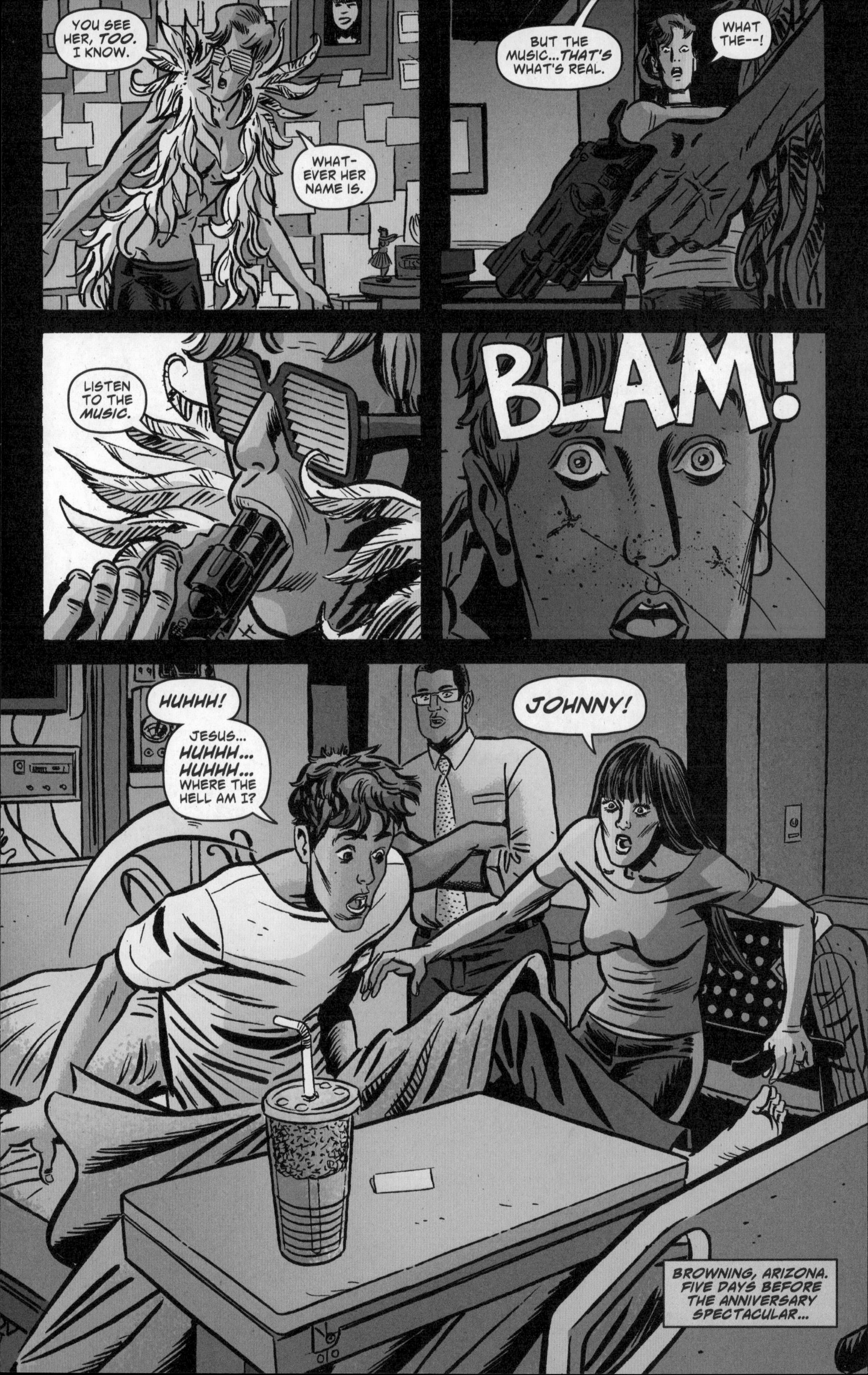
YOU SEE HER, *TOO.* I KNOW.
WHAT-EVER HER NAME IS.
BUT THE MUSIC...*THAT'S* WHAT'S REAL.
WHAT THE--!
LISTEN TO THE *MUSIC.*
BLAM!
HUHHH!
JESUS... *HUHHH... HUHHH...* WHERE THE HELL AM I?
JOHNNY!
BROWNING, ARIZONA. FIVE DAYS BEFORE THE ANNIVERSARY SPECTACULAR...

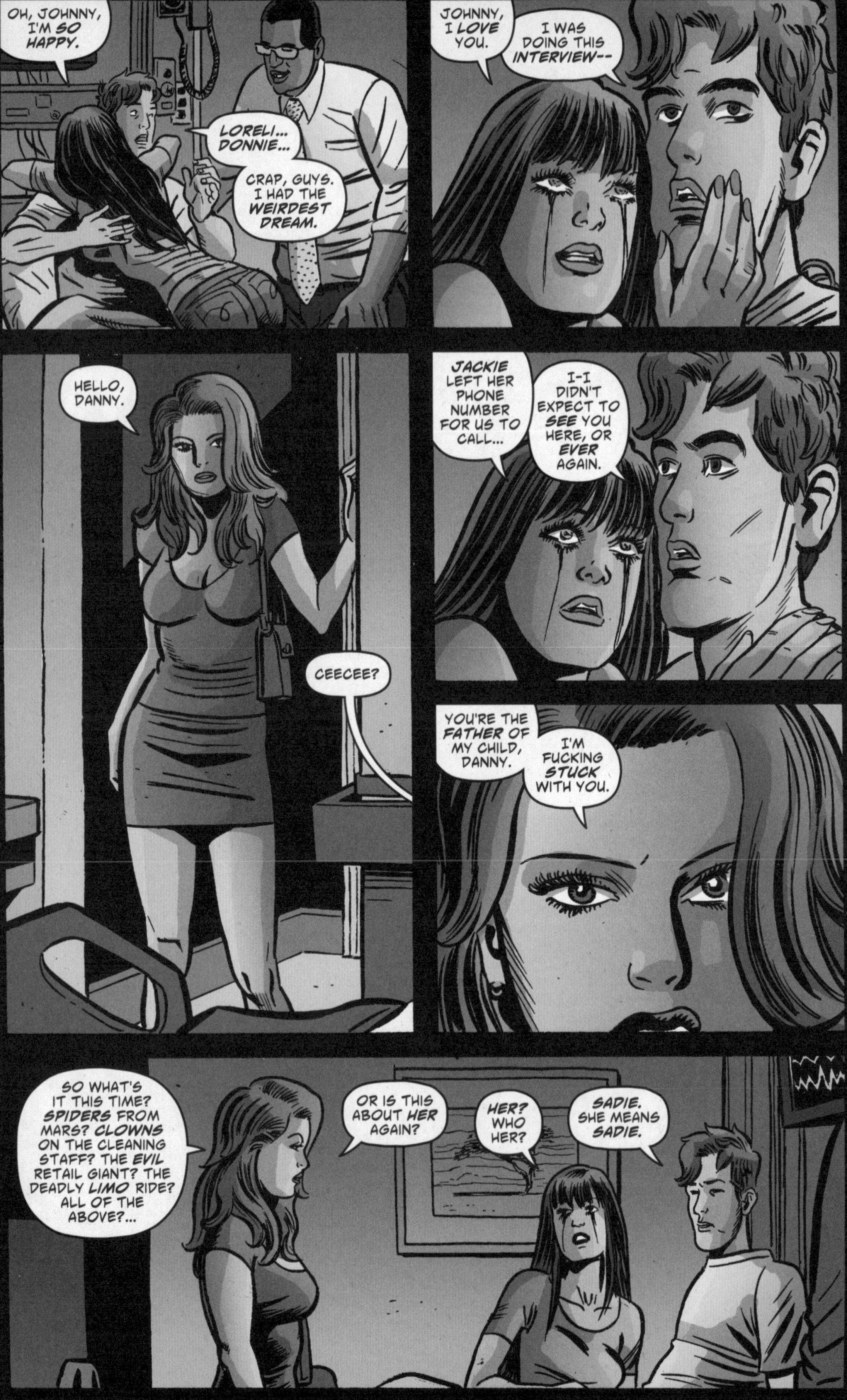
OH, JOHNNY, I'M SO HAPPY.
LORELI... DONNIE...
CRAP, GUYS. I HAD THE WEIRDEST DREAM.
JOHNNY, I LOVE YOU.
I WAS DOING THIS INTERVIEW--
HELLO, DANNY.
CEECEE?
JACKIE LEFT HER PHONE NUMBER FOR US TO CALL...
I-I DIDN'T EXPECT TO SEE YOU HERE, OR EVER AGAIN.
YOU'RE THE FATHER OF MY CHILD, DANNY.
I'M FUCKING STUCK WITH YOU.
SO WHAT'S IT THIS TIME? SPIDERS FROM MARS? CLOWNS ON THE CLEANING STAFF? THE EVIL RETAIL GIANT? THE DEADLY LIMO RIDE? ALL OF THE ABOVE?...
OR IS THIS ABOUT HER AGAIN?
HER? WHO HER?
SADIE. SHE MEANS SADIE.

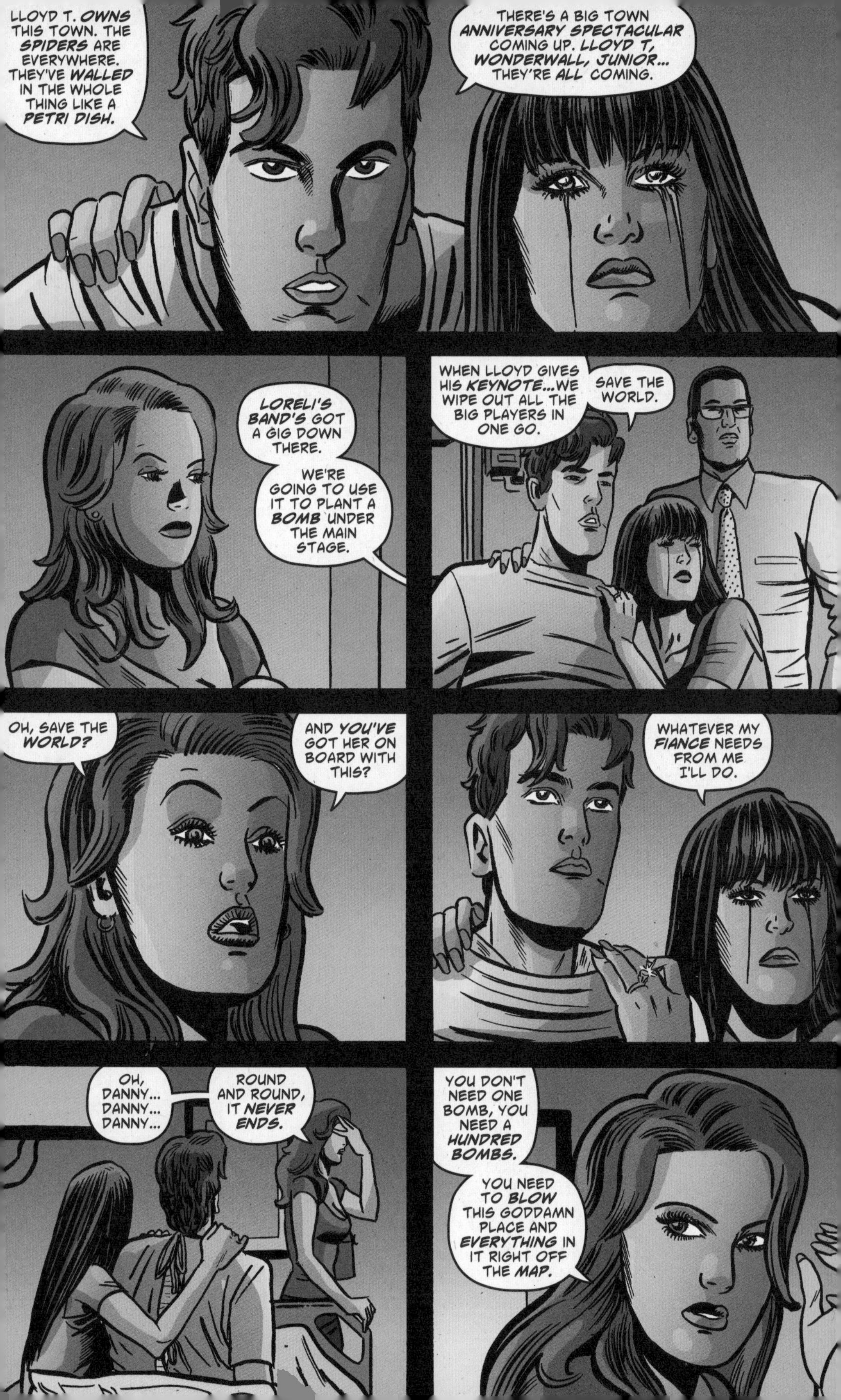
LLOYD T. OWNS THIS TOWN. THE SPIDERS ARE EVERYWHERE. THEY'VE WALLED IN THE WHOLE THING LIKE A PETRI DISH.
THERE'S A BIG TOWN ANNIVERSARY SPECTACULAR COMING UP. LLOYD T, WONDERWALL, JUNIOR... THEY'RE ALL COMING.
LORELI'S BAND'S GOT A GIG DOWN THERE.
WE'RE GOING TO USE IT TO PLANT A BOMB UNDER THE MAIN STAGE.
WHEN LLOYD GIVES HIS KEYNOTE...WE WIPE OUT ALL THE BIG PLAYERS IN ONE GO.
SAVE THE WORLD.
OH, SAVE THE WORLD?
AND YOU'VE GOT HER ON BOARD WITH THIS?
WHATEVER MY FIANCE NEEDS FROM ME I'LL DO.
OH, DANNY... DANNY... DANNY...
ROUND AND ROUND, IT NEVER ENDS.
YOU DON'T NEED ONE BOMB, YOU NEED A HUNDRED BOMBS.
YOU NEED TO BLOW THIS GODDAMN PLACE AND EVERYTHING IN IT RIGHT OFF THE MAP.

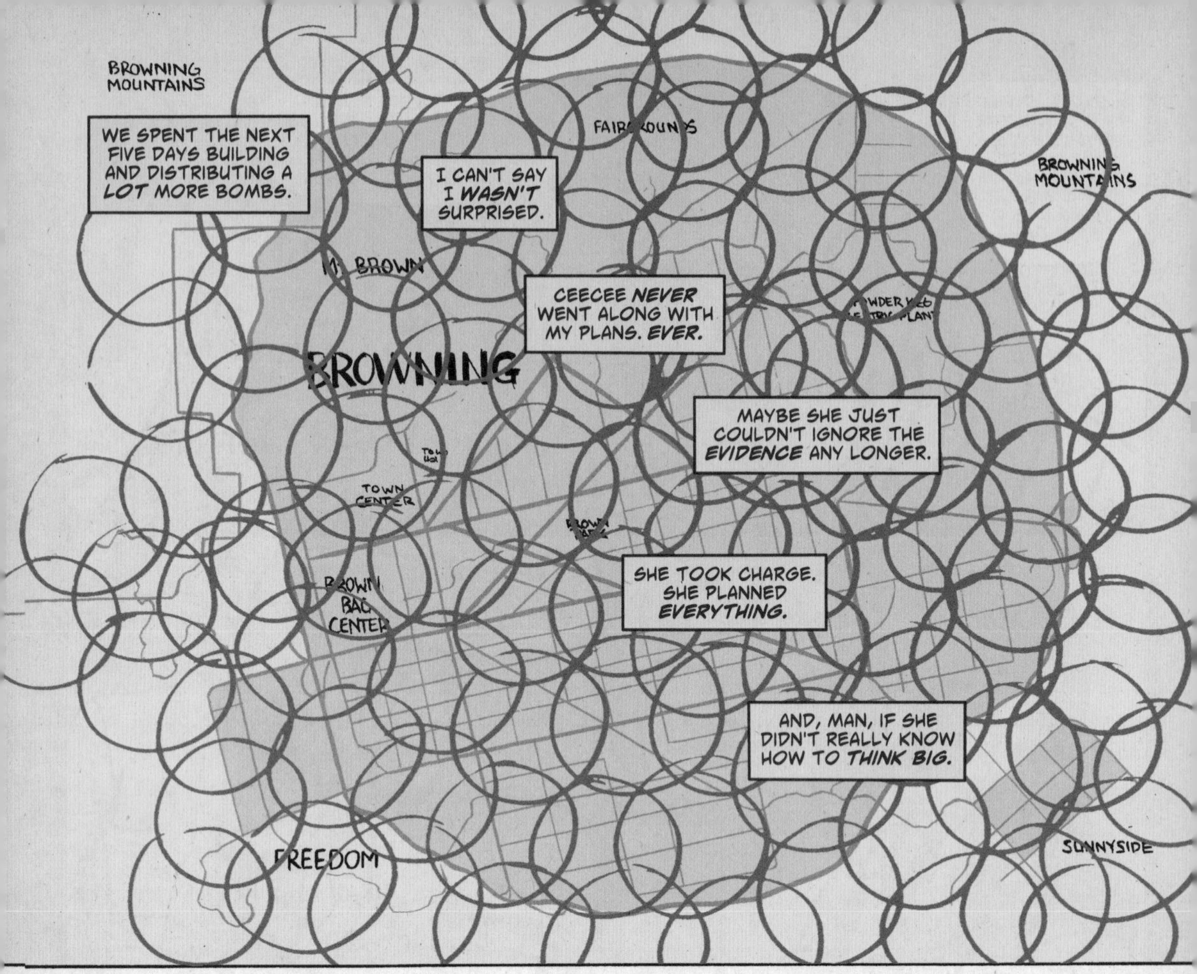
BROWNING MOUNTAINS
WE SPENT THE NEXT FIVE DAYS BUILDING AND DISTRIBUTING A *LOT* MORE BOMBS.
I CAN'T SAY I *WASN'T* SURPRISED.
BROWNING MOUNTAINS
CEECEE *NEVER* WENT ALONG WITH MY PLANS. *EVER.*
BROWNING
MAYBE SHE JUST COULDN'T IGNORE THE *EVIDENCE* ANY LONGER.
TOWN CENTER
SHE TOOK CHARGE. SHE PLANNED *EVERYTHING.*
AND, MAN, IF SHE DIDN'T REALLY KNOW HOW TO *THINK BIG.*
FREEDOM
SUNNYSIDE

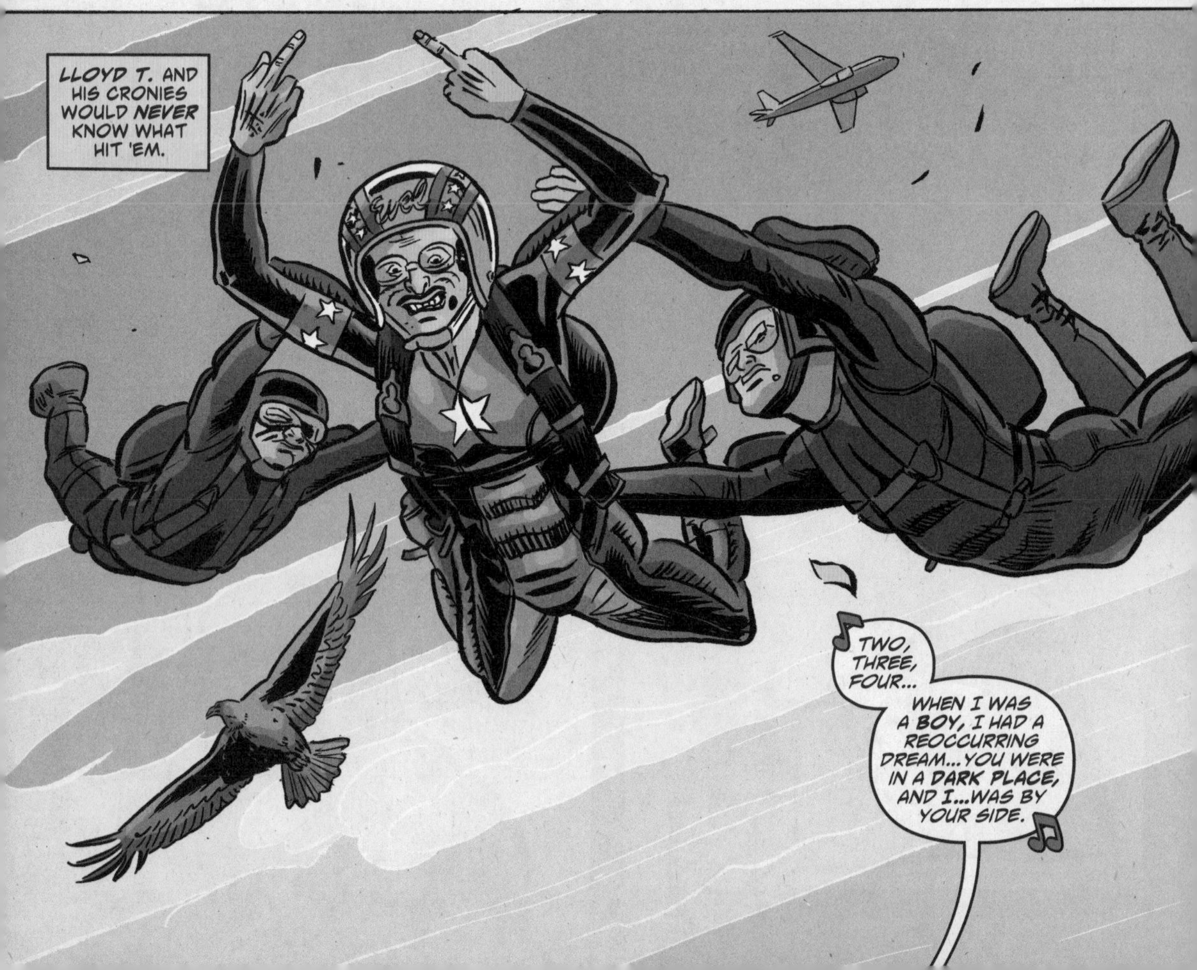
LLOYD T. AND HIS CRONIES WOULD *NEVER* KNOW WHAT HIT 'EM.
TWO, THREE, FOUR...
WHEN I WAS A *BOY*, I HAD A REOCCURRING DREAM...YOU WERE IN A *DARK PLACE*, AND I...WAS BY YOUR SIDE.

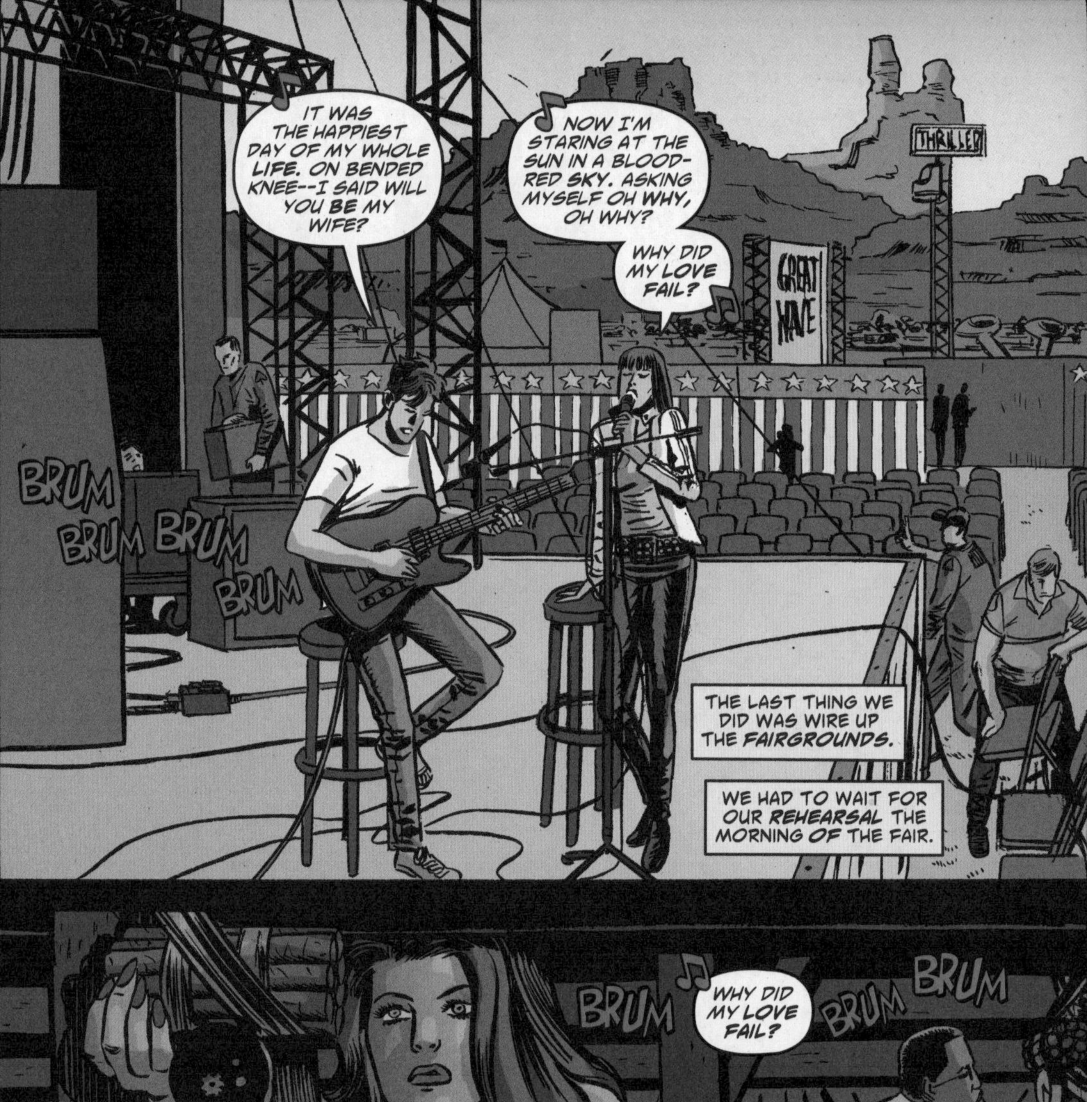
IT WAS THE HAPPIEST DAY OF MY WHOLE LIFE. ON BENDED KNEE--I SAID WILL YOU BE MY WIFE?
NOW I'M STARING AT THE SUN IN A BLOOD-RED SKY. ASKING MYSELF OH WHY, OH WHY?
WHY DID MY LOVE FAIL?
THRILLED
GREAT WAVE
BRUM
BRUM BRUM
BRUM
THE LAST THING WE DID WAS WIRE UP THE FAIRGROUNDS.
WE HAD TO WAIT FOR OUR REHEARSAL THE MORNING OF THE FAIR.

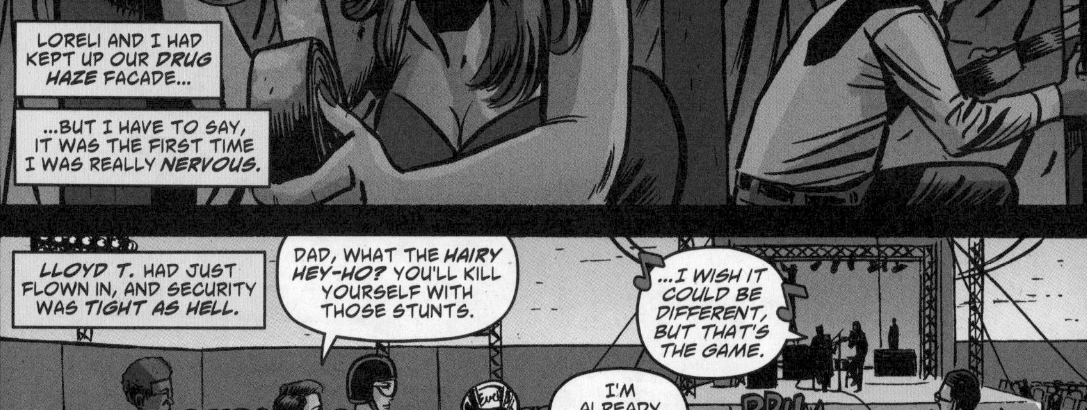
BRUM
WHY DID MY LOVE FAIL?
BRUM BRUM
LORELI AND I HAD KEPT UP OUR DRUG HAZE FACADE...
...BUT I HAVE TO SAY, IT WAS THE FIRST TIME I WAS REALLY NERVOUS.

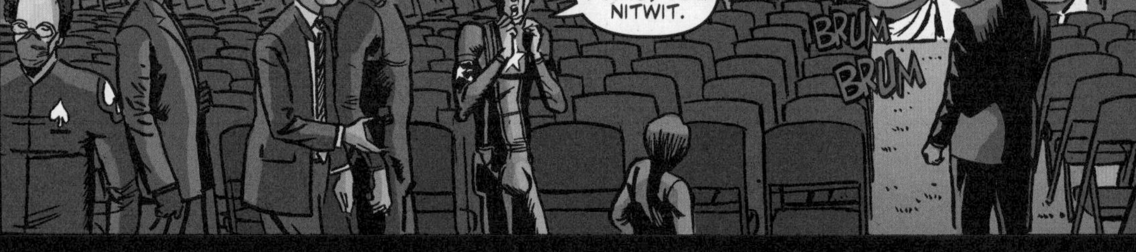
LLOYD T. HAD JUST FLOWN IN, AND SECURITY WAS TIGHT AS HELL.
DAD, WHAT THE HAIRY HEY-HO? YOU'LL KILL YOURSELF WITH THOSE STUNTS.
...I WISH IT COULD BE DIFFERENT, BUT THAT'S THE GAME.
I'M ALREADY DYING, YOU NITWIT.
BRUM
BRUM
BRUM

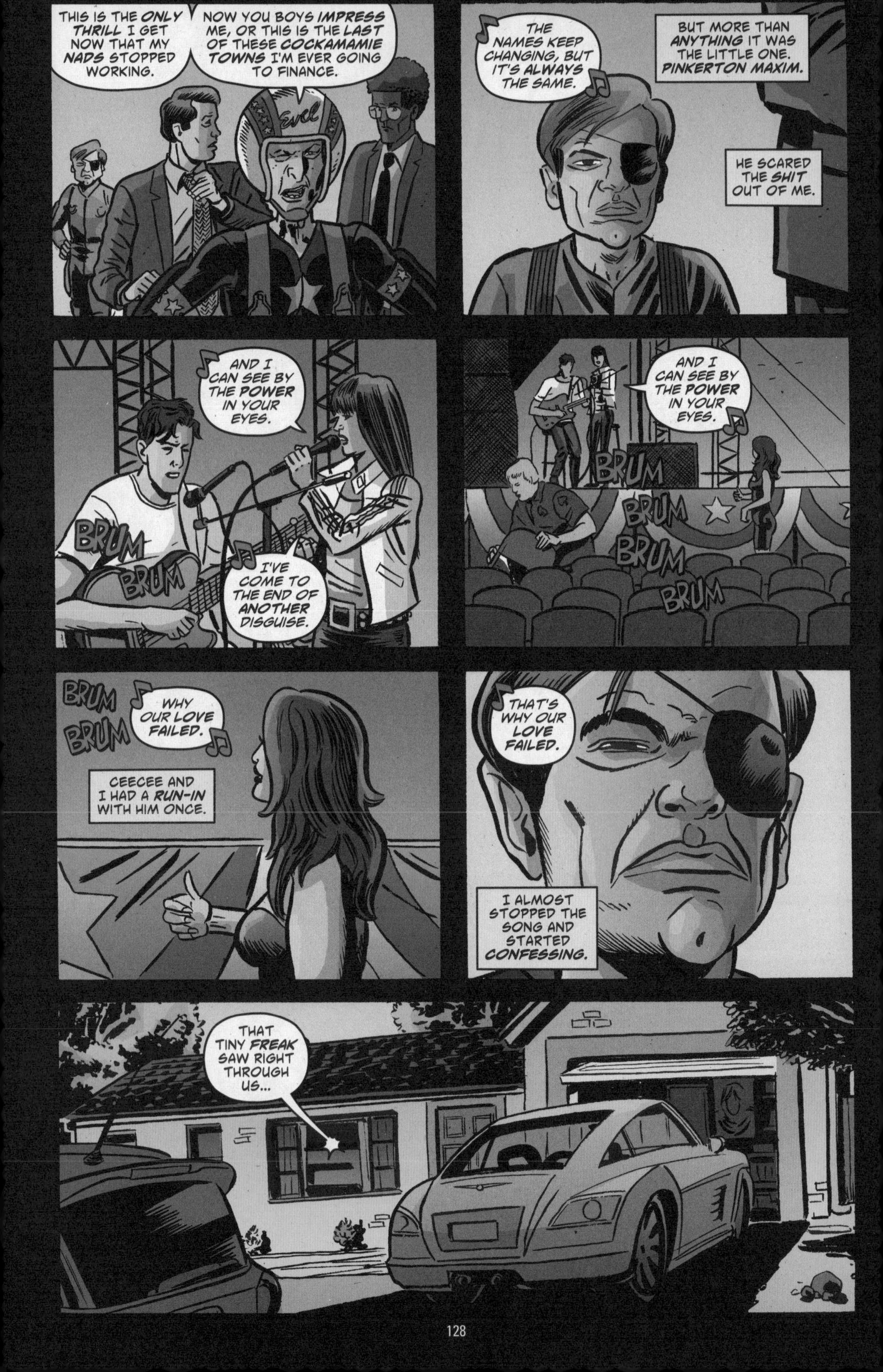
THIS IS THE *ONLY THRILL* I GET NOW THAT MY *NADS* STOPPED WORKING.
NOW YOU BOYS *IMPRESS* ME, OR THIS IS THE *LAST* OF THESE *COCKAMAMIE TOWNS* I'M EVER GOING TO FINANCE.
THE NAMES KEEP CHANGING, BUT IT'S *ALWAYS* THE SAME.
BUT MORE THAN *ANYTHING* IT WAS THE LITTLE ONE. *PINKERTON MAXIM.*
HE SCARED THE *SHIT* OUT OF ME.
AND I CAN SEE BY THE *POWER* IN YOUR EYES.
BRUM
BRUM
I'VE COME TO THE END OF *ANOTHER* DISGUISE.
AND I CAN SEE BY THE *POWER* IN YOUR EYES.
BRUM
BRUM
BRUM
BRUM
BRUM
BRUM
WHY OUR *LOVE* FAILED.
CEECEE AND I HAD A *RUN-IN* WITH HIM ONCE.
THAT'S WHY OUR *LOVE* FAILED.
I ALMOST STOPPED THE SONG AND STARTED *CONFESSING.*
THAT TINY *FREAK* SAW RIGHT THROUGH US...

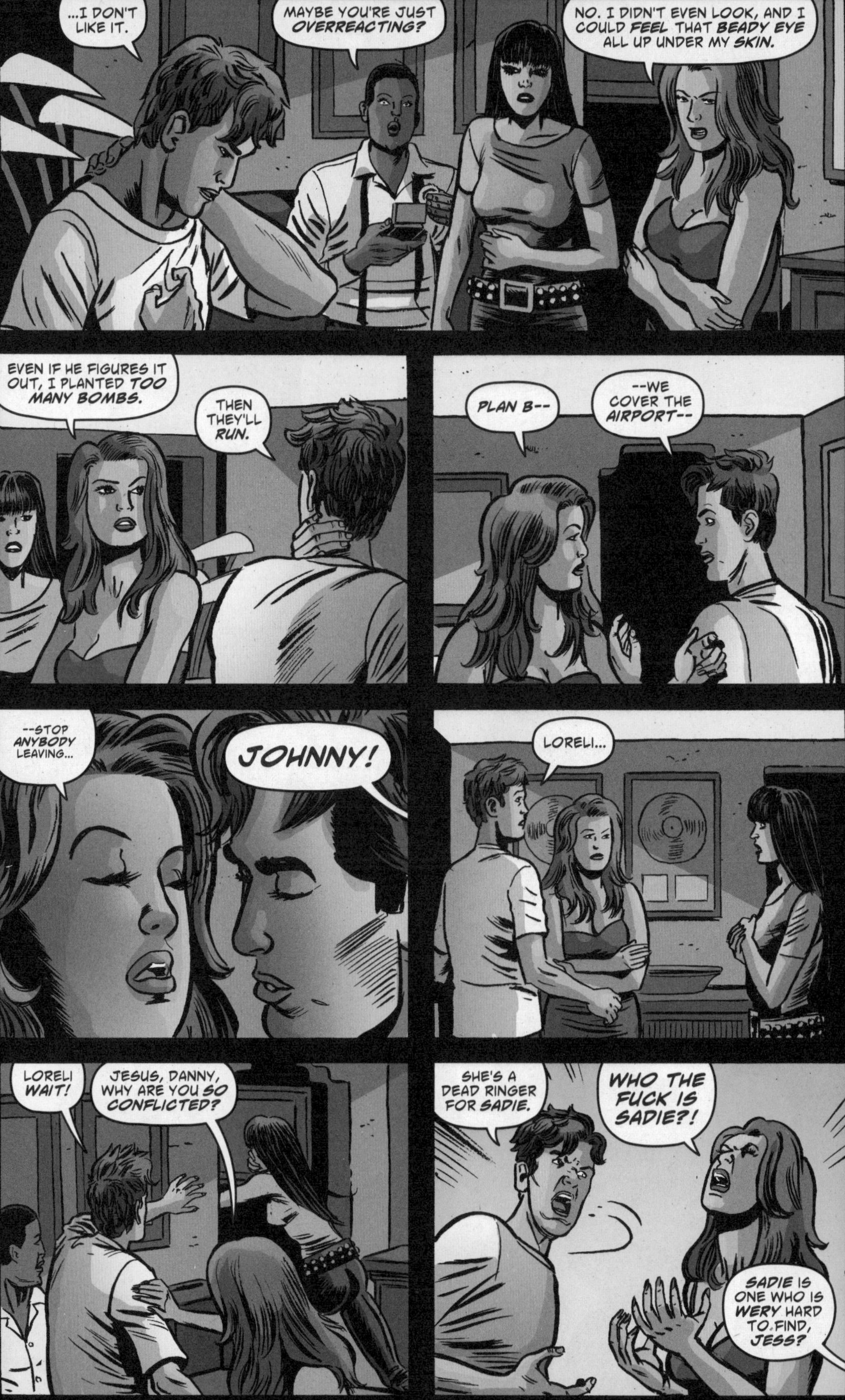
...I DON'T LIKE IT.
MAYBE YOU'RE JUST OVERREACTING?
NO. I DIDN'T EVEN LOOK, AND I COULD FEEL THAT BEADY EYE ALL UP UNDER MY SKIN.
EVEN IF HE FIGURES IT OUT, I PLANTED TOO MANY BOMBS.
THEN THEY'LL RUN.
PLAN B--
--WE COVER THE AIRPORT--
--STOP ANYBODY LEAVING...
JOHNNY!
LORELI...
LORELI WAIT!
JESUS, DANNY, WHY ARE YOU SO CONFLICTED?
SHE'S A DEAD RINGER FOR SADIE.
WHO THE FUCK IS SADIE?!
SADIE IS ONE WHO IS WERY HARD TO FIND, JESS?

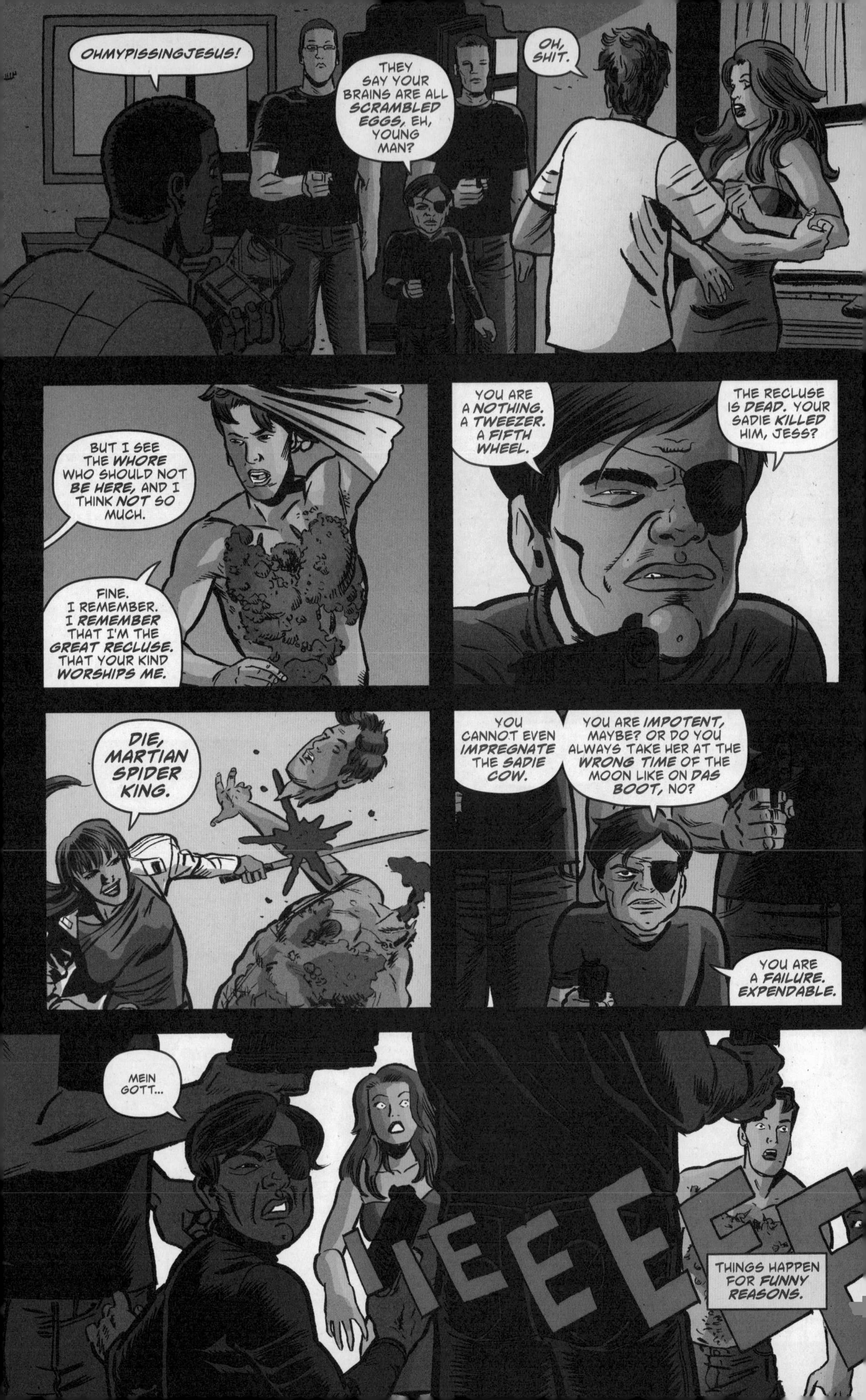
OHMYPISSINGJESUS!
THEY SAY YOUR BRAINS ARE ALL SCRAMBLED EGGS, EH, YOUNG MAN?
OH, SHIT.
BUT I SEE THE WHORE WHO SHOULD NOT BE HERE, AND I THINK NOT SO MUCH.
FINE. I REMEMBER. I REMEMBER THAT I'M THE GREAT RECLUSE. THAT YOUR KIND WORSHIPS ME.
YOU ARE A NOTHING. A TWEEZER. A FIFTH WHEEL.
THE RECLUSE IS DEAD. YOUR SADIE KILLED HIM, JESS?
DIE, MARTIAN SPIDER KING.
YOU CANNOT EVEN IMPREGNATE THE SADIE COW.
YOU ARE IMPOTENT, MAYBE? OR DO YOU ALWAYS TAKE HER AT THE WRONG TIME OF THE MOON LIKE ON DAS BOOT, NO?
YOU ARE A FAILURE. EXPENDABLE.
MEIN GOTT...
IEEE
THINGS HAPPEN FOR FUNNY REASONS.

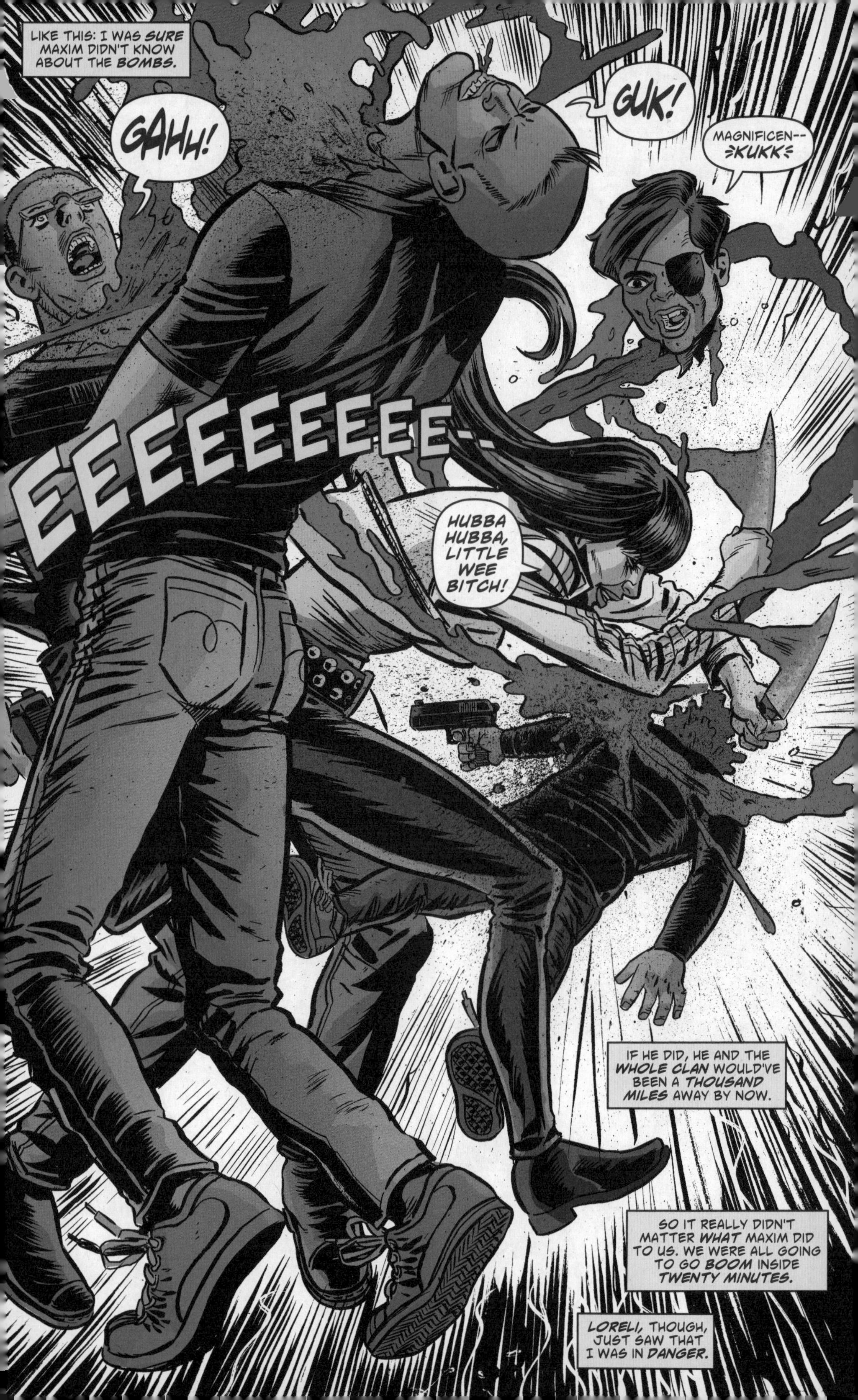
LIKE THIS: I WAS *SURE* MAXIM DIDN'T KNOW ABOUT THE *BOMBS*.
GAHH!
GUK!
MAGNIFICEN-- *KUKK*
EEEEEEEEE--
HUBBA HUBBA, LITTLE WEE BITCH!
IF HE DID, HE AND THE *WHOLE CLAN* WOULD'VE BEEN A *THOUSAND MILES* AWAY BY NOW.
SO IT REALLY DIDN'T MATTER *WHAT* MAXIM DID TO US. WE WERE ALL GOING TO GO *BOOM* INSIDE *TWENTY MINUTES*.
LORELI, THOUGH, JUST SAW THAT I WAS IN *DANGER*.

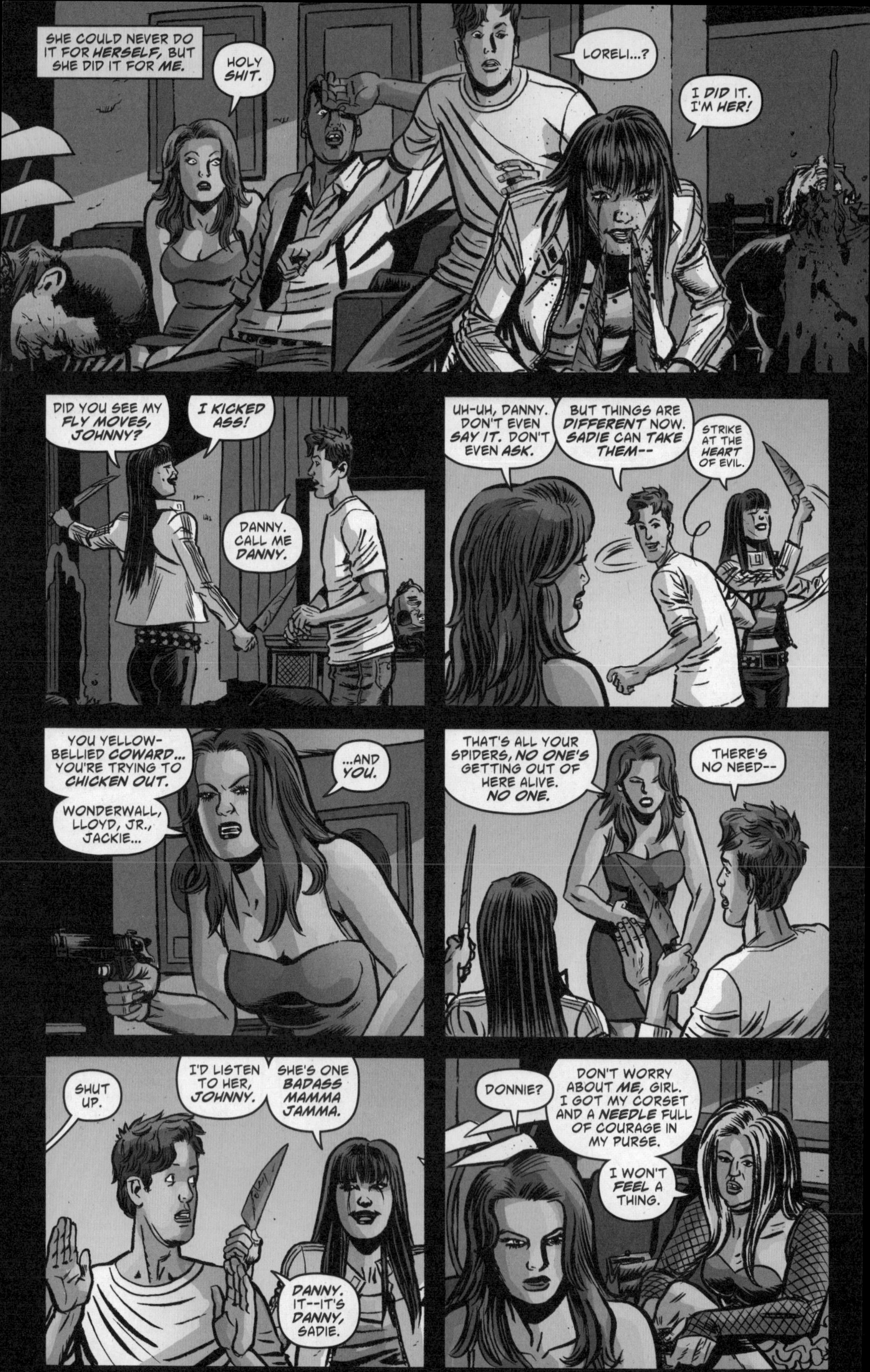
SHE COULD NEVER DO IT FOR *HERSELF*, BUT SHE DID IT FOR *ME*.
HOLY *SHIT*.
LORELI...?
I *DID* IT. I'M *HER!*
DID YOU SEE MY *FLY MOVES*, *JOHNNY?*
I KICKED ASS!
DANNY. CALL ME *DANNY*.
UH-UH, DANNY. DON'T EVEN *SAY IT*. DON'T EVEN *ASK*.
BUT THINGS ARE *DIFFERENT* NOW. *SADIE* CAN *TAKE THEM--*
STRIKE AT THE *HEART* OF EVIL.
YOU YELLOW-BELLIED *COWARD...* YOU'RE TRYING TO *CHICKEN OUT*.
...AND *YOU*.
WONDERWALL, LLOYD, JR., JACKIE...
THAT'S ALL YOUR SPIDERS, *NO ONE'S* GETTING OUT OF HERE ALIVE. *NO ONE*.
THERE'S NO NEED--
SHUT UP.
I'D LISTEN TO HER, *JOHNNY*.
SHE'S ONE *BADASS MAMMA JAMMA*.
DANNY. IT--IT'S *DANNY*, SADIE.
DONNIE?
DON'T WORRY ABOUT *ME*, GIRL. I GOT MY CORSET AND A *NEEDLE* FULL OF COURAGE IN MY PURSE.
I WON'T *FEEL* A THING.

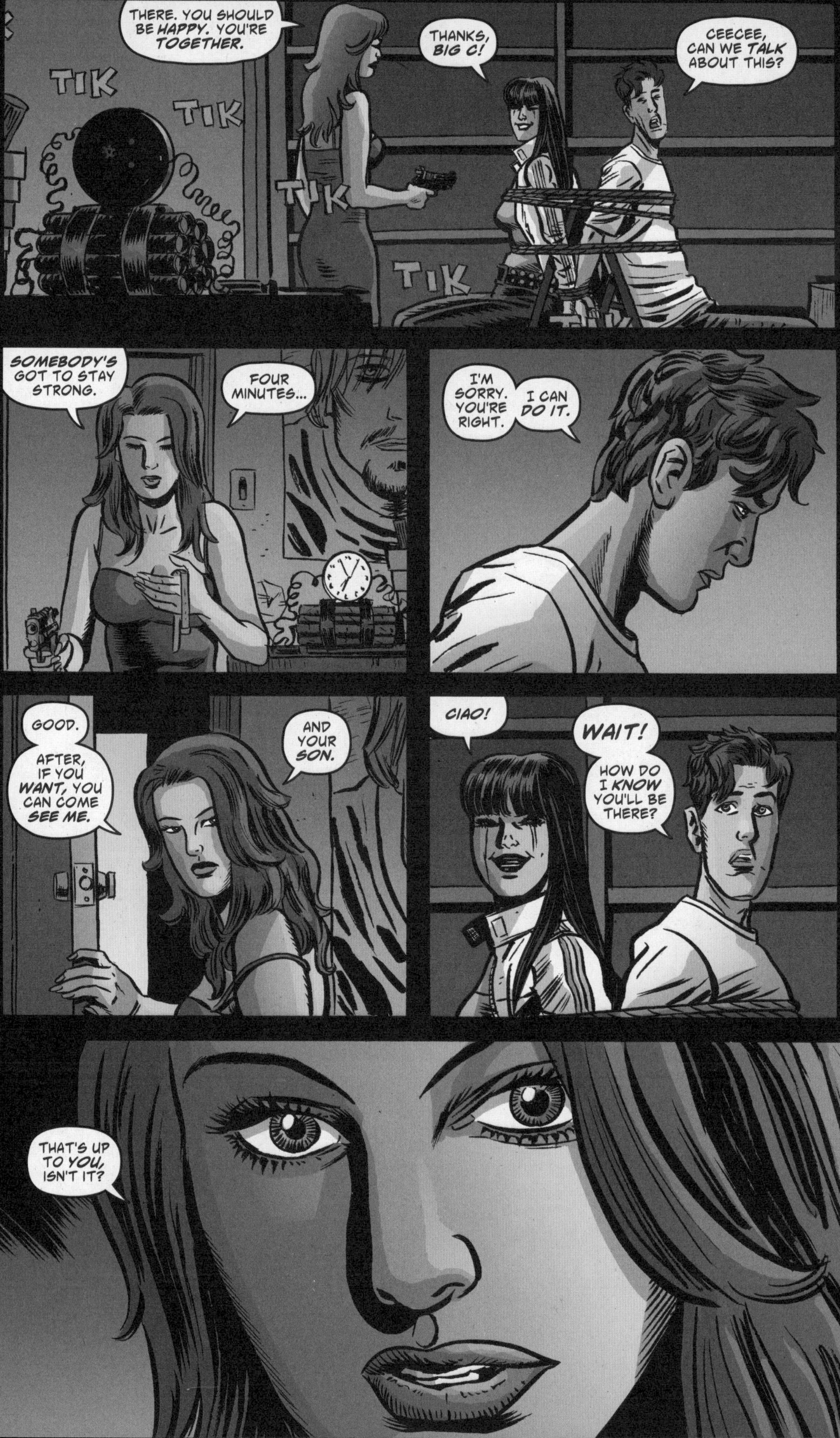
THERE. YOU SHOULD BE *HAPPY*. YOU'RE *TOGETHER*.
THANKS, *BIG C!*
CEECEE, CAN WE *TALK* ABOUT THIS?
TIK
TIK
TIK
TIK
SOMEBODY'S GOT TO STAY STRONG.
FOUR MINUTES...
I'M SORRY. YOU'RE RIGHT.
I CAN *DO IT.*
GOOD.
AFTER, IF YOU *WANT,* YOU CAN COME *SEE ME.*
AND YOUR *SON.*
CIAO!
WAIT!
HOW DO I *KNOW* YOU'LL BE THERE?
THAT'S UP TO *YOU,* ISN'T IT?

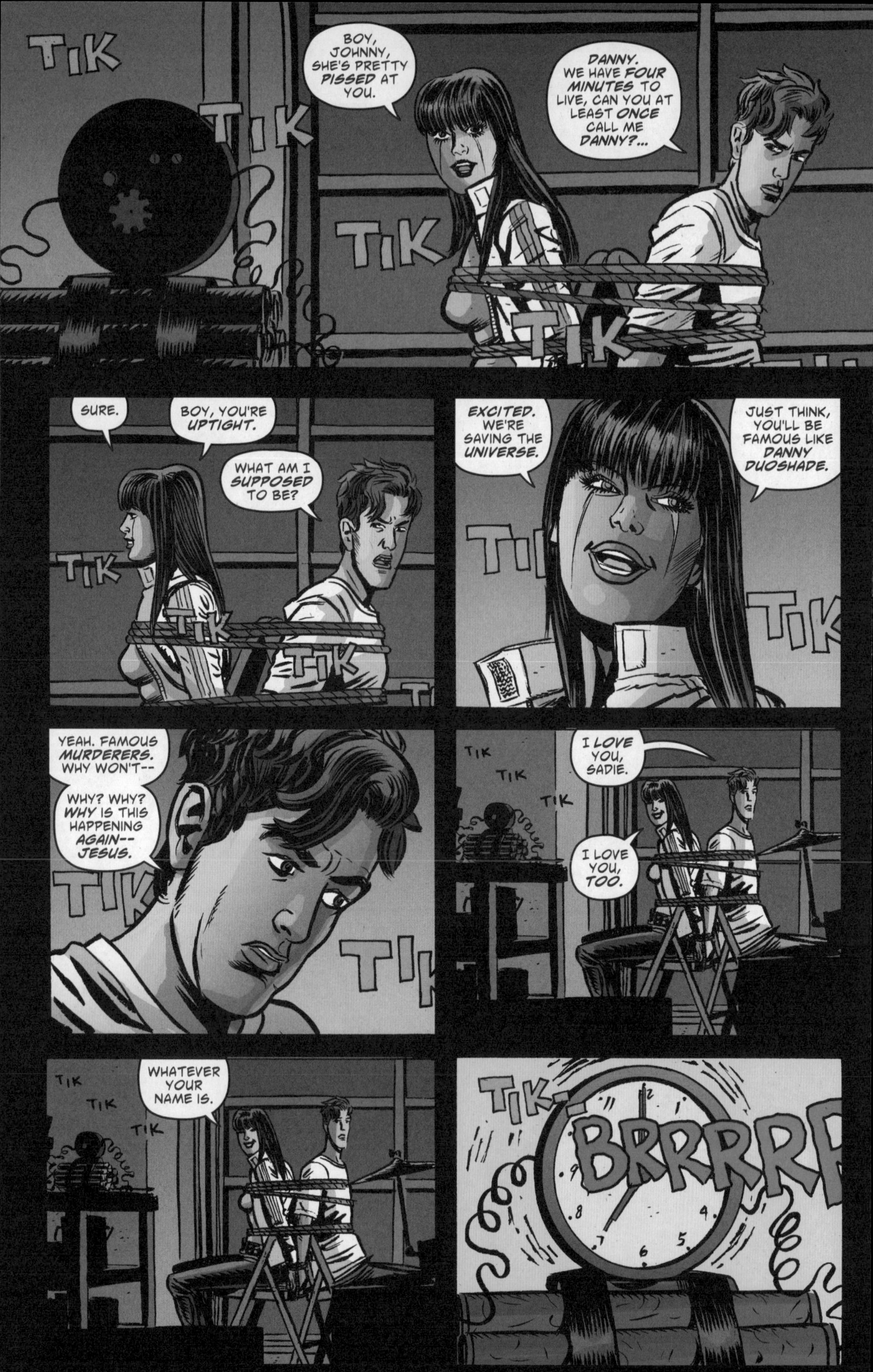
TIK
BOY, JOHNNY, SHE'S PRETTY PISSED AT YOU.
DANNY. WE HAVE FOUR MINUTES TO LIVE, CAN YOU AT LEAST ONCE CALL ME DANNY?...
TIK
TIK
TIK
SURE.
BOY, YOU'RE UPTIGHT.
WHAT AM I SUPPOSED TO BE?
TIK
TIK
TIK
EXCITED. WE'RE SAVING THE UNIVERSE.
JUST THINK, YOU'LL BE FAMOUS LIKE DANNY DUOSHADE.
TIK
YEAH. FAMOUS MURDERERS. WHY WON'T--
WHY? WHY? WHY IS THIS HAPPENING AGAIN-- JESUS.
TIK
TIK
I LOVE YOU, SADIE.
TIK
TIK
TIK
I LOVE YOU, TOO.
TIK
TIK
TIK
WHATEVER YOUR NAME IS.
TIK-
BRRRRR

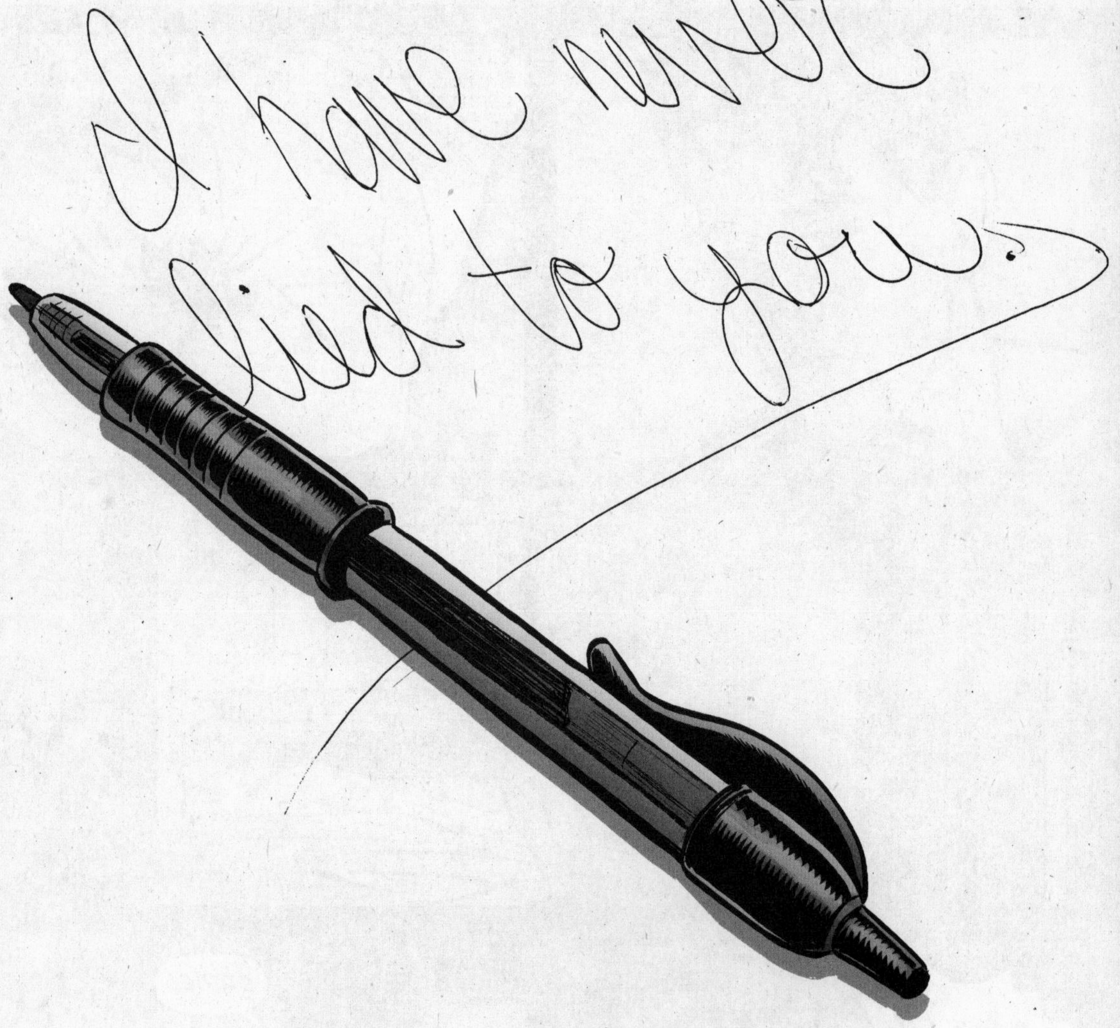
I have never lied to you.

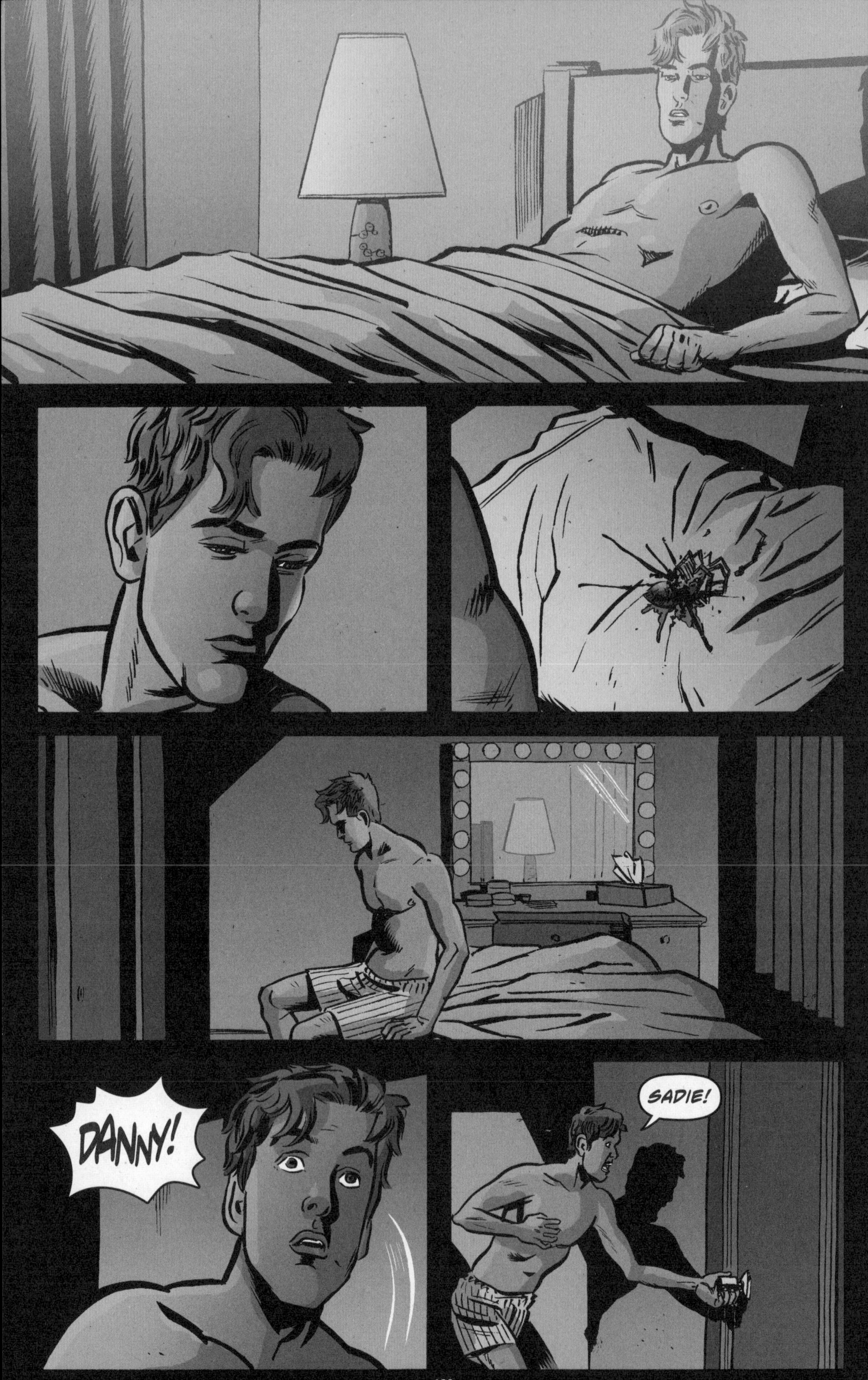
DANNY!
SADIE!

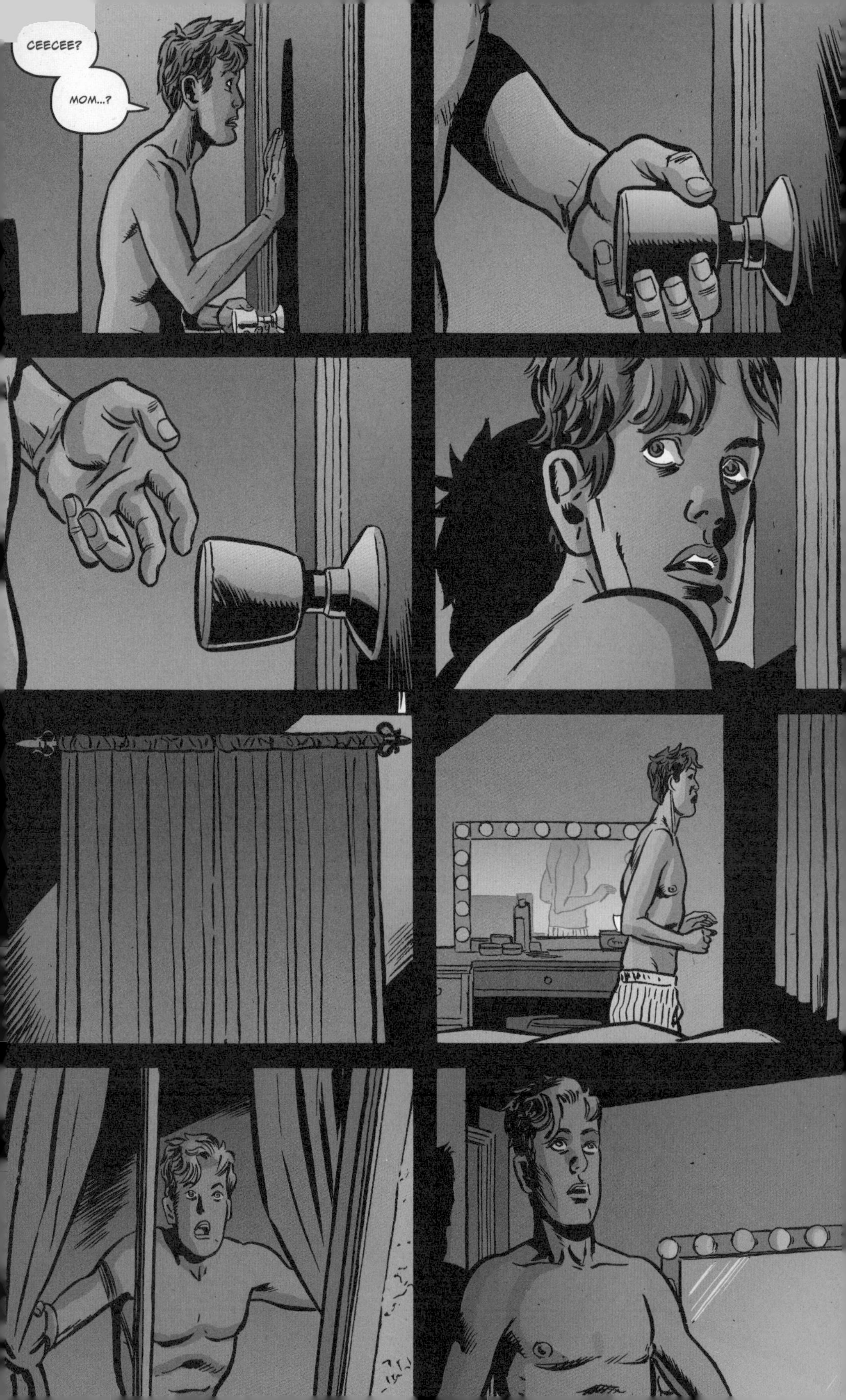
CEECEE?
MOM...?

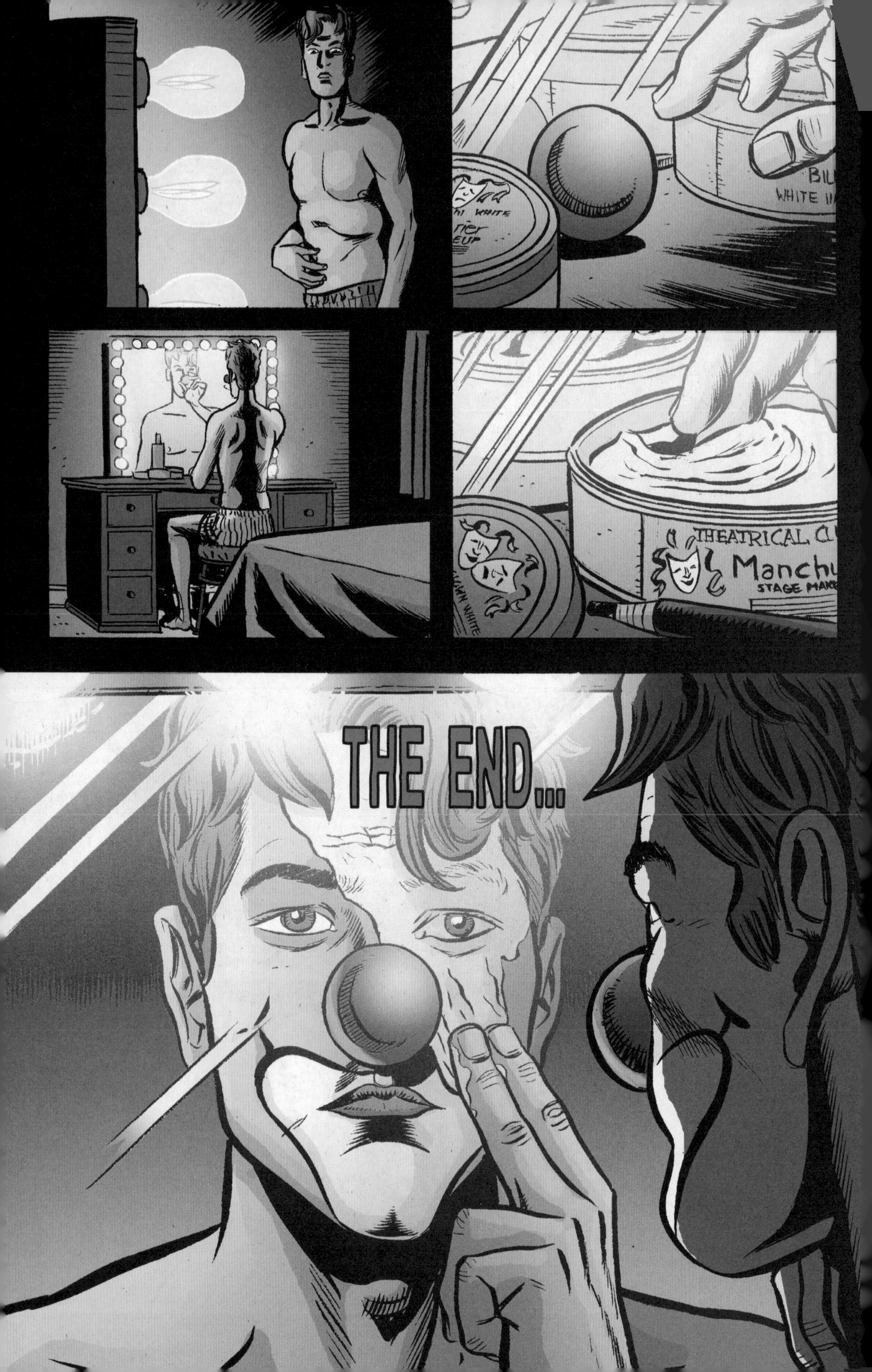
THEATRICAL CL
Manchu
STAGE MAKE
THE END...

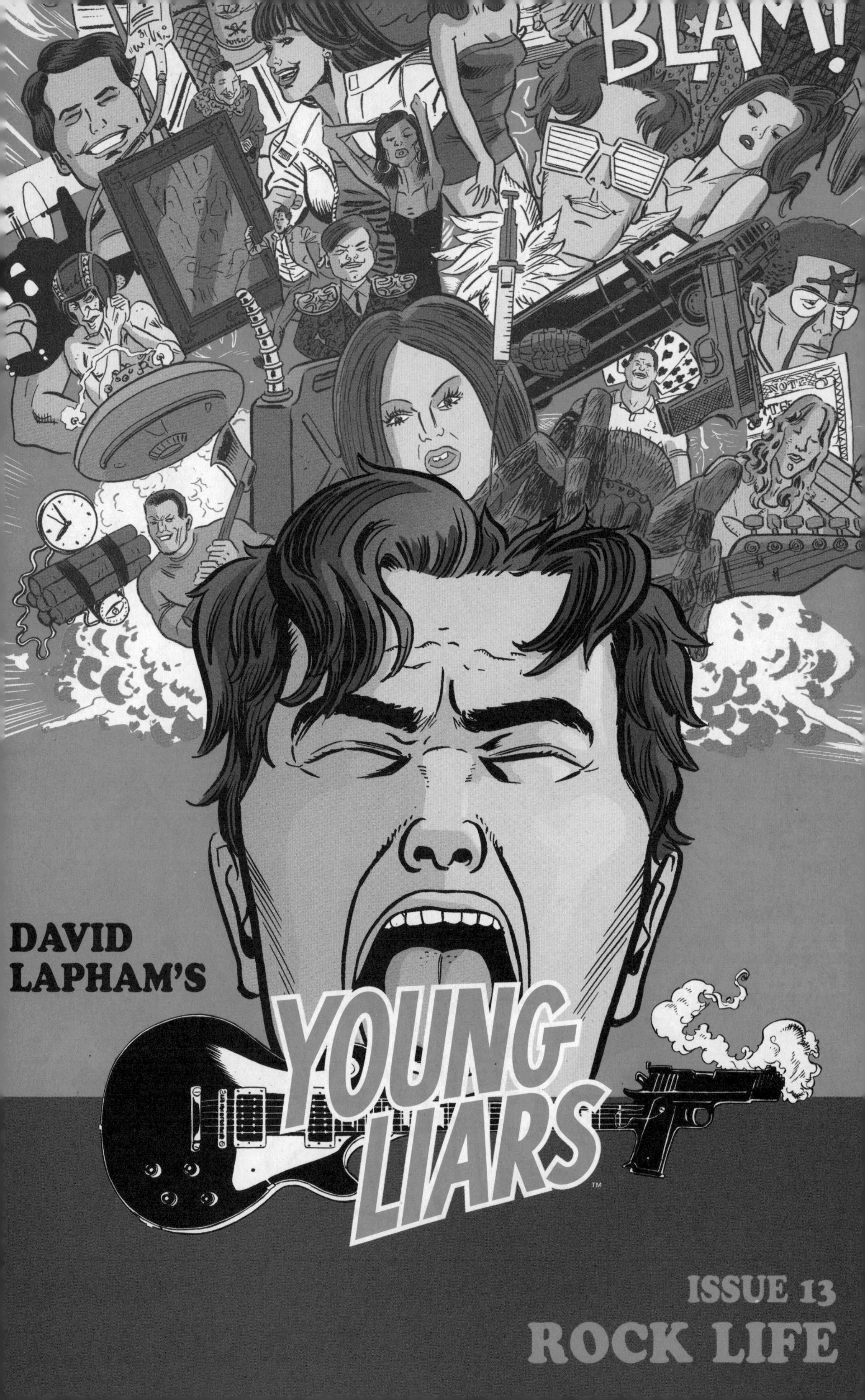
BLAM!
DAVID
LAPHAM'S
YOUNG
LIARS™
ISSUE 13
ROCK LIFE

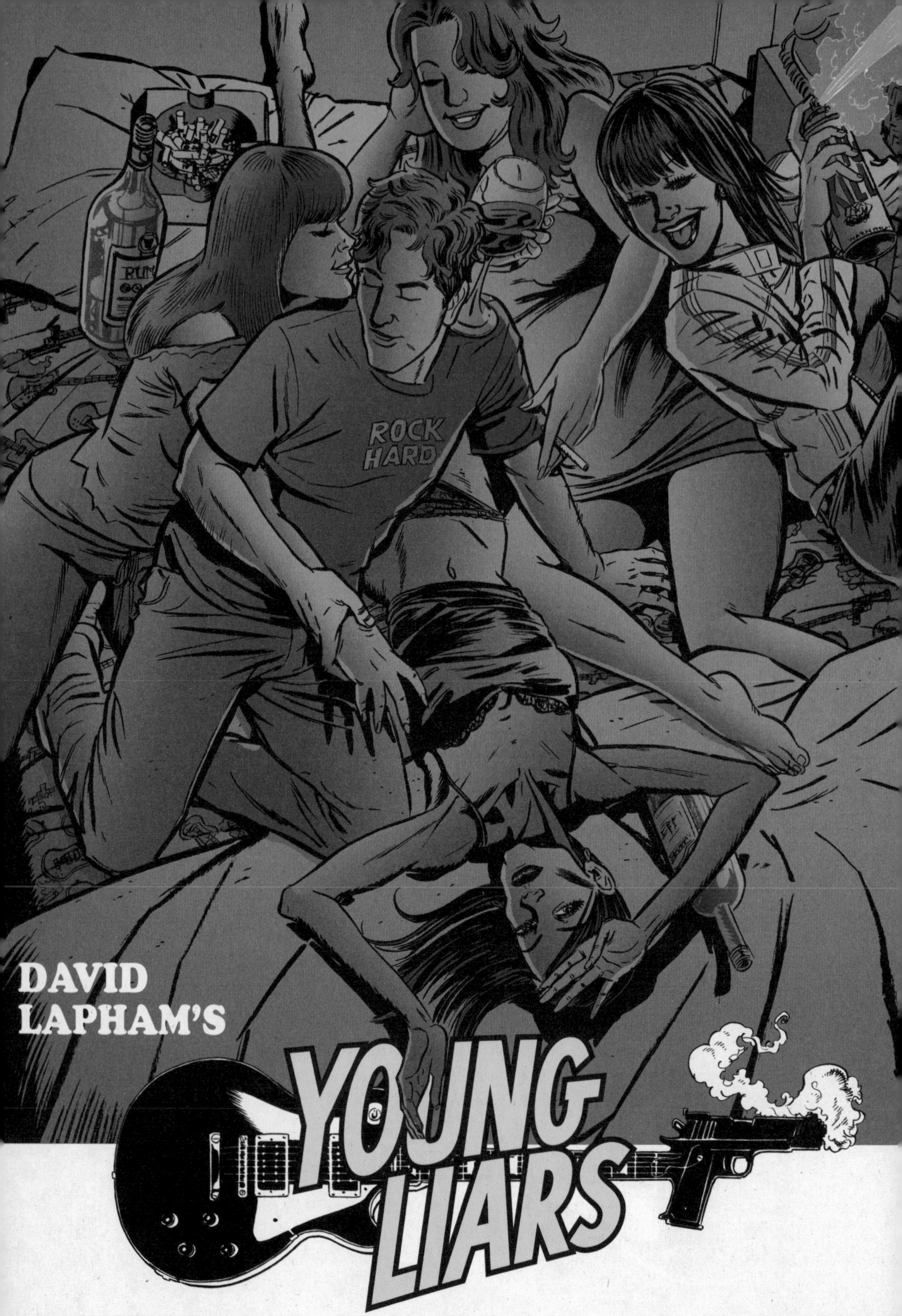
ROCK
HARD
RUM
DAVID
LAPHAM'S
YOUNG
LIARS

ISSUE 14

PENCIL ROT

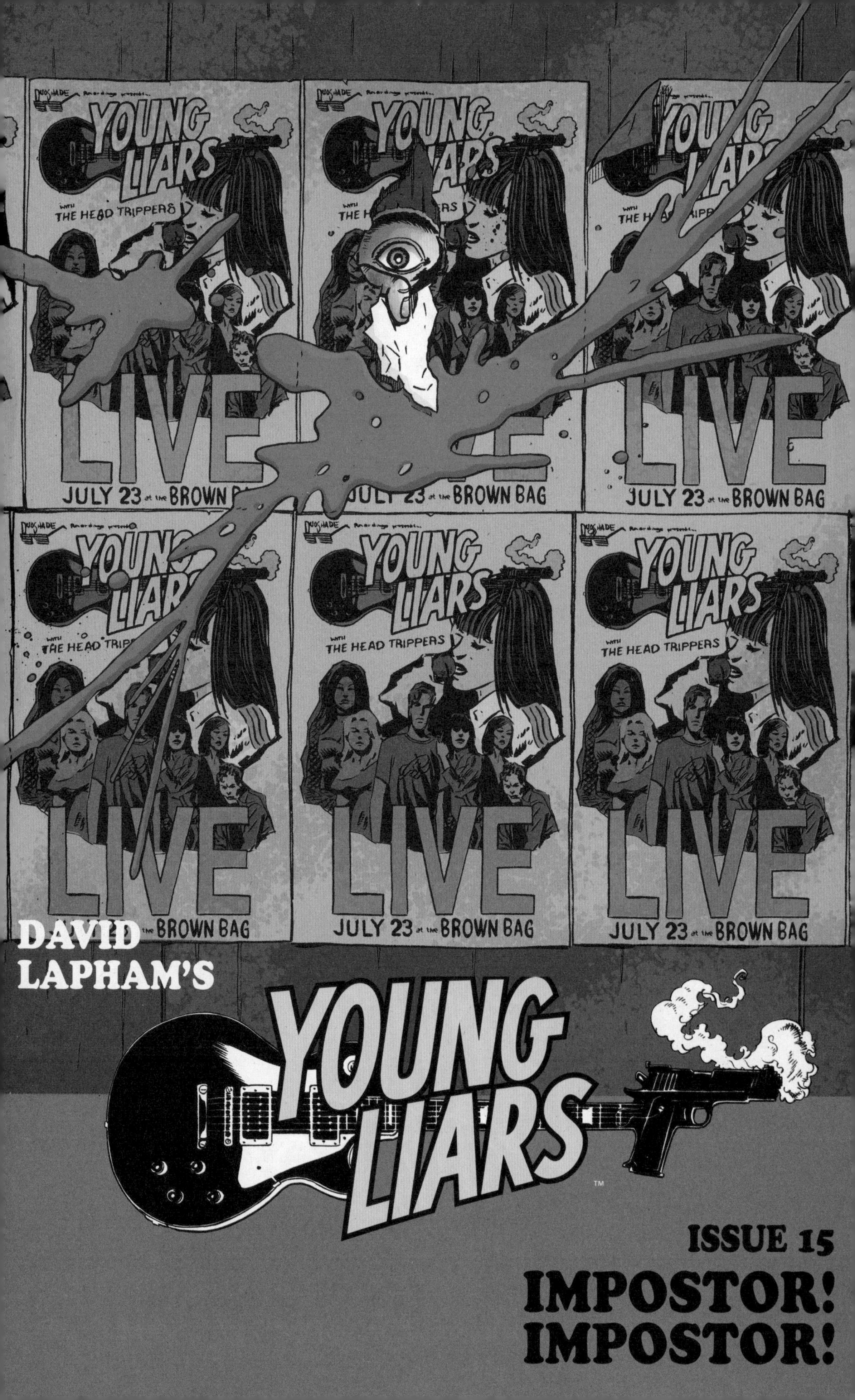

YOUNG LIARS
WITH THE HEAD TRIPPERS
LIVE
JULY 23 at the BROWN BAG
DAVID LAPHAM'S
YOUNG LIARS™
ISSUE 15
IMPOSTOR! IMPOSTOR!

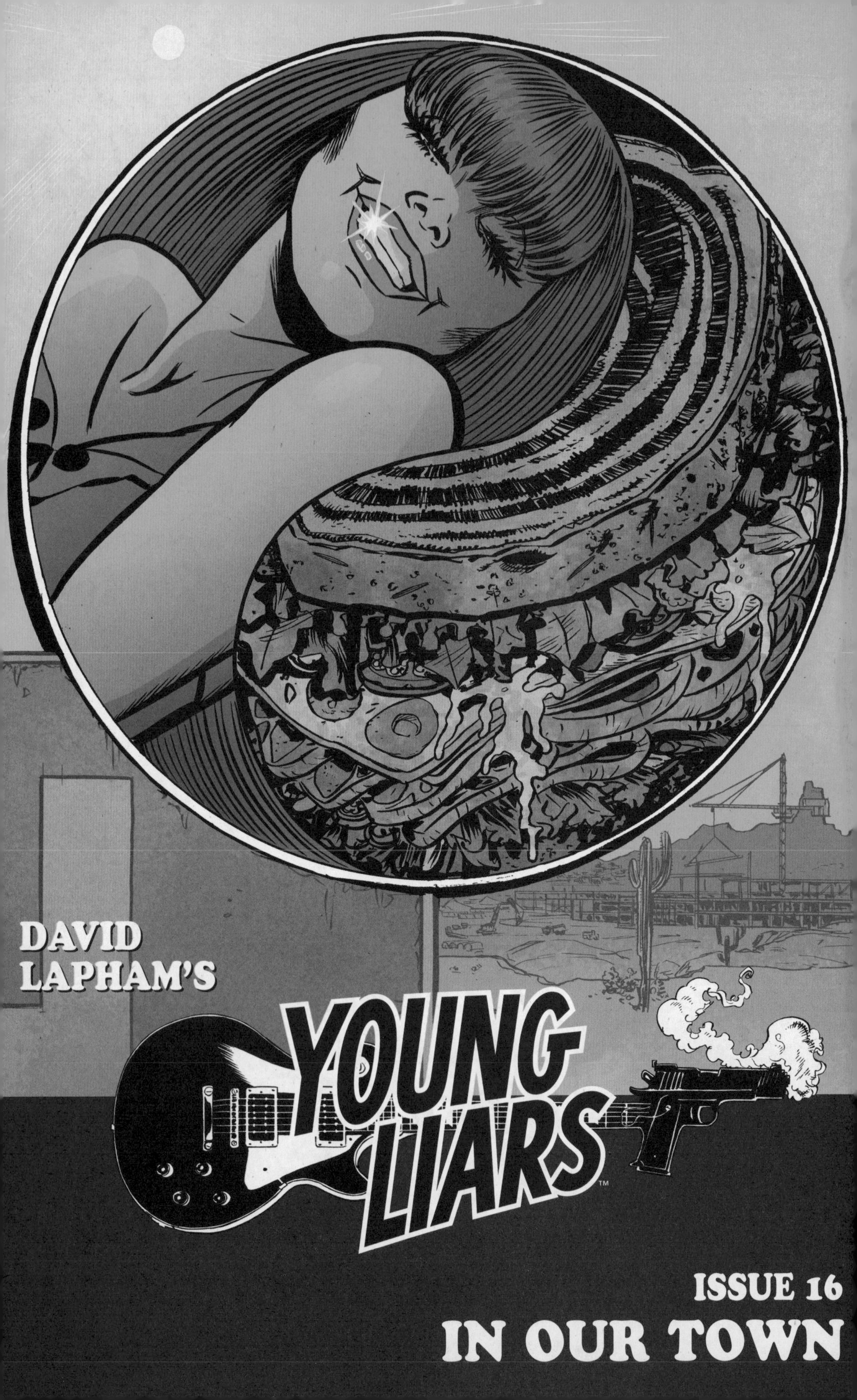
DAVID
LAPHAM'S
YOUNG LIARS™
ISSUE 16
IN OUR TOWN

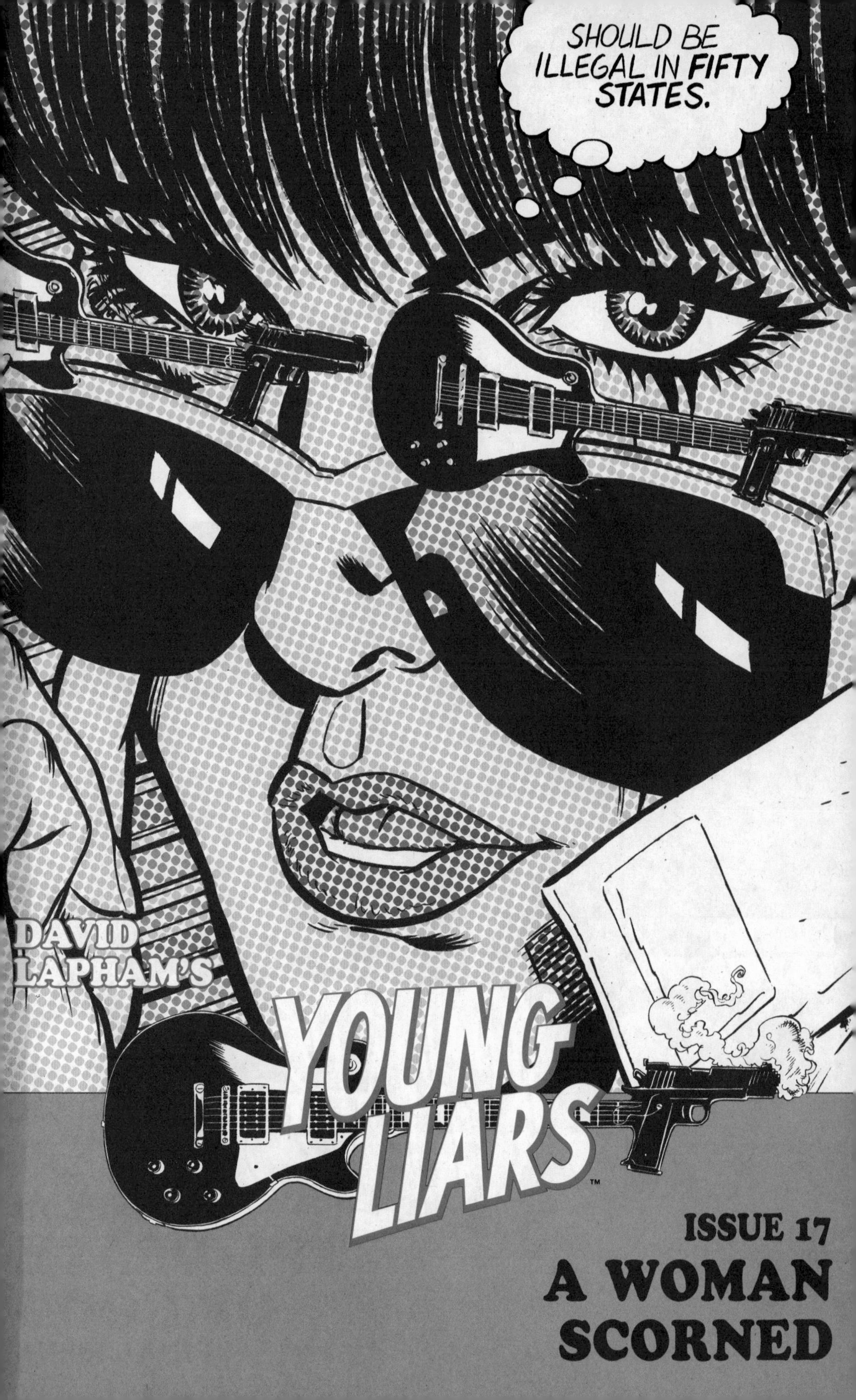
SHOULD BE ILLEGAL IN FIFTY STATES.
DAVID LAPHAM'S
YOUNG LIARS™
ISSUE 17
A WOMAN SCORNED

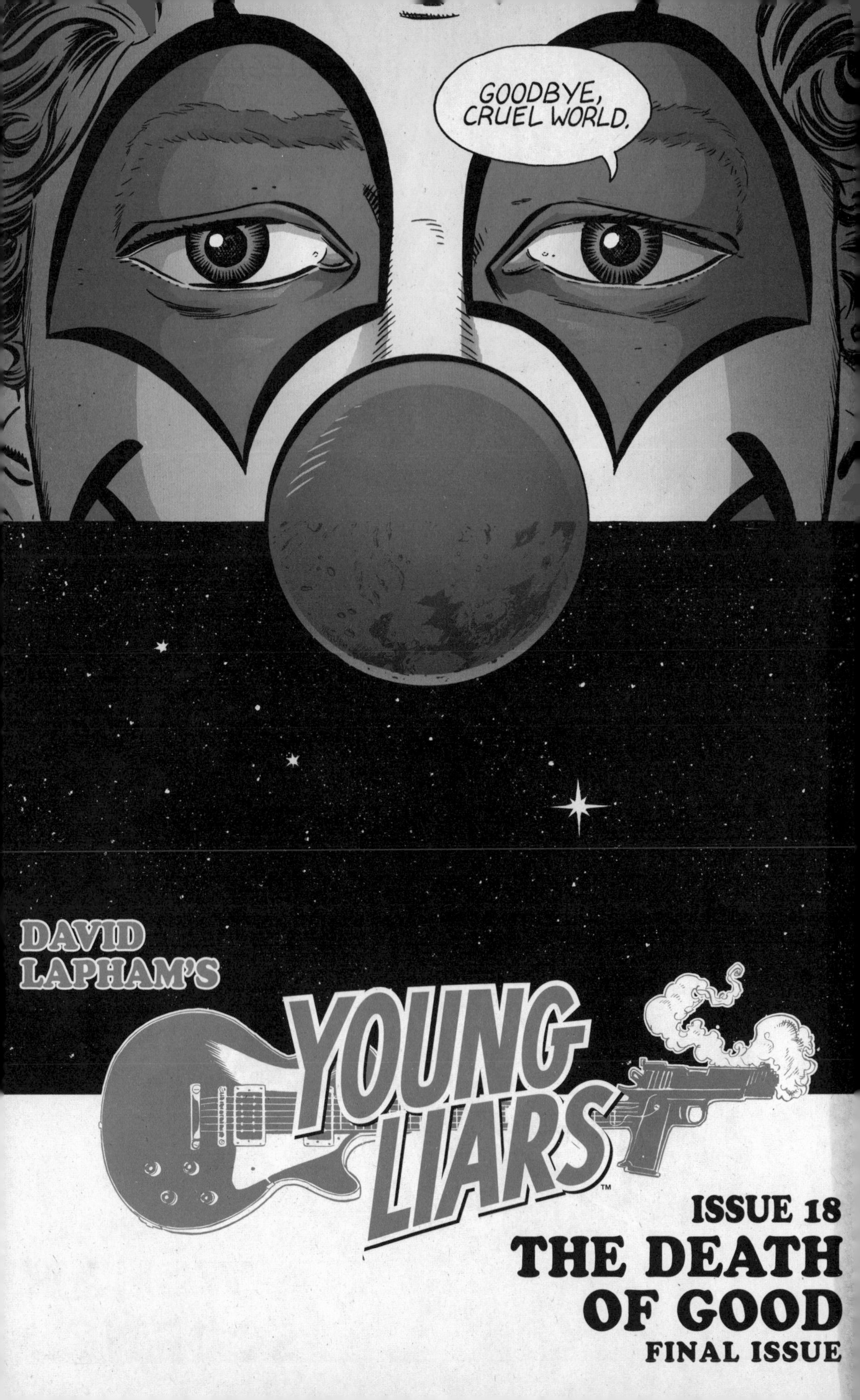
GOODBYE, CRUEL WORLD.
DAVID LAPHAM'S
YOUNG LIARS™
ISSUE 18
THE DEATH OF GOOD
FINAL ISSUE